T0255199

Data-Centric Systems and Applications

More information about this series at http://www.springer.com/series/5258

Edward Sciore

Database Design and Implementation

Second Edition

Edward Sciore
Boston College
Chestnut Hill, MA, USA

ISSN 2197-9723 ISSN 2197-974X (electronic)
Data-Centric Systems and Applications
ISBN 978-3-030-33835-0 ISBN 978-3-030-33836-7 (eBook)
https://doi.org/10.1007/978-3-030-33836-7

The first edition of this book was published by John Wiley & Sons, Inc.

This Springer imprint is published by the registered company Springer Nature Switzerland AG.
The registered company address is: Gewerbestrasse 11, 6330 Cham, Switzerland

Preface

A database system is a common, visible tool in the corporate world—employees frequently interact directly with database systems to submit data or create reports. Database systems are also common, but invisible, as components of software systems. For example, consider an e-commerce website that uses a server-side database to hold customer, product, and sales information. Or consider a GPS navigation system that uses an embedded database to manage the road maps. In both of these examples, the presence of the database system is hidden from the user; the application code performs all of the database interaction.

From the point of view of a software developer, learning to use a database directly is rather mundane, because modern database systems contain sophisticated front ends that make the creation of queries and reports straightforward. On the other hand, the possibility of incorporating database functionality into a software application is exciting, because it opens up a wealth of new and unexplored opportunities.

But what does "incorporating database functionality" mean? A database system provides many things, such as persistence, transactional support, and query processing. Which of these features are needed, and how should they be integrated into the software? Suppose, for example, that a programmer is asked to modify an existing application, say to add the ability to save state, or to increase reliability, or to improve the efficiency of file access. The programmer is faced with several architectural options. She could:

- Purchase a full-featured general-purpose database system and then modify the application to connect to the database as a client
- Obtain a more specialized system that contains only the desired features and whose code can be embedded directly into the application
- Write the necessary functionality herself

In order to make the proper choice, the programmer needs to understand what each of these options entail. She needs to know not only what database systems do but also how they do it and why.

This text examines database systems from the point of view of the software developer. This perspective allows us to investigate *why* database systems are the way they are. It is, of course, important to be able to write queries, but it is equally important to know how they are processed. We don't want to just use JDBC, we want to know why the API contains the classes and methods that it does. We need a sense of how hard is it to write a disk cache or logging facility. And what exactly *is* a database driver, anyway?

Organization of the Text

The first two chapters provide a quick overview of database systems and their use. Chapter 1 discusses the purpose and features of a database system and introduces you to the Derby and SimpleDB systems. Chapter 2 explains how to write a database application using Java. It presents the basics of JDBC, which is the fundamental API for Java programs that interact with a database.

Chapters 3–11 examine the internals of a typical database engine. Each of its chapters covers a different database component, starting with the lowest level of abstraction (the disk and file manager) and ending with the highest (the JDBC client interface). The chapter for each component explains the issues and considers possible design decisions. As a result, you can see exactly what services each component provides and how it interacts with the other components in the system. By the end of this part, you will have witnessed the gradual development of a simple but completely functional system.

The remaining four chapters focus on efficient query processing. They examine the sophisticated techniques and algorithms that can replace the simple design choices described earlier. Topics include indexing, sorting, intelligent buffer usage, and query optimization.

Text Prerequisites

This text is intended for upper-level undergraduate or beginning graduate courses in computer science. It assumes that the reader is comfortable with basic Java programming; for example, it uses the classes in `java.util` extensively, particularly collections and maps. Advanced Java concepts (such as RMI and JDBC) are fully explained in the text.

The material in this book is typically studied as a second course in database systems. However, I have had success teaching it to students with no database experience. To that end, this book assumes no prior database knowledge other than a passing acquaintance with SQL. And students without such knowledge of SQL will find it easy to pick up what they need.

The SimpleDB Software

In my experience, it is much easier for students to grasp conceptual ideas (such as concurrency control, buffer management, and query optimization algorithms) than to grasp how these ideas interact. Ideally, a student should write an entire database system as part of his coursework, just as the student would write an entire compiler in a compiler course. However, a database system is much more complex than a compiler, so that approach is not practical. My solution was to write a simple but fully functional database system, called *SimpleDB*. Students can apply their conceptual knowledge by examining SimpleDB code and modifying it.

SimpleDB "looks" like a commercial database system, both in its function and structure. Functionally, it is a multiuser, transaction-oriented database server that executes SQL statements and interacts with clients via JDBC. Structurally, it contains the same basic components as a commercial system, with similar APIs. Each component of SimpleDB has a corresponding chapter in the text, which discusses the component's code and the design decisions behind it.

SimpleDB is a useful educational tool because its code is small, easily readable, and easily modifiable. It omits all unnecessary functionality, implements only a tiny portion of SQL, and uses only the simplest (and often very impractical) algorithms. There consequently are numerous opportunities for students to extend the system with additional features and more efficient algorithms; many of these extensions appear as end-of-chapter exercises.

SimpleDB can be downloaded from the *http://cs.bc.edu/~sciore/simpledb*. Details on installing and using SimpleDB appear on that web page and in Chap. 1. I welcome suggestions for improving the code, as well as reports of any bugs. You can email me at sciore@bc.edu.

End-of-Chapter Readings

This text is motivated by two questions: What functionality do database systems provide? What algorithms and design decisions will best implement this functionality? Entire shelves can be filled with books that address different aspects of these questions. Since there is no way that a single text could hope to be comprehensive, I have chosen to present only those algorithms and techniques that most clearly illustrate the issues involved. My overriding goal is to teach the principles behind a technique, even if it means omitting (or reducing) discussion of the most commercially viable version of it. Instead, the end of each chapter contains a "suggested readings" section. Those sections discuss interesting ideas and research directions that went unmentioned in the text and provide references to relevant web pages, research articles, reference manuals, and books.

End-of-Chapter Exercises

The end of each chapter contains numerous exercises. Some exercises are of the pencil-and-paper variety, designed to reinforce concepts taught in the chapter. Other exercises suggest interesting modifications to SimpleDB, and many of them make excellent programming projects. I have written solutions to most of the exercises. If you are the instructor of a course using this textbook and would like a copy of the solution manual, please email me at sciore@bc.edu.

Contents

About the Author

Edward Sciore is a recently retired associate professor in the Computer Science Department at Boston College. He is the author of numerous research articles about database systems, which span both theory and practice. His favorite activity, however, is to teach database courses to captive students. These teaching experiences, accumulated over a 35-year period, are what led to the writing of this text.

Chapter 1
Database Systems

Database systems play an important role in the computer industry. Some database systems (such as Oracle) are enormously complex and typically run on large, high-end machines. Others (such as SQLite) are small, streamlined, and intended for the storage of application-specific data. Despite their wide range of uses, all database systems have similar features. This chapter examines the issues that a database system must address and the capabilities it is expected to have. It also introduces the Derby and SimpleDB database systems, which will be discussed in this book.

1.1 Why a Database System?

A *database* is a collection of data stored on a computer. The data in a database is typically organized into *records*, such as employee records, medical records, sales records, etc. Figure 1.1 depicts a database that holds information about students in a university and the courses they have taken. This database will be used as a running example throughout the book. The database of Fig. 1.1 contains five types of records:

- There is a STUDENT record for each student that has attended the university. Each record contains the student's ID number, name, graduation year, and ID of the student's major department.
- There is a DEPT record for each department in the university. Each record contains the department's ID number and name.
- There is a COURSE record for each course offered by the university. Each record contains the course's ID number, title, and the ID of the department that offers it.
- There is a SECTION record for each section of a course that has ever been given. Each record contains the section's ID number, the year the section was offered, the ID of the course, and the professor teaching that section.

E. Sciore, *Database Design and Implementation*, Data-Centric Systems and Applications, https://doi.org/10.1007/978-3-030-33836-7_1

STUDENT	SId	SName	GradYear	MajorId
	1	joe	2021	10
	2	amy	2020	20
	3	max	2022	10
	4	sue	2022	20
	5	bob	2020	30
	6	kim	2020	20
	7	art	2021	30
	8	pat	2019	20
	9	lee	2021	10

DEPT	DId	DName
	10	compsci
	20	math
	30	drama

COURSE	CId	Title	DeptId
	12	db systems	10
	22	compilers	10
	32	calculus	20
	42	algebra	20
	52	acting	30
	62	elocution	30

ENROLL	EId	StudentId	SectionId	Grade
	14	1	13	A
	24	1	43	C
	34	2	43	B+
	44	4	33	B
	54	4	53	A
	64	6	53	A

SECTION	SectId	CourseId	Prof	YearOffered
	13	12	turing	2018
	23	12	turing	2016
	33	32	newton	2017
	43	32	einstein	2018
	53	62	brando	2017

Fig. 1.1 Some records for a university database

- There is an ENROLL record for each course taken by a student. Each record contains the enrollment ID number, the ID numbers of the student and the section of the course taken, and the grade the student received for the course.

Figure 1.1 is just a conceptual picture of some records. It does not indicate anything about how the records are stored or how they are accessed. There are many available software products, called *database systems*, which provide an extensive set of features for managing records.

What does it mean to "manage" records? What features must a database system have, and which features are optional? The following five requirements seem fundamental:

- *Databases must be persistent.* Otherwise, the records would disappear as soon as the computer is turned off.
- *Databases can be shared.* Many databases, such as our university database, are intended to be shared by multiple concurrent users.
- *Databases must be kept accurate.* If users cannot trust the contents of a database, it becomes useless and worthless.
- *Databases can be very large.* The database of Fig. 1.1 contains only 29 records, which is ridiculously small. It is not unusual for a database to contain millions (or even billions) of records.
- *Databases must be usable.* If users are not able to easily get at the data they want, their productivity will suffer, and they will clamor for a different product.

1 TAB j o e TAB 2 0 2 1 TAB 1 0 RET 2 TAB a m y TAB 2 0 2 0 TAB 2 0 RET 3 TAB m a x ...

Fig. 1.2 Implementing the STUDENT records in a text file

The following subsections examine the implications of these requirements. Each requirement forces the database system to contain increasingly more features, resulting in more complexity than you might have expected.

1.1.1 Record Storage

A common way to make a database persistent is to store its records in files. The simplest and most straightforward approach is for a database system to store records in text files, one file per record type; each record could be a line of text, with its values separated by tabs. Figure 1.2 depicts the beginning of the text file for the STUDENT records.

This approach has the advantage that a user could examine and modify the files with a text editor. Unfortunately, the approach is too inefficient to be useful, for two reasons.

The first reason is that large text files take too long to update. Suppose, for example, that someone deletes Joe's record from the STUDENT file. The database system would have no choice but to rewrite the file beginning at Amy's record, moving each succeeding record to the left. Although the time required to rewrite a small file is negligible, rewriting a 1 gigabyte file could easily take several minutes, which is unacceptably long. A database system needs to be much more clever about how it stores records, so that updates to the file require only small, local rewrites.

The second reason is that large text files take too long to read. Consider searching the STUDENT file for the students in the class of 2019. The only way is to scan the file sequentially. Sequential scanning can be very inefficient. You probably know several in-memory data structures, such as trees and hash tables, which enable fast searching. A database system needs to use analogous data structures to implement its files. For example, a database system might organize the records in a file using a structure that facilitates one particular type of search (e.g., on student name, graduation year or major), or it might create multiple auxiliary files, each facilitating a different type of search. These auxiliary files are called *indexes* and are the subject of Chap. 12.

1.1.2 Multi-user Access

When many users share a database, there is a good chance that they will be accessing some of its data files concurrently. Concurrency is a good thing, because each user can be served quickly without having to wait for the other users to finish. But too much concurrency is bad, because it can cause the database to become inaccurate. For example, consider a travel-planning database. Suppose that two users try to reserve a seat on a flight that has 40 seats remaining. If both users concurrently read the same flight record, they both will see the 40 available seats. They both then modify the record so that the flight now has 39 available seats. Oops. Two seats have been reserved, but only one reservation has been recorded in the database.

A solution to this problem is to limit concurrency. The database system should allow the first user to read the flight record and see the 40 available seats and then block the second user until the first user finishes. When the second user resumes, it will see 39 available seats and modify it to 38, as it should. In general, a database system must be able to detect when a user is about to perform an action that conflicts with an action of another user and then (and only then) block that user from executing until the first user has finished.

Users also may need to undo database updates they have made. For example, suppose that a user has searched the travel-planning database for a trip to Madrid and found a date for which there is both an available flight and a hotel with a vacancy. Now suppose that the user reserves the flight, but while the reservation process is occurring, all of the hotels for that date fill up. In this case, the user may need to undo the flight reservation and try for a different date.

An update that is undoable should not be visible to the other users of the database. Otherwise, another user may see the update, think that the data is "real," and make a decision based on it. The database system must therefore provide users with the ability to specify when their changes are permanent; the user is said to *commit* the changes. Once a user commits, the changes become visible and cannot be undone. Chapter 5 examines these issues.

1.1.3 Dealing with Catastrophe

Suppose that you are running a program that gives a pay raise to all professors, when the database system unexpectedly crashes. After the system restarts, you realize that some of the professors have a new salary, but others don't. What should you do? You can't just rerun the program because that would give some professors a double pay raise. Instead, you need the database system to recover gracefully from the crash, undoing the updates of all programs that were running when the crash occurred. The mechanism for doing so is interesting and nontrivial, and is examined in Chap. 5.

1.1.4 Memory Management

Databases need to be stored in persistent memory, such as disk drives or flash drives. Flash drives are about 100 times faster than disk drives but are also significantly more expensive. Typical access times are about 6 ms for disk and 60 μs for flash. However, both of these times are orders of magnitude slower than main memory (or RAM), which has access times of about 60 ns. That is, RAM is about 1000 times faster than flash and 100,000 times faster than disk.

To see the effect of this performance difference and the consequent problems faced by a database system, consider the following analogy. Suppose you crave a chocolate chip cookie. There are three ways to get one: from your kitchen, at the neighborhood grocery store, or via mail order. In this analogy, your kitchen corresponds to RAM, the neighborhood store corresponds to a flash drive, and the mail order company corresponds to a disk. Suppose that it takes 5 seconds to get the cookie from your kitchen. Getting the cookie from the analogous store would require 5000 seconds, which is over an hour. This means going to the store, waiting in a very long line, buying the cookie, and returning. And getting the cookie from the analogous mail order company would require 500,000 seconds, which is over 5 days. That means ordering the cookie online and having it shipped using standard delivery. From this point of view, flash and disk memory look terribly slow.

Wait! It gets worse. Database support for concurrency and reliability slows things down even more. If someone else is using the data you want, then you may be forced to wait until the data is released. In our analogy, this corresponds to arriving at the grocery store and discovering that the cookies are sold out, forcing you to wait until they are restocked.

In other words, a database system is faced with the following conundrum: It must manage *more* data than main memory systems, using *slower* devices, with *multiple people* fighting over access to the data, and make it *completely recoverable*, all the while maintaining a reasonable response time.

A large part of the solution to this conundrum is to use *caching*. Whenever the database system needs to process a record, it loads it into RAM and keeps it there for as long as possible. Main memory will thus contain the portion of the database that is currently in use. All reading and writing occur in RAM. This strategy has the advantage that fast main memory is used instead of slow persistent memory but has the disadvantage that the persistent version of the database can become out of date. The database system needs to implement techniques for keeping the persistent version of the database synchronized with the RAM version, even in the face of a system crash (when the contents of RAM is destroyed). Chapter 4 considers various caching strategies.

1.1.5 Usability

A database is not very useful if its users cannot easily extract the data they want. For example, suppose that a user wants to know the names of all students who graduated in 2019. In the absence of a database system, the user would be forced to write a program to scan the student file. Figure 1.3 gives the Java code for such a program, assuming that the file is stored as text. Note that most of the Java code deals with decoding the file, reading each record and splitting it into an array of values to be examined. The code to determine the desired student names (in bold) is hidden within the uninteresting file-manipulation code.

```
public static List<String> getStudents2019() {
   List<String> result = new ArrayList<>();
   FileReader rdr = new FileReader("students.txt");
   BufferedReader br = new BufferedReader(rdr);
   String line = br.readLine();
   while (line != null) {
      String[] vals = line.split("\t");
      String gradyear = vals[2];
      if (gradyear.equals("2019"))
         result.add(vals[1]);
      line = br.readLine();
   }
   return result;
}
```

Fig. 1.3 Retrieving the name of students graduating in 2019

Consequently, most database systems support a *query language*, so that users can easily specify their desired data. The standard query language for relational databases is SQL. The code of Fig. 1.3 can be expressed by the single SQL statement:

```
select SName from STUDENT where GradYear = 2019
```

This SQL statement is much shorter and clearer than the Java program, primarily because it specifies the values to be extracted from the file without having to specify how to retrieve them.

1.2 The Derby Database System

Learning database concepts is much more effective if you can use a database system to follow along interactively. Although there are a wide variety of available database systems, I suggest that you use *Derby* database system because it is Java-based, free, easy to install, and easy to use. The latest version of Derby can be downloaded from the `downloads` tab at the URL `db.apache.org/derby`. The downloaded distribution file unpacks to a folder containing several directories. For example, the `docs` directory contains reference documentation, the *demo* directory contains a sample database, and so on. The full system contains many more features than can be covered here; the interested reader can peruse the various guides and manuals in the `docs` directory.

Derby has many features that are not needed in this book. In fact, you only need to add four files from Derby's `lib` directory to your classpath: `derby.jar`, `derbynet.jar`, `derbyclient.jar`, and `derbytools.jar`. There are many ways to change your classpath, depending on your Java platform and operating system. I will explain how to do it using the Eclipse development platform. If you are not familiar with Eclipse, you can download its code and documentation from `eclipse.org`. If you use a different development platform, then you should be able to adapt my Eclipse directions to fit your environment.

First, create an Eclipse project for Derby. Then configure its build path, as follows. From the `Properties` window, select "Java Build Path." Click on the "Libraries" tab and then "Add External JARS," and use the file chooser to select the four jar files you need. That's it.

The Derby distribution contains an application, called `ij`, which enables you to create and access Derby databases. Because Derby is written completely in Java, `ij` is actually the name of a Java class, located in the package `org.apache.derby.tools`. You run `ij` by executing its class. To execute the class from Eclipse, go to "Run Configurations" in the Run menu. Add a new configuration to your Derby project; call it "Derby ij." In the field for the configuration's main class, enter "org.apache.derby.tools.ij." When you run the configuration, `ij` displays a console window that asks for input.

Input to `ij` is a sequence of commands. A command is a string that ends with a semicolon. Commands can be split over several lines of text; the `ij` client will not execute a command until it encounters a line ending in a semicolon. Any SQL statement is a legal command. In addition, `ij` supports commands to connect and disconnect from a database and to exit the session.

The `connect` command specifies the database that `ij` should connect to, and the `disconnect` command disconnects from it. A given session can connect and disconnect multiple times. The *`exit`* command ends the session. Figure 1.4 shows an example *`ij`* session. The session has two parts. In the first part, the user connects to a new database, creates a table, inserts a record into that table, and disconnects. In the second part, the user reconnects to that database, retrieves the inserted values, and disconnects.

The argument to the `connect` command is called its *connection string*. The connection string has three substrings, separated by colons. The first two substrings are "jdbc" and "derby," indicating that you want to connect to a Derby database using the JDBC protocol. (JDBC is the topic of Chap. 2.) The third substring

```
ij> connect 'jdbc:derby:ijtest;create=true';
ij> create table T(A int, B varchar(9));
0 rows inserted/updated/deleted
ij> insert into T(A,B) values(3, 'record3');
1 row inserted/updated/deleted
ij> disconnect;
ij> connect 'jdbc:derby:ijtest';
ij> select * from T;
A          |B
--------------------
3          |record3

1 row selected
ij> disconnect;
ij> exit;
```

Fig. 1.4 An example *ij* session

identifies the database. The string "ijtest" is the name of the database; its files will be in a folder named "ijtest", located in the directory from which the `ij` program was launched. For example, if you ran the program from Eclipse, the database folder will be in the project directory. The string "create = true" tells Derby to create a new database; if it is omitted (as in the second *connection* command), then Derby expects to find an existing database.

1.3 Database Engines

A database application such as `ij` is comprised of two independent parts: the user interface (or UI), and the code to access the database. This latter code is called the *database engine*. Separating the UI from the database engine is good system design, as it simplifies the development of the application. A well-known example of this separation occurs in the Microsoft Access database system. It has a graphical UI that allows a user to interact with the database by clicking the mouse and filling in values, and an engine that handles the data storage. When the UI determines that it needs information from the database, it constructs a request and sends it to the engine. The engine then executes the request and sends values back to the UI.

This separation also adds flexibility to the system: an application designer can use the same user interface with different database engines or build different user interfaces for the same database engine. Microsoft Access provides an example of each case. A form built using the Access UI can connect to the Access engine or any other database engine. And the cells in an Excel spreadsheet can contain formulas that query the Access engine.

A UI accesses a database by connecting to the desired engine and then calling methods from the engine's API. As an example, note that the Derby `ij` program is really just a UI. Its *connect* command establishes a connection to the specified database engine, and each SQL command sends the SQL statement to the engine, retrieves the results, and displays them.

Database engines typically support multiple standard APIs. When a Java program connects to an engine, the API of choice is called *JDBC*. Chapter 2 discusses JDBC in detail and shows how to write an `ij`-like application using JDBC.

A connection from a UI to a database engine can be *embedded* or *server-based*. In an embedded connection, the code for the database engine runs in the same process as the code for the UI, which gives the UI exclusive access to the engine. An application should use an embedded connection only when the database "belongs" to that application and is stored on the same machine as the application. Other applications need to use server-based connections.

In a server-based connection, the code for the database engine executes inside a dedicated server program. This server program is always running, waiting for client connections, and need not be on the same machine as its clients. After a client establishes a connection with the server, the client sends JDBC requests to it and receives responses.

A server can be connected to multiple clients simultaneously. While the server is processing one client's request, other clients can be sending their own requests. The server contains a *scheduler*, which queues up requests waiting for service and determines when they get executed. Each client is unaware of the other clients and (apart from delays due to scheduling) has the pleasant illusion that the server is dealing with it exclusively.

The `ij` session of Fig. 1.4 used an embedded connection. It created the database "ijtest" on the machine that was running the session, and no server was involved. To execute an analogous server-based `ij` session, two things must change: the Derby engine must run as a server, and the *connect* command must be modified so that it identifies the server.

The code for the Derby server is in the Java class `NetworkServerControl`, in the package `org.apache.derby.drda`. To run the server from Eclipse, go to "Run Configurations" in the Run menu. Add a new configuration to your Derby project and call it "Derby Server." In the field for the main class, enter "org.apache.derby.drda.NetworkServerControl." In the Arguments tab, enter the program argument "start -h localhost." Each time you run the configuration, a console window should appear indicating that the Derby server is running.

What is the purpose of the program argument "start -h localhost"? The first word is the command "start," which tells the class to start the server. You can stop the server by executing the same class with the argument "shutdown" (or you can simply terminate the process from the console window). The string "-h localhost" tells the server to only accept requests from clients on the same machine. If you replace "localhost" by a domain name or IP address, then the server will only accept requests from that machine. Using the IP address "0.0.0.0" tells the server to accept requests from anywhere.[1]

A connection string for a server-based connection must specify the network or IP address of the server machine. In particular, consider the following *ij connect* commands:

```
ij> connect 'jdbc:derby:ijtest'
ij> connect 'jdbc:derby://localhost/ijtest'
ij> connect 'jdbc:derby://cs.bc.edu/ijtest'
```

The first command establishes an embedded connection to the "ijtest" database. The second command establishes a server-based connection to "ijtest" using the server running on the machine "localhost," that is, on the local machine. The third command establishes a server-based connection to "ijtest" using the server running on the machine "cs.bc.edu."

Note how the connect string completely encapsulates the decision to use an embedded or server-side connection. For example, consider again Fig. 1.4. You can modify the session to use server-side connections instead of embedded ones by

[1]Of course, if you allow clients to connect from anywhere, then you expose the database to hackers and other unscrupulous users. Typically, you would either place such a server inside of a firewall, enable Derby's authentication mechanism, or both.

simply changing the *connect* commands. The other commands in the session are unaffected.

1.4 The SimpleDB Database System

Derby is a sophisticated, full-featured database system. This complexity, however, means that its source code is not readily understandable or modifiable. I wrote the SimpleDB database system to be the opposite of Derby—its code is small, easily readable, and easily modifiable. It omits all unnecessary functionality, implements only a tiny portion of SQL, and uses only the simplest (and often very impractical) algorithms. Its purpose is to give you a clear look at each component of a database engine and how these components interact.

The latest version of SimpleDB can be downloaded from its website at the URL `cs.bc.edu/~sciore/simpledb`. The downloaded file unpacks to the folder `SimpleDB_3.x`; this folder contains directories `simpledb`, `simpleclient`, and `derbyclient`. The `simpledb` folder contains code for the database engine. Unlike Derby, this code is not packed into a jar file; instead, every file is explicit within the folder.

To install the SimpleDB engine, you must add the `simpledb` folder to your classpath. To do so using Eclipse, first, create a new project; call it "SimpleDB Engine." Then from the operating system, copy the subfolder of your `SimpleDB_3.x` folder named "simpledb" to the `src` folder of the project. Finally, refresh the project from Eclipse, using the `refresh` command in the File menu.

The `derbyclient` folder contains example programs that call the Derby engine. Use the operating system to copy the contents of this folder (not the folder itself) to the `src` folder of your Derby project, and refresh it. These client programs will be discussed in Chap. 2.

The `simpleclient` folder contains example programs that call the SimpleDB engine. You should create a new project for them; call it "SimpleDB Clients." To ensure that the example programs can find the SimpleDB engine code, you should add the `SimpleDB Engine` project to the build path of `SimpleDB Clients`. Then use the operating system to copy the contents of `simpleclient` into the `src` directory of `SimpleDB Clients`.

SimpleDB supports both embedded and server-based connections. One of the programs in the `simpleclient` folder is `SimpleIJ`, which is a simplified version of the Derby `ij` program. One difference from `ij` is that you can only connect once, at the beginning of the session. When you execute the program, it asks you for a connection string. The syntax of the connection string is similar to that in `ij`. For example, consider the following SimpleDB connection strings:

```
jdbc:simpledb:testij
jdbc:simpledb://localhost
jdbc:simpledb://cs.bc.edu
```

The first connection string specifies an embedded connection to the "testij" database. Like Derby, the database will be located in the directory of the executing program, which is the `SimpleDB Clients` project. Unlike Derby, SimpleDB will create the database if it does not exist, so there is no need for an explicit "create = true" flag.

The second and third connection strings specify a server-based connection to a SimpleDB server running on the local machine or on `cs.bc.edu`. Unlike Derby, the connection string does not specify a database. The reason is that the SimpleDB engine can handle only one database at a time, which is specified when the server is started.

`SimpleIJ` repeatedly prints a prompt asking you to enter a single line of text containing an SQL statement. Unlike Derby, the line must contain the entire statement, and no semicolon is needed at the end. The program then executes that statement. If the statement is a query, then the output table is displayed. If the statement is an update command, then the number of affected records is printed. If the statement is ill-formed, then an error message will be printed. SimpleDB understands a very limited subset of SQL, and `SimpleIJ` will throw an exception if given an SQL statement that the engine does not understand. These limitations are described in the next section.

The SimpleDB engine can be run as a server. The main class is *StartServer* in the package *simpledb.server*. To run the server from Eclipse, go to "Run Configurations" in the Run menu. Add a new configuration to your `SimpleDB Engine` project called "SimpleDB Server." In the field for the main class, enter "simpledb.server.StartServer." Use the Arguments tab to enter the name of the desired database. For convenience, the server will use the database named "studentdb" if you omit the argument. When you run the configuration, a console window should appear indicating that the SimpleDB server is running.

The SimpleDB server accepts client connections from anywhere, corresponding to Derby's "*-h 0.0.0.0*" command-line option. The only way to shut down the server is to kill its process from the console window.

1.5 The SimpleDB Version of SQL

Derby implements nearly all of standard SQL. SimpleDB, on the other hand, implements only a tiny subset of standard SQL and imposes restrictions not present in the SQL standard. This section briefly indicates these restrictions. Other chapters of the book explain them in more detail, and many end-of-chapter exercises will ask you to implement some of the omitted features.

A query in SimpleDB consists only of *select-from-where* clauses in which the `select` clause contains a list of field names (without the AS keyword), and the `from` clause contains a list of table names (without range variables).

The terms in the optional `where` clause can be connected only by the boolean operator `and`. Terms can only compare constants and fieldnames for equality.

Unlike standard SQL, there are no other comparison operators, no other boolean operators, no arithmetic operators or built-in functions, and no parentheses. Consequently, nested queries, aggregation, and computed values are not supported.

Because there are no range variables and no renaming, all field names in a query must be disjoint. And because there are no `group by` or `order by` clauses, grouping and sorting are not supported. Other restrictions are:

- The "*" abbreviation in the `select` clause is not supported.
- There are no null values.
- There are no explicit joins or outer joins in the `from` clause.
- The `union` keyword is not supported.
- An `insert` statement takes explicit values only. That is, an insertion cannot be specified by a query.
- An `update` statement can have only one assignment in the `set` clause.

1.6 Chapter Summary

- A *database* is a collection of data stored on a computer. The data in a database is typically organized into *records*. A *database system* is software that manages the records in a database.
- A database system must be able to handle large shared databases, storing its data on slow persistent memory. It must provide a high-level interface to its data and ensure data accuracy in the face of conflicting user updates and system crashes. Database systems meet these requirements by having the following features:
  - The ability to store records in a file, using a format that can be accessed more efficiently than the file system typically allows
  - Complex algorithms for indexing data in files, to support fast access
  - The ability to handle concurrent accesses from multiple users over a network, blocking users when necessary
  - Support for committing and rolling back changes
  - The ability to cache database records in main memory and to manage the synchronization between the persistent and main-memory versions of the database, restoring the database to a reasonable state if the system crashes
  - A language compiler/interpreter, for translating user queries on tables to executable code on files
  - Query optimization strategies, for transforming inefficient queries into more efficient ones
- The *database engine* is the component of the database system that maintains the data. A database application is responsible for user input and output; it calls the database engine to obtain the data it needs.
- A connection to the database engine can be either *embedded* or *server-based*. A program having an embedded connection has exclusive access to the database

engine. A program having a server-based connection shares the engine with other concurrent programs.

- Two Java-based database systems are *Derby* and *SimpleDB*. Derby implements the full SQL standard, whereas SimpleDB implements only a limited subset of SQL. SimpleDB is useful because its code is easy to understand. The rest of this book starting in Chap. 3 will examine this code in detail.

1.7 Suggested Reading

Database systems have undergone dramatic changes over the years. A good account of these changes can be found in Chap. 6 of National Research Council (1999) and in Haigh (2006). The Wikipedia entry at `en.wikipedia.org/wiki/Database_management_system#History` is also interesting.

The client-server paradigm is useful in numerous areas of computing, not just databases. A general overview of the field can be found in Orfali et al. (1999). Documentation on the various features and configuration options of the Derby server can be found at the URL `db.apache.org/derby/manuals/index.html`.

Haigh, T. (2006). “A veritable bucket of facts”. Origins of the data base management system. *ACM SIGMOD Record, 35*(2), 33–49.

National Research Council Committee on Innovations in Computing and Communications. (1999). *Funding a revolution*. National Academy Press. Available from `www.nap.edu/read/6323/chapter/8#159`

Orfali, R., Harkey, D., & Edwards, J. (1999). *Client/server survival guide* (3rd ed.). Wiley.

1.8 Exercises

Conceptual Exercises

1.1. Suppose that an organization needs to manage a relatively small number of shared records (say, 100 or so).

(a) Would it make sense to use a commercial database system to manage these records?
(b) What features of a database system would not be required?
(c) Would it be reasonable to use a spreadsheet to store these records? What are the potential problems?

1.2. Suppose you want to store a large amount of personal data in a database. What features of a database system wouldn't you need?

1.3. Consider some data that you typically manage without a database system (such as a shopping list, address book, checking account info, etc.).

(a) How large would the data have to get before you would break down and store it in a database system?
(b) What changes to how you use the data would make it worthwhile to use a database system?

1.4. If you know how to use a version control system (such as Git or Subversion), compare its features to those of a database system.

(a) Does a version control system have a concept of a record?
(b) How does check-in/checkout correspond to database concurrency control?
(c) How does a user perform a commit? How does a user undo uncommitted changes?
(d) Many version control systems save updates in *difference files*, which are small files that describe how to transform the previous version of the file into the new one. If a user needs to see the current version of the file, the system starts with the original file and applies all of the difference files to it. How well does this implementation strategy satisfy the needs of a database system?

Project-Based Exercises

1.5. Investigate whether your school administration or company uses a database system. If so:

(a) What employees explicitly use the database system in their job? (As opposed to those employees who run "canned" programs that use the database without their knowledge.) What do they use it for?
(b) When a user needs to do something new with the data, does the user write his own query, or does someone else do it?

1.6. Install and run the Derby and SimpleDB servers.

(a) Run the `ij` and `SimpleIJ` programs from the server machine.
(b) If you have access to a second machine, modify the demo clients and run them remotely from that machine as well.

Chapter 2
JDBC

A database application interacts with a database engine by calling the methods of its API. The API used by Java applications is called *JDBC* (for *Java DataBase Connectivity*). The JDBC library consists of five Java packages, most of which implement advanced features useful only in large commercial applications. This chapter is interested in the core JDBC functionality found in the package `java.sql`. This core functionality can be divided into two parts: *basic JDBC*, which contains the classes and methods required for rudimentary usage, and *advanced JDBC*, which contains optional features that provide added convenience and flexibility.

2.1 Basic JDBC

The basic functionality of JDBC is embodied in five interfaces: `Driver`, `Connection`, `Statement`, `ResultSet`, and `ResultSetMetadata`. Moreover, only a very few methods of these interfaces are essential. Figure 2.1 lists these methods.

The example programs of this section illustrate the use of these methods. The first example program is `CreateTestDB`, which illustrates how a program connects to and disconnects from a Derby engine. Its code appears in Fig. 2.2, with the JDBC-related code highlighted in bold. The following subsections examine this code in detail.

2.1.1 Connecting to a Database Engine

Each database engine will have its own (and possibly proprietary) mechanism for making connections with clients. Clients, on the other hand, want to be as server independent as possible. That is, a client doesn't want to know the nitty-gritty details

E. Sciore, *Database Design and Implementation*, Data-Centric Systems and Applications, https://doi.org/10.1007/978-3-030-33836-7_2

```
Driver
public Connection connect(String url, Properties prop)
                                         throws SQLException;
Connection
public Statement createStatement() throws SQLException;
public void      close()           throws SQLException;

Statement
public ResultSet executeQuery(String qry)  throws SQLException;
public int       executeUpdate(String cmd) throws SQLException;
public void      close()                   throws SQLException;

ResultSet
public boolean   next()                   throws SQLException;
public int       getInt()                 throws SQLException;
public String    getString()              throws SQLException;
public void      close()                  throws SQLException;
public ResultSetMetaData getMetaData()    throws SQLException;

ResultSetMetaData
public int        getColumnCount()            throws SQLException;
public String     getColumnName(int column)   throws SQLException;
public int        getColumnType(int column)   throws SQLException;
public int getColumnDisplaySize(int column)   throws SQLException;
```

Fig. 2.1 The APIs for basic JDBC

```
import java.sql.Driver;
import java.sql.Connection;
import org.apache.derby.jdbc.ClientDriver;

public class CreateTestDB {
   public static void main(String[] args) {
      String url = "jdbc:derby://localhost/testdb;create=true";
      Driver d = new ClientDriver();
      try {
         Connection conn = d.connect(url, null);
         System.out.println("Database Created");
         conn.close();
      }
      catch(SQLException e) {
         e.printStackTrace();
      }
   }
}
```

Fig. 2.2 The JDBC code for the CreateTestDB client

of how to connect to an engine; it simply wants the engine to provide a class for the client to call. Such a class is called a *driver*.

JDBC driver classes implement the interface `Driver`. Derby and SimpleDB each have two driver classes: one for server-based connections and one for embedded connections. A server-based connection to the Derby engine uses the class `ClientDriver`, whereas an embedded connection uses `EmbeddedDriver`; both classes are in package `org.apache.derby.jdbc`. A server-based connection to the SimpleDB engine uses the class `NetworkDriver` (in package `simpledb.jdbc.network`), whereas an embedded connection uses `EmbeddedDriver` (in package `simpledb.jdbc.embedded`).

A client connects to a database engine by calling a `Driver` object's *connect* method. For example, the following three lines of Fig. 2.2 make a server-based connection to a Derby database:

```
String url = "jdbc:derby://localhost/testdb;create=true";
Driver d = new ClientDriver();
Connection conn = d.connect(url, null);
```

The `connect` method takes two arguments. The first argument to the method is a URL that identifies the driver, the server (for server-based connections), and the database. This URL is called the *connection string* and has the same syntax as the `ij` (or `SimpleIJ`) server-based connection strings of Chap. 1. The connection string in Fig. 2.2 consists of four parts:

- The substring "jdbc:derby:" describes the protocol used by the client. Here, the protocol says that this client is a Derby client that speaks JDBC.
- The substring "//localhost" describes the machine where the server is located. Instead of *localhost*, you could substitute any domain name or IP address.
- The substring "/testdb" describes the path to the database on the server. For a Derby server, the path begins at the current directory of the user that started the server. The end of the path (here, "testdb") is the directory where all data files for this database will be stored.
- The remainder of the connection string consists of property values to be sent to the engine. Here, the substring is ";create = true", which tells the engine to create a new database. In general, several property values can be sent to a Derby engine. For example, if the engine requires user authentication, then values for the properties `username` and `password` would also be specified. The connection string for the user "einstein" might look like this:

```
"jdbc:derby://localhost/testdb;create=true;user=einstein;
password=emc2"
```

The second argument to `connect` is an object of type `Properties`. This object provides another way to pass property values to the engine. In Fig. 2.2, the value of this argument is `null` because all properties are specified in the connection string. Alternatively, you could have put the property specification into the second argument, as follows:

```
String url = "jdbc:derby://localhost/testdb";
Properties prop = new Properties();
prop.put("create", "true");
prop.put("username", "einstein");
prop.put("password", "emc2");
Driver d = new ClientDriver();
Connection conn = d.connect(url, prop);
```

Each database engine has its own connection string syntax. A server-based connection string for SimpleDB differs from Derby in that it contains only a protocol and machine name. (It doesn't make sense for the string to contain the name of the database, because the database is specified when the SimpleDB server is started. And the connection string doesn't specify properties because the SimpleDB server doesn't support any.) For example, the following three lines of code make a connection to a SimpleDB server:

```
String url = "jdbc:simpledb://localhost";
Driver d = new NetworkDriver();
conn = d.connect(url, null);
```

Although the driver class and connection string syntax are vendor-specific, the rest of a JDBC program is completely vendor-neutral. For example, consider the variables `d` and `conn` in Fig. 2.2. Their corresponding JDBC types, `Driver` and `Connection`, are interfaces. You can tell from the code that variable `d` is assigned to a `ClientDriver` object. However, `conn` is assigned to the `Connection` object returned by the method `connect`, and there is no way to know its actual class. This situation is true for all JDBC programs. Apart from the name of the driver class and its connection string, a JDBC program only knows about and cares about the vendor-neutral JDBC interfaces. Consequently, a basic JDBC client will import from two packages:

- The built-in package `java.sql`, to obtain the vendor-neutral JDBC interface definitions
- The vendor-supplied package that contains the driver class

2.1.2 Disconnecting from a Database Engine

During the time that a client is connected to a database engine, the engine may allocate resources for the client's use. For example, a client may request locks from its server that keep other clients from accessing portions of the database. Even the ability to connect to an engine can be a resource. A company may have a site license with a commercial database system that restricts the number of simultaneous connections, which means that holding a connection could deprive another client from connecting. Because connections hold valuable resources, clients are expected to disconnect from the engine as soon as the database is no longer needed. A client program disconnects from its engine by calling the `close` method of its `Connection` object. This call to `close` can be seen in Fig. 2.2.

2.1.3 SQL Exceptions

The interaction between a client and database engine can generate exceptions for many reasons. Examples are as follows:

- The client asks the engine to execute a badly formed SQL statement or an SQL query that accesses a nonexistent table or that compares two incompatible values.
- The engine aborts the client because of a deadlock between it and a concurrent client.
- There is a bug in the engine code.
- The client cannot access the engine (for a server-based connection). Perhaps the host name is wrong, or the host has become unreachable.

Different database engines have their own internal way of dealing with these exceptions. SimpleDB, for example, throws a `RemoteException` on a network problem, a `BadSyntaxException` on an SQL statement problem, a `BufferAbortException` or `LockAbortException` on a deadlock, and a generic `RuntimeException` on a server problem.

In order to make exception handling vendor independent, JDBC provides its own exception class, called `SQLException`. When a database engine encounters an internal exception, it wraps it in an SQL exception and sends it to the client program.

The message string associated with an SQL exception identifies the internal exception that caused it. Each database engine is free to provide its own messages. Derby, for example, has nearly 900 error messages, whereas SimpleDB lumps all of the possible problems into six messages: "network problem," "illegal SQL statement," "server error," "operation not supported," and two forms of "transaction abort."

Most JDBC methods (and all of the methods in Fig. 2.1) throw an SQL exception. SQL exceptions are *checked*, which means that clients must explicitly deal with them either by catching them or throwing them onward. The two JDBC methods in Fig. 2.2 are performed inside a `try` block; if either causes an exception, the code prints a stack trace and returns.

Note that the code of Fig. 2.2 has a problem, namely, that its connection is not closed when an exception is thrown. This is an example of a *resource leak*—the engine cannot easily reclaim the connection's resources after the client dies. One way to fix the problem is to close the connection within the `catch` block. However, the `close` method needs to be called from within a `try` block, which means the `catch` block of Fig. 2.2 really ought to look like this:

```
catch(SQLException e) {
  e.printStackTrace();
  try {
    conn.close();
  }
  catch (SQLException ex) {}
}
```

This is starting to look ugly. Moreover, what should the client do if the `close` method throws an exception? The above code ignores it, but that doesn't seem quite right.

A better solution is to let Java close the connection automatically, via its *try-with-resources* syntax. To use it, you create the `Connection` object within parentheses after the `try` keyword. When the `try` block ends (either normally or via exception), Java will implicitly call the object's `close` method. The improved `try` block for Fig. 2.2 looks like this:

```
try (Connection conn = d.connect(url, null)) {
  System.out.println("Database Created");
}
catch (SQLException e) {
  e.printStackTrace();
}
```

This code handles all exceptions properly, without losing the simplicity of Fig. 2.2.

2.1.4 Executing SQL Statements

A connection can be thought of as a "session" with the database engine, during which the engine executes SQL statements for the client. JDBC supports this idea as follows.

A `Connection` object has the method `createStatement`, which returns a `Statement` object. The `Statement` object has two ways to execute SQL statements: the methods `executeQuery` and `executeUpdate`. It also has the method `close`, for deallocating resources held by the object.

Figure 2.3 shows a client program that calls `executeUpdate` to modify the `MajorId` value of Amy's STUDENT record. The argument to the method is a string denoting the SQL update statement; the method returns the number of records that were updated.

The `Statement` object, like the `Connection` object, needs to be closed. The easiest solution is to autoclose both objects in the `try` block.

The specification of the SQL command illustrates an interesting point. Since the command is stored as a Java string, it is encased in double quotes. On the other hand, strings in SQL use single quotes. This distinction makes your life easy, because you

```
public class ChangeMajor {
   public static void main(String[] args) {
      String url = "jdbc:derby://localhost/studentdb";
      String cmd = "update STUDENT set MajorId=30 where SName='amy'";

      Driver d = new ClientDriver();
      try ( Connection conn = d.connect(url, null);
            Statement stmt = conn.createStatement()) {
         int howmany = stmt.executeUpdate(cmd);
         System.out.println(howmany + " records changed.");
      }
      catch(SQLException e) {
         e.printStackTrace();
      }
   }
}
```

Fig. 2.3 JDBC code for the ChangeMajor client

don't have to worry about a quote character having two different meanings—SQL strings use single quotes, and Java strings use double quotes.

The ChangeMajor code assumes that a database named "studentdb" exists. The SimpleDB distribution contains the class CreateStudentDB, which creates the database and populates it with the tables of Fig. 1.1. It should be the first program called when using the university database. Its code appears in Fig. 2.4. The code executes SQL statements to create five tables and insert records into them. For brevity, only the code for STUDENT is shown.

2.1.5 Result Sets

A statement's executeQuery method executes an SQL query. The argument to this method is a string denoting an SQL query, and it returns an object of type ResultSet. A ResultSet object represents the query's output records. The client can search through the result set to examine these records.

For an example program that illustrates the use of result sets, consider the class StudentMajor shown in Fig. 2.5. Its call to executeQuery returns a result set containing the name and major of each student. The subsequent while loop prints each record in the result set.

Once a client obtains a result set, it iterates through the output records by calling the method next. This method moves to the next record, returning true if the move is successful and false if there are no more records. Typically, a client uses a loop to move through all the records, processing each one in turn.

A new ResultSet object is always positioned before the first record, and so you need to call next before you can look at the first record. Because of this requirement, the typical way to loop through the records looks like this:

```
public class CreateStudentDB {
   public static void main(String[] args) {
      String url = "jdbc:derby://localhost/studentdb;create=true";
      Driver d = new ClientDriver();
      try (Connection conn = d.connect(url, null);
            Statement stmt = conn.createStatement()) {

         String s = "create table STUDENT(SId int,
                 SName varchar(10), MajorId int, GradYear int)";
         stmt.executeUpdate(s);
         System.out.println("Table STUDENT created.");

         s = "insert into STUDENT(SId, SName,
                                 MajorId, GradYear) values ";
         String[] studvals = {"(1, 'joe', 10, 2021)",
               "(2, 'amy', 20, 2020)",
               "(3, 'max', 10, 2022)",
               "(4, 'sue', 20, 2022)",
               "(5, 'bob', 30, 2020)",
               "(6, 'kim', 20, 2020)",
               "(7, 'art', 30, 2021)",
               "(8, 'pat', 20, 2019)",
               "(9, 'lee', 10, 2021)"};
         for (int i=0; i<studvals.length; i++)
            stmt.executeUpdate(s + studvals[i]);
         System.out.println("STUDENT records inserted.");

         ...

      }
      catch(SQLException e) {
         e.printStackTrace();
      }
   }
}
```

Fig. 2.4 JDBC code for the `CreateStudentDB` client

```
String qry = "select ...";
ResultSet rs = stmt.executeQuery(qry);
while (rs.next()) {
  ... // process the record
}
```

An example of such a loop appears in Fig. 2.5. During the `nth` pass through this loop, variable `rs` will be positioned at the `nth` record of the result set. The loop will end when there are no more records to process.

When processing a record, a client uses the methods `getInt` and `getString` to retrieve the values of its fields. Each of the methods takes a field name as argument and returns the value of that field. In Fig. 2.5, the code retrieves and prints the values of fields `SName` and `DName` for each record.

```
public class StudentMajor {
   public static void main(String[] args) {
      String url = "jdbc:derby://localhost/studentdb";
      String qry = "select SName, DName from DEPT, STUDENT "
            + "where MajorId = DId";

      Driver d = new ClientDriver();
      try ( Connection conn = d.connect(url, null);
            Statement stmt = conn.createStatement();
            ResultSet rs = stmt.executeQuery(qry)) {
         System.out.println("Name\tMajor");
         while (rs.next()) {
            String sname = rs.getString("SName");
            String dname = rs.getString("DName");
            System.out.println(sname + "\t" + dname);
         }
      }
      catch(SQLException e) {
         e.printStackTrace();
      }
   }
}
```

Fig. 2.5 JDBC code for the `StudentMajor` client

Result sets tie up valuable resources on the engine. The method `close` releases these resources and makes them available for other clients. A client should therefore strive to be a "good citizen" and close result sets as soon as possible. One option is to call `close` explicitly, typically at the end of the above while-loop. Another option, used in Fig. 2.5, is to use the Java autoclose mechanism.

2.1.6 Using Query Metadata

The *schema* of a result set is defined to be the name, type, and display size of each field. This information is made available through the interface `ResultSetMetaData`.

When a client executes a query, it usually knows the schema of the output table. For example, hardcoded into the `StudentMajor` client is the knowledge that its result set contains the two string fields `SName` and `DName`.

However, suppose that a client program allows users to submit queries as input. The program can call the method `getMetaData` on the query's result set, which returns an object of type `ResultSetMetaData`. It can then call the methods of this object to determine the output table's schema. For example, the code in Fig. 2.6 uses `ResultSetMetaData` to print the schema of an argument result set.

```
void printSchema(ResultSet rs) throws SQLException {
   ResultSetMetaData md = rs.getMetaData();
   for(int i=1; i<=md.getColumnCount(); i++) {
      String name    = md.getColumnName(i);
      int size       = md.getColumnDisplaySize(i);
      int typecode = md.getColumnType(i);
      String type;
      if (typecode == Types.INTEGER)
         type = "int";
      else if (typecode == Types.VARCHAR)
         type = "string";
      else
         type = "other";
      System.out.println(name + "\t" + type + "\t" + size);
   }
}
```

Fig. 2.6 Using ResultSetMetaData to print the schema of a result set

This code illustrates the typical use of a ResultSetMetaData object. It first calls the method getColumnCount to return the number of fields in the result set; it then calls the methods getColumnName, getColumnType, and getColumnDisplaySize to determine the name, type, and size of the field at each column. Note that column numbers start at 1, not 0 as you might expect.

The method getColumnType returns an integer that encodes the field type. These codes are defined as constants in the JDBC class Types. This class contains codes for 30 different types, which should give you an idea of how extensive the SQL language is. The actual values for these types are not important, because a JDBC program should always refer to the codes by name, not value.

A good example of a client that requires metadata knowledge is a command interpreter. The program SimpleIJ from Chap. 1 is such a program; its code appears in Fig. 2.7. As this is your first example of a nontrivial JDBC client, you should examine its code closely.

The main method begins by reading a connection string from the user and using it to determine the proper driver to use. The code looks for the characters "//" in the connection string. If those characters appear, then the string must be specifying a server-based connection, and otherwise an embedded connection. The method then establishes the connection by passing the connection string into the appropriate driver's connect method.

The main method processes one line of text during each iteration of its while loop. If the text is an SQL statement, the method doQuery or doUpdate is called, as appropriate. The user can exit the loop by entering "exit," at which point the program exits.

```
public class SimpleIJ {
   public static void main(String[] args) {
      Scanner sc = new Scanner(System.in);
      System.out.println("Connect> ");
      String s = sc.nextLine();
      Driver d = (s.contains("//")) ? new NetworkDriver()
                                    : new EmbeddedDriver();

      try (Connection conn = d.connect(s, null);
          Statement stmt = conn.createStatement()) {
         System.out.print("\nSQL> ");
         while (sc.hasNextLine()) {
            // process one line of input
            String cmd = sc.nextLine().trim();
            if (cmd.startsWith("exit"))
               break;
            else if (cmd.startsWith("select"))
               doQuery(stmt, cmd);
            else
               doUpdate(stmt, cmd);
            System.out.print("\nSQL> ");
         }
      }
      catch (SQLException e) {
         e.printStackTrace();
      }
      sc.close();
   }

   private static void doQuery(Statement stmt, String cmd) {
      try (ResultSet rs = stmt.executeQuery(cmd)) {
         ResultSetMetaData md = rs.getMetaData();
         int numcols = md.getColumnCount();
         int totalwidth = 0;

         // print header
         for(int i=1; i<=numcols; i++) {
            String fldname = md.getColumnName(i);
            int width = md.getColumnDisplaySize(i);
            totalwidth += width;
            String fmt = "%" + width + "s";
            System.out.format(fmt, fldname);
         }
```

Fig. 2.7 The JDBC code for the SimpleIJ client

```
            System.out.println();
            for(int i=0; i<totalwidth; i++)
               System.out.print("-");
            System.out.println();

            // print records
            while(rs.next()) {
               for (int i=1; i<=numcols; i++) {
                  String fldname = md.getColumnName(i);
                  int fldtype = md.getColumnType(i);
                  String fmt = "%" + md.getColumnDisplaySize(i);
                  if (fldtype == Types.INTEGER) {
                     int ival = rs.getInt(fldname);
                     System.out.format(fmt + "d", ival);
                  }
                  else {
                     String sval = rs.getString(fldname);
                     System.out.format(fmt + "s", sval);
                  }
               }
               System.out.println();
            }
         }
         catch (SQLException e) {
            System.out.println("SQL Exception: " + e.getMessage());
         }
      }

      private static void doUpdate(Statement stmt, String cmd) {
         try {
            int howmany = stmt.executeUpdate(cmd);
            System.out.println(howmany + " records processed");
         }
         catch (SQLException e) {
            System.out.println("SQL Exception: " + e.getMessage());
         }
      }
   }
```

Fig. 2.7 (continued)

The method doQuery executes the query and obtains the result set and metadata of the output table. Most of the method is concerned with determining proper spacing for the values. The calls to getColumnDisplaySize return the space requirements for each field; the code uses these numbers to construct a format string that will allow the field values to line up properly. The complexity of this code illustrates the maxim "the devil is in the details." That is, the conceptually difficult tasks are easily coded, thanks to the ResultSet and ResultSetMetaData methods, whereas the trivial task of lining up the data takes most of the coding effort.

The methods `doQuery` and `doUpdate` trap exceptions by printing an error message and returning. This error-handling strategy allows the main loop to continue to accept statements until the user enters the "exit" command.

2.2 Advanced JDBC

Basic JDBC is relatively simple to use, but it provides a fairly limited set of ways to interact with the database engine. This section considers some additional features of JDBC that give the client more control over how the database is accessed.

2.2.1 Hiding the Driver

In basic JDBC, a client connects to a database engine by obtaining an instance of a `Driver` object and calling its `connect` method. A problem with this strategy is that it places vendor-specific code into the client program. JDBC contains two vendor-neutral classes for keeping driver information out of client programs: `DriverManager` and `DataSource`. Let's consider each in turn.

Using `DriverManager`

The class `DriverManager` holds a collection of drivers. It contains static methods to add a driver to the collection and to search the collection for a driver that can handle a given connection string. Two of these methods appear in Fig. 2.8.

The idea is that a client repeatedly calls `registerDriver` to register the driver for each database that it might use. When the client wants to connect to a database, it only needs to call the `getConnection` method and provide it with a connection string. The driver manager tries the connection string on each driver in its collection until one of them returns a non-null connection.

For example, consider the code of Fig. 2.9. The first two lines register the server-based Derby and SimpleDB drivers with the driver manager. The last two lines establish a connection to the Derby server. The client does not need to specify the driver when it calls `getConnection`; it only specifies the connection string. The driver manager determines which of its registered drivers to use.

```
static public void registerDriver(Driver driver)
                                        throws SQLException;
static public Connection getConnection(String url, Properties p)
                                        throws SQLException;
```

Fig. 2.8 Two methods of the `DriverManager` class

```
DriverManager.registerDriver(new ClientDriver());
DriverManager.registerDriver(new NetworkDriver());
String url   = "jdbc:derby://localhost/studentdb";
Connection c = DriverManager.getConnection(url);
```

Fig. 2.9 Connecting to a Derby server using `DriverManager`

The use of `DriverManager` in Fig. 2.9 is not especially satisfying, because the driver information hasn't been hidden—it is right there in the calls to `registerDriver`. JDBC resolves this issue by allowing the drivers to be specified in the Java system-properties file. For example, the Derby and SimpleDB drivers can be registered by adding the following line to the file:

```
jdbc.drivers=
org.apache.derby.jdbc.ClientDriver:simpledb.remote.NetworkDriver
```

Placing the driver information in the properties file is an elegant way to remove driver specifications from client code. By changing this one file, you can revise the driver information used by all JDBC clients without having to recompile any code.

Using `DataSource`

Although the driver manager can hide the drivers from the JDBC clients, it cannot hide the connection string. In particular, the connection string in the above example contains "jdbc:derby," so it is evident which driver is intended. A more recent addition to JDBC is the interface `DataSource` in the package `javax.sql`. This is currently the preferred strategy for managing drivers.

A `DataSource` object encapsulates both the driver and the connection string, thereby enabling a client to connect to an engine without knowing any connection details. To create data sources in Derby, you need the Derby-supplied classes `ClientDataSource` (for server-based connections) and `EmbeddedDataSource` (for embedded connections), both of which implement `DataSource`. The client code might look like this:

```
ClientDataSource ds = new ClientDataSource();
ds.setServerName("localhost");
ds.setDatabaseName("studentdb");
Connection conn = ds.getConnection();
```

Each database vendor supplies its own classes that implement `DataSource`. Since these classes are vendor-specific, they can encapsulate the details of its driver, such as the driver name and the syntax of the connection string. A program that uses them only needs to specify the requisite values.

The nice thing about using a data source is that the client no longer needs to know the name of the driver or the syntax of the connection string. Nevertheless, the class is still vendor-specific, and so client code is still not completely vendor independent. This problem can be addressed in various ways.

One solution is for the database administrator to save the `DataSource` object in a file. The DBA can create the object and use Java serialization to write it to the file. A client can then obtain the data source by reading the file and de-serializing it back to a `DataSource` object. This solution is similar to using a properties file. Once the `DataSource` object is saved in the file, it can be used by any JDBC client. And the DBA can make changes to the data source by simply replacing the contents of that file.

A second solution is to use a name server (such as a JNDI server) instead of a file. The DBA places the `DataSource` object on the name server, and clients then request the data source from the server. Given that name servers are a common part of many computing environments, this solution is often easy to implement, although the details are beyond the scope of this book.

2.2.2 Explicit Transaction Handling

Each JDBC client runs as a series of *transactions*. Conceptually, a transaction is a "unit of work," meaning that all its database interactions are treated as a unit. For example, if one update in a transaction fails, the engine will ensure that all updates made by that transaction will fail.

A transaction *commits* when its current unit of work has completed successfully. The database engine implements a commit by making all modifications permanent and releasing any resources (e.g., locks) that were assigned to that transaction. Once the commit is complete, the engine starts a new transaction.

A transaction *rolls back* when it cannot commit. The database engine implements a rollback by undoing all changes made by that transaction, releasing locks, and starting a new transaction. A transaction that has committed or rolled back is said to have *completed*.

Transactions are implicit in basic JDBC. The database engine chooses the boundaries of each transaction, deciding when a transaction should be committed and whether it should be rolled back. This situation is called *autocommit*.

During autocommit, the engine executes each SQL statement in its own transaction. The engine commits the transaction if the statement successfully completes and rolls back the transaction otherwise. An update command completes as soon as the `executeUpdate` method has finished, and a query completes when the query's result set is closed.

A transaction accrues locks, which are not released until the transaction has committed or rolled back. Because these locks can cause other transactions to wait, shorter transactions enable more concurrency. This principle implies that clients running in autocommit mode should close their result sets as soon as possible.

Autocommit is a reasonable default mode for JDBC clients. Having one transaction per SQL statement leads to short transactions and often is the right thing to do. However, there are circumstances when a transaction ought to consist of several SQL statements.

One situation where autocommit is undesirable is when a client needs to have two statements active at the same time. For example, consider the code fragment of Fig. 2.10. This code first executes a query that retrieves all courses. It then loops

```
DataSource ds = ...
Connection conn = ds.getConnection();
Statement stmt1 = conn.createStatement();
Statement stmt2 = conn.createStatement();
ResultSet rs = stmt1.executeQuery("select * from COURSE");
while (rs.next()) {
   String title = rs.getString("Title");
   boolean goodCourse = getUserDecision(title);
   if (!goodCourse) {
       int id = rs.getInt("CId");
       stmt2.executeUpdate("delete from COURSE where CId =" + id);
   }
}
rs.close();
```

Fig. 2.10 Code that could behave incorrectly in autocommit mode

```
DataSource ds = ...
Connection conn = ds.getConnection();
Statement stmt = conn.createStatement();
String cmd1 = "update SECTION set Prof= 'brando' where SectId = 43";
String cmd2 = "update SECTION set Prof= 'einstein' where SectId = 53";
stmt.executeUpdate(cmd1);
// suppose that the engine crashes at this point
stmt.executeUpdate(cmd2);
```

Fig. 2.11 More code that could behave incorrectly in autocommit mode

through the result set, asking the user whether each course should be deleted. If so, it executes an SQL deletion statement to do so.

The problem with this code is that the deletion statement will be executed while the record set is still open. Because a connection supports only one transaction at a time, it must preemptively commit the query's transaction before it can create a new transaction to execute the deletion. And since the query's transaction has committed, it doesn't really make sense to access the remainder of the record set. The code will either throw an exception or have unpredictable behavior.[1]

Autocommit is also undesirable when multiple modifications to the database need to happen together. The code fragment of Fig. 2.11 provides an example. The intent of the code is to swap the professors teaching sections 43 and 53. However, the database will become incorrect if the engine crashes after the first call to `executeUpdate` but before the second one. This code needs both SQL statements

---

[1]The actual behavior of this code depends on the *holdability* of the result set, whose default value is engine dependent. If the holdability is `CLOSE_CURSORS_AT_COMMIT`, then the result set will become invalid, and an exception will be thrown. If the holdability is `HOLD_CURSORS_OVER_COMMIT`, then the result set will stay open, but its locks will be released. The behavior of such a result set is unpredictable and similar to the read-uncommitted isolation mode to be discussed in Sect. 2.2.3.

```
public void setAutoCommit(boolean ac) throws SQLException;
public void commit()                  throws SQLException;
public void rollback()                throws SQLException;
```

Fig. 2.12 The `Connection` methods for explicit transaction handling

to occur in the same transaction, so that they are either committed together or rolled back together.

Autocommit mode can also be inconvenient. Suppose that your program is performing multiple insertions, say by loading data from a text file. If the engine crashes while the program is running, then some of the records will be inserted and some will not. It could be tedious and time-consuming to determine where the program failed and to rewrite it to insert only the missing records. A better alternative is to place all the insertion commands in the same transaction. Then all of them would get rolled back after a system crash, and it would be possible to simply rerun the client.

The `Connection` interface contains three methods that allow the client to handle its transactions explicitly. Figure 2.12 gives their API. A client turns off autocommit by calling `setAutoCommit(false)`. The client completes the current transaction and starts a new one by calling `commit` or `rollback`, as desired.

When a client turns off autocommit, it takes on the responsibility for rolling back failed SQL statements. In particular, if an exception gets thrown during a transaction, then the client must roll back that transaction inside its exception-handling code.

For an example, consider again the incorrect code fragment of Fig. 2.10. A corrected version appears in Fig. 2.13. The code calls `setAutoCommit` immediately after the connection is created and calls `commit` immediately after the statements have completed. The `catch` block contains the call to `rollback`. This call needs to be placed inside its own `try` block, in case it throws an exception.

At first glance, an exception during rollback seems like it could corrupt the database, as in Fig. 2.11. Fortunately, database rollback algorithms are designed to handle such possibilities; Chap. 5 contains the remarkable details. Thus, the code in Fig. 2.13 can legitimately ignore a failed rollback, knowing that the database engine will make things right.

2.2.3 Transaction Isolation Levels

A database server typically has several clients active at the same time, each running their own transaction. By executing these transactions concurrently, the server can improve their throughput and response time. Thus, concurrency is a good thing. However, *uncontrolled* concurrency can cause problems, because a transaction can interfere with another transaction by modifying the data used by that other transaction in unexpected ways. Here are three examples that demonstrate the kinds of problems that can occur.

```
DataSource ds = ...
try (Connection conn = ds.getConnection()) {
   conn.setAutoCommit(false);
   Statement stmt = conn.createStatement();
   ResultSet rs = stmt.executeQuery("select * from COURSE");
   while (rs.next()) {
      String title = rs.getString("Title");
      boolean goodCourse = getUserDecision(title);
      if (!goodCourse) {
         int id = rs.getInt("CId");
         stmt.executeUpdate("delete from COURSE where CId =" + id);
      }
   }
   rs.close();
   stmt.close();
   conn.commit();
}
catch (SQLException e) {
   e.printStackTrace();
   try {
      if (conn != null)
         conn.rollback();
   }
   catch (SQLException e2) {}
}
```

Fig. 2.13 A revision of Fig. 2.10 that handles transactions explicitly

Example 1: Reading Uncommitted Data

Consider again the code for Fig. 2.11 that swaps the professors of two sections and assume that it runs as a single transaction (i.e., with autocommit turned off). Call this transaction T1. Suppose also that the university has decided to give bonuses to its professors, based on the number of sections taught; it therefore executes a transaction T2 that counts the sections taught by each professor. Furthermore, suppose that these two transactions happen to run concurrently—in particular, suppose that T2 begins and executes to completion immediately after the first update statement of T1. The result is that Professors Brando and Einstein will get credited, respectively, with one extra and one fewer course than they deserve, which will affect their bonuses.

What went wrong? Each of the transactions is correct in isolation, but together they cause the university to give out the wrong bonuses. The problem is that T2 incorrectly assumed that the records it read were *consistent*, that is, that they made sense together. However, data written by an uncommitted transaction may not always be consistent. In the case of T1, the inconsistency occurred at the point where only one of the two modifications was made. When T2 read the uncommitted modified records at that point, the inconsistency caused it to make incorrect calculations.

Example 2: Unexpected Changes to an Existing Record

For this example, assume that the STUDENT table contains a field `MealPlanBal`, which denotes how much money the student has for buying food in the cafeteria.

```
DataSource ds = ...
Connection conn = ds.getConnection();
conn.setAutoCommit(false);
Statement stmt = conn.createStatement();
ResultSet rs = stmt.executeQuery("select MealPlanBal from STUDENT "
                                + "where SId = 1");
rs.next();
int balance = rs.getInt("MealPlanBal");
rs.close();

int newbalance = balance - 10;
if (newbalance < 0)
  throw new NoFoodAllowedException("You cannot afford this meal");

stmt.executeUpdate("update STUDENT "
                 + "set MealPlanBal = " + newbalance
                 + " where SId = 1");
conn.commit();
```

(a)

```
DataSource ds = ...
Connection conn = ds.getConnection();
conn.setAutoCommit(false);
Statement stmt = conn.createStatement();
stmt.executeUpdate("update STUDENT "
                 + "set MealPlanBal = MealPlanBal + 1000 "
                 + "where SId = 1");
conn.commit();
```

(b)

Fig. 2.14 Two concurrent transactions that can manage to "lose" an update. (**a**) Transaction T1 decrements the meal plan balance, (**b**) Transaction T2 increments the meal plan balance

Consider the two transactions of Fig. 2.14. Transaction T1 executed when Joe bought a $10 lunch. The transaction runs a query to find out his current balance, verifies that the balance is sufficient, and decrements his balance appropriately. Transaction T2 executed when Joe's parents sent in a check for $1000 to be added to his meal plan balance. That transaction simply runs an SQL update statement to increment Joe's balance.

Now suppose that these two transactions happen to run concurrently at a time when Joe has a $50 balance. In particular, suppose that T2 begins and executes to completion immediately after T1 calls `rs.close`. Then T2, which commits first, will modify the balance to $1050. However, T1 is unaware of this change and still thinks that the balance is $50. It thus modifies the balance to $40 and commits. The result is that the $1000 deposit is not credited to his balance, that is, the update got "lost."

The problem here is that transaction T1 incorrectly assumed that the value of the meal plan balance would not change between the time that T1 read the value and the time that T1 modified the value. Formally, this assumption is called *repeatable read*, because the transaction assumes that repeatedly reading an item from the database will always return the same value.

Example 3: Unexpected Changes to the Number of Records
Suppose that the university dining services made a profit of $100,000 last year. The university feels bad that it overcharged its students, so it decides to divide the profit equally among them. That is, if there are 1000 current students, then the university will add $100 to each meal plan balance. The code appears in Fig. 2.15.

The problem with this transaction is that it assumes that the number of current students will not change between the calculation of the rebate amount and the updating of the STUDENT records. But suppose that several new STUDENT records got inserted into the database between the closing of the record set and the execution of the update statement. These new records will incorrectly get the precalculated rebate, and the university will wind up spending more than $100,000 on rebates. These new records are known as *phantom records*, because they mysteriously appear after the transaction has started.

These examples illustrate the kind of problems that can arise when two transactions interact. The only way to guarantee that an arbitrary transaction will not have problems is to execute it in complete isolation from the other transactions. This form of isolation is called *serializability* and is discussed in considerable detail in Chap. 5.

Unfortunately, serializable transactions can run very slowly, because they require the database engine to significantly reduce the amount of concurrency it allows. JDBC therefore defines four isolation levels, which allow clients to specify how much isolation a transaction should have:

```
DataSource ds = ...
Connection conn = ds.getConnection();
conn.setAutoCommit(false);
Statement stmt = conn.createStatement();
String qry = "select count(SId) as HowMany from STUDENT "
          + "where GradYear >= extract(year, current_date)"
ResultSet rs = stmt.executeQuery(qry);
rs.next();
int count = rs.getInt("HowMany");
rs.close();

int rebate = 100000 / count;
String cmd = "update STUDENT "
          + "set MealPlanBalance = MealPlanBalance + " + rebate
          + " where GradYear >= extract(year, current_date)";
stmt.executeUpdate(cmd);
conn.commit();
```

Fig. 2.15 A transaction that could give out more rebates than expected

- *Read-Uncommitted* isolation means no isolation at all. Such a transaction could suffer any of the problems from the above three examples.
- *Read-Committed* isolation forbids a transaction from accessing uncommitted values. Problems related to nonrepeatable reads and phantoms are still possible.
- *Repeatable-Read* isolation extends read-committed so that reads are always repeatable. The only possible problems are due to phantoms.
- *Serializable* isolation guarantees that no problems will ever occur.

A JDBC client specifies the isolation level it wants by calling the `Connection` method `setTransactionIsolation`. For example, the following code fragment sets the isolation level to serializable:

```
DataSource ds = ...
Connection conn = ds.getConnection();
conn.setAutoCommit(false);
conn.setTransactionIsolation(
                    Connection.TRANSACTION_SERIALIZABLE);
```

These four isolation levels exhibit a trade-off between execution speed and potential problems. That is, the faster you want your transaction to run, the greater the risk you must accept that the transaction might run incorrectly. This risk can be mitigated by a careful analysis of the client.

For example, you might be able to convince yourself that phantoms and nonrepeatable reads will not be a problem. This would be the case, for example, if your transaction performs only insertions, or if it deletes specific existing records (as in "delete from STUDENT where SId = 1"). In this case, an isolation level of read-committed will be fast and correct.

For another example, you might convince yourself that any potential problems are uninteresting. Suppose that your transaction calculates, for each year, the average grade given during that year. You decide that even though grade changes can occur during the execution of the transaction, those changes are not likely to affect the resulting statistics significantly. In this case, you could reasonably choose the isolation level of read-committed or even read-uncommitted.

The default isolation level for many database servers (including Derby, Oracle, and Sybase) is read-committed. This level is appropriate for the simple queries posed by naïve users in autocommit mode. However, if your client programs perform critical tasks, then it is equally critical that you carefully determine the most appropriate isolation level. A programmer that turns off autocommit mode must be very careful to choose the proper isolation level of each transaction.

2.2.4 Prepared Statements

Many JDBC client programs are *parameterized*, in the sense that they accept an argument value from the user and execute an SQL statement based on that argument. An example of such a client is the demo client `FindMajors`, whose code appears in Fig. 2.16.

```
public class FindMajors {
   public static void main(String[] args) {
   System.out.print("Enter a department name: ");
   Scanner sc = new Scanner(System.in);
   String major = sc.next();
   sc.close();
   String qry = "select sname, gradyear from student, dept "
        + "where did = majorid and dname = '" + major + "'";

   ClientDataSource ds = new ClientDataSource();
   ds.setServerName("localhost");
   ds.setDatabaseName("studentdb");
   try ( Connection conn = ds.getConnection();
         Statement stmt = conn.createStatement();
         ResultSet rs = stmt.executeQuery(qry)) {

      System.out.println("Here are the " + major + " majors");
      System.out.println("Name\tGradYear");
      while (rs.next()) {
         String sname = rs.getString("sname");
         int gradyear = rs.getInt("gradyear");
         System.out.println(sname + "\t" + gradyear);
      }
   }
   catch(Exception e) {
      e.printStackTrace();
   }
  }
}
```

Fig. 2.16 The JDBC code for the `FindMajors` client

This client begins by asking the user for a department name. It then incorporates this name into the SQL query that it executes. For example, suppose that the user entered the value "math." Then the generated SQL query would be as follows:

```
select SName, GradYear from STUDENT, DEPT
where DId = MajorId and DName = 'math'
```

Note how the code explicitly adds the single quotes surrounding the department name when it generates the query. Instead of generating an SQL statement dynamically this way, the client can use a *parameterized* SQL statement. A parameterized statement is an SQL statement in which '?' characters denote missing parameter values. A statement can have several parameters, all denoted by '?'. Each parameter has an *index value* that corresponds to its position in the string. For example, the following parameterized statement deletes all students having a yet-unspecified graduation year and major. The value for `GradYear` is assigned index 1, and the value for `MajorId` is assigned index 2.

```
public class PreparedFindMajors {
   public static void main(String[] args) {
      System.out.print("Enter a department name: ");
      Scanner sc = new Scanner(System.in);
      String major = sc.next();
      sc.close();
      String qry = "select sname, gradyear from student, dept "
               + "where did = majorid and dname = ?";
      ClientDataSource ds = new ClientDataSource();
      ds.setServerName("localhost");
      ds.setDatabaseName("studentdb");
      try ( Connection conn = ds.getConnection();
         PreparedStatement pstmt = conn.prepareStatement(qry)) {
         pstmt.setString(1, major);
         ResultSet rs = pstmt.executeQuery();
         System.out.println("Here are the " + major + " majors");
         System.out.println("Name\tGradYear");
         while (rs.next()) {
            String sname = rs.getString("sname");
            int gradyear = rs.getInt("gradyear");
            System.out.println(sname + "\t" + gradyear);
         }
         rs.close();
      }
      catch(Exception e) {
         e.printStackTrace();
      }
   }
}
```

Fig. 2.17 Revising the `FindMajors` client to use prepared statements

```
delete from STUDENT where GradYear = ? and MajorId = ?
```

The JDBC class `PreparedStatement` handles parameterized statements. A client processes a prepared statement in three steps:

- It creates a `PreparedStatement` object for a specified parameterized SQL statement.
- It assigns values to the parameters.
- It executes the prepared statement.

For example, Fig. 2.17 revises the `FindMajors` client to use prepared statements. Changes are in bold. The last three statements in bold correspond to the above three bullet points. First, the client creates the `PreparedStatement` object by calling the method `prepareStatement` and passing the parameterized SQL statement as an argument. Second, the client calls the `setString` method to assign a value to the first (and only) parameter. Third, the method calls `executeQuery` to execute the statement.

```
public ResultSet executeQuery()                     throws SQLException;
public int  executeUpdate()                         throws SQLException;
public void setInt(int index, int val)              throws SQLException;
public void setString(int index, String val) throws SQLException;
```

Fig. 2.18 Part of the API for PreparedStatement

```
// Prepare the query
String qry = "select SName, GradYear from STUDENT, DEPT "
          + "where DId = MajorId and DName = ?";
PreparedStatement pstmt = conn.prepareStatement(qry);

// Repeatedly get parameters and execute the query
String major = getUserInput();
while (major != null) {
   pstmt.setString(1, major);
   ResultSet rs = pstmt.executeQuery();
   displayResultSet(rs);
   major = getUserInput();
}
```

Fig. 2.19 Using a prepared statement in a loop

Figure 2.18 gives the API for the most common PreparedStatement methods. The methods executeQuery and executeUpdate are similar to the corresponding methods in Statement; the difference is that they do not require any arguments. The methods setInt and setString assign values to parameters. In Fig. 2.17, the call to setString assigned a department name to the first index parameter. Note that the setString method automatically inserts the single quotes around its value, so that the client doesn't have to.

Most people find it more convenient to use prepared statements than to create the SQL statements explicitly. Prepared statements are also the more efficient option when statements are generated in a loop, as shown in Fig. 2.19. The reason is that the database engine is able to compile a prepared statement without knowing its parameter values. It compiles the statement once and then executes it repeatedly inside of the loop without further recompilation.

2.2.5 Scrollable and Updatable Result Sets

Result sets in basic JDBC are *forward-only* and *non-updatable*. Full JDBC also allows result sets to be *scrollable* and *updatable*. Clients can position such result sets at arbitrary records, update the current record, and insert new records. Figure 2.20 gives the API for these additional methods.

The method beforeFirst positions the result set before the first record, and the method afterLast positions the result set after the last record. The method absolute positions the result set at exactly the specified record and returns false

<u>*Methods used by scrollable result sets*</u>

```
public void    beforeFirst()          throws SQLException;
public void    afterLast()            throws SQLException;
public boolean previous()             throws SQLException;
public boolean next()                 throws SQLException;
public boolean absolute(int pos)      throws SQLException;
public boolean relative(int offset)   throws SQLException;
```

<u>*Methods used by updatable result sets*</u>

```
public void updateInt(String fldname, int val) throws SQLException;
public void updateString(String fldname, String val)
                                       throws SQLException;
public void updateRow()          throws SQLException;
public void deleteRow()          throws SQLException;
public void moveToInsertRow()    throws SQLException;
public void moveToCurrentRow()   throws SQLException;
```

Fig. 2.20 Part of the API for `ResultSet`

if there is no such record. The method `relative` positions the result set a relative number of rows. In particular, `relative(1)` is identical to `next`, and `relative(-1)` is identical to `previous`.

The methods `updateInt` and `updateString` modify the specified field of the current record on the client. However, the modification is not sent to the database until `updateRow` is called. The need to call `updateRow` is somewhat awkward, but it allows JDBC to batch updates to several fields of a record into a single call to the engine.

Insertions are handled by the concept of an *insert row*. This row does not exist in the table (e.g., you cannot scroll to it). Its purpose is to serve as a staging area for new records. The client calls `moveToInsertRow` to position the result set at the insert row, then the `updateXXX` methods to set the values of its fields, then `updateRow` to insert the record into the database, and finally `moveToCurrentRow` to reposition the record set to where it was before the insertion.

By default, record sets are forward-only and non-updatable. If a client wants a more powerful record set, it specifies so in the `createStatement` method of `Connection`. In addition to the no-arg `createStatement` method of basic JDBC, there is also a two-arg method in which the client specifies scrollability and updatability. For example, consider the following statement:

```
Statement stmt =
conn.createStatement(ResultSet.TYPE_SCROLL_INSENSITIVE,
                     ResultSet.CONCUR_UPDATABLE);
```

All result sets generated from this statement will be scrollable and updatable. The constant TYPE_FORWARD_ONLY specifies a non-scrollable result set, and CONCUR_READ_ONLY specifies a non-updatable result set. These constants can be mixed and matched to obtain the desired scrollability and updatability.

For an example, recall the code of Fig. 2.10, which allowed a user to iterate through the COURSE table, deleting desired records. Figure 2.21 revises that code to

```
DataSource ds = ...
Connection conn = ds.getConnection();
conn.setAutocommit(false);

Statement stmt = conn.createStatement(ResultSet.TYPE_FORWARD_ONLY,
                                      ResultSet.CONCUR_UPDATABLE);

ResultSet rs = stmt.executeQuery("select * from COURSE");
while (rs.next()) {
   String title = rs.getString("Title");
   boolean goodCourse = getUserDecision(title);
   if (!goodCourse)
      rs.deleteRow();
}
rs.close();
  stmt.close();
conn.commit();
```

Fig. 2.21 Revising the code of Fig. 2.10

use updatable result sets. Note that a deleted row remains current until the call to `next`.

A scrollable result set has limited use, because most of the time the client knows what it wants to do with the output records and doesn't need to examine them twice. A client would typically need a scrollable result set only if it allowed users to interact with the result of a query. For example, consider a client that wants to display the output of a query as a Swing `JTable` object. The `JTable` will display a scrollbar when there are too many output records to fit on the screen and allow the user to move back and forth through the records by clicking on the scrollbar. This situation requires the client to supply a scrollable result set to the `JTable` object, so that it can retrieve previous records when the user scrolls back.

2.2.6 Additional Data Types

In addition to integer and string values, JDBC also contains methods to manipulate numerous other types. For example, consider the interface `ResultSet`. In addition to the methods `getInt` and `getString`, there are also methods `getFloat`, `getDouble`, `getShort`, `getTime`, `getDate`, and several others. Each of these methods will read the value from the specified field of the current record and convert it (if possible) to the indicated Java type. In general, of course, it makes most sense to use numeric JDBC methods (such as `getInt`, `getFloat`, etc.) on numeric SQL fields and so on. But JDBC will attempt to convert any SQL value to the Java type indicated by the method. In particular, it is always possible to convert any SQL value to a Java string.

2.3 Computing in Java vs. SQL

Whenever a programmer writes a JDBC client, an important decision must be made: What part of the computation should be performed by the database engine, and what part should be performed by the Java client? This section examines these questions.

Consider again the `StudentMajor` demo client of Fig. 2.5. In that program, the engine performs all of the computation, by executing an SQL query to compute the join of the STUDENT and DEPT tables. The client's only responsibility is to retrieve the query output and print it.

In contrast, you could have written the client so that it does all of the computation, as shown in Fig. 2.22. In that code, the engine's only responsibility is to create result sets for the STUDENT and DEPT tables. The client does all the rest of the work, computing the join and printing the result.

Which of these two versions is better? Clearly, the original version is more elegant. Not only does it have less code, but the code is easier to read. But what about efficiency? As a rule of thumb, it is always more efficient to do as little as possible in the client. There are two main reasons:

- There is usually less data to transfer from engine to client, which is especially important if they are on different machines.
- The engine contains detailed specialized knowledge about how each table is implemented and the possible ways to compute complex queries (such as joins). It is highly unlikely that a client can compute a query as efficiently as the engine.

For example, the code of Fig. 2.22 computes the join by using two nested loops. The outer loop iterates through the STUDENT records. For each student, the inner loop searches for the DEPT record matching that student's major. Although this is a reasonable join algorithm, it is not particularly efficient. Chapters 13 and 14 discuss several techniques that lead to much more efficient execution.

Figures 2.5 and 2.22 exemplify the extremes of really good and really bad JDBC code, and so comparing them was pretty easy. But sometimes, the comparison is more difficult. For example, consider again the *PreparedFindMajors* demo client of Fig. 2.17, which returns the students having a specified major department. That code asks the engine to execute an SQL query that joins STUDENT and MAJOR. Suppose that you know that executing a join can be time-consuming. After some serious thought, you realize that you can get the data you need without using a join. The idea is to use two single-table queries. The first query scans through the DEPT table looking for the record having the specified major name and returning its `DId`-value. The second query then uses that value to search the `MajorID` values of STUDENT records. The code for this algorithm appears in Fig. 2.23.

This algorithm is simple, elegant, and efficient. All it requires is a sequential scan through each of two tables and ought to be much faster than a join. You can be proud of your effort.

Unfortunately, your effort is wasted. The new algorithm isn't really new but just a clever implementation of a join—in particular, it is a *multibuffer product* of

```
public class BadStudentMajor {
  public static void main(String[] args) {
     ClientDataSource ds = new ClientDataSource();
     ds.setServerName("localhost");
     ds.setDatabaseName("studentdb");
     Connection conn = null;
     try {
        conn = ds.getConnection();
        conn.setAutoCommit(false);
        try (Statement stmt1 = conn.createStatement();
             Statement stmt2 = conn.createStatement(
                   ResultSet.TYPE_SCROLL_INSENSITIVE,
                   ResultSet.CONCUR_READ_ONLY);
             ResultSet rs1 = stmt1.executeQuery(
                        "select * from STUDENT");
             ResultSet rs2 = stmt2.executeQuery(
                        "select * from DEPT") ) {
           System.out.println("Name\tMajor");
           while (rs1.next()) {
              // get the next student
              String sname = rs1.getString("SName");
              String dname = null;
              rs2.beforeFirst();
              while (rs2.next())
                 // search for the major department of that student
                 if (rs2.getInt("DId") == rs1.getInt("MajorId")) {
                    dname = rs2.getString("DName");
                    break;
                 }
              System.out.println(sname + "\t" + dname);
           }
        }
        conn.commit();
        conn.close();
     }
     catch(SQLException e) {
        e.printStackTrace();
        try {
           if (conn != null) {
              conn.rollback();
              conn.close();
           }
        }
        catch (SQLException e2) {}
     }
  }
}
```

Fig. 2.22 An alternative (but bad) way to code the StudentMajor client

```
public class CleverFindMajors {
   public static void main(String[] args) {
      String major = args[0];
      String qry1 = "select DId from DEPT where DName = ?";
      String qry2 = "select * from STUDENT where MajorId = ?";

      ClientDataSource ds = new ClientDataSource();
      ds.setServerName("localhost");
      ds.setDatabaseName("studentdb");
      try (Connection conn = ds.getConnection()) {
         PreparedStatement stmt1 = conn.prepareStatement(qry1);
         stmt1.setString(1, major);
         ResultSet rs1 = stmt1.executeQuery();
         rs1.next();
         int deptid = rs1.getInt("DId");  // get the major's ID
         rs1.close();
         stmt1.close();

         PreparedStatement stmt2 = conn.prepareStatement(qry2);
         stmt2.setInt(1, deptid);
         ResultSet rs2 = stmt2.executeQuery();
         System.out.println("Here are the " + major + " majors");
         System.out.println("Name\tGradYear");
         while (rs2.next()) {
            String sname = rs2.getString("sname");
            int gradyear = rs2.getInt("gradyear");
            System.out.println(sname + "\t" + gradyear);
         }
         rs2.close();
         stmt2.close();
      }
      catch(Exception e) {
         e.printStackTrace();
      }
   }
}
```

Fig. 2.23 A clever way to implement the `FindMajors` client

Chap. 14 with a materialized inner table. A well-written database engine would know about this algorithm (among several others) and would use it to compute the join if it turned out to be most efficient. All of your cleverness has thus been preempted by the database engine. The moral is the same as with the `StudentMajor` client: Letting the engine do the work tends to be the most efficient strategy (as well as the easiest one to code).

One of the mistakes that beginning JDBC programmers make is that they try to do too much in the client. The programmer might think that he or she knows a really clever way to implement a query in Java. Or the programmer might not be sure how to express a query in SQL and feels more comfortable coding the query in Java. In each of these cases, the decision to code the query in Java is almost always wrong. The programmer must trust that the database engine will do its job.[2]

2.4 Chapter Summary

- The JDBC methods manage the transfer of data between a Java client and a database engine.
- Basic JDBC consists of five interfaces: `Driver`, `Connection`, `Statement`, `ResultSet`, and `ResultSetMetaData`.
- A `Driver` object encapsulates the low-level details for connecting with the engine. If a client wants to connect to an engine, it must obtain a copy of the appropriate driver class. The driver class and its connection string are the only vendor-specific code in a JDBC program. Everything else refers to vendor-neutral JDBC interfaces.
- Result sets and connections hold resources that other clients might need. A JDBC client should always close them as soon as it can.
- Every JDBC method can throw an `SQLException`. A client is obligated to check for these exceptions.
- The methods of `ResultSetMetaData` provide information about the schema of the output table, that is, the name, type, and display size of each field. This information is useful when the client accepts queries directly from the user, as in an SQL interpreter.
- A basic JDBC client calls the driver class directly. Full JDBC provides the class `DriverManager` and the interface `DataSource` to simplify the connection process and make it more vendor-neutral.
- The class `DriverManager` holds a collection of drivers. A client registers its drivers with the driver manager, either explicitly or (preferably) via a system properties file. When the client wants to connect to a database, it provides a connection string to the driver manager, and it makes the connection for the client.
- A `DataSource` object is even more vendor-neutral, because it encapsulates both the driver and the connection string. A client can therefore connect to a database engine without knowing any of the connection details. The database administrator can create various `DataSource` objects and place them on a server for clients to use.
- A basic JDBC client ignores the existence of transactions. The database engine executes these clients in *autocommit* mode, which means that each SQL statement is its own transaction.

---

[2]At least, you should start by trusting that the engine will be efficient. If you discover that your application is running slowly because the engine is not executing the join efficiently, then you can recode the program as in Fig. 2.23. But it is always best to avoid premature cleverness.

- All of the database interactions in a transaction are treated as a unit. A transaction *commits* when its current unit of work has completed successfully. A transaction *rolls back* when it cannot commit. The database engine implements a rollback by undoing all changes made by that transaction.
- Autocommit is a reasonable default mode for simple, unimportant JDBC clients. If a client performs critical tasks, then its programmer should carefully analyze its transactional needs. A client turns off autocommit by calling `setAutoCommit(false)`. This call causes the engine to start a new transaction. The client then calls `commit` or `rollback` when it needs to complete the current transaction and begin a new one. When a client turns off autocommit, it must handle failed SQL statements by rolling back the associated transaction.
- A client can also use the method `setTransactionIsolation` to specify its isolation level. JDBC defines four isolation levels:
  - *Read-Uncommitted* isolation means no isolation at all. The transaction could have problems resulting from reading uncommitted data, nonrepeatable reads, or phantom records.
  - *Read-Committed* isolation forbids a transaction from accessing uncommitted values. Problems related to nonrepeatable reads and phantoms are still possible.
  - *Repeatable-Read* isolation extends read-committed so that reads are always repeatable. The only possible problems are due to phantoms.
  - *Serializable* isolation guarantees that no problems will ever occur.
- Serializable isolation is clearly to be preferred, but its implementation tends to cause transactions to run slowly. The programmer must analyze the risk of possible concurrency errors with the client and choose a less restrictive isolation level only if the risk seems tolerable.
- A *prepared statement* has an associated SQL statement, which can have placeholders for parameters. The client can then assign values to the parameters at a later time and then execute the statement. Prepared statements are a convenient way to handle dynamically generated SQL statements. Moreover, a prepared statement can be compiled before its parameters are assigned, which means that executing a prepared statement multiple times (such as in a loop) will be very efficient.
- Full JDBC allows result sets to be *scrollable* and *updatable*. By default, record sets are forward-only and non-updatable. If a client wants a more powerful record set, it specifies so in the `createStatement` method of `Connection`.
- The rule of thumb when writing a JDBC client is to let the engine do as much work as possible. Database engines are remarkably sophisticated and usually know the most efficient way to obtain the desired data. It is almost always a good idea for the client to determine an SQL statement that retrieves exactly the desired data and submit it to the engine. In short, the programmer must trust the engine to do its job.

2.5 Suggested Reading

A comprehensive and well-written book on JDBC is Fisher et al. (2003), part of which exists as an online tutorial at `docs.oracle.com/javase/tutorial/jdbc`. In addition, every database vendor supplies documentation explaining the use of its drivers, as well as other vendor-specific issues. If you intend to write clients for a specific engine, then it is imperative to be familiar with the documentation.

Fisher, M., Ellis, J., & Bruce, J. (2003). *JDBC API tutorial and reference* (3rd ed.). Addison Wesley.

2.6 Exercises

Conceptual Exercises

2.1. The Derby documentation recommends that you turn off autocommit when executing a sequence of inserts. Explain why you think it makes this recommendation.

Programming Exercises

2.2. Write some SQL queries for the university database. For each query, write a program using Derby that executes that query and prints its output table.

2.3. The `SimpleIJ` program requires each SQL statement to be a single line of text. Revise it so that a statement can comprise multiple lines and terminate with a semicolon, similar to Derby's `ij` program.

2.4. Write a class `NetworkDataSource` for SimpleDB that works similarly to the Derby class `ClientDataSource`. Add this class to the package `simpledb.jdbc.network`. Your code need not implement all of the methods of the interface `javax.sql.DataSource` (and its superclasses); in fact, the only one of those methods that it needs to implement is the no-arg method `getConnection()`. What vendor-specific methods should `NetworkDataSource` have?

2.5. It is often useful to be able to create a text file that contains SQL commands. These commands can then be executed in batch by a JDBC program. Write a JDBC program that reads commands from a specified text file and executes them. Assume that each line of the file is a separate command.

2.6. Investigate how a result set can be used to populate a Java `JTable` object. (Hint: You will need to extend the class `AbstractTableModel`.) Then revise the demo client `FindMajors` to have a GUI interface that displays its output in a `JTable`.

2.7. Write JDBC code for the following tasks:

(a) Import data from a text file into an existing table. The text file should have one record per line, with each field separated by tabs. The first line of the file should be the names of the fields. The client should take the name of the file and the name of the table as input, and insert the records into the table.

(b) Export data to a text file. The client should take the name of the file and the name of the table as input, and write the contents of each record into the file. The first line of the file should be the names of the fields.

2.8. This chapter has ignored the possibility of null values in a result set. To check for null values, you use the method `wasNull` in `ResultSet`. Suppose you call `getInt` or `getString` to retrieve a field value. If you call `wasNull` immediately afterward, it will return `true` if the retrieved value was null. For example, the following loop prints out graduation years, assuming that some of them might be null:

```
while(rs.next()) {
  int gradyr = rs.getInt("gradyear");
  if (rs.wasNull())
     System.out.println("null");
  else
     System.out.println(gradyr);
}
```

(a) Rewrite the code for the `StudentMajor` demo client under the assumption that student names might be null.

(b) Modify the `SimpleIJ` demo client so that it connects to Derby (instead of SimpleDB). Then rewrite the code under the assumption that any field value might be null.

Chapter 3
Disk and File Management

Database engines keep their data on persistent storage devices such as disks and flash drives. This chapter investigates the properties of these devices and considers techniques (such as RAID) that can improve their speed and reliability. It also examines the two interfaces that the operating system provides for interacting with these devices—a block-level interface and a file-level interface—and proposes a combination of the two interfaces that is most appropriate for a database system. Finally, it considers the SimpleDB file manager in detail, studying its API and its implementation.

3.1 Persistent Data Storage

The contents of a database must be kept *persistent*, so that the data will not be lost if the database system or the computer goes down. This section examines two particularly useful hardware technologies: *disk drives* and *flash drives*. Flash drives are not yet as widespread as disk drives, although their importance will increase as their technology matures. Let's begin with disk drives.

3.1.1 Disk Drives

A *disk drive* contains one or more rotating *platters*. A platter has concentric *tracks*, and each track consists of a sequence of bytes. Bytes are read from (and written to) the platter by means of a movable arm with a read/write head. The arm is positioned at the desired track, and the head can read (or write) the bytes as they rotate under it. Figure 3.1 depicts the top view of a one-platter disk drive. Of course, this figure is not drawn to scale, because a typical platter has many thousands of tracks.

Modern disk drives typically have multiple platters. For space efficiency, pairs of platters are usually joined back-to-back, creating what looks like a two-sided platter;

E. Sciore, *Database Design and Implementation*, Data-Centric Systems and Applications, https://doi.org/10.1007/978-3-030-33836-7_3

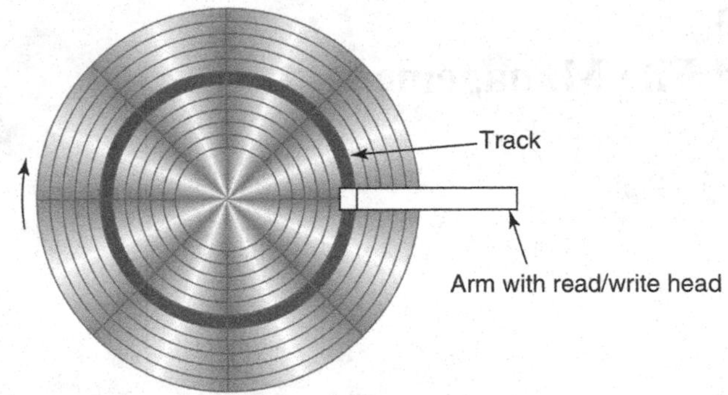

Fig. 3.1 The top view of a one-platter disk drive

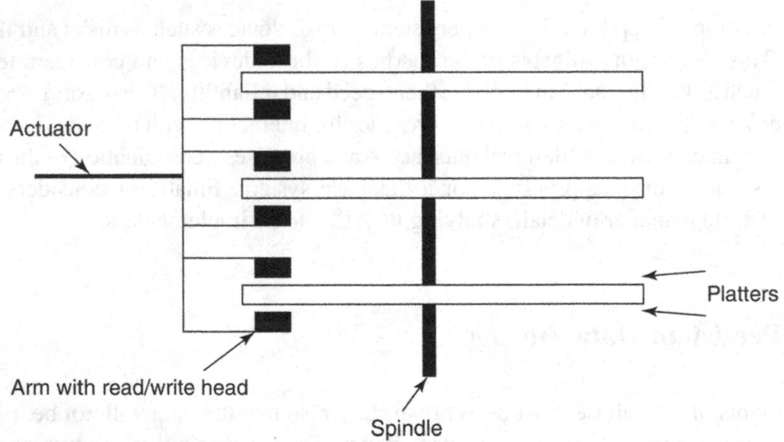

Fig. 3.2 The side view of a multi-platter disk drive

but conceptually, each side is still a separate platter. Each platter has its own read/write head. These heads do not move independently; instead, they are all connected to a single *actuator*, which moves them simultaneously to the same track on each platter. Moreover, only one read/write head can be active at a time, because there is only one datapath to the computer. Figure 3.2 depicts the side view of a multi-platter disk drive.

The general performance of a disk drive can be measured by four values: its capacity, rotation speed, transfer rate, and seek time.

The *capacity* of a drive is the number of bytes that can be stored. This value depends on the number of platters, the number of tracks per platter, and the number of bytes per track. Given that the platters tend to come in more or less standard sizes, manufacturers increase capacity primarily by increasing the density of a platter, that is, by squeezing more tracks per platter and more bytes per track. Platter capacities of over 40 GB are now common.

The *rotation speed* is the rate at which the platters spin and is usually given as revolutions per minute. Typical speeds range from 5400 rpm to 15,000 rpm.

The *transfer rate* is the speed at which bytes pass by the disk head, to be transferred to/from memory. For example, an entire track's worth of bytes can be transferred in the time it takes for the platter to make a single revolution. The transfer rate is thus determined by both the rotation speed and the number of bytes per track. Rates of 100 MB/s are common.

The *seek time* is the time it takes for the actuator to move the disk head from its current location to a requested track. This value depends on how many tracks need to be traversed. It can be as low as 0 (if the destination track is the same as the starting track) and as high as 15–20 ms (if the destination and starting tracks are at different ends of the platter). The average seek time usually provides a reasonable estimate of actuator speed. Average seek times on modern disks are about 5 ms.

Consider the following example. Suppose that a four-platter disk drive spins at 10,000 rpm with an average seek time of 5 ms. Each platter contains 10,000 tracks, with each track containing 500,000 bytes. Here are some calculated values[1]:

The capacity of the drive:

```
500,000 bytes/track x 10,000 tracks/platter x 4 platters/drive
= 20,000,000,000 bytes, or approximately 20GB
```

The transfer rate:

```
500,000 bytes/revolution x 10,000 revolutions/60 seconds
= 83,333,333 bytes/second, or approximately 83MB/s
```

3.1.2 Accessing a Disk Drive

A *disk access* is a request to read some bytes from the disk drive into memory or to write some bytes from memory to disk. These bytes must be on a contiguous portion of a track on some platter. The disk drive executes a disk access in three stages:

- It moves the disk head to the specified track. This time is called the *seek time*.
- It waits for the platter to rotate until the first desired byte is beneath the disk head. This time is called the *rotational delay*.
- As the platter continues to rotate, it reads each byte (or writes each byte) that appears under the disk head, until the last desired byte appears. This time is called the *transfer time*.

The time required to execute a disk access is the sum of the seek time, rotational delay, and transfer time. Each of these times is constrained by the mechanical

[1]Technically, 1 KB = 1024 bytes, 1 MB = 1,048,576 bytes, and 1 GB = 1,073,741,824 bytes. For convenience, I round them down to one thousand, one million, and one billion bytes, respectively.

movement of the disk. Mechanical movement is significantly slower than electrical movement, which is why disk drives are so much slower than RAM. The seek time and rotational delay are especially annoying. These two times are nothing but overhead that every disk operation is forced to wait for.

Calculating the exact seek time and rotational delay of a disk access is impractical, because it requires knowing the previous state of the disk. Instead, you can estimate these times by using their average. You already know about the average seek time. The average rotational delay is easily calculated. The rotational delay can be as low as 0 (if the first byte just happens to be under the head) and as high as the time for a complete rotation (if the first byte just passed by the head). On the average, you will have to wait ½ rotation until the platter is positioned where you want it. Thus the average rotational delay is half of the rotation time.

The transfer time is also easily calculated from the transfer rate. In particular, if the transfer rate is `r` bytes/second and you are transferring `b` bytes, then the transfer time is `b/r` seconds.

For an example, consider the disk drive spinning at 10,000 rpm, having an average seek time of 5 ms and a transfer rate of 83 MB/s. Here are some calculated costs:

Average rotational delay:
```
60 seconds/minute x 1 minute/10,000 revolutions x ½ revolution
= 0.003 seconds or 3 ms
```

Transfer time for 1 byte:
```
1 byte x 1 second/83,000,000 bytes
= 0.000000012 seconds or 0.000012 ms
```

Transfer time for 1000 bytes:
```
1,000 bytes x 1 second/83,000,000 bytes
= 0.000012 seconds or 0.012 ms
```

Estimated time to access 1 byte:
```
5 ms (seek) + 3 ms (rotational delay) + 0.000012 ms (transfer)
= 8.000012 ms
```

Estimated time to access 1000 bytes:
```
5 ms (seek) + 3 ms (rotational delay) + 0.012 ms (transfer)
= 8.012 ms
```

Note that the estimated access time for 1000 bytes is essentially the same as for 1 byte. In other words, it makes no sense to access a few bytes from disk. In fact, you couldn't even if you wanted to. Modern disks are built so that each track is divided into fixed-length *sectors*; a disk read (or write) must operate on an entire sector at a time. The size of a sector may be determined by the disk manufacturer, or it may be chosen when the disk is formatted. A typical sector size is 512 bytes.

3.1.3 Improving Disk Access Time

Because disk drives are so slow, several techniques have been developed to help improve access times. This section considers three techniques: disk caches, cylinders, and disk striping.

Disk Caches

A *disk cache* is memory that is bundled with the disk drive and is usually large enough to store the contents of thousands of sectors. Whenever the disk drive reads a sector from disk, it saves the contents of that sector in its cache; if the cache is full, the new sector replaces an old sector. When a sector is requested, the disk drive checks the cache. If the sector happens to be in the cache, it can be returned immediately to the computer without an actual disk access.

Suppose that an application requests the same sector more than once in a relatively short period. The first request will bring the sector into the cache and subsequent requests will retrieve it from the cache, thereby saving on disk accesses. However, this feature is not particularly useful for a database engine, because it is already doing its own caching (as you shall see in Chap. 4). If a sector is requested multiple times, the engine will find the sector in its own cache and not even bother to go to the disk.

The real value of a disk cache is its ability to *pre-fetch* sectors. Instead of reading just a requested sector, the disk drive can read the entire track containing that sector into the cache, in the hope that other sectors of the track will be requested later. The point is that reading an entire track is not that much more time-consuming than reading a single sector. In particular, there is no rotational delay, because the disk can read the track starting from whatever sector happens to be under the read/write head and continue reading throughout the rotation. Compare the access times:

```
Time to read a sector = seek time + ½ rotation time + sector rotation time
Time to read a track  = seek time + rotation time
```

That is, the difference between reading a single sector and a track full of sectors is less than half the disk rotation time. If the database engine happens to request just one other sector on the track, then reading the entire track into the cache will have saved time.

Cylinders

The database system can improve disk access time by storing related information in nearby sectors. For example, the ideal way to store a file is to place its contents on the same track of a platter. This strategy is clearly best if the disk does track-based caching, because the entire file will be read in a single disk access. But the strategy is good even without caching, because it eliminates seek time—each time another sector is read, the disk head will already be located at the proper track.[2]

---

[2]A file whose contents are wildly scattered across different tracks of the disk is said to be *fragmented*. Many operating systems provide a defragmentation utility that improves access time by relocating each file so that its sectors are as contiguous as possible.

Suppose that a file occupies more than one track. A good idea is to store its contents in nearby tracks of the platter so that the seek time between tracks is as small as possible. An even better idea, however, is to store its contents on the same track of other platters. Since the read/write heads of each platter all move together, all of the tracks having the same track number can be accessed without any additional seek time.

The set of tracks having the same track number is called a *cylinder*, because if you look at those tracks from the top of the disk, they describe the outside of a cylinder. Practically speaking, a cylinder can be treated as if it were a very large track, because all its sectors can be accessed with zero additional seeks.

Disk Striping

Another way to improve disk access time is to use multiple disk drives. Two small drives are faster than one large drive because they contain two independent actuators and thus can respond to two different sector requests simultaneously. For example, two 20 GB disks, working continuously, will be about twice as fast as a single 40 GB disk. This speedup scales well: in general, N disks will be about N times as fast as a single disk. (Of course, several smaller drives are also more expensive than a single large drive, so the added efficiency comes at a cost.)

However, the efficiency of multiple small disks will be lost if they cannot be kept busy. Suppose, for example, that one disk contains the frequently used files, while the other disks contain the little-used, archived files. Then the first disk would be doing all of the work, with the other disks standing idle most of the time. This setup would have about the same efficiency as a single disk.

So the problem is how to balance the workload among the multiple disks. The database administrator could try to analyze file usage in order to best distribute the files on each disk, but that approach is not practical: It is difficult to do, hard to guarantee, and would have to be continually reevaluated and revised over time. Fortunately, there is a much better approach, known as *disk striping*.

The disk striping strategy uses a controller to hide the smaller disks from the operating system, giving it the illusion of a single large disk. The controller maps sector requests on the virtual disk to sector requests on the actual disks. The mapping works as follows. Suppose there are N small disks, each having k sectors. The virtual disk will have N∗k sectors; these sectors are assigned to sectors of the real disks in an alternating pattern. Disk 0 will contain virtual sectors 0, N, 2N, etc. Disk 1 will contain virtual sectors 1, N+1, 2N+1, etc., and so on. The term *disk striping* comes from the following imagery: If you imagine that each small disk is painted in a different color, then the virtual disk looks like it has stripes, with its sectors painted in alternating colors.[3] See Fig. 3.3.

---

[3]Most controllers allow a user to define a stripe to be of any size, not just a sector. For example, a track makes a good stripe if the disk drives are also performing track-based disk caching. The optimal stripe size depends on many factors and is often determined by trial and error.

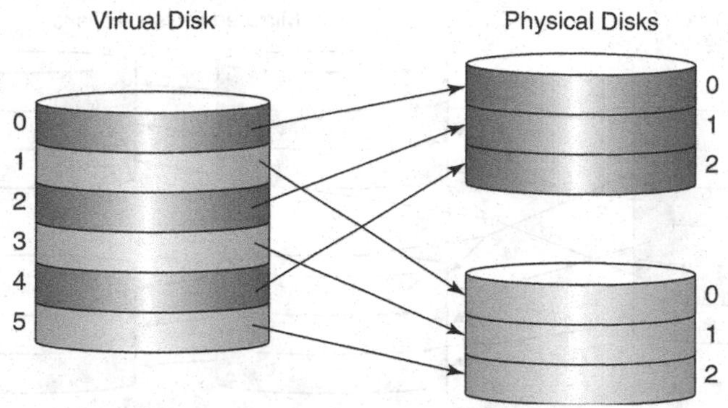

Fig. 3.3 Disk striping

Disk striping is effective because it distributes the database equally among the small disks. If a request arrives for a random sector, then that request will be sent to one of the small disks with equal probability. And if several requests arrive for contiguous sectors, they will be sent to different disks. Thus the disks are guaranteed to be working as uniformly as possible.

3.1.4 Improving Disk Reliability by Mirroring

Users of a database expect that their data will remain safe on disk and will not get lost or become corrupted. Unfortunately, disk drives are not completely reliable. The magnetic material on a platter can degenerate, causing sectors to become unreadable. Or a piece of dust or a jarring movement could cause a read/write head to scrape against a platter, ruining the affected sectors (a "head crash").

The most obvious way to guard against disk failure is to keep a copy of the disk's contents. For example, you could make nightly backups of the disk; when a disk fails, you simply buy a new disk and copy the backup onto it. The problem with this strategy is that you lose all of the changes to the disk that occurred between the time that the disk was backed up and the time when it failed. The only way around this problem is to replicate every change to the disk at the moment it occurs. In other words, you need to keep two identical versions of the disk; these versions are said to be *mirrors* of each other.

As with striping, a controller is needed to manage the two mirrored disks. When the database system requests a disk read, the controller can access the specified sector of either disk. When a disk write is requested, the controller performs the same write to both disks. In theory, these two disk writes could be performed in parallel, which would require no additional time. In practice, however, it is important to write the mirrors sequentially to guard against a system crash. The problem is that if the system crashes in the middle of a disk write, the contents of that sector are lost. So if both mirrors are written in parallel, both copies of the sector could be lost, whereas if

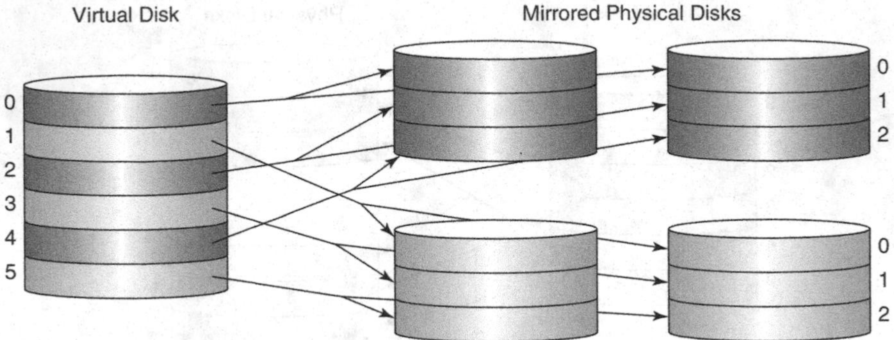

Fig. 3.4 Disk striping with mirrors

the mirrors are written sequentially, then at least one of the mirrors will be uncorrupted.

Suppose that one disk from a mirrored pair fails. The database administrator can recover the system by performing the following procedure:

1. Shut down the system.
2. Replace the failed disk with a new disk.
3. Copy the data from the good disk onto the new disk.
4. Restart the system.

Unfortunately, this procedure is not fool-proof. Data can still get lost if the good disk fails while it is in the middle of copying to the new disk. The chance of both disks failing within a couple of hours of each other is small (it is about 1 in 60,000 with today's disks), but if the database is important, this small risk might be unacceptable. You can reduce the risk by using three mirrored disks instead of two. In this case, the data would be lost only if all three disks failed within the same couple of hours; such a possibility, while nonzero, is so remote that it can comfortably be ignored.

Mirroring can coexist with disk striping. A common strategy is to mirror the striped disks. For example, one could store 40 GB of data on four 20 GB drives: Two of the drives would be striped, and the other two would be mirrors of the striped drives. Such a configuration is both fast and reliable. See Fig. 3.4.

3.1.5 Improving Disk Reliability by Storing Parity

The drawback to mirroring is that it requires twice as many disks to store the same amount of data. This burden is particularly noticeable when disk striping is used—if you want to store 300 GB of data using 15 20 GB drives, then you will need to buy another 15 drives to be their mirrors. It is not unusual for large database installations to create a huge virtual disk by striping many small disks, and the prospect of buying an equal number of disks just to be mirrors is unappealing. It would be nice to be able to recover from a failed disk without using so many mirror disks.

In fact, there is a clever way to use a single disk to back up any number of other disks. The strategy works by storing *parity* information on the backup disk. Parity is defined for a set S of bits as follows:

- The parity of S is 1 if it contains an odd number of 1s.
- The parity of S is 0 if it contains an even number of 1s.

In other words, if you add the parity bit to S, you will always have an even number of 1s.

Parity has the following interesting and important property: The value of any bit can be determined from the value of the other bits, as long as you also know the parity. For example, suppose that S = {1, 0, 1}. The parity of S is 0 because it has an even number of 1s. Suppose you lose the value of the first bit. Because the parity is 0, the set {?, 0, 1} must have had an even number of 1s; thus, you can infer that the missing bit must be a 1. Similar deductions can be made for each of the other bits (including the parity bit).

This use of parity extends to disks. Suppose you have N + 1 identically sized disks. You choose one of the disks to be the parity disk and let the other N disks hold the striped data. Each bit of the parity disk is computed by finding the parity of the corresponding bit of all the other disks. If any disk fails (including the parity disk), the contents of that disk can be reconstructed by looking, bit by bit, at the contents of the other disks. See Fig. 3.5.

The disks are managed by a controller. Read and write requests are handled basically the same as with striping—the controller determines which disk holds the requested sector and performs that read/write operation. The difference is that write requests must also update the corresponding sector of the parity disk. The controller can calculate the updated parity by determining which bits of the modified sector changed; the rule is that if a bit changes, then the corresponding parity bit must also change. Thus, the controller requires four disk accesses to implement a sector-write

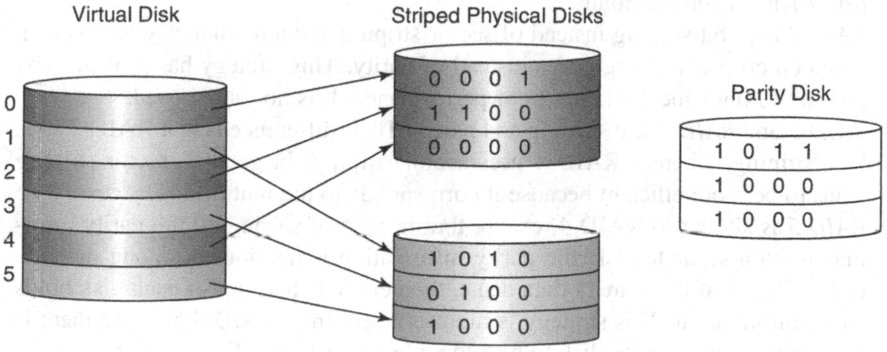

Fig. 3.5 Disk striping with parity

operation: it must read the sector and the corresponding parity sector (in order to calculate the new parity bits), and it must write the new contents of both sectors.

This use of parity information is somewhat magical, in the sense that one disk is able to reliably back up any number of other disks. However, this magic is accompanied by two drawbacks.

The first drawback to using parity is that a sector-write operation is more time-consuming, as it requires both a read and a write from two disks. Experience indicates that using parity reduces the efficiency of striping by a factor of about 20%.

The second drawback to parity is that the database is more vulnerable to a non-recoverable multi-disk failure. Consider what happens when a disk fails—all of the other disks are needed to reconstruct the failed disk, and the failure of any one of them is disastrous. If the database is comprised of many small disks (say, around 100), then the possibility of a second failure becomes very real. Contrast this situation with mirroring, in which a recovery from a failed disk only requires that its mirror not fail, which is much less likely.

3.1.6 RAID

The previous sections considered three ways to use multiple disks: *striping* to speed up disk access time, and *mirroring* and *parity* to guard against disk failure. These strategies use a controller to hide the existence of the multiple disks from the operating system and provide the illusion of a single, virtual disk. The controller maps each virtual read/write operation to one or more operations on the underlying disks. The controller can be implemented in software or hardware, although hardware controllers are more widespread.

These strategies are part of a larger collection of strategies known as *RAID*, which stands for *Redundant Array of Inexpensive Disks*. There are seven RAID levels.

- *RAID-0* is striping, without any guard against disk failure. If one of the striped disks fails, then the entire database is potentially ruined.
- *RAID-1* is mirrored striping.
- *RAID-2* uses bit striping instead of sector striping and a redundancy mechanism based on error-correcting codes instead of parity. This strategy has proven to be difficult to implement and has poor performance. It is no longer used.
- *RAID-3* and *RAID-4* use striping and parity. Their difference is that RAID-3 uses byte striping, whereas RAID-4 uses sector striping. In general, sector striping tends to be more efficient because it corresponds to the unit of disk access.
- *RAID-5* is similar to RAID-4, except that instead of storing all the parity information on a separate disk, the parity information is distributed among the data disks. That is, if there are N data disks, then every Nth sector of each disk holds parity information. This strategy is more efficient than RAID-4 because there is no longer a single parity disk to become a bottleneck. See Exercise 3.5.

- *RAID-6* is similar to RAID-5, except that it keeps two kinds of parity information. This strategy is therefore able to handle two concurrent disk failures but needs another disk to hold the additional parity information.

The two most popular RAID levels are RAID-1 and RAID-5. The choice between them is really one of mirroring vs. parity. Mirroring tends to be the more solid choice in a database installation, first because of its speed and robustness and second because the cost of the additional disk drives has become so low.

3.1.7 Flash Drives

Disk drives are commonplace in current database systems, but they have an insurmountable drawback—their operation depends entirely on the mechanical activity of spinning platters and moving actuators. This drawback makes disk drives inherently slow compared to electronic memory and also susceptible to damage from falling, vibration, and other shocks.

Flash memory is a more recent technology that has the potential to replace disk drives. It uses semiconductor technology, similar to RAM, but does not require an uninterrupted power supply. Because its activity is entirely electrical, it can access data much more quickly than disk drives and has no moving parts to get damaged.

Flash drives currently have a seek time of around 50 microseconds, which is about 100 times faster than disk drives. The transfer rate of current flash drives depends on the bus interface is it connected to. Flash drives connected by fast internal buses are comparable to those of disk drives; however, external USB flash drives are slower than disk drives.

Flash memory wears out. Each byte can be rewritten a fixed number of times; attempting to write to a byte that has hit its limit will cause the flash drive to fail. Currently, this maximum is in the millions, which is reasonably high for most database applications. High-end drives employ "wear-leveling" techniques that automatically move frequently written bytes to less-written locations; this technique allows the drive to operate until all bytes on the drive reach their rewrite limit.

A flash drive presents a sector-based interface to the operating system, which makes the flash drive look like a disk drive. It is possible to employ RAID techniques with flash drives, although striping is less important because the seek time of a flash drive is so low.

The main impediment to flash drive adoption is its price. Prices are currently about 100 times the price of a comparable disk drive. Although the price of both flash and disk technology will continue to decrease, eventually flash drives will be cheap enough to be treated as mainstream. At that point, disk drives may be relegated to archival storage and the storage of extremely large databases.

Flash memory can also be used to enhance a disk drive by serving as a persistent front end. If the database fits entirely in the flash memory, then the disk drive will never get used. But as the database gets larger, the less frequently used sectors will migrate to disk.

As far as the database engine is concerned, a flash drive has the same properties as a disk drive: it is persistent, slow, and accessed in sectors. (It just happens to be less slow than a disk drive.) Consequently, I shall conform to current terminology and refer to persistent memory as "the disk" throughout the rest of this book.

3.2 The Block-Level Interface to the Disk

Disks may have different hardware characteristics—for example, they need not have the same sector size, and their sectors may be addressed in different ways. The operating system is responsible for hiding these (and other) details, providing its applications with a simple interface for accessing disks.

The notion of a *block* is central to this interface. A block is similar to a sector except that its size is determined by the OS. Each block has the same fixed size for all disks. The OS maintains the mapping between blocks and sectors. The OS also assigns a *block number* to each block of a disk; given a block number, the OS determines the actual sector addresses.

The contents of a block cannot be accessed directly from the disk. Instead, the sectors comprising the block must first be read into a memory *page* and accessed from there. To modify the contents of a block, a client must read the block into a page, modify the bytes in the page, and then write the page back to the block on disk.

An OS typically provides several methods to access disk blocks, such as:

- `readblock(n,p)` reads the bytes at block `n` of the disk into page `p` of memory.
- `writeblock(n,p)` writes the bytes in page `p` of memory to block `n` of the disk.
- `allocate(k,n)` finds `k` contiguous unused blocks on disk, marks them as used, and returns the block number of the first one. The new blocks should be located as close to block `n` as possible.
- `deallocate(k,n)` marks the `k` contiguous blocks starting with block `n` as unused.

The OS keeps track of which blocks on disk are available for allocation and which are not. There are two basic strategies that it can adopt: a disk map or a free list.

A *disk map* is a sequence of bits, one bit for each block on the disk. A bit value of 1 means the block is free, and a 0 means that the block is already allocated. The disk map is stored on the disk, usually in its first several blocks. The OS can deallocate block `n` by simply changing bit `n` of the disk map to 1. It can allocate `k` contiguous blocks by searching the disk map for `k` bits in a row having the value 1 and then setting those bits to 0.

A *free list* is a chain of *chunks*, where a chunk is a contiguous sequence of unallocated blocks. The first block of each chunk stores two values: the length of the

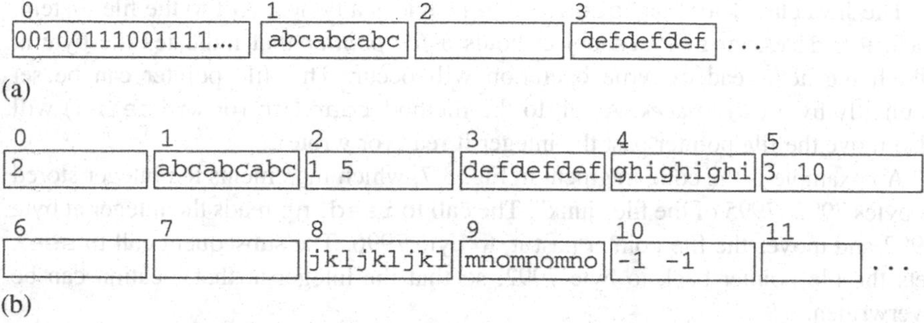

Fig. 3.6 Two ways to keep track of free blocks. **(a)** A disk map, **(b)** A free list

chunk and the block number of the next chunk on the chain.[4] The first block of the disk contains a pointer to the first chunk on the chain. When the OS is asked to allocate k contiguous blocks, it searches the free list for a sufficiently large chunk. It then has the choice of removing the entire chunk from the free list and allocating it or of splitting off a piece of length k and allocating only those blocks. When asked to deallocate a chunk of blocks, the OS simply inserts it into the free list.

Figure 3.6 illustrates these two techniques for a disk that has blocks 0, 1, 3, 4, 8, and 9 allocated. Part (a) shows the disk map stored in block 0 of the disk; a bit value of 0 indicates an allocated block. Part (b) shows the corresponding free list. Block 0 contains the value 2, meaning that the first chunk of the free list begins at block 2. Block 2 contains the two values 1 and 5, indicating that the chunk contains 1 block and that the next chunk begins at block 5. Similarly, the contents of block 5 indicate that its chunk is 3 blocks long, and the next chunk is at block 10. The value of −1 in block 10 indicates that it is the last chunk, which contains all remaining blocks.

The free list technique requires minimal extra space; all you need is to store an integer in block 0 to point to the first block in the list. On the other hand, the disk map technique requires space to hold the map. Figure 3.6a assumes that the map can fit into a single block. In general, however, several blocks may be required; see Exercise 3.7. The advantage of a disk map is that it gives the OS a better picture of where the "holes" in the disk are. For example, disk maps are often the strategy of choice if the OS needs to support the allocation of multiple blocks at a time.

3.3 The File-Level Interface to the Disk

The OS provides another, higher-level interface to the disk, called the *file system*. A client views a file as a named sequence of bytes. There is no notion of block at this level. Instead, a client can read (or write) any number of bytes starting at any position in the file.

[4]Since the block is unallocated, its contents can be used by the OS for any purpose whatsoever. In this case, it is a simple matter to use the first 8 bytes of the block to store these two integers.

The Java class `RandomAccessFile` provides a typical API to the file system. Each `RandomAccessFile` object holds a *file pointer* that indicates the byte at which the next read or write operation will occur. This file pointer can be set explicitly by a call to *seek*. A call to the method `readInt` (or `writeInt`) will also move the file pointer past the integer it read (or wrote).

An example is the code fragment in Fig. 3.7, which increments the integer stored at bytes 7992–7995 of the file "junk". The call to `readInt` reads the integer at byte 7992 and moves the file pointer past it, to byte 7996. The subsequent call to `seek` sets the file pointer back to byte 7992, so that the integer at that location can be overwritten.

Note that the calls to `readInt` and `writeInt` act as if the disk were being accessed directly, hiding the fact that disk blocks must be accessed through pages. An OS typically reserves several pages of memory for its own use; these pages are called *I/O buffers*. When a file is opened, the OS assigns an I/O buffer to the file, unbeknownst to the client.

The file-level interface enables a file to be thought of as a sequence of blocks. For example, if blocks are 4096 bytes long (i.e., 4K bytes), then byte 7992 is in block 1 of the file (i.e., its second block). Block references like "block 1 of the file" are called *logical* block references, because they tell us where the block is with respect to the file, but not where the block is on disk.

Given a particular file location, the `seek` method determines the actual disk block that holds that location. In particular, `seek` performs two conversions:

- It converts the specified byte position to a logical block reference.
- It converts the logical block reference to a physical block reference.

The first conversion is easy—the logical block number is just the byte position divided by the block size. For example, assuming 4K-byte blocks, byte 7992 is in block 1 because $7992/4096 = 1$ (integer division).

The second conversion is harder and depends on how a file system is implemented. The remainder of this section considers three file implementation strategies: *contiguous allocation*, *extent-based allocation*, and *indexed allocation*. Each of these three strategies stores its information about file locations on disk, in a *file system directory*. The *seek* method accesses the blocks of this directory when it converts logical block references to physical block references. You can think of these disk accesses as a hidden "overhead" imposed by the file system. Operating systems try to minimize this overhead, but they cannot eliminate it.

```
RandomAccessFile f = new RandomAccessFile("junk", "rws");
f.seek(7992);
int n = f.readInt();
f.seek(7992);
f.writeInt(n+1);
f.close();
```

Fig. 3.7 Using the file-system interface to the disk

Continuous Allocation

Contiguous allocation is the simplest strategy, storing each file as a sequence of contiguous blocks. To implement contiguous allocation, the file system directory holds the length of each file and the location of its first block. Mapping logical to physical block references is easy—if the file begins at disk block `b`, then block `N` of the file is in disk block `b + N`. Figure 3.8 depicts the directory for a file system containing two files: a 48-block long file named "junk" that begins at block 32 and a 16-block long file named "temp" that begins at block 80.

Contiguous allocation has two problems. The first problem is that a file cannot be extended if there is another file immediately following it. The file "junk" in Fig. 3.8 is an example of such a file. Thus, clients must create their files with the maximum number of blocks they might need, which leads to wasted space when the file is not full. This problem is known as *internal fragmentation*. The second problem is that as the disk gets full, it may have lots of small-sized chunks of unallocated blocks, but no large chunks. Thus, it may not be possible to create a large file, even though the disk contains plenty of free space. This problem is known as *external fragmentation*. In other words:

- Internal fragmentation is the wasted space inside a file.
- External fragmentation is the wasted space is outside all the files.

Extent-Based Allocation

The extent-based allocation strategy is a variation of contiguous allocation that reduces both internal and external fragmentation. Here, the OS stores a file as a sequence of fixed-length *extents*, where each extent is a contiguous chunk of blocks. A file is extended one extent at a time. The file system directory for this strategy contains, for each file, a list of the first blocks of each extent of the file.

For example, suppose that the OS stores files in 8-block extents. Figure 3.9 depicts the file system directory for the two files "junk" and "temp." These files have the same size as before but are now split into extents. The file "junk" has six extents, and the file "temp" has two extents.

To find the disk block that holds block `N` of the file, the `seek` method searches the file system directory for the extent list for that file; it then searches the extent list to

Name	First Block	Length
junk	32	48
temp	80	16

Fig. 3.8 A file system directory for contiguous allocation

Name	Extents
junk	32, 480, 696, 72, 528, 336
temp	64, 8

Fig. 3.9 A file system directory for extent-based allocation

determine the extent that contains block `N`, from which it can calculate the location of the block. For example, consider the file directory of Fig. 3.9. The location of block 21 of the file "junk" can be calculated as follows:

1. Block `21` is in extent `2` of the file, because `21/8` = `2` (integer division).
2. Extent `2` begins at logical block `2*8` = `16` of the file.
3. So block `21` is in block `21-16` = `5` of that extent.
4. The file's extent list says that extent `2` begins at physical block `696`.
5. Thus the location of block 21 is `696 + 5` = `701`.

Extent-based allocation reduces internal fragmentation because a file can waste no more than an extent's worth of space. And external fragmentation is eliminated because all extents are the same size.

Indexed Allocation

Indexed allocation takes a different approach—it doesn't even try to allocate files in contiguous chunks. Instead, each block of the file is allocated individually (in one-block-long extents, if you will). The OS implements this strategy by allocating a special *index block* with each file, which keeps track of the disk blocks allocated to that file. That is, an index block `ib` can be thought of as an array of integers, where the value of `ib[N]` is the disk block that holds logical block `N` of the file. Calculating the location of any logical block is thus trivial—you just look it up in the index block.

Figure 3.10a depicts the file system directory for the two files "junk" and "temp." The index block for "junk" is block 34. Figure 3.10b gives the first few integers in that block. From this figure, it is easy to see that block 1 of file "junk" is at block 103 of the disk.

This approach has the advantage that blocks are allocated one at a time, so there is no fragmentation. Its main problem is that files will have a maximum size, because they can have only as many blocks as there are values in an index block. The UNIX file system addresses this problem by supporting multiple levels of index block, thereby allowing the maximum file size to be very large. See Exercises 3.12 and 3.13.

Name	Index Block
junk	34
temp	439

(a)

```
Block 34:
        32 103 16 17 98 ...
```

(b)

Fig. 3.10 A file system directory for indexed allocation. (**a**) The directory table, (**b**) The contents of index block 34

3.4 The Database System and the OS

The OS provides two levels of support for disk access: block-level support and file-level support. Which level should the implementers of a database engine choose?

Choosing to use block-level support has the advantage of giving the engine complete control over which disk blocks are used for what purposes. For example, frequently used blocks can be stored in the middle of the disk, where the seek time will be less. Similarly, blocks that tend to be accessed together can be stored near each other. Another advantage is that the database engine is not constrained by OS limitations on files, allowing it to support tables that are larger than the OS limit or span multiple disk drives.

On the other hand, the use of the block-level interface has several disadvantages: such a strategy is complex to implement; it requires that the disk be formatted and mounted as a *raw disk*, that is, a disk whose blocks are not part of the file system; and it requires that the database administrator have extensive knowledge about block access patterns in order to fine-tune the system.

The other extreme is for the database engine to use the OS file system as much as possible. For example, every table could be stored in a separate file, and the engine would access records using file-level operations. This strategy is much easier to implement, and it allows the OS to hide the actual disk accesses from the database system. This situation is unacceptable for two reasons. First, the database system needs to know where the block boundaries are, so that it can organize and retrieve data efficiently. And second, the database system needs to manage its own pages, because the OS way of managing I/O buffers is inappropriate for database queries. You shall encounter these issues in later chapters.

A compromise strategy is for the database system to store all of its data in one or more OS files, but to treat the files as if they were raw disks. That is, the database system accesses its "disk" using logical file blocks. The OS is responsible for mapping each logical block reference to its corresponding physical block, via the `seek` method. Because `seek` may incur disk accesses when it examines the file system directory, the database system will not be in complete control of the disk. However, these additional blocks are usually insignificant compared with the large number of blocks accessed by the database system. Thus the database system is able to use the high-level interface to the OS while maintaining significant control over disk accesses.

This compromise strategy is used in many database systems. Microsoft Access keeps everything in a single `.mdb` file, whereas Oracle, Derby, and SimpleDB use multiple files.

3.5 The SimpleDB File Manager

The portion of the database engine that interacts with the operating system is called the *file manager*. This section examines the file manager for SimpleDB. Section 3.5.1 examines how clients use the file manager; Sect. 3.5.2 examines its implementation.

3.5.1 Using the File Manager

A SimpleDB database is stored in several files. There is a file for each table and each index, as well as a log file and several catalog files. The SimpleDB file manager provides block-level access to these files, via the package `simpledb.file`. This package exposes three classes: `BlockId`, `Page`, and `FileMgr`. Their API appears in Fig. 3.11.

A `BlockId` object identifies a specific block by its file name and logical block number. For example, the statement,

```
BlockId blk = new BlockId("student.tbl", 23)
```

BlockId
```
public BlockId(String filename, int blknum);
public String filename();
public int    number();
```

Page
```
public Page(int blocksize);
public Page(byte[] b);
public int     getInt(int offset);
public byte[]  getBytes(int offset);
public String  getString(int offset);
public void    setInt(int offset, int val);
public void    setBytes(int offset, byte[] val);
public void    setString(int offset, String val);
public int     maxLength(int strlen);
```

FileMgr
```
public FileMgr(String dbDirectory, int blocksize);
public void     read(BlockId blk, Page p);
public void     write(BlockId blk, Page p);
public BlockId  append(String filename);
public boolean  isNew();
public int      length(String filename);
public int      blockSize();
```

Fig. 3.11 The API for the SimpleDB file manager

creates a reference to block 23 of the file `student.tbl`. The methods `filename` and `number` return its file name and block number.

A `Page` object holds the contents of a disk block. Its first constructor creates a page that gets its memory from an operating system I/O buffer; this constructor is used by the buffer manager. Its second constructor creates a page that gets its memory from a Java array; this constructor is used primarily by the log manager. The various `get` and `set` methods enable clients to store or access values at specified locations of the page. A page can hold three value types: ints, strings, and "blobs" (i.e., arbitrary arrays of bytes). Corresponding methods for additional types can be added if desired; see Exercise 3.17. A client can store a value at any offset of the page but is responsible for knowing what values have been stored where. An attempt to get a value from the wrong offset will have unpredictable results.

The `FileMgr` class handles the actual interaction with the OS file system. Its constructor takes two arguments: a string denoting the name of the database and an integer denoting the size of each block. The database name is used as the name of the folder that contains the files for the database; this folder is located in the engine's current directory. If no such folder exists, then a folder is created for a new database. The method `isNew` returns `true` in this case and `false` otherwise. This method is needed for the proper initialization of a new database.

The `read` method reads the contents of the specified block into the specified page. The `write` method performs the inverse operation, writing the contents of a page to the specified block. The `length` method returns the number of blocks in the specified file.

The engine has one `FileMgr` object, which is created during system startup. The class `SimpleDB` (in package `simpledb.server`) creates the object, and its method `fileMgr` returns the created object.

The class `FileTest` in Fig. 3.12 illustrates the use of these methods. This code has three sections. The first section initializes the `SimpleDB` object; the three arguments specify that the engine should use the database named "studentdb," using 400-byte blocks and a pool of 8 buffers. The 400-byte block size is the default for SimpleDB. It is artificially small so that you can easily create demo databases having a lot of blocks. In a commercial database system, this value would be set to the block size defined by the operating system; a typical block size is 4K bytes. The buffer pool will be discussed in Chap. 4.

The second section of Fig. 3.12 writes the string "abcdefghijklm" locations 88 of the second block of the file "testfile." It then calls the `maxLength` method to determine the maximum length of the string, so it can determine the location following the string. It then writes the integer 345 to that location.

The third section reads this block into another page and extracts the two values from it.

```
public class FileTest {
   public static void main(String[] args) throws IOException {
      SimpleDB db = new SimpleDB("filetest", 400, 8);
      FileMgr fm = db.fileMgr();

      BlockId blk = new BlockId("testfile", 2);
      Page p1 = new Page(fm.blockSize());
      int pos1 = 88;
      p1.setString(pos1, "abcdefghijklm");
      int size = Page.maxLength("abcdefghijklm".length());
      int pos2 = pos1 + size;
      p1.setInt(pos2, 345);
      fm.write(blk, p1);

      Page p2 = new Page(fm.blockSize());
      fm.read(blk, p2);
      System.out.println("offset " + pos2 +
                         " contains " + p2.getInt(pos2));
      System.out.println("offset " + pos1 +
                         " contains " + p2.getString(pos1));
   }
}
```

Fig. 3.12 Testing the SimpleDB file manager

3.5.2 Implementing the File Manager

This subsection examines the implementation of the three file manager classes.

The class `BlockId`
The code for class `BlockId` appears in Fig. 3.13. In addition to straightforward implementations of the methods `fileName` and `number`, the class also implements `equals`, `hashCode`, and `toString`.

The class `Page`
The code to implement class `Page` appears in Fig. 3.14. Each page is implemented using a Java `ByteBuffer` object. A `ByteBuffer` object wraps a byte array with methods to read and write values at arbitrary locations of the array. These values can be primitive values (such as integers) as well as smaller byte arrays. For example, `Page`'s `setInt` method saves an integer in the page by calling the `ByteBuffer`'s `putInt` method. `Page`'s `setBytes` method saves a blob as two values: first the number of bytes in the specified blob and then the bytes themselves. It calls `ByteBuffer`'s `putInt` method to write the integer and the method `put` to write the bytes.

The `ByteBuffer` class does not have methods to read and write strings, so `Page` chooses to write string values as blobs. The Java `String` class has a method `getBytes`, which converts a string into a byte array; it also has a constructor that converts the byte array back to a string. Thus, `Page`'s `setString` method calls

```
public class BlockId {
   private String filename;
   private int blknum;

   public BlockId(String filename, int blknum) {
      this.filename = filename;
      this.blknum   = blknum;
   }

   public String fileName() {
      return filename;
   }

   public int number() {
      return blknum;
   }

   public boolean equals(Object obj) {
      BlockId blk = (BlockId) obj;
      return filename.equals(blk.filename) && blknum == blk.blknum;
   }

   public String toString() {
      return "[file " + filename + ", block " + blknum + "]";
   }

   public int hashCode() {
      return toString().hashCode();
   }
}
```

Fig. 3.13 The code for the SimpleDB class `BlockId`

`getBytes` to convert the string to bytes and then writes those bytes as a blob. Similarly, `Page`'s `getString` method reads a blob from the byte buffer and then converts the bytes to a string.

The conversion between a string and its byte representation is determined by a *character encoding*. Several standard encodings exist, such as ASCII and Unicode-16. The Java `Charset` class contains objects that implement many of these encodings. The constructor for `String` and its `getBytes` method take a `Charset` argument. In Fig. 3.14 you can see that `Page` uses the ASCII encoding, but you can change the `CHARSET` constant to get an encoding of your preference.

A charset chooses how many bytes each character encodes to. ASCII uses one byte per character, whereas Unicode-16 uses between 2 bytes and 4 bytes per character. Consequently, a database engine may not know exactly how many bytes a given string will encode to. `Page`'s `maxLength` method calculates the maximum size of the blob for a string having a specified number of characters. It does so by multiplying the number of characters by the max number of bytes per character and adding 4 bytes for the integer that is written with the bytes.

```
public class Page {
   private ByteBuffer bb;
   public static final Charset CHARSET = StandardCharsets.US_ASCII;

   // A constructor for creating data buffers
   public Page(int blocksize) {
      bb = ByteBuffer.allocateDirect(blocksize);
   }

   // A constructor for creating log pages
   public Page(byte[] b) {
      bb = ByteBuffer.wrap(b);
   }

   public int getInt(int offset) {
      return bb.getInt(offset);
   }

   public void setInt(int offset, int n) {
      bb.putInt(offset, n);
   }

   public byte[] getBytes(int offset) {
      bb.position(offset);
      int length = bb.getInt();
      byte[] b = new byte[length];
      bb.get(b);
      return b;
   }

   public void setBytes(int offset, byte[] b) {
      bb.position(offset);
      bb.putInt(b.length);
      bb.put(b);
   }

   public String getString(int offset) {
      byte[] b = getBytes(offset);
      return new String(b, CHARSET);
   }

   public void setString(int offset, String s) {
      byte[] b = s.getBytes(CHARSET);
      setBytes(offset, b);
   }

   public static int maxLength(int strlen) {
      float bytesPerChar = CHARSET.newEncoder().maxBytesPerChar();
      return Integer.BYTES + (strlen * (int)bytesPerChar);
   }

   // a package private method, needed by FileMgr
   ByteBuffer contents() {
      bb.position(0);
      return bb;
   }
}
```

Fig. 3.14 The code for the SimpleDB class Page

The byte array that underlies a `ByteBuffer` object can come either from a Java array or from the operating system's I/O buffers. The `Page` class has two constructors, each corresponding to a different kind of underlying byte array. Since I/O buffers are a valuable resource, the use of the first constructor is carefully controlled by the buffer manager and will be discussed in the next chapter. Other components of the database engine (such as the log manager) use the other constructor.

The class `FileMgr`

The code for class `FileMgr` appears in Fig. 3.15. Its primary job is to implement methods that read and write pages to disk blocks. Its `read` method seeks to the appropriate position in the specified file and reads the contents of that block to the byte buffer of the specified page. The `write` method is similar. The `append` method seeks to the end of the file and writes an empty array of bytes to it, which causes the OS to automatically extend the file. Note how the file manager always reads or writes a block-sized number of bytes from a file and always at a block boundary. In doing so, the file manager ensures that each call to `read`, `write`, or `append` will incur exactly one disk access.

Each `RandomAccessFile` object in the map `openFiles` corresponds to an open file. Note that files are opened in "rws" mode. The "rw" portion specifies that the file is open for reading and writing. The "s" portion specifies that the operating system should not delay disk I/O in order to optimize disk performance; instead, every `write` operation must be written immediately to the disk. This feature ensures that the database engine knows exactly when disk writes occur, which will be especially important for implementing the data recovery algorithms of Chap. 5.

The methods `read`, `write`, and `append` are *synchronized*, which means that only one thread can be executing them at a time. Synchronization is needed to maintain consistency when methods share updateable objects, such as the `RandomAccessFile` objects. For example, the following scenario could occur if `read` were not synchronized: Suppose that two JDBC clients, each running in their own thread, are trying to read different blocks from the same file. Thread A runs first. It starts to execute `read` but gets interrupted right after the call to `f.seek`, that is, it has set the file position but has not yet read from it. Thread B runs next and executes `read` to completion. When thread A resumes, the file position will have changed, but the thread will not notice it; thus, it will incorrectly read from the wrong block.

There is only one `FileMgr` object in SimpleDB, which is created by the `SimpleDB` constructor in package `simpledb.server`. The `FileMgr` constructor determines if the specified database folder exists and creates it if necessary. The constructor also removes any temporary files that might have been created by the materialized operators of Chap. 13.

3.6 Chapter Summary

- A *disk drive* contains one or more rotating *platters*. A platter has concentric *tracks*, and each track consists of *sectors*. The size of a sector is determined by the disk manufacturer; a common sector size is 512 bytes.

```
public class FileMgr {
   private File dbDirectory;
   private int blocksize;
   private boolean isNew;
   private Map<String,RandomAccessFile> openFiles = new HashMap<>();

   public FileMgr(File dbDirectory, int blocksize) {
      this.dbDirectory = dbDirectory;
      this.blocksize = blocksize;
      isNew = !dbDirectory.exists();

      // create the directory if the database is new
      if (isNew)
         dbDirectory.mkdirs();

      // remove any leftover temporary tables
      for (String filename : dbDirectory.list())
         if (filename.startsWith("temp"))
               new File(dbDirectory, filename).delete();
   }

   public synchronized void read(BlockId blk, Page p) {
      try {
         RandomAccessFile f = getFile(blk.fileName());
         f.seek(blk.number() * blocksize);
         f.getChannel().read(p.contents());
      }
      catch (IOException e) {
         throw new RuntimeException("cannot read block " + blk);
      }
   }
   public synchronized void write(BlockId blk, Page p) {
      try {
         RandomAccessFile f = getFile(blk.fileName());
         f.seek(blk.number() * blocksize);
         f.getChannel().write(p.contents());
      }
      catch (IOException e) {
         throw new RuntimeException("cannot write block" + blk);
      }
   }

   public synchronized BlockId append(String filename) {
      int newblknum = size(filename);
      BlockId blk = new BlockId(filename, newblknum);
      byte[] b = new byte[blocksize];
      try {
         RandomAccessFile f = getFile(blk.fileName());
         f.seek(blk.number() * blocksize);
         f.write(b);
      }
```

Fig. 3.15 The code for the SimpleDB class `FileMgr`

```
      catch (IOException e) {
         throw new RuntimeException("cannot append block" + blk);
      }
      return blk;
   }

   public  int length(String filename) {
      try {
         RandomAccessFile f = getFile(filename);
         return (int)(f.length() / blocksize);
      }
      catch (IOException e) {
         throw new RuntimeException("cannot access " + filename);
      }
   }

   public boolean isNew() {
      return isNew;
   }

   public int blockSize() {
      return blocksize;
   }
   private RandomAccessFile getFile(String filename)
                                    throws IOException {
      RandomAccessFile f = openFiles.get(filename);
      if (f == null) {
         File dbTable = new File(dbDirectory, filename);
         f = new RandomAccessFile(dbTable, "rws");
         openFiles.put(filename, f);
      }
      return f;
   }
}
```

Fig. 3.15 (continued)

- Each platter has its own read/write head. These heads do not move independently; instead, they are all connected to a single *actuator*, which moves them simultaneously to the same track on each platter.
- A disk drive executes a disk access in three stages:
  - The actuator moves the disk head to the specified track. This time is called the *seek time*.
  - The drive waits for the platter to rotate until the first desired byte is beneath the disk head. This time is called the *rotational delay*.
  - The bytes rotating under the disk head are read (or written). This time is called the *transfer time*.
- Disk drives are slow because their activity is mechanical. Access times can be improved by using *disk caches*, *cylinders*, and *disk striping*. A disk cache allows

the disk to pre-fetch sectors by reading an entire track at a time. A cylinder consists of the tracks on each platter having the same track number. Blocks on the same cylinder can be accessed with no additional seek time. Disk striping distributes the contents of a virtual disk among several small disks. Speedup occurs because the small disks can operate simultaneously.

- *RAID* techniques can be used to improve disk reliability. The basic RAID levels are:
  - RAID-0 is striping, with no additional reliability. If a disk fails, the entire database is effectively ruined.
  - RAID-1 adds mirroring to the striped disks. Each disk has an identical mirror disk. If a disk fails, its mirror can be used to reconstruct it.
  - RAID-4 uses striping with an additional disk to hold redundant parity information. If a disk fails, its contents can be reconstructed by combining the information on the other disks with the parity disk.
- The RAID techniques require a *controller* to hide the existence of the multiple disks from the operating system and provide the illusion of a single, virtual disk. The controller maps each virtual read/write operation to one or more operations on the underlying disks.
- Disk technology is being challenged by *flash memory*. Flash memory is persistent but faster than disk because it is completely electronic. However, since flash is still significantly slower than RAM, the operating system treats a flash drive the same as a disk drive.
- The operating system hides the physical details of disk and flash drives from its clients by providing a block-based interface to them. A *block* is similar to a sector, except that its size is OS-defined. A client accesses the contents of a device by block number. The OS keeps track of which blocks on disk are available for allocation, by using either a *disk map* or a *free list*.
- A *page* is a block-sized area of memory. A client modifies a block by reading its contents into a page, modifying the page, and then writing the page back to the block.
- The operating system also provides a file-level interface to the disk. A client views a file as a named sequence of bytes.
- An operating system can implement files using *contiguous allocation*, *extent-based allocation*, or *indexed allocation*. Contiguous allocation stores each file as a sequence of contiguous blocks. Extent-based allocation stores a file a sequence of *extents*, where each extent is a contiguous chunk of blocks. Indexed allocation allocates each block of the file individually. A special *index block* is kept with each file, to keep track of the disk blocks allocated to that file.
- A database system can choose to use either the block-level or the file-level interface to the disk. A good compromise is to store the data in files but to access the files at the block level.

3.7 Suggested Reading

The article Chen et al. (1994) provides a detailed survey of the various RAID strategies and their performance characteristics. A good book that discusses UNIX-based file systems is von Hagen (2002), and one that discusses Windows NTFS is Nagar (1997). Brief overviews of various file system implementations can be found in many operating systems textbooks, such as Silberschatz et al. (2004).

Flash memory has the property that overwriting an existing value is significantly slower than writing a completely new value. Consequently, there has been a lot of research aimed at flash-based file systems that do not overwrite values. Such file systems store updates in a log, similar to the log of Chap. 4. The articles Wu and Kuo (2006) and Lee and Moon (2007) examine these issues.

Chen, P., Lee, E., Gibson, G., & Patterson, D. (1994) RAID: High-performance, reliable secondary storage. *ACM Computing Surveys, 26*(2), 145–185.

Lee, S., & Moon, B. (2007) Design of flash-based DBMS: An in-page logging approach. *Proceedings of the ACM-SIGMOD Conference*, pp. 55–66.

Nagar, R. (1997) *Windows NT file system internals*. O'Reilly.

Silberschatz, A., Gagne, G., & Galvin, P. (2004) *Operating system concepts*. Addison Wesley.

von Hagen, W. (2002) *Linux filesystems*. Sams Publishing.

Wu, C., & Kuo, T. (2006) The design of efficient initialization and crash recovery for log-based file systems over flash memory. *ACM Transactions on Storage, 2*(4), 449–467.

3.8 Exercises

Conceptual Exercises

3.1. Consider a single-platter disk containing 50,000 tracks and spinning at 7200 rpm. Each track holds 500 sectors, and each sector contains 512 bytes.

(a) What is the capacity of the platter?
(b) What is the average rotational delay?
(c) What is the maximum transfer rate?

3.2. Consider an 80 GB disk drive spinning at 7200 rpm with a transfer rate of 100 MB/s. Assume that each track contains the same number of bytes.

(a) How many bytes does each track contain? How many tracks does the disk contain?
(b) If the disk were spinning at 10,000 rpm, what would the transfer rate be?

3.3. Suppose that you have 10 20 GB disk drives, each of which has 500 sectors per track. Suppose that you want to create a virtual 200 GB drive by striping the small disks, with the size of each stripe being an entire track instead of just a single sector.

(a) Suppose that the controller receives a request for virtual sector M. Give the formula that computes the corresponding actual drive and sector number.
(b) Give a reason why track-sized stripes might be more efficient than sector-sized stripes.
(c) Give a reason why track-sized stripes might be less efficient than sector-sized stripes.

3.4. All of the failure-recovery procedures discussed in this chapter require the system to be shut down while the failed disk is replaced. Many systems cannot tolerate downtime of any amount, and yet they also don't want to lose data.

(a) Consider the basic mirroring strategy. Give an algorithm for restoring a failed mirror without any downtime. Does your algorithm increase the risk of a second disk failure? What should be done to reduce this risk?
(b) Modify the parity strategy to similarly eliminate downtime. How do you deal with the risk of a second disk failure?

3.5. One consequence of the RAID-4 parity strategy is that the parity disk gets accessed for every disk write operation. One suggested improvement is to omit the parity disk and instead "stripe" the data disks with the parity information. For example, sectors 0, N, 2N, etc. of disk 0 will contain parity information, as will sectors 1, N + 1, 2N + 1, etc. of disk 1, and so on. This improvement is called *RAID-5*.

(a) Suppose a disk fails. Explain how it will get recovered.
(b) Show that with this improvement, disk reads and writes still require the same number of disk accesses as RAID-4.
(c) Explain why this improvement nevertheless leads to more efficient disk accesses.

3.6. Consider Fig. 3.5, and suppose that one of the striped disks fails. Show how to reconstruct its contents using the parity disk.

3.7. Consider a 1 GB database, stored in a file whose block size is 4K bytes.

(a) How many blocks will the file contain?
(b) Suppose that the database system uses a disk map to manage its free blocks. How many additional blocks are needed to hold the disk map?

3.8. Consider Fig. 3.6. Draw a picture of the disk map and the free list after the following operations have been executed:

```
allocate(1,4); allocate(4,10); allocate(5,12);
```

3.9. Figure 3.16 depicts a RAID-4 system in which one of the disks has failed. Use the parity disk to reconstruct its values.

3.10. The free list allocation strategy can wind up with two contiguous chunks on the free list.

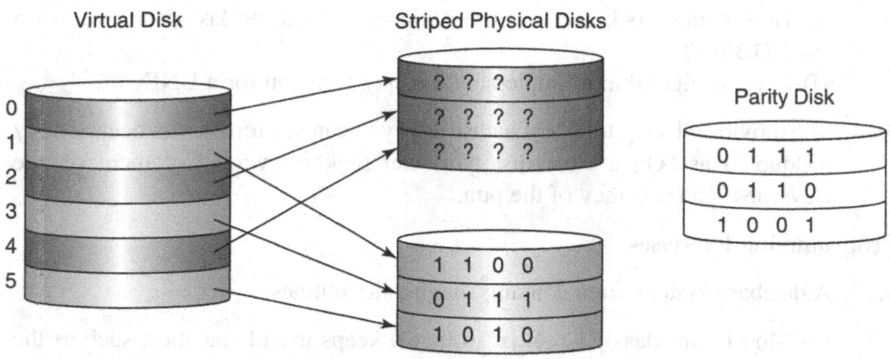

Fig. 3.16 A failed physical disk in a RAID-4 system

(a) Explain how to modify the free-list technique so that contiguous chunks can be merged.
(b) Explain why merging unallocated chunks is a good idea when files are allocated contiguously.
(c) Explain why merging is not important for extent-based or indexed file allocation.

3.11. Suppose that the OS uses extent-based file allocation using extents of size 12, and suppose that the extent list for a file is [240, 132, 60, 252, 12, 24].

(a) What is the size of the file?
(b) Calculate the physical disk block of logical blocks 2, 12, 23, 34, and 55 of the file.

3.12. Consider a file implementation that uses indexed file allocation. Assuming that the block size is 4K bytes, what is the size of the largest possible file?

3.13. In UNIX, the directory entry for a file points to a block called an *inode*. In one implementation of an inode, the beginning of the block holds various header information, and its last 60 bytes contains 15 integers. The first 12 of these integers are the physical locations of the first 12 data blocks in the file. The next two integers are the location of two *index blocks*, and the last integer is the location of a *double-index block*. An index block consists entirely of block numbers of the next data blocks in the file; a double-index block consists entirely of block numbers of index blocks (whose contents point to data blocks).

(a) Assuming again that the block size is 4K bytes, how many data blocks does an index block refer to?
(b) Ignoring the double-index block, what is the largest possible UNIX file size?
(c) How many data blocks does a double-index block refer to?
(d) What is the largest possible UNIX file size?

(e) How many block accesses are required to read the last data block of a 1 GB file?

(f) Give an algorithm to implement the *seek* function for a UNIX file.

3.14. The movie and song title "On a clear day you can see forever" is occasionally misquoted as "On a clear disk you can seek forever." Comment on the cleverness and accuracy of the pun.

Programming Exercises

3.15. A database system often contains diagnostic routines.

(a) Modify the class `FileMgr` so that it keeps useful statistics, such as the number of blocks read/written. Add new method(s) to the class that will return these statistics.

(b) Modify the methods `commit` and `rollback` of the class `RemoteConnectionImpl` (in the `simpledb.jdbc.network` package) so that they print these statistics. Do the same for the class `EmbeddedConnection` (in the `simpledb.jdbc.embedded` package). The result will be that the engine prints the statistics for each SQL statement it executes.

3.16. The methods `setInt`, `setBytes`, and `setString` of class `Page` do not check that the new value fits in the page.

(a) Modify the code to perform the checks. What should you do if the check fails?

(b) Give a reason why it is reasonable to not perform the checks.

3.17. The class `Page` has methods to get/set integers, blobs, and strings. Modify the class to handle other types, such as short integers, booleans, and dates.

3.18. The class `Page` implements a string by creating a blob from the string's characters. Another way to implement a string is to write each character individually, appending a delimiter character at the end. A reasonable delimiter character in Java is '\0'. Modify the class accordingly.

Chapter 4
Memory Management

This chapter studies two components of the database engine: the *log manager* and the *buffer manager*. Each of these components is responsible for certain files: The log manager is responsible for the log file, and the buffer manager is responsible for the data files.

Both components face the problem of how to efficiently manage the reading and writing of disk blocks with main memory. The contents of a database is typically much larger than main memory, and so these components may need to shuttle blocks in and out of memory. This chapter examines their memory needs and the memory-management algorithms they use. The log manager supports only sequential access to the log file and has a simple, optimal memory-management algorithm. On the other hand, the buffer manager must support arbitrary access to user files, which is a much more difficult challenge.

4.1 Two Principles of Database Memory Management

Recall that the only way that a database engine can read a disk value is to read the block containing it into a page of memory, and the only way to write a disk value is to write the modified page back to its block. Database engines follow two important principles when they move data between the disk and memory: *minimize disk accesses*, and *don't rely on virtual memory*.

Principle 1: Minimize Disk Accesses

Consider an application that reads data from the disk, searches through the data, performs various computations, makes some changes, and writes the data back. How can you estimate the amount of time this will take? Recall that RAM operations are over 1000 times faster than flash and 100,000 times faster than disk. This means that in most practical situations, the time it takes to read/write the block from disk is at

E. Sciore, *Database Design and Implementation*, Data-Centric Systems and Applications, https://doi.org/10.1007/978-3-030-33836-7_4

least as large as the time it takes to process the block in RAM. Consequently, the single most important thing a database engine can do is minimize block accesses.

One way to minimize block accesses is to avoid accessing a disk block multiple times. This kind of problem occurs in many areas of computing and has a standard solution known as *caching*. For example, a CPU has a local hardware cache of previously executed instructions; if the next instruction is in the cache, the CPU does not have to load it from RAM. For another example, a browser keeps a cache of previously accessed web pages; if a user requests a page that happens to be in the cache (say, by hitting the browser's Back button), the browser can avoid retrieving it from the network.

A database engine uses memory pages to cache disk blocks. By keeping track of which pages contain the contents of which blocks, the engine may be able to satisfy a client request by using an existing page and thereby avoid a disk read. Similarly, the engine writes pages to disk only when necessary, in the hope that multiple changes to a page can be made via a single disk write.

The need to minimize disk accesses is so important that it pervades the entire implementation of the database engine. For example, the retrieval algorithms used by the engine are chosen specifically because of the frugal way that they access the disk. And when an SQL query has several possible retrieval strategies, the planner will choose the strategy that it thinks will require the fewest number of disk accesses.

Principle 2: Don't Rely on Virtual Memory

Modern operating systems support *virtual memory*. The operating system gives each process the illusion that it has a very large amount of memory in which to store its code and data. A process can allocate objects arbitrarily in its virtual memory space; the operating system maps each virtual page to an actual page of physical memory.

The virtual memory space supported by an operating system is usually far larger than a computer's physical memory. Since not all virtual pages fit in physical memory, the OS must store some of them on disk. When a process accesses a virtual page not in memory, a *page swap* occurs. The OS chooses a physical page, writes the contents of that page to disk (if it had been modified), and reads the saved contents of the virtual page from disk to that page.

The most straightforward way for the database engine to manage disk blocks is to give each block its own virtual page. For example, it could keep an array of pages for each file, having one slot for each block of the file. These arrays would be huge, but they would fit in virtual memory. As the database system accessed these pages, the virtual memory mechanism would swap them between disk and physical memory, as needed. This is a simple, easily implemented strategy. Unfortunately, it has a serious problem, which is that the operating system, not the database engine, controls when pages get written to disk. Two issues arise.

The first issue is that the operating system's page-swapping strategy can impair the database engine's ability to recover after a system crash. The reason, as you shall see in Chap. 5, is that a modified page will have some associated log records, and these log records *must* be written to disk before the page. (Otherwise, the log records will not be available to help the database recover after a system crash.) Since the OS does not know about the log, it may swap out a modified page without writing its log records and thereby subvert the recovery mechanism.[1]

The second issue is that the operating system has no idea which pages are currently in use and which pages the database engine no longer cares about. The OS can make an educated guess, such as choosing to swap the page that was least recently accessed. But if the OS guesses incorrectly, it will swap out a page that will be needed again, causing two unnecessary disk accesses. The database engine, on the other hand, has a much better idea of what pages are needed and can make much more intelligent guesses.

Therefore, a database engine must manage its own pages. It does so by allocating a relatively small number of pages that it knows will fit in physical memory; these pages are known as the database's *buffer pool*. The engine keeps track of which pages are available for swapping. When a block needs to be read into a page, the database engine (and not the operating system) chooses an available page from the buffer pool, writes its contents (and its log record) to disk if necessary, and only then reads in the specified block.

4.2 Managing Log Information

Whenever a user changes the database, the database engine must keep track of that change in case it needs to be undone. The values describing a change are kept in a *log record*, and the log records are stored in a *log file*. New log records are appended to the end of the log.

The *log manager* is the database engine component responsible for writing log records to the log file. The log manager does not understand the contents of the log records—that responsibility belongs to the recovery manager of Chap. 5. Instead, the log manager treats the log as just an ever-increasing sequence of log records.

This section examines how the log manager can manage memory as it writes log records to the log file. Consider the algorithm of Fig. 4.1, which is the most straightforward way to append a record to the log.

This algorithm requires a disk read and a disk write for every appended log record. It is simple but very inefficient. Figure 4.2 illustrates the operation of the log

1. Allocate a page in memory.
2. Read the last block of the log file into that page.
3a. If there is room, place the log record after the other records on the page, and write the page back to disk.
3b. If there is no room, then allocate a new, empty page, place the log record in that page, and append the page to a new block at the end of the log file.

Fig. 4.1 A simple (but inefficient) algorithm for appending a new record to the log

[1]Actually, there do exist operating systems that address this issue, but they are not commonplace.

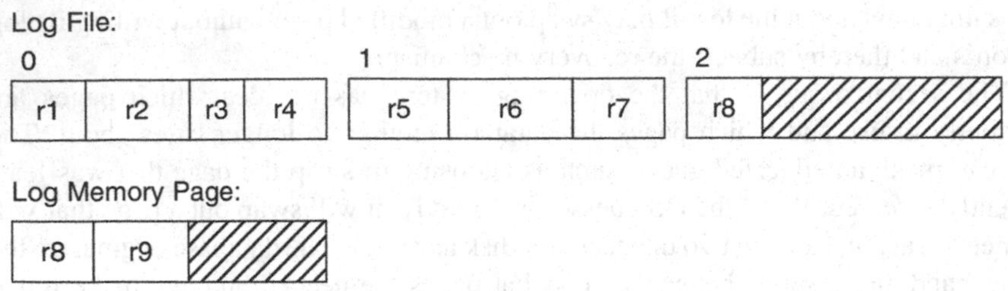

Fig. 4.2 Adding a new log record r9

manager halfway through step 3a of the algorithm. The log file contains three blocks that hold eight records, labeled r1 through r8. Log records can have varying sizes, which is why four records fit into block 0 but only three fit into block 1. Block 2 is not yet full and contains just one record. The memory page contains the contents of block 2. In addition to record r8, a new log record (record r9) has just been placed in the page.

Suppose now that the log manager completes the algorithm by writing the page back to block 2 of the file. When the log manager is eventually asked to add another log record to the file, it will perform steps 1 and 2 of the algorithm and read block 2 into a page. But note that this disk read is completely unnecessary, because the existing log page already contains the contents of block 2! Consequently, steps 1 and 2 of the algorithm are unnecessary. The log manager just needs to permanently allocate a page to contain the contents of the last log block. As a result, all of the disk reads are eliminated.

It is also possible to reduce the disk writes. In the above algorithm, the log manager writes its page to disk every time a new record is added to the page. Looking at Fig. 4.2, you can see that there is no need to write record r9 immediately to the disk. Each new log record can be simply added to the page as long as the page has room. When the page becomes full, the log manager can write the page to disk, clear its contents, and start anew. This new algorithm would result in exactly one disk write for each log block, which is clearly optimum.

This algorithm has one glitch: A log page may need to be written to the disk before it is full, due to circumstances beyond the control of the log manager. The issue is that the buffer manager cannot write a modified data page to disk until that page's associated log records have also been written to disk. If one of those log records happen to be in the log page but not yet on disk, then the log manager must write its page to disk, regardless of whether the page is full. This issue will be addressed in Chap. 5.

Figure 4.3 gives the resulting log management algorithm. This algorithm has two places where a memory page gets written to disk: when a log record needs to be forced to disk and when the page is full. Consequently, a memory page might get written to the same log block multiple times. But since these disk writes are absolutely necessary and cannot be avoided, you can conclude that the algorithm is optimal.

1. Permanently allocate one memory page to hold the contents of the last block of the log file. Call this page P.
2. When a new log record is submitted:
   a) If there is no room in P, then:
      Write P to disk and clear its contents.
   b) Append the new log record to P.
3. When the database system requests that a particular log record be written to disk:
   a) Determine if that log record is in P.
   b) If so, then write P to disk.

Fig. 4.3 The optimal log management algorithm

4.3 The SimpleDB Log Manager

This section examines the log manager of the SimpleDB database system. Section 4.3.1 illustrates the use of the log manager. Section 4.3.2 examines its implementation.

4.3.1 The API for the Log Manager

The SimpleDB log manager implementation is in the package *simpledb.log*. This package exposes the class `LogMgr`, whose API appears in Fig. 4.4.

The database engine has one `LogMgr` object, which is created during system startup. The arguments to the constructor are a reference to the file manager and the name of the log file.

The method `append` adds a record to the log and returns an integer. As far as the log manager is concerned, a log record is an arbitrarily sized byte array; it saves the array in the log file but has no idea what its contents denote. The only constraint is that the array must fit inside a page. The return value from `append` identifies the new log record; this identifier is called its *log sequence number* (or *LSN*).

Appending a record to the log does not guarantee that the record will get written to disk; instead, the log manager chooses when to write log records to disk, as in the algorithm of Fig. 4.3. A client can force a specific log record to disk by calling the method `flush`. The argument to `flush` is the LSN of a log record; the method ensures that this log record (and all previous log records) is written to disk.

A client calls the method `iterator` to read the records in the log; this method returns a Java iterator for the log records. Each call to the iterator's `next` method

LogMgr

```
public LogMgr(FileMgr fm, String logfile);
public int  append(byte[] rec);
public void flush(int lsn);
public Iterator<byte[]> iterator();
```

Fig. 4.4 The API for the SimpleDB log manager

will return a byte array denoting the next record in the log. The records returned by the iterator method are in reverse order, starting at the most recent record and moving backwards through the log file. The records are returned in this order because that is how the recovery manager wants to see them.

The class LogTest in Fig. 4.5 provides an example of how to use the log manager API. The code creates 70 log records, each consisting of a string and an integer. The integer is the record number N, and the string is the value "recordN." The code prints the records once after the first 35 have been created and then again after all 70 have been created.

If you run the code, you will discover that only 20 records are printed after the first call to printLogRecords. The reason is those records filled the first log block and were flushed to disk when the 21st log record was created. The other 15 log records remained in the in-memory log page and were not flushed. The second call to createRecords creates records 36 through 70. The call to flush tells the log manager to ensure that record 65 is on disk. But since records 66–70 are in the same page as record 65, they are also written to disk. Consequently, the second call to printLogRecords will print all 70 records, in reverse order.

Note how the method createLogRecord allocates a byte array to be the log record. It creates a Page object to wrap that array, so that it can use the page's setInt and setString methods to place the string and integer at appropriate offsets in the log record. The code then returns the byte array. Similarly, the method printLogRecords creates a Page object to wrap the log record, so that it can extract the string and integer from the record.

4.3.2 Implementing the Log Manager

The code for LogMgr appears in Fig. 4.6. Its constructor uses the provided string as the name of the log file. If the log file is empty, the constructor appends a new empty block to it. The constructor also allocates a single page (called logpage) and initializes it to contain the contents of the last log block in the file.

Recall that a log sequence number (or LSN) identifies a log record. The method append assigns LSNs sequentially, starting from 1, using the variable latestLSN. The log manager keeps track of the next available LSN and the LSN of the most recent log record written to disk. The method flush compares the most recent LSN against the specified LSN. If the specified LSN is smaller, then the desired log record must have already been written to disk; otherwise, logpage is written to disk, and the latest LSN becomes the most recent one.

The append method calculates the size of the log record to determine if it will fit in the current page. If not, it writes the current page to disk and calls appendNewBlock to clear the page and append the now-empty page to the log file. This strategy is slightly different from the algorithm of Fig. 4.3; namely, the log manager extends the log file by appending an empty page to it, instead of extending the file by appending a full page. This strategy is simpler to implement because it allows flush to assume that the block is already on disk.

```
public class LogTest {
   private static LogMgr lm;

   public static void main(String[] args) {
      SimpleDB db = new SimpleDB("logtest", 400, 8);
      lm = db.logMgr();
      createRecords(1, 35);
      printLogRecords("The log file now has these records:");
      createRecords(36, 70);
      lm.flush(65);
      printLogRecords("The log file now has these records:");
   }

   private static void printLogRecords(String msg) {
      System.out.println(msg);
      Iterator<byte[]> iter = lm.iterator();
      while (iter.hasNext()) {
         byte[] rec = iter.next();
         Page p = new Page(rec);
         String s = p.getString(0);
         int npos = Page.maxLength(s.length());
         int val = p.getInt(npos);
         System.out.println("[" + s + ", " + val + "]");
      }
      System.out.println();
   }

   private static void createRecords(int start, int end) {
      System.out.print("Creating records: ");
      for (int i=start; i<=end; i++) {
         byte[] rec = createLogRecord("record"+i, i+100);
         int lsn = lm.append(rec);
         System.out.print(lsn + " ");
      }
      System.out.println();
   }

   private static byte[] createLogRecord(String s, int n) {
      int npos = Page.maxLength(s.length());
      byte[] b = new byte[npos + Integer.BYTES];
      Page p = new Page(b);
      p.setString(0, s);
      p.setInt(npos, n);
      return b;
   }
}
```

Fig. 4.5 Testing the log manager

```
public class LogMgr {
   private FileMgr fm;
   private String logfile;
   private Page logpage;
   private BlockId currentblk;
   private int latestLSN = 0;
   private int lastSavedLSN = 0;

   public LogMgr(FileMgr fm, String logfile) {
      this.fm = fm;
      this.logfile = logfile;
      byte[] b = new byte[fm.blockSize()];
      logpage = new Page(b);
      int logsize = fm.length(logfile);
      if (logsize == 0)
         currentblk = appendNewBlock();
      else {
         currentblk = new BlockId(logfile, logsize-1);
         fm.read(currentblk, logpage);
      }
   }

   public void flush(int lsn) {
      if (lsn >= lastSavedLSN)
         flush();
   }
   public Iterator<byte[]> iterator() {
      flush();
      return new LogIterator(fm, currentblk);
   }
   public synchronized int append(byte[] logrec) {
      int boundary = logpage.getInt(0);
      int recsize = logrec.length;
      int bytesneeded = recsize + Integer.BYTES;
      if (boundary - bytesneeded < Integer.BYTES) { // It doesn't fit
         flush();                     // so move to the next block.
         currentblk = appendNewBlock();
         boundary = logpage.getInt(0);
      }
      int recpos = boundary - bytesneeded;
      logpage.setBytes(recpos, logrec);
      logpage.setInt(0, recpos); // the new boundary
      latestLSN += 1;
      return latestLSN;
   }
   private BlockId appendNewBlock() {
      BlockId blk = fm.append(logfile);
      logpage.setInt(0, fm.blockSize());
      fm.write(blk, logpage);
      return blk;
   }
   private void flush() {
      fm.write(currentblk, logpage);
      lastSavedLSN = latestLSN;
   }
}
```

Fig. 4.6 The code for the SimpleDB class `LogMgr`

Note that `append` places the log records in the page from right to left. The variable `boundary` contains the offset of the most recently added record. This strategy enables the log iterator to read records in reverse order by reading from left to right. The boundary value is written to the first four bytes of the page so that the iterator will know where the records begin.

The `iterator` method flushes the log (in order to ensure that the entire log is on disk) and then returns a `LogIterator` object. The class `LogIterator` is a package-private class that implements the iterator; its code appears in Fig. 4.7. A `LogIterator` object allocates a page to hold the contents of a log block. The constructor positions the iterator at the first record in the last block of the log (which is, remember, where the last log record was written). The method `next` moves to the next record in the page; when there are no more records, it reads the previous block

```
class LogIterator implements Iterator<byte[]> {
   private FileMgr fm;
   private BlockId blk;
   private Page p;
   private int currentpos;
   private int boundary;
   public LogIterator(FileMgr fm, BlockId blk) {
      this.fm = fm;
      this.blk = blk;
      byte[] b = new byte[fm.blockSize()];
      p = new Page(b);
      moveToBlock(blk);
   }

   public boolean hasNext() {
      return currentpos<fm.blockSize() || blk.number()>0;
   }

   public byte[] next() {
      if (currentpos == fm.blockSize()) {
         blk = new BlockId(blk.fileName(), blk.number()-1);
         moveToBlock(blk);
      }
      byte[] rec = p.getBytes(currentpos);
      currentpos += Integer.BYTES + rec.length;
      return rec;
   }

   private void moveToBlock(BlockId blk) {
      fm.read(blk, p);
      boundary = p.getInt(0);
      currentpos = boundary;
   }
}
```

Fig. 4.7 The code for the SimpleDB class `LogIterator`

into the page and returns its first record. The `hasNext` method returns false when there are no more records in the page and no more previous blocks.

4.4 Managing User Data

Log records are used in a limited, well-understood way. The log manager can therefore fine-tune its use of memory; in particular, it is able to perform its job optimally with a single dedicated page. Similarly, each `LogIterator` object only needs a single page.

JDBC applications, on the other hand, access their data completely unpredictably. There is no way to know which block an application will request next and whether it will ever access a previous block again. And even after an application is completely finished with its blocks, you can't know whether another application will access any of those same blocks in the near future. This section describes how the database engine can efficiently manage memory in such a situation.

4.4.1 The Buffer Manager

The *buffer manager* is the component of the database engine responsible for the pages that hold user data. The buffer manager allocates a fixed set of pages, called the *buffer pool*. As mentioned in the beginning of this chapter, the buffer pool should fit into the computer's physical memory, and these pages should come from the I/O buffers held by the operating system.

In order to access a block, a client interacts with the buffer manager according to the protocol given in Fig. 4.8.

A page is said to be *pinned* if some client is currently pinning it; otherwise, the page is *unpinned*. The buffer manager is obligated to keep a page available to its clients for as long as it is pinned. Conversely, once a page becomes unpinned, the buffer manager is allowed to assign it to another block.

When a client asks the buffer manager to pin a page to a block, the buffer manager will encounter one of these four possibilities:

- The contents of the block is in some page in the buffer, and:
  - The page is pinned.
  - The page is unpinned.

1. The client asks the buffer manager to *pin* a page from the buffer pool to that block.
2. The client accesses the contents of the page as much as it desires.
3. When the client is done with the page, it tells the buffer manager to *unpin* it.

Fig. 4.8 The protocol for accessing a disk block

- The contents of the block is not currently in any buffer, and:
  - There exists at least one unpinned page in the buffer pool.
  - All pages in the buffer pool are pinned.

The first case occurs when one or more clients are currently accessing the contents of the block. Since a page can be pinned by multiple clients, the buffer manager simply adds another pin to the page and returns the page to the client. Each client that is pinning the page is free to concurrently read and modify its values. The buffer manager is not concerned about potential conflicts that may occur; that responsibility belongs to the concurrency manager of Chap. 5.

The second case occurs when the client(s) that were using the buffer have finished with it, but the buffer has not yet been reassigned. Since the contents of the block are still in the buffer page, the buffer manager can reuse the page by simply pinning it and returning it to the client.

The third case requires the buffer manager to read the block from disk into a buffer page. Several steps are involved. The buffer manager must first select an unpinned page to reuse (because pinned pages are still being used by clients). Second, if the selected page has been modified, then the buffer manager must write the page contents to disk; this action is called *flushing* the page. Finally, the requested block can be read into the selected page, and the page can be pinned.

The fourth case occurs when the buffers are heavily used, such as in the query-processing algorithms of Chap. 14. In this case, the buffer manager cannot satisfy the client request. The best solution is for the buffer manager to place the client on a wait list until an unpinned buffer page becomes available.

4.4.2 Buffers

Each page in the buffer pool has associated status information, such as whether it is pinned and, if so, what block it is assigned to. A *buffer* is the object that contains this information. Every page in the buffer pool has an associated buffer. Each buffer observes the changes to its page and is responsible for writing its modified page to disk. Just as with the log, a buffer can reduce disk accesses if it can delay writing its page. For example, if page is modified several times, then it is more efficient to write the page once, after all modifications have been made. A reasonable strategy is to have the buffer postpone writing its page to disk until the page is unpinned.

Actually, the buffer can wait even longer than that. Suppose a modified page becomes unpinned but is not written to disk. If the page gets pinned again to the same block (as in the second case above), the client will see the modified contents exactly as it had been left. This has the same effect as if the page had been written to disk and then read back, but without the disk accesses. In a sense, the buffer's page acts as the in-memory version of its disk block. Any client wishing to use the block will simply be directed to the buffer page, which the client can read or modify without incurring any disk accesses.

In fact, there are only two reasons why a buffer will ever need to write a modified page to disk: either the page is being replaced because the buffer is getting pinned to a different block (as in the third case above) or the recovery manager needs to write its contents to disk to guard against a possible system crash (to be discussed in Chap. 5).

4.4.3 Buffer Replacement Strategies

The pages in the buffer pool begin unallocated. As pin requests arrive, the buffer manager primes the buffer pool by assigning requested blocks to unallocated pages. Once all pages have been allocated, the buffer manager will begin replacing pages. The buffer manager may choose any unpinned page in the buffer pool for replacement.

If the buffer manager needs to replace a page and all buffer pages are pinned, then the requesting client must wait. Consequently, each client has the responsibility to "be a good citizen" and unpin a page as soon as it is no longer needed.

When more than one buffer page is unpinned, the buffer manager must decide which one to replace. This choice can have a dramatic effect on the efficiency of the database system. For example, the worst choice would be to replace the page that will be accessed next, because the buffer manager would then have to immediately replace another page. It turns out that the best choice is to always replace the page that will be unused for the longest amount of time.

Since the buffer manager cannot predict which pages will be accessed next, it is forced to guess. Here, the buffer manager is in almost exactly the same situation as the operating system when it swaps pages in virtual memory. However, there is one big difference: Unlike the operating system, the buffer manager *knows* whether a page is currently being used or not, because the pages in use are exactly the ones that are pinned. The burden of not being able to replace pinned pages turns out to be a blessing. Clients, by pinning pages responsibly, keep the buffer manager from making the really bad guesses. The buffer replacement strategy only has to choose from among the currently unwanted pages, which is far less critical.

Given the set of unpinned pages, the buffer manager needs to decide which of those pages will not be needed for the longest amount of time. For example, a database usually has several pages (such as the catalog files of Chap. 7) that are used constantly throughout the lifetime of the database. The buffer manager ought to avoid replacing such pages, since they will almost certainly be re-pinned fairly soon. There are several replacement strategies that try to make the best guess. This section considers four of them: *Naïve*, *FIFO*, *LRU*, and *Clock*.

Figure 4.9 introduces an example that will allow us to compare the behavior of these replacement algorithms. Part (a) gives a sequence of operations that pin and unpin five blocks of a file, and part (b) depicts the resulting state of the buffer pool, assuming that it contains four buffers. The only page replacement occurred when the fifth block (i.e., block 50) was pinned. However, since only one buffer was unpinned at that time, the buffer manager had no choice. In other words, the buffer pool would look like Fig. 4.9b, regardless of the page replacement strategy.

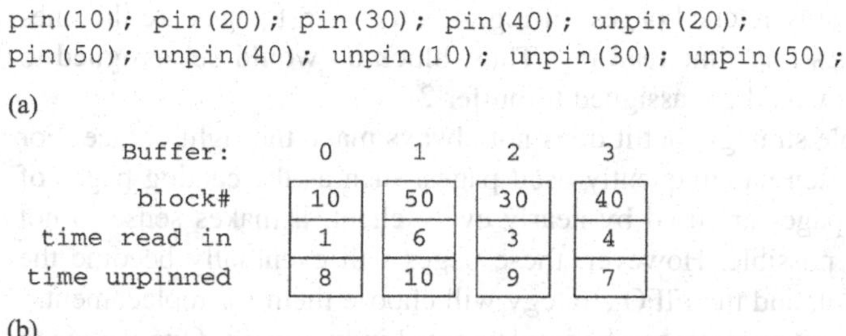

pin(10); pin(20); pin(30); pin(40); unpin(20);
pin(50); unpin(40); unpin(10); unpin(30); unpin(50);
(a)
Buffer: 0 1 2 3
block# 10 50 30 40
time read in 1 6 3 4
time unpinned 8 10 9 7
(b)

Fig. 4.9 The effect of some pin/unpin operations on a pool of four buffers. (**a**) A sequence of ten *pin/unpin* operations, (**b**) The resulting state of the buffer pool

Each buffer in Fig. 4.9b holds three pieces of information: its block number, the time it was read into the buffer, and the time it became unpinned. The times in the figure correspond to the position of the operation in Fig. 4.9a.

The buffers of Fig. 4.9b are all unpinned. Suppose now that the buffer manager receives two more pin requests:

```
pin(60); pin(70);
```

The buffer manager will need to replace two buffers. All of the buffers are available; which ones should it choose? Each of the following replacement algorithms will give a different answer.

The Naïve Strategy

The simplest replacement strategy is to traverse the buffer pool sequentially, replacing the first unpinned buffer found. Using the example of Fig. 4.9, block 60 will be assigned to buffer 0, and block 70 will be assigned to buffer 1.

This strategy is easy to implement but has little else to recommend it. For example, consider again the buffers of Fig. 4.9, and suppose a client repeatedly pins and unpins blocks 60 and 70, like this:

```
pin(60); unpin(60); pin(70); unpin(70); pin(60); unpin(60);...
```

The naïve replacement strategy will use buffer 0 for both blocks, which means that the blocks will need to be read in from disk each time they are pinned. The problem is that the buffer pool is not evenly utilized. Had the replacement strategy chosen two different buffers for blocks 60 and 70, then the blocks would have been read from disk once each—which is a tremendous improvement in efficiency.

The FIFO Strategy

The naïve strategy chooses a buffer based only on convenience. The FIFO strategy tries to be more intelligent, by choosing the buffer that was least recently replaced, that is, the page that has been sitting in the buffer pool the longest. This strategy usually works better than the naïve strategy, because older pages are less likely to be needed than more recently fetched pages. In Fig. 4.9, the oldest pages are the ones with the smallest values for "time read in." Thus, block 60 would get assigned to buffer 0, and block 70 would get assigned to buffer 2.

FIFO is a reasonable strategy, but it does not always make the right choice. For example, a database often has frequently used pages, such as the catalog pages of Chap. 7. Since these pages are used by nearly every client, it makes sense to not replace them if at all possible. However, these pages will eventually become the oldest pages in the pool, and the FIFO strategy will choose them for replacement.

The FIFO replacement strategy can be implemented in two ways. One way is to have each buffer hold the time when its page was last replaced, as in Fig. 4.9b. The replacement algorithm would then scan the buffer pool, choosing the unpinned page having the earliest replacement time. A second, more efficient way would be for the buffer manager to keep a list of pointers to its buffers, ordered by replacement time. The replacement algorithm searches the list; the first unpinned page found is replaced, and the pointer to it is moved to the end of the list.

The LRU Strategy

The FIFO strategy bases its replacement decision on when a page was *added* to the buffer pool. A similar strategy would be to make the decision based on when a page was last *accessed*, the rationale being that a page that has not been used in the near past will also not be used in the near future. This strategy is called LRU, which stands for *least recently used*. In the example of Fig. 4.9, the "time unpinned" value corresponds to when the buffer was last used. Thus block 60 would be assigned to buffer 3, and block 70 would be assigned to buffer 0.

The LRU strategy tends to be an effective general-purpose strategy and avoids replacing commonly used pages. Both implementation options for FIFO can be adapted to LRU. The only change that must be made is that the buffer manager must update the timestamp (for the first option) or update the list (for the second option) each time a page becomes *unpinned*, instead of when it gets replaced.

The Clock Strategy

This strategy is an interesting combination of the above strategies that has an easy and straightforward implementation. As in the naïve strategy, the clock replacement algorithm scans through the buffer pool, choosing the first unpinned page it finds. The difference is that the algorithm always starts its scan at the page after the previous replacement. If you visualize the buffer pool as forming a circle, then the replacement algorithm scans the pool like the hand of an analog clock, stopping when a page is replaced and starting when another replacement is required.

The example of Fig. 4.9b does not indicate the clock position. But the last replacement it made was buffer 1, which means that the clock is positioned immediately after that. Thus, block 60 will be assigned to buffer 2, and block 70 will be assigned to buffer 3.

The clock strategy attempts to use the buffers as evenly as possible. If a page is pinned, the clock strategy will skip past it and not consider it again until it has examined all other buffers in the pool. This feature gives the strategy an LRU flavor. The idea is that if a page is frequently used, there is a high probability that it will be pinned when its turn for replacement arrives. If so, then it is skipped over and given "another chance."

4.5 The SimpleDB Buffer Manager

This section examines the buffer manager of the SimpleDB database system. Section 4.5.1 covers the buffer manager's API and gives examples of its use. Section 4.5.2 then shows how these classes can be implemented in Java.

4.5.1 An API for the Buffer Manager

The SimpleDB buffer manager is implemented by the package `simpledb.buffer`. This package exposes the two classes `BufferMgr` and `Buffer`; their API appears in Fig. 4.10.

Each database system has one `BufferMgr` object, which is created during system startup. Its constructor has three arguments: the size of the buffer pool and a reference to the file manager and log manager.

A `BufferMgr` object has methods to pin and unpin a page. The method `pin` returns a `Buffer` object pinned to a page containing the specified block, and the `unpin` method unpins the page. The `available` method returns the number of unpinned buffer pages. And the method `flushAll` ensures that all pages modified by the specified transaction have been written to disk.

Given a `Buffer` object, a client can call its `contents` method to obtain the associated page. If the client modifies the page, then it is also responsible for generating an appropriate log record and calling the buffer's `setModified` method.

BufferMgr

```
public BufferMgr(FileMgr fm, LogMgr lm, int numbuffs);
public Buffer pin(BlockId blk);
public void   unpin(Buffer buff);
public int    available();
public void   flushAll(int txnum);
```

Buffer

```
public Buffer(FileMgr fm, LogMgr lm);
public Page    contents();
public BlockId block();
public boolean isPinned();
public void    setModified(int txnum, int lsn);
public int     modifyingTx();
```

Fig. 4.10 The API for the SimpleDB buffer manager

The method has two arguments: an integer that identifies the modifying transaction and the LSN of the generated log record.

The code in Fig. 4.11 tests the `Buffer` class. It prints "The new value is 1" the first time you execute it, and each subsequent execution increments the printed value. The code behaves as follows. It creates a `SimpleDB` object having three buffers. It pins a page to block 1, increments the integer at offset 80, and calls `setModified` to indicate that the page has been modified. The arguments to `setModified` should be the transaction number and LSN of the generated log file. The details behind these two values will be discussed in Chap. 5, so until then, the given arguments are reasonable placeholders.

The buffer manager hides the actual disk accesses from its clients. A client has no idea exactly how many disk accesses occur on its behalf and when they occur. A disk read can occur only during a call to `pin`—in particular, when the specified block is not currently in a buffer. A disk write can occur only during a call to `pin` or `flushAll`. A call to `pin` will cause a disk write if the replaced page has been modified, and a call to `flushAll` will cause a disk write for each page modified by the specified transaction.

For example, the code of Fig. 4.11 contains two modifications to block 1. Neither of these modifications is explicitly written to disk. Executing the code shows that the

```
public class BufferTest {
   public static void main(String[] args) {
      SimpleDB db = new SimpleDB("buffertest", 400, 3);
      BufferMgr bm = db.bufferMgr();

      Buffer buff1 = bm.pin(new BlockId("testfile", 1));
      Page p = buff1.contents();
      int n = p.getInt(80);
      p.setInt(80, n+1);            // This modification will
      buff1.setModified(1, 0);      // get written to disk.
      System.out.println("The new value is " + (n+1));
      bm.unpin(buff1);
      // One of these pins will flush buff1 to disk:
      Buffer buff2 = bm.pin(new BlockId("testfile", 2));
      Buffer buff3 = bm.pin(new BlockId("testfile", 3));
      Buffer buff4 = bm.pin(new BlockId("testfile", 4));

      bm.unpin(buff2);
      buff2 = bm.pin(new BlockId("testfile", 1));
      Page p2 = buff2.contents();
      p2.setInt(80, 9999);          // This modification
      buff2.setModified(1, 0);      // won't get written to disk.
      bm.unpin(buff2);
   }
}
```

Fig. 4.11 Testing the `Buffer` class

first modification is written to disk but the second one is not. Consider the first modification. Since there are only three buffers in the buffer pool, the buffer manager will need to replace the page for block 1 (and thereby write it to disk) in order to pin pages for blocks 2, 3, and 4. On the other hand, the page for block 1 does not need to be replaced after the second modification, so the page does not get written to disk, and its modifications are lost. The issue of lost modifications will be discussed in Chap. 5.

Suppose that the database engine has a lot of clients, all of whom are using a lot of buffers. It is possible for every buffer page to be pinned. In this case, the buffer manager cannot immediately satisfy a `pin` request. Instead, it places the client on a wait list. When a buffer becomes available, the buffer manager takes the client off the wait list so that it can complete the `pin` request. In other words, the client will not be aware of the buffer contention; the client will only notice that the engine seems to have slowed down.

There is one situation where buffer contention can cause a serious problem. Consider a scenario where clients A and B each need two buffers, but only two buffers are available. Suppose client A pins the first buffer. There is now a race for the second buffer. If client A gets it before client B, then B will be added to the wait list. Client A will eventually finish and unpin the buffers, at which time client B can pin them. This is a good scenario. Now suppose instead that client B gets the second buffer before client A. Then both A and B will be on the wait list. If these are the only two clients in the system, then no buffers will ever get unpinned, and both A and B will be on the wait list forever. This is a bad scenario. Clients A and B are said to be *deadlocked*.

In a real database system with thousands of buffers and hundreds of clients, this kind of deadlock is highly unlikely. Nevertheless, the buffer manager must be prepared to deal with the possibility. The solution taken by SimpleDB is to keep track of how long a client has been waiting for a buffer. If it has waited too long (say, 10 seconds), then the buffer manager assumes that the client is in deadlock and throws an exception of type `BufferAbortException`. The client is responsible for handling the exception, typically by rolling back the transaction and possibly restarting it.

The code in Fig. 4.12 tests the buffer manager. It again creates a `SimpleDB` object having only three buffers, and then calls the buffer manager to pin their pages to blocks 0, 1, and 2 of file "testfile." It then unpins block 1, repins block 2, and pins block 1 again. These three actions will not cause any disk reads and will leave no available buffers. The attempt to pin block 3 will place the thread on a waiting list. However, since the thread already holds all of the buffers, none of them will be unpinned, and the buffer manager will throw an exception after ten seconds of waiting. The program catches the exception and continues. It unpins block 2. Its attempt to pin block 3 will now be successful because a buffer has become available.

```
public class BufferMgrTest {
   public static void main(String[] args) throws Exception {
      SimpleDB db = new SimpleDB("buffermgrtest", 400, 3);
      BufferMgr bm = db.bufferMgr();

      Buffer[] buff = new Buffer[6];
      buff[0] = bm.pin(new BlockId("testfile", 0));
      buff[1] = bm.pin(new BlockId("testfile", 1));
      buff[2] = bm.pin(new BlockId("testfile", 2));
      bm.unpin(buff[1]); buff[1] = null;
      buff[3] = bm.pin(new BlockId("testfile", 0));
      buff[4] = bm.pin(new BlockId("testfile", 1));
      System.out.println("Available buffers: " + bm.available());
      try {
         System.out.println("Attempting to pin block 3...");
         buff[5] = bm.pin(new BlockId("testfile", 3));
      }
      catch(BufferAbortException e) {
         System.out.println("Exception: No available buffers\n");
      }
      bm.unpin(buff[2]); buff[2] = null;
      buff[5] = bm.pin(new BlockId("testfile", 3)); // now this works

      System.out.println("Final Buffer Allocation:");
      for (int i=0; i<buff.length; i++) {
         Buffer b = buff[i];
         if (b != null)
            System.out.println("buff["+i+"] pinned to block "
                                    + b.block());
      }
   }
}
```

Fig. 4.12 Testing the buffer manager

4.5.2 Implementing the Buffer Manager

Figure 4.13 contains the code for class `Buffer`. A `Buffer` object keeps track of four kinds of information about its page:

- *A reference to the block assigned to its page*. If no block is assigned, then the value is `null`.
- *The number of times the page is pinned*. The pin count is incremented on each pin and decremented on each unpin.
- *An integer indicating if the page has been modified*. A value of −1 indicates that the page has not been changed; otherwise, the integer identifies the transaction that made the change.
- *Log information*. If the page has been modified, then the buffer holds the LSN of the most recent log record. LSN values are never negative. If a client calls

```
public class Buffer {
   private FileMgr fm;
   private LogMgr lm;
   private Page contents;
   private BlockId blk = null;
   private int pins = 0;
   private int txnum = -1;
   private int lsn = -1;

   public Buffer(FileMgr fm, LogMgr lm) {
      this.fm = fm;
      this.lm = lm;
      contents = new Page(fm.blockSize());
   }

   public Page contents() {
      return contents;
   }

   public BlockId block() {
      return blk;
   }

   public void setModified(int txnum, int lsn) {
      this.txnum = txnum;
      if (lsn>=0) this.lsn = lsn;
   }
   public boolean isPinned() {
      return pins > 0;
   }

   public int modifyingTx() {
      return txnum;
   }

   void assignToBlock(BlockId b) {
      flush();
      blk = b;
      fm.read(blk, contents);
      pins = 0;
   }

   void flush() {
      if (txnum >= 0) {
         lm.flush(lsn);
         fm.write(blk, contents);
         txnum = -1;
      }
   }

   void pin() {
      pins++;
   }

   void unpin() {
      pins--;
   }
}
```

Fig. 4.13 The code for the SimpleDB class `Buffer`

setModified with a negative LSN, it indicates that a log record was not generated for that update.

The method flush ensures that the buffer's assigned disk block has the same values as its page. If the page has not been modified, then the method need not do anything. If it has been modified, then the method first calls LogMgr.flush to ensure that the corresponding log record is on disk; then it writes the page to disk.

The method assignToBlock associates the buffer with a disk block. The buffer is first flushed, so that any modifications to the previous block are preserved. The buffer is then associated with the specified block, reading its contents from disk.

The code for BufferMgr appears in Fig. 4.14. The method pin assigns a buffer to the specified block. It does so by calling the private method tryToPin. That method has two parts. The first part, findExistingBuffer, tries to find a buffer that is already assigned to the specified block. The buffer is returned if found. Otherwise the second part of the algorithm, chooseUnpinnedBuffer, uses naïve replacement to choose an unpinned buffer. The chosen buffer's assignToBlock method is called, which handles the writing of the existing page to disk (if necessary) and the reading of the new page from disk. The method returns null if it cannot find an unpinned buffer.

If tryToPin returns null, the pin method will call the Java method wait. In Java, every object has a wait list. The object's wait method interrupts the execution of the calling thread and places it on that list. In Fig. 4.14, the thread will stay on that list until one of two conditions occurs:

- Another thread calls notifyAll (which occurs from a call to unpin).
- MAX_TIME milliseconds have elapsed, which means that the thread has been waiting too long.

When a waiting thread resumes, it continues in its loop, trying to obtain a buffer (together with all the other threads that were waiting). The thread will keep getting placed back on the wait list until either it gets the buffer or it has exceeded its time limit.

The unpin method unpins the specified buffer and then checks to see if that buffer is still pinned. If not, then notifyAll is called to remove all client threads from the wait list. Those threads will fight for the buffer; whichever is scheduled first will win. When one of the other threads is scheduled, it may find that all buffers are still allocated; if so, it will be placed back on the wait list.

4.6 Chapter Summary

- A database engine must strive to minimize disk accesses. It therefore carefully manages the in-memory pages that it uses to hold disk blocks. The database components that manage these pages are the *log manager* and the *buffer manager*.

```
public class BufferMgr {
   private Buffer[] bufferpool;
   private int numAvailable;
   private static final long MAX_TIME = 10000; // 10 seconds

   public BufferMgr(FileMgr fm, LogMgr lm, int numbuffs) {
      bufferpool = new Buffer[numbuffs];
      numAvailable = numbuffs;
      for (int i=0; i<numbuffs; i++)
         bufferpool[i] = new Buffer(fm, lm);
   }

   public synchronized int available() {
      return numAvailable;
   }

   public synchronized void flushAll(int txnum) {
      for (Buffer buff : bufferpool)
         if (buff.modifyingTx() == txnum)
            buff.flush();
   }


   public synchronized void unpin(Buffer buff) {
      buff.unpin();
      if (!buff.isPinned()) {
         numAvailable++;
         notifyAll();
      }
   }

   public synchronized Buffer pin(BlockId blk) {
      try {
         long timestamp = System.currentTimeMillis();
         Buffer buff = tryToPin(blk);
         while (buff == null && !waitingTooLong(timestamp)) {
            wait(MAX_TIME);
            buff = tryToPin(blk);
         }
         if (buff == null)
            throw new BufferAbortException();
         return buff;
      }
      catch(InterruptedException e) {
         throw new BufferAbortException();
      }
   }
```

Fig. 4.14 The code for the SimpleDB class `BufferMgr`

```
   private boolean waitingTooLong(long starttime) {
      return System.currentTimeMillis() - starttime > MAX_TIME;
   }

   private Buffer tryToPin(BlockId blk) {
      Buffer buff = findExistingBuffer(blk);
      if (buff == null) {
         buff = chooseUnpinnedBuffer();
         if (buff == null)
            return null;
         buff.assignToBlock(blk);
      }
      if (!buff.isPinned())
         numAvailable--;
      buff.pin();
      return buff;
   }

   private Buffer findExistingBuffer(BlockId blk) {
      for (Buffer buff : bufferpool) {
         BlockId b = buff.block();
         if (b != null && b.equals(blk))
            return buff;
      }
      return null;
   }

   private Buffer chooseUnpinnedBuffer() {
      for (Buffer buff : bufferpool)
         if (!buff.isPinned())
            return buff;
      return null;
   }
}
```

Fig. 4.14 (continued)

- The log manager is responsible for saving log records in the log file. Because log records are always appended to the log file and are never modified, the log manager can be very efficient. It only needs to allocate a single page and has a simple algorithm for writing that page to disk as few times as possible.
- The buffer manager allocates several pages, called the *buffer pool*, to handle user data. The buffer manager *pins* and *unpins* buffer pages to disk blocks, at the request of clients. A client accesses a buffer's page after it is pinned and unpins the buffer when finished.
- A modified buffer will get written to disk in two circumstances: when the page is being replaced and when the recovery manager needs it to be on disk.

- When a client asks to pin a page to a block, the buffer manager chooses the appropriate buffer. If a page for that block is already in a buffer, then that buffer is used; otherwise, the buffer manager replaces the contents of an existing buffer.
- The algorithm that determines which buffer to replace is called the *buffer replacement strategy*. Four interesting replacement strategies are:
  - *Naïve*: Choose the first unpinned buffer it finds.
  - *FIFO*: Choose the unpinned buffer whose contents were replaced least recently.
  - *LRU*: Choose the unpinned buffer whose contents were unpinned least recently.
  - *Clock*: Scan the buffers sequentially from the last replaced buffer; choose the first unpinned buffer found.

4.7 Suggested Reading

The article Effelsberg et al. (1984) contains a well-written and comprehensive treatment of buffer management that extends many of the ideas in this chapter. Chapter 13 of Gray and Reuter (1993) contains an in-depth discussion of buffer management, illustrating their discussion with a C-based implementation of a typical buffer manager.

Oracle's default buffer replacement strategy is LRU. However, it uses FIFO replacement when scanning large tables. The rationale is that a table scan will typically not need a block after it is unpinned, and so LRU winds up saving the wrong blocks. Details can be found in Chap. 14 of Ashdown et al. (2019).

Several researchers have investigated how to make the buffer manager itself more intelligent. The basic idea is that a buffer manager can keep track of the pin requests of each transaction. If it detects a pattern (say, the transaction repeatedly reads the same N blocks of a file), it will try to avoid replacing those pages, even if they are not pinned. The article Ng et al. (1991) describes the idea in more detail and provides some simulation results.

Ashdown, L., et al. (2019). *Oracle database concepts*. Document E96138-01, Oracle Corporation. Available from https://docs.oracle.com/en/database/oracle/oracle-database/19/cncpt/database-concepts.pdf

Effelsberg, W., & Haerder, T. (1984). Principles of database buffer management. *ACM Transactions on Database Systems, 9*(4), 560–595.

Gray, J., & Reuter, A. (1993). *Transaction processing: concepts and techniques*. Morgan Kaufman.

Ng, R., Faloutsos, C., & Sellis, T. (1991). Flexible buffer allocation based on marginal gains. *Proceedings of the ACM SIGMOD Conference*, pp. 387–396.

4.8 Exercises

Conceptual Exercises

4.1. The code for `LogMgr.iterator` calls flush. Is this call necessary? Explain.

4.2. Explain why the method `BufferMgr.pin` is synchronized. What problem could occur if it wasn't?

4.3. Can more than one buffer ever be assigned to the same block? Explain.

4.4. The buffer replacement strategies in this chapter do not distinguish between modified and unmodified pages when looking for an available buffer. A possible improvement is for the buffer manager to always replace an unmodified page whenever possible.

(a) Give one reason why this suggestion could reduce the number of disk accesses made by the buffer manager.
(b) Give one reason why this suggestion could increase the number of disk accesses made by the buffer manager.
(c) Do you think strategy is worthwhile? Explain.

4.5. Another possible buffer replacement strategy is *least recently modified*: the buffer manager chooses the modified buffer having the lowest LSN. Explain why such a strategy might be worthwhile.

4.6. Suppose that a buffer page has been modified several times without being written to disk. The buffer saves only the LSN of the most recent change and sends only this LSN to the log manager when the page is finally flushed. Explain why the buffer doesn't need to send the other LSNs to the log manager.

4.7. Consider the example pin/unpin scenario of Fig. 4.9a, together with the additional operations `pin(60); pin(70)`. For each of the four replacement strategies given in the text, draw the state of the buffers, assuming that the buffer pool contains five buffers.

4.8. Starting from the buffer state of Fig. 4.9b, give a scenario in which:

(a) The FIFO strategy requires the fewest disk accesses
(b) The LRU strategy requires the fewest disk accesses
(c) The clock strategy requires the fewest disk accesses

4.9. Suppose that two different clients each want to pin the same block but are placed on the wait list because no buffers are available. Consider the implementation of the SimpleDB class `BufferMgr`. Show that when a single buffer becomes available, both clients will be able to use it.

4.10. Consider the adage "Virtual is its own reward." Comment on the cleverness of the pun, and discuss its applicability to the buffer manager.

Programming Exercises

4.11. The SimpleDB log manager allocates its own page and writes it explicitly to disk. Another design option is for it to pin a buffer to the last log block and let the buffer manager handle the disk accesses.

(a) Work out a design for this option. What are the issues that need to be addressed? Is it a good idea?
(b) Modify SimpleDB to implement your design.

4.12. Each `LogIterator` object allocates a page to hold the log blocks it accesses.

(a) Explain why using a buffer instead of a page would be much more efficient.
(b) Modify the code to use a buffer instead of a page. How should the buffer get unpinned?

4.13. This exercise examines whether a JDBC program could maliciously pin all of the buffers in the buffer pool.

(a) Write a JDBC program to pin all of the buffers of the SimpleDB buffer pool. What happens when all of the buffers are pinned?
(b) The Derby database system does buffer management differently than SimpleDB. When a JDBC client requests a buffer, Derby pins the buffer, sends a copy of the buffer to the client, and unpins the buffer. Explain why your code will not be malicious to other Derby clients.
(c) Derby avoids SimpleDB's problem by always copying pages from engine to client. Explain the consequences of this approach. Do you prefer it to the SimpleDB approach?
(d) Another way to keep a rogue client from monopolizing all of the buffers is to allow each transaction to pin no more than a certain percentage (say, 10%) of the buffer pool. Implement and test this modification to the SimpleDB buffer manager.

4.14. Modify class `BufferMgr` to implement each of the other replacement strategies described in this chapter.

4.15. Exercise 4.4 suggests a page replacement strategy that chooses unmodified pages over modified ones. Implement this replacement strategy.

4.16. Exercise 4.5 suggests a page replacement strategy that chooses the modified page having the lowest LSN. Implement this strategy.

4.17. The SimpleDB buffer manager traverses the buffer pool sequentially when searching for buffers. This search will be time-consuming when there are thousands of buffers in the pool. Modify the code, adding data structures (such as special-purpose lists and hash tables) that will improve the search times.

4.18. In Exercise 3.15, you were asked to write code that maintained statistics about disk usage. Extend this code to also give information about buffer usage.

Chapter 5
Transaction Management

The buffer manager allows multiple clients to access the same buffer concurrently, arbitrarily reading and writing its values. The result can be chaos: A page might have different (and even inconsistent) values each time a client looks at it, making it impossible for the client to get an accurate picture of the database. Or two clients can unwittingly overwrite the values of each other, thereby corrupting the database.

Consequently, a database engine has a *concurrency manager* and a *recovery manager*, whose jobs are to maintain order and ensure database integrity. Each client program is written as a sequence of *transactions*. The concurrency manager regulates the execution of these transactions so that they behave consistently. The recovery manager reads and writes records to the log, so that changes made by uncommitted transactions can be undone if necessary. This chapter covers the functionality of these managers and the techniques used to implement them.

5.1 Transactions

Consider an airline reservation database, having two tables with the following fields:

```
SEATS(FlightId, NumAvailable, Price)
CUST(CustId, BalanceDue)
```

Figure 5.1 contains JDBC code to purchase a ticket for a specified customer on a specified flight. Although this code has no bugs, various problems can occur when it is being used concurrently by multiple clients or when the server crashes. The following three scenarios illustrate these problems.

E. Sciore, *Database Design and Implementation*, Data-Centric Systems and Applications, https://doi.org/10.1007/978-3-030-33836-7_5

```
public void reserveSeat(Connection conn, int custId,
                        int flightId) throws SQLException {
   Statement stmt = conn.createStatement();
   String s;

   // step 1: Get availability and price
   s  = "select NumAvailable, Price from SEATS " +
        "where FlightId = " + flightId;
   ResultSet rs = stmt.executeQuery(s);
   if (!rs.next()) {
      System.out.println("Flight doesn't exist");
      return;
   }
   int numAvailable = rs.getInt("NumAvailable");
   int price = rs.getInt("Price");
   rs.close();

   if (numAvailable == 0) {
      System.out.println("Flight is full");
      return;
   }

   // step 2: Update availability
   int newNumAvailable = numAvailable - 1;
   s  = "update SEATS set NumAvailable = " + newNumAvailable +
        " where FlightId = " + flightId;
   stmt.executeUpdate(s);

   // step 3: Get and update customer balance
   s = "select BalanceDue from CUST where CustID = " + custId;
   rs = stmt.executeQuery(s);
   int newBalance = rs.getInt("BalanceDue") + price;
   rs.close();

   s  =  "update CUST set BalanceDue = " + newBalance +
         " where CustId = " + custId;
   stmt.executeUpdate(s);
}
```

Fig. 5.1 JDBC code to reserve a seat on a flight

In the first scenario, suppose that both clients A and B run the JDBC code concurrently, with the following sequence of actions:

- Client A executes all of step 1 and is then interrupted.
- Client B executes to completion.
- Client A completes its execution.

In this case, both threads will use the same value for `numAvailable`. The result is that two seats will be sold, but the number of available seats will be decremented only once.

In the second scenario, suppose that while a client is running the code, the server crashes just after step two executes. In this case, the seat will be reserved, but the customer will not be charged for it.

In the third scenario, suppose that a client runs the code to completion, but the buffer manager does not immediately write the modified pages to disk. If the server crashes (possibly several days later), then there is no way to know which of the pages (if any) were eventually written to disk. If the first update was written but not the second, then the customer receives a free ticket; if the second update was written but not the first, then the customer is charged for a nonexistent ticket. And if neither page was written, then the entire interaction will be lost.

The above scenarios show how data can get lost or corrupted when client programs are able to run indiscriminately. Database engines solve this problem by forcing client programs to consist of *transactions*. A transaction is a group of operations that behaves as a single operation. The meaning of "as a single operation" can be characterized by the following so-called *ACID* properties: *atomicity*, *consistency*, *isolation*, and *durability*.

- Atomicity means that a transaction is "all or nothing." That is, either all its operations succeed (the transaction *commits*) or they all fail (the transaction does a *rollback*).
- Consistency means that every transaction leaves the database in a consistent state. This implies that each transaction is a complete work unit that can be executed independently of other transactions.
- Isolation means that a transaction behaves as if it is the only thread using the engine. If multiple transactions are running concurrently, then their result should be the same as if they were all executed serially in some order.
- Durability means that changes made by a committed transaction are guaranteed to be permanent.

Each of the above scenarios results from some violation of the ACID properties. The first scenario violated the isolation property, because both clients read the same value for `numAvailable`, whereas in any serial execution, the second client would have read the value written by the first. The second scenario violated atomicity, and the third scenario violated durability.

The atomicity and durability properties describe the proper behavior of the commit and rollback operations. A committed transaction must be durable, and an uncommitted transaction (either due to an explicit rollback or a system crash) must have its changes completely undone. These features are the responsibility of the *recovery manager* and are the topic of Sect. 5.3.

The consistency and isolation properties describe the proper behavior of concurrent clients. The database engine must keep clients from conflicting with each other. A typical strategy is to detect when a conflict is about to occur and to make one of the clients wait until that conflict is no longer possible. These features are the responsibility of the *concurrency manager* and are the topic of Sect. 5.4.

Transaction

```
public Transaction(FileMgr fm, LogMgr lm, BufferMgr bm);
public void commit();
public void rollback();
public void recover();

public void pin(BlockId blk);
public void unpin(BlockId blk);
public int  getInt(BlockId blk, int offset);
public String getString(BlockId blk, int offset);
public void setInt(BlockId blk, int offset, int val,
                   boolean okToLog);
public void setString(BlockId blk, int offset, String val,
                   boolean okToLog);
public int  availableBuffs();

public int   size(String filename);
public Block append(String filename);
public int   blockSize();
```

Fig. 5.2 The API for SimpleDB transactions

5.2 Using Transactions in SimpleDB

Before getting into details about how the recovery and concurrency managers do their job, it will help to get a feel for how clients use transactions. In SimpleDB, every JDBC transaction has its own `Transaction` object; its API appears in Fig. 5.2.

The methods of `Transaction` fall into three categories. The first category consists of methods related to the transaction's lifespan. The constructor begins a new transaction, the `commit` and `rollback` methods terminate it, and the method `recover` rolls back all uncommitted transactions. The `commit` and `rollback` methods automatically unpin the transaction's pinned buffer pages.

The second category consists of methods to access buffers. A transaction hides the existence of buffers from its client. When a client calls `pin` on a block, the transaction saves the buffer internally and does not return it to the client. When the client calls a method such as `getInt`, it passes in a `BlockId` reference. The transaction finds the corresponding buffer, calls the `getInt` method on the buffer's page, and passes the result back to the client.

The transaction hides the buffer from the client so it can make the necessary calls to the concurrency and recovery managers. For example, the code for `setInt` will acquire the appropriate locks (for concurrency control) and write the value that is currently in the buffer to the log (for recovery) before modifying the buffer. The fourth argument to `setInt` and `setString` is a boolean that indicates whether the update should be logged. This value is usually `true`, but there are certain cases (such as formatting a new block or undoing a transaction) where logging is not appropriate and the value should be `false`.

```
public class TxTest {
   public static void main(String[] args) throws Exception {
      SimpleDB db = new SimpleDB("txtest", 400, 8);
      FileMgr fm = db.fileMgr();
      LogMgr lm = db.logMgr();
      BufferMgr bm = db.bufferMgr();

      Transaction tx1 = new Transaction(fm, lm, bm);
      BlockId blk = new BlockId("testfile", 1);
      tx1.pin(blk);
      // Don't log initial block values.
      tx1.setInt(blk, 80, 1, false);
      tx1.setString(blk, 40, "one", false);
      tx1.commit();

      Transaction tx2 = new Transaction(fm, lm, bm);
      tx2.pin(blk);
      int ival = tx2.getInt(blk, 80);
      String sval = tx2.getString(blk, 40);
      System.out.println("initial value at location 80 = " + ival);
      System.out.println("initial value at location 40 = " + sval);
      int newival = ival + 1;
      int newsval = sval + "!";
      tx2.setInt(blk, 80, newival, true);
      tx2.setString(blk, 40, newsval, true);
      tx2.commit();

      Transaction tx3 = new Transaction(fm, lm, bm);
      tx3.pin(blk);
      System.out.println("new value at location 80 = "
                        + tx3.getInt(blk, 80));
      System.out.println("new value at location 40 = "
                        + tx3.getString(blk, 40));
      tx3.setInt(blk, 80, 9999, true);
      System.out.println("pre-rollback value at location 80 = "
                        + tx3.getInt(blk, 80));
      tx3.rollback();

      Transaction tx4 = new Transaction(fm, lm, bm);
      tx4.pin(blk);
      System.out.println("post-rollback at location 80 = "
                        + tx4.getInt(blk, 80));

      tx4.commit();
   }
}
```

Fig. 5.3 Testing the SimpleDB `Transaction` class

The third category consists of three methods related to the file manager. The method `size` reads the end of the file marker, and `append` modifies it; these methods must call the concurrency manager to avoid potential conflicts. The method `blockSize` exists as a convenience to clients who might need it.

Figure 5.3 illustrates a simple use of the `Transaction` methods. The code consists of four transactions, which perform similar tasks as the `BufferTest` class of Fig. 4.11. All four transactions access block 1 of file "testfile." Transaction `tx1` initializes the values at offsets 80 and 40; these updates are not logged. Transaction `tx2` reads those values, prints them, and increments them. Transaction `tx3` reads and prints the incremented values. Then it sets the integer to 9999 and rolls back. Transaction `tx4` reads the integer to verify that the rollback did in fact occur.

Compare this code to the code from Chap. 4 and observe what the `Transaction` class does for you: it manages your buffers; it generates log records for each update and writes them to the log file; and it is able to roll back your transaction on demand. But equally important is how this class works behind the scenes to ensure that the code satisfies the ACID properties. For example, suppose you randomly abort the program while it is executing. When you subsequently restart the database engine, the modifications of all transactions that had committed will be on disk (durability), and the modifications of the transaction that happened to be running will be rolled back (atomicity).

Moreover, the `Transaction` class also guarantees that this program will satisfy the ACID isolation property. Consider the code for transaction `tx2`. The variables `newival` and `newsval` (see the bold code) are initialized as follows:

```
int newival = ival + 1;
String newsval = sval + "!";
```

This code assumes that the values at locations 80 and 40 of the block have not changed. Without concurrency control, however, this assumption might not be true. The issue is the "non-repeatable read" scenario of Sect. 2.2.3. Suppose that `tx2` gets interrupted immediately after initializing `ival` and `sval`, and another program modifies the values at offsets 80 and 40. Then the values of `ival` and `sval` are now out of date, and `tx2` must call `getInt` and `getString` again to obtain their correct values. The `Transaction` class is responsible for making sure that such a possibility will not occur, so that this code is guaranteed to be correct.

5.3 Recovery Management

The *recovery manager* is the portion of the database engine that reads and processes the log. It has three functions: to write log records, to roll back a transaction, and to recover the database after a system crash. This section investigates these functions in detail.

```
<START, 1>
<COMMIT, 1>
<START,  2>
<SETINT, 2, testfile, 1, 80, 1, 2>
<SETSTRING, 2, testfile, 1, 40, one, one!>
<COMMIT, 2>
<START, 3>
<SETINT, 3, testfile, 1, 80, 2, 9999>
<ROLLBACK, 3>
<START, 4>
<COMMIT, 4>
```

Fig. 5.4 The log records generated from Fig. 5.3

5.3.1 Log Records

In order to be able to roll back a transaction, the recovery manager logs information about the transaction's activities. In particular, it writes a *log record* to the log each time a loggable activity occurs. There are four basic kinds of log record: *start records*, *commit records*, *rollback records*, and *update records*. I shall follow SimpleDB and assume two kinds of update record: one for updates to integers and one for updates to strings.

Log records are generated by the following loggable activities:

- A start record is written when a transaction begins.
- A commit or rollback record is written when a transaction completes.
- An update record is written when a transaction modifies a value.

Another potentially loggable activity is appending a block to the end of a file. Then if the transaction rolls back, the new block allocated by `append` can be deallocated from the file. For simplicity, I shall ignore this possibility. Exercise 5.48 addresses the issue.

As an example, consider the code of Fig. 5.3, and suppose that the id of `tx1` is 1 and so on. Figure 5.4 shows the log records generated by this code.

Each log record contains a description of what type of record it is (`START`, `SETINT`, `SETSTRING`, `COMMIT`, or `ROLLBACK`) and the ID of its transaction. Update records contain five additional values: the name and block number of the modified file, the offset where the modification occurred, the old value at that offset, and the new value at that offset.

In general, multiple transactions will be writing to the log concurrently, and so the log records for a given transaction will be interspersed through the log.

5.3.2 Rollback

One use of the log is to help the recovery manager *roll back* a specified transaction T. The recovery manager rolls back a transaction by undoing its modifications. Since

1. Set the current record to be the most recent log record.
2. Do until the current record is the start record for T:
   a) If the current record is an update record for T then:
      Write the saved old value to the specified location.
   b) Move to the previous record in the log.
3. Append a rollback record to the log.

Fig. 5.5 The algorithm for rolling back transaction T

these modifications are listed in the update log records, it is a relatively simple matter to scan the log, find each update record, and restore the original contents of each modified value. Figure 5.5 presents the algorithm.

There are two reasons why this algorithm reads the log backwards from the end, instead of forward from the beginning. The first reason is that the beginning of the log file will contain records from long-ago completed transactions. It is most likely that the records you are looking for are at the end of the log, and thus it is more efficient to read from the end. The second, more important reason is to ensure correctness. Suppose that the value at a location was modified several times. Then there will be several log records for that location, each having a different value. The value to be restored should come from the earliest of these records. If the log records are processed in reverse order, then this will in fact occur.

5.3.3 Recovery

Another use of the log is to *recover* the database. Recovery is performed each time the database engine starts up. Its purpose is to restore the database to a reasonable state. The term "reasonable state" means two things:

- All uncompleted transactions should be rolled back.
- All committed transactions should have their modifications written to disk.

When a database engine starts up following a normal shutdown, it should already be in a reasonable state, because the normal shutdown procedure is to wait until the existing transactions complete and then flush all buffers. However, if a crash had caused the engine to go down unexpectedly, then there may be uncompleted transactions whose executions were lost. Since there is no way the engine can complete them, their modifications must be undone. There may also be committed transactions whose modifications were not yet flushed to disk; these modifications must be redone.

The recovery manager assumes that a transaction completed if the log file contains a commit or rollback record for it. So if a transaction had committed prior to the system crash but its commit record did not make it to the log file, then the recovery manager will treat the transaction as if it did not complete. This situation might not seem fair, but there is really nothing else that the recovery manager can do. All it knows is what is contained in the log file, because everything else about the transaction was wiped out in the system crash.

// The undo stage
1. For each log record (reading backwards from the end):
    a) If the current record is a commit record then:
        Add that transaction to the list of committed transactions.
    b) If the current record is a rollback record then:
        Add that transaction to the list of rolled-back transactions.
    c) If the current record is an update record for a transaction not on the
        committed or rollback list, then: Restore the old value at the specified location.

// The redo stage
2. For each log record (reading forwards from the beginning):
    If the current record is an update record and that transaction is on the committed
    list, then: Restore the new value at the specified location.

Fig. 5.6 The undo-redo algorithm for recovering a database

Actually, rolling back a committed transaction is not only unfair; it violates the ACID property of *durability*. Consequently, the recovery manager must ensure that such a scenario cannot occur. It does so by flushing the commit log record to disk before it completes a commit operation. Recall that flushing a log record also flushes all previous log records. So when the recovery manager finds a commit record in the log, it knows that all of the update records for that transaction are also in the log.

Each update log record contains both the old value and the new value of the modification. The old value is used when you want to undo the modification, and the new value is used when you want to redo the modification. Figure 5.6 presents the recovery algorithm.

Stage 1 undoes the uncompleted transactions. As with the rollback algorithm, the log must be read backwards from the end to ensure correctness. Reading the log backwards also means that a commit record will always be found before its update records; so when the algorithm encounters an update record, it knows whether that record needs to be undone or not.

It is important for stage 1 to read the entire log. For example, the very first transaction might have made a change to the database before going into an infinite loop. That update record will not be found unless you read to the very beginning of the log.

Stage 2 redoes the committed transactions. Since the recovery manager cannot tell which buffers were flushed and which were not, it redoes all changes made by all committed transactions.

The recovery manager performs stage 2 by reading the log forward from the beginning. The recovery manager knows which update records need to be redone, because it computed the list of committed transaction during stage 1. Note that the log *must* be read forward during the redo stage. If several committed transactions happened to modify the same value, then the final recovered value should be due to the most recent modification.

The recovery algorithm is oblivious to the current state of the database. It writes old or new values to the database without looking at what the current values are at those locations, because the log tells it *exactly* what the contents of the database should be. There are two consequences to this feature:

- Recovery is idempotent.
- Recovery may cause more disk writes than necessary.

By *idempotent*, I mean that performing the recovery algorithm several times has the same result as performing it once. In particular, you will get the same result even if you re-run the recovery algorithm immediately after having run just part of it. This property is essential to the correctness of the algorithm. For example, suppose that the database system crashes while it is in the middle of the recovery algorithm. When the database system restarts, it will run the recovery algorithm again, from the beginning. If the algorithm were not idempotent, then re-running it would corrupt the database.

Because this algorithm does not look at the current contents of the database, it may make unnecessary changes. For example, suppose that the modifications made by a committed transaction have been written to disk; then redoing those changes during stage 2 will set the modified values to the contents that they already have. The algorithm can be revised so that it does not make these unnecessary disk writes; see Exercise 5.44.

5.3.4 Undo-Only and Redo-Only Recovery

The recovery algorithm of the previous section performs both undo and redo operations. A database engine may choose to simplify the algorithm to perform only undo operations or only redo operations, that is, it executes either stage 1 or stage 2 of the algorithm, but not both.

5.3.4.1 Undo-Only Recovery

Stage 2 can be omitted if the recovery manager is sure that all committed modifications have been written to disk. The recovery manager can do so by forcing the buffers to disk *before* it writes the commit record to the log. Figure 5.7 expresses this approach as an algorithm. The recovery manager must follow the steps of this algorithm in exactly the order given.

Which is better, undo-only recovery or undo-redo recovery? Undo-only recovery is faster, because it requires only one pass through the log file, instead of two. The log is also a bit smaller, because update records no longer need to contain the new modified value. On the other hand, the *commit* operation is much slower, because it must flush the modified buffers. If you assume that system crashes are infrequent, then undo-redo recovery wins. Not only do transactions commit faster, but there should be fewer overall disk writes due to the postponed buffer flushes.

1. Flush the transaction's modified buffers to disk.
2. Write a commit record to the log.
3. Flush the log page containing the commit record.

Fig. 5.7 The algorithm for committing a transaction, using undo-only recovery

5.3.4.2 Redo-Only Recovery

Stage 1 can be omitted if uncommitted buffers are never written to disk. The recovery manager can ensure this property by having each transaction keep its buffers pinned until the transaction completes. A pinned buffer will not get chosen for replacement, and thus its contents will not get flushed. In addition, a rolled back transaction will need its modified buffers to be "erased." Figure 5.8 gives the necessary revisions to the rollback algorithm.

Redo-only recovery is faster than undo-redo recovery, because uncommitted transactions can be ignored. However, it requires that each transaction keep a buffer pinned for every block that it modifies, which increases the contention for buffers in the system. With a large database, this contention can seriously impact the performance of all transactions, which makes redo-only recovery a risky choice.

It is interesting to think about whether it is possible to combine the undo-only and redo-only techniques, to create a recovery algorithm that doesn't require either stage 1 or stage 2. See Exercise 5.19.

5.3.5 Write-Ahead Logging

Step 1 of the recovery algorithm in Fig. 5.6 needs further examination. Recall that this step iterates through the log, performing an undo for each update record from an uncompleted transaction. In justifying the correctness of this step, I made the following assumption: *all updates for an uncompleted transaction will have a corresponding log record in the log file.* Otherwise, the database will be corrupted because there would be no way to undo the update.

Since the system could crash at any time, the only way to satisfy this assumption is to have the log manager flush each update log record to disk as soon as it is written. But as Sect. 4.2 demonstrated, this strategy is painfully inefficient. There must be a better way.

Let's analyze the kinds of things that can go wrong. Suppose that an uncompleted transaction modified a page and created a corresponding update log record. If the server crashes, there are four possibilities:

(a) Both the page and the log record got written to disk.
(b) Only the page got written to disk.
(c) Only the log record got written to disk.
(d) Neither got written to disk.

For each buffer modified by the transaction:

a) Mark the buffer as unallocated. (In SimpleDB, set its block number to `-1`)
b) Mark the buffer as unmodified.
c) Unpin the buffer.

Fig. 5.8 The algorithm for rolling back a transaction, using redo-only recovery

Consider each possibility in turn. If (a), then the recovery algorithm will find the log record and undo the change to the data block on disk; no problem. If (b), then the recovery algorithm won't find the log record, and so it will not undo the change to the data block. This is a serious problem. If (c), then the recovery algorithm will find the log record and undo the nonexistent change to the block. Since the block wasn't actually changed, this is a waste of time, but not incorrect. If (d), then the recovery algorithm won't find the log record, but since there was no change to the block there is nothing to undo anyway; no problem.

Thus (b) is the only problem case. The database engine avoids this case by flushing an update log record to disk before flushing the corresponding modified buffer page. This strategy is called using a *write-ahead log*. Note that the log may describe modifications to the database that never wind up occurring (as in possibility (c) above), but if the database does get modified, the log record for that modification will always be on disk.

The standard way to implement a write-ahead log is for each buffer to keep track of the LSN of its most recent modification. Before a buffer replaces a modified page, it tells the log manager to flush the log up to that LSN. As a result, the log record corresponding to a modification will always be on disk before the modification gets saved to disk.

5.3.6 *Quiescent Checkpointing*

The log contains the history of every modification to the database. As time passes, the size of the log file can become very large—in some cases, larger than the data files. The effort to read the entire log during recovery and undo/redo every change to the database can become overwhelming. Consequently, recovery strategies have been devised for reading only a portion of the log. The basic idea is that the recovery algorithm can stop searching the log as soon as it knows two things:

- All earlier log records were written by completed transactions.
- The buffers for those transactions have been flushed to disk.

The first bullet point applies to the undo stage of the recovery algorithm. It ensures that there are no more uncommitted transactions to be rolled back. The second bullet point applies to the redo stage and ensures that all earlier committed transactions do not need to be redone. Note that if the recovery manager implements undo-only recovery then the second bullet point will always be true.

At any point in time, the recovery manager can perform a *quiescent checkpoint* operation, as shown in Fig. 5.9. Step 2 of that algorithm ensures that the first bullet point is satisfied, and step 3 ensures that the second bullet point is satisfied.

The quiescent checkpoint record acts as a marker in the log. When stage 1 of the recovery algorithm encounters the checkpoint record as it moves backwards through

1. Stop accepting new transactions.
2. Wait for existing transactions to finish.
3. Flush all modified buffers.
4. Append a quiescent checkpoint record to the log and flush it to disk.
5. Start accepting new transactions.

Fig. 5.9 The algorithm for performing a quiescent checkpoint

```
<START, 0>
<SETINT, 0, junk, 33, 8, 542, 543>
<START, 1>
<START, 2>
<COMMIT, 1>
<SETSTRING, 2, junk, 44, 20, hello, ciao>
   //The quiescent checkpoint procedure starts here
<SETSTRING, 0, junk, 33, 12, joe, joseph>
<COMMIT, 0>
   //tx 3 wants to start here, but must wait
<SETINT, 2, junk, 66, 8, 0, 116>
<COMMIT, 2>
<CHECKPOINT>
<START, 3>
<SETINT, 3, junk, 33, 8, 543, 120>
```

Fig. 5.10 A log using quiescent checkpointing

the log, it knows that all earlier log records can be ignored; it therefore can begin stage 2 from that point in the log and move forward. In other words, the recovery algorithm never needs to look at log records prior to a quiescent checkpoint record.

A good time to write a quiescent checkpoint record is during system startup, after recovery has completed and before new transactions have begun. Since the recovery algorithm has just finished processing the log, the checkpoint record ensures that it will never need to examine those log records again.

For an example, consider the log shown in Fig. 5.10. This example log illustrates three things: First, no new transactions can start once the checkpoint process begins; second, the checkpoint record was written as soon as the last transaction completed and the buffers were flushed; and third, other transactions may start as soon as the checkpoint record is written.

5.3.7 *Nonquiescent Checkpointing*

Quiescent checkpointing is simple to implement and easy to understand. However, it requires that the database be unavailable while the recovery manager waits for existing transactions to complete. In many database applications, this is a serious shortcoming—companies don't want their databases to occasionally stop responding

1. Let T1,...,Tk be the currently running transactions.
2. Stop accepting new transactions.
3. Flush all modified buffers.
4. Write the record `<NQCKPT T1,..., Tk>` into the log.
5. Start accepting new transactions.

Fig. 5.11 The algorithm for adding a nonquiescent checkpoint record

for arbitrary periods of time. Consequently, a checkpointing algorithm has been developed that doesn't require quiescence. The algorithm appears in Fig. 5.11.

This algorithm uses a different kind of checkpoint record, called a *nonquiescent checkpoint record*. A nonquiescent checkpoint record contains a list of the currently running transactions.

The recovery algorithm is revised as follows. Stage 1 of the algorithm reads the log backwards as before and keeps track of the completed transactions. When it encounters a nonquiescent checkpoint record <NQCKPT T1,..., Tk>, it determines which of these transactions are still running. It can then continue reading the log backwards until it encounters the start record for the earliest of those transactions. All log records prior to this start record can be ignored.

For an example, consider again the log of Fig. 5.10. With nonquiescent checkpointing, the log would appear as in Fig. 5.12. Note that the <NQCKPT...> record appears in this log in the place where the checkpoint process began in Fig. 5.10 and states that transactions 0 and 2 are still running at that point. This log differs from that of Fig. 5.10 in that transaction 2 never commits.

If the recovery algorithm sees this log during system startup, it would enter stage 1 and proceed as follows.

- When it encounters the <SETINT, 3, ...> log record, it will check to see if transaction 3 was on the list of committed transactions. Since that list is currently empty, the algorithm will perform an undo, writing the integer 543 to offset 8 of block 33 of file "junk".

```
<START, 0>
<SETINT, 0, junk, 33, 8, 542, 543>
<START, 1>
<START, 2>
<COMMIT, 1>
<SETSTRING, 2, junk, 44, 20, hello, ciao>
<NQCKPT, 0, 2>
<SETSTRING, 0, junk, 33, 12, joe, joseph>
<COMMIT, 0>
<START, 3>
<SETINT, 2, junk, 66, 8, 0, 116>
<SETINT, 3, junk, 33, 8, 543, 120>
```

Fig. 5.12 A log using nonquiescent checkpointing

- The log record `<SETINT, 2, ...>` will be treated similarly, writing the integer 0 to offset 8 of block 66 of "junk".
- The `<COMMIT, 0>` log record will cause 0 to be added to the list of committed transactions.
- The `<SETSTRING, 0, ...>` log record will be ignored, because 0 is in the committed transaction list.
- When it encounters the `<NQCKPT 0,2>` log record, it knows that transaction 0 has committed, and thus it can ignore all log records prior to the start record for transaction 2.
- When it encounters the `<START, 2>` log record, it enters stage 2 and begins moving forward through the log.
- The `<SETSTRING, 0,...>` log record will be redone, because 0 is in the committed transaction list. The value 'joseph' will be written to offset 12 of block 33 of "junk".

5.3.8 Data Item Granularity

The recovery-management algorithms of this section use values as the unit of logging. That is, a log record is created for each value that is modified, with the log record containing the previous and new versions of the value. This unit of logging is called a *recovery data item*. The size of a data item is called its *granularity*.

Instead of using values as data items, the recovery manager could choose to use blocks or files. For example, suppose that blocks were chosen as the data item. In this case, an update log record would be created each time a block was modified, with the previous and new values of the block being stored in the log record.

The advantage to logging blocks is that fewer log records are needed if you use undo-only recovery. Suppose that a transaction pins a block, modifies several values, and then unpins it. You could save the original contents of the block in a single log record, instead of having to write one log record for each modified value. The disadvantage, of course, is that the update log records are now very large; the entire contents of the block gets saved, regardless of how many of its values actually change. Thus, logging blocks makes sense only if transactions tend to do a lot of modifications per block.

Now consider what it would mean to use files as data items. A transaction would generate one update log record for each file that it changed. Each log record would contain the entire original contents of that file. To roll back a transaction, you would just need to replace the existing files with their original versions. This approach is almost certainly less practical than using values or blocks as data items, because each transaction would have to make a copy of the entire file, no matter how many values changed.

Although file-granularity data items are impractical for database systems, they are often used by non-database applications. Suppose, for example, that your computer crashes while you are editing a file. After the system reboots, some word processors are able to show you two versions of the file: the version that you most recently saved and the version that existed at the time of the crash. The reason is that those word processors do not write your modifications directly to the original file but to a copy; when you save, the modified file is copied to the original one. This strategy is a crude version of file-based logging.

5.3.9 The SimpleDB Recovery Manager

The SimpleDB recovery manager is implemented via the class `RecoveryMgr` in package `simpledb.tx.recovery`. The API for `RecoveryMgr` appears in Fig. 5.13.

Each transaction has its own `RecoveryMgr` object, whose methods write the appropriate log records for that transaction. For example, the constructor writes a start log record to the log; the `commit` and `rollback` methods write corresponding log records; and the `setInt` and `setString` methods extract the old value from the specified buffer and write an update record to the log. The `rollback` and `recover` methods perform the rollback (or recovery) algorithms.

A `RecoveryMgr` object uses undo-only recovery with value-granularity data items. Its code can be divided into two areas of concern: code to implement log records, and code to implement the rollback and recovery algorithms.

5.3.9.1 Log Records

As mentioned in Sect. 4.2, the log manager sees each log record as a byte array. Each kind of log record has its own class, which is responsible for embedding the appropriate values in the byte array. The first value in each array will be an integer that denotes the *operator* of the record; the operator can be one of the constants `CHECKPOINT`, `START`, `COMMIT`, `ROLLBACK`, `SETINT`, or `SETSTRING`. The remaining values depend on the operator—a quiescent checkpoint record has no other values, an update record has five other values, and the other records have one other value.

<u>*RecoveryMgr*</u>

```
public RecoveryMgr(Transaction tx, int txnum, LogMgr lm,
                   BufferMgr bm);
public void commit();
public void rollback();
public void recover();
public int  setInt(Buffer buff, int offset, int newval);
public int  setString(Buffer buff, int offset, String newval);
```

Fig. 5.13 The API for the SimpleDB recovery manager

Each log record class implements the interface LogRecord, which is shown in Fig. 5.14. The interface defines three methods that extract the components of the log record. Method op returns the record's operator. Method txNumber returns the ID of the transaction that wrote the log record. This method makes sense for all log records except checkpoint records, which return a dummy ID value. The method undo restores any changes stored in that record. Only the setint and setstring log records will have a non-empty undo method; the method for those records will pin a buffer to the specified block, write the specified value at the specified offset, and unpin the buffer.

The classes for the individual kinds of log record all have similar code; it should suffice to examine one of the classes, say SetStringRecord, whose code appears in Fig. 5.15.

The class has two significant methods: a static method writeToLog, which encodes the six values of a SETSTRING log record into a byte array, and the constructor, which extracts those six values from that byte array. Consider the implementation of writeToLog. It first calculates the size of the byte array and the offset within that array of each value. It then creates a byte array of that size, wraps it in a Page object, and uses the page's setInt and setString methods

```
public interface LogRecord {
   static final int CHECKPOINT = 0, START = 1, COMMIT = 2,
                    ROLLBACK  = 3, SETINT = 4, SETSTRING = 5;
   int op();
   int txNumber();
   void undo(int txnum);

   static LogRecord createLogRecord(byte[] bytes) {
      Page p = new Page(bytes);
      switch (p.getInt(0)) {
      case CHECKPOINT:
         return new CheckpointRecord();
      case START:
         return new StartRecord(p);
      case COMMIT:
         return new CommitRecord(p);
      case ROLLBACK:
         return new RollbackRecord(p);
      case SETINT:
         return new SetIntRecord(p);
      case SETSTRING:
         return new SetStringRecord(p);
      default:
         return null;
      }
   }
}
```

Fig. 5.14 The code for the SimpleDB LogRecord interface

```
public class SetStringRecord implements LogRecord {
   private int txnum, offset;
   private String val;
   private BlockId blk;

   public SetStringRecord(Page p) {
      int tpos = Integer.BYTES;
      txnum = p.getInt(tpos);
      int fpos = tpos + Integer.BYTES;
      String filename = p.getString(fpos);
      int bpos = fpos + Page.maxLength(filename.length());
      int blknum = p.getInt(bpos);
      blk = new BlockId(filename, blknum);
      int opos = bpos + Integer.BYTES;
      offset = p.getInt(opos);
      int vpos = opos + Integer.BYTES;
      val = p.getString(vpos);
   }
   public int op() {
      return SETSTRING;
   }

   public int txNumber() {
      return txnum;
   }

   public String toString() {
     return "<SETSTRING " + txnum + " " + blk + " " + offset + " "
                                                + val + ">";
   }

   public void undo(Transaction tx) {
      tx.pin(blk);
      tx.setString(blk, offset, val, false); // don't log the undo!
      tx.unpin(blk);
   }

   public static int writeToLog(LogMgr lm, int txnum, BlockId blk,
                                int offset, String val) {
      int tpos = Integer.BYTES;
      int fpos = tpos + Integer.BYTES;
      int bpos = fpos + Page.maxLength(blk.fileName().length());
      int opos = bpos + Integer.BYTES;
      int vpos = opos + Integer.BYTES;
      int reclen = vpos + Page.maxLength(val.length());
      byte[] rec = new byte[reclen];
      Page p = new Page(rec);
      p.setInt(0, SETSTRING);
      p.setInt(tpos, txnum);
      p.setString(fpos, blk.fileName());
      p.setInt(bpos, blk.number());
      p.setInt(opos, offset);
      p.setString(vpos, val);
      return lm.append(rec);
   }
}
```

Fig. 5.15 The code for the class `SetStringRecord`

to write the values in the appropriate locations. The constructor is analogous. It determines the offset of each value within the page and extracts them.

The undo method has one argument, which is the transaction performing the undo. The method has the transaction pin the block denoted by the record, write the saved value, and unpin the block. The method that calls undo (either rollback or recover) is responsible for flushing the buffer contents to disk.

5.3.9.2 Rollback and Recover

The class RecoveryMgr implements the undo-only recovery algorithm; its code appears in Fig. 5.16. The commit and rollback methods flush the transaction's buffers before writing their log record, and the doRollback and doRecover methods make a single backward pass through the log.

The doRollback method iterates through the log records. Each time it finds a log record for that transaction, it calls the record's undo method. It stops when it encounters the start record for that transaction.

The doRecover method is implemented similarly. It reads the log until it hits a quiescent checkpoint record or reaches the end of the log, keeping a list of committed transaction numbers. It undoes uncommitted update records the same as in rollback, the difference being that it handles all uncommitted transactions, not just a specific one. This method is slightly different from the recovery algorithm of Fig. 5.6, because it will undo transactions that have already been rolled back. Although this difference does not make the code incorrect, it does make it less efficient. Exercise 5.50 asks you to improve it.

5.4 Concurrency Management

The *concurrency manager* is the component of the database engine that is responsible for the correct execution of concurrent transactions. This section examines what it means for execution to be "correct" and studies some algorithms that ensure correctness.

5.4.1 Serializable Schedules

The *history* of a transaction is its sequence of calls to methods that access the database files—in particular, the get/set methods.[1] For example, the histories of each transaction in Fig. 5.3 could be written, somewhat tediously, as shown in Fig. 5.17a. Another way to express the history of a transaction is in terms of the

[1]The size and append methods also access a database file but more subtly than do the get/set methods. Section 5.4.5 will consider the effect of size and append.

```
public class RecoveryMgr {
   private LogMgr lm;
   private BufferMgr bm;
   private Transaction tx;
   private int txnum;

   public RecoveryMgr(Transaction tx, int txnum, LogMgr lm,
                                                    BufferMgr bm) {

      this.tx = tx;
      this.txnum = txnum;
      this.lm = lm;
      this.bm = bm;
      StartRecord.writeToLog(lm, txnum);
   }

   public void commit() {
      bm.flushAll(txnum);
      int lsn = CommitRecord.writeToLog(lm, txnum);
      lm.flush(lsn);
   }

   public void rollback() {
      doRollback();
      bm.flushAll(txnum);
      int lsn = RollbackRecord.writeToLog(lm, txnum);
      lm.flush(lsn);
   }

   public void recover() {
      doRecover();
      bm.flushAll(txnum);
      int lsn = CheckpointRecord.writeToLog(lm);
      lm.flush(lsn);
   }

   public int setInt(Buffer buff, int offset, int newval) {
      int oldval = buff.contents().getInt(offset);
      BlockId blk = buff.block();
      return SetIntRecord.writeToLog(lm, txnum, blk, offset,
      oldval);
   }

   public int setString(Buffer buff, int offset, String newval)
   {
      String oldval = buff.contents().getString(offset);
      BlockId blk = buff.block();
      return SetStringRecord.writeToLog(lm, txnum, blk, offset,
      oldval);
   }

   private void doRollback() {
      Iterator<byte[]> iter = lm.iterator();
      while (iter.hasNext()) {
```

Fig. 5.16 The code for the class RecoveryMgr

```
         byte[] bytes = iter.next();
         LogRecord rec = LogRecord.createLogRecord(bytes);
         if (rec.txNumber() == txnum) {
            if (rec.op() == START)
               return;
            rec.undo(tx);
         }
      }
   }

   private void doRecover() {
      Collection<Integer> finishedTxs = new ArrayList<Integer>();
      Iterator<byte[]> iter = lm.iterator();
      while (iter.hasNext()) {
         byte[] bytes = iter.next();
         LogRecord rec = LogRecord.createLogRecord(bytes);
         if (rec.op() == CHECKPOINT)
            return;
         if (rec.op() == COMMIT || rec.op() == ROLLBACK)
            finishedTxs.add(rec.txNumber());
         else if (!finishedTxs.contains(rec.txNumber()))
            rec.undo(tx);
      }
   }
}
```

Fig. 5.16 (continued)

affected blocks, as shown in Fig. 5.17b. For example, the history for `tx2` states that it reads twice from block `blk` and then writes twice to `blk`.

Formally, the history of a transaction is the sequence of *database actions* made by that transaction. The term "database action" is deliberately vague. Part (a) of Fig. 5.17 treated a database action as the modification of a value, and part (b) treated it as the read/write of a disk block. Other granularities are possible, which are discussed in Sect. 5.4.8. Until then, I shall assume that a database action is the reading or writing of a disk block.

When multiple transactions are running concurrently, the database engine will interleave the execution of their threads, periodically interrupting one thread and resuming another. (In SimpleDB, the Java runtime environment does this automatically.) Thus, the actual sequence of operations performed by the concurrency manager will be an unpredictable interleaving of the histories of its transactions. That interleaving is called a *schedule*.

The purpose of concurrency control is to ensure that only correct schedules get executed. But what does "correct" mean? Well, consider the simplest possible schedule—one in which all transactions run serially (such as in Fig. 5.17). The operations in this schedule will not be interleaved, that is, the schedule will simply be the back-to-back histories of each transaction. This kind of schedule is called a *serial schedule*.

Concurrency control is predicated on the assumption that a serial schedule *has* to be correct, since there is no concurrency. The interesting thing about defining

```
tx1: setInt(blk, 80, 1, false);
     setString(blk, 40, "one", false);

tx2: getInt(blk, 80);
     getString(blk, 40);
     setInt(blk, 80, newival, true);
     setString(blk, 40, newsval, true);

tx3: getInt(blk, 80));
     getString(blk, 40));
     setInt(blk, 80, 9999, true);
     getInt(blk, 80));

tx4: getInt(blk, 80));
```

(a)

```
tx1: W(blk); W(blk)
tx2: R(blk); R(blk); W(blk); W(blk)
tx3: R(blk); R(blk); W(blk); R(blk)
tx4: R(blk)
```

(b)

Fig. 5.17 Transaction histories from Fig. 5.3. (**a**) Data access histories, (**b**) Block access histories

correctness in terms of serial schedules is that different serial schedules of the same transactions can give different results. For example, consider the two transactions T1 and T2, having the following identical histories:

```
T1: W(b1); W(b2)
T2: W(b1); W(b2)
```

Although these transactions have the same history (i.e., they both write block b1 first and then block b2), they are not necessarily identical as transactions—for example, T1 might write an 'X' at the beginning of each block, whereas T2 might write a 'Y.' If T1 executes before T2, the blocks will contain the values written by T2, but if they execute in the reverse order, the blocks will contain the values written by T1.

In this example, T1 and T2 have different opinions about what blocks b1 and b2 should contain. And since all transactions are equal in the eyes of the database engine, there is no way to say that one result is more correct than another. Thus, you are forced to admit that the result of *either* serial schedule is correct. That is, there can be several correct results.

A non-serial schedule is said to be *serializable* if it produces the same result as some serial schedule.[2] Since serial schedules are correct, it follows that serializable

[2]The term *serializable* is also used in Java—a serializable class is one whose objects can be written as a stream of bytes. Unfortunately, that use of the term has absolutely nothing to do with the database usage of it.

schedules must also be correct. For an example, consider the following non-serial schedule of the above transactions:

```
W1(b1); W2(b1); W1(b2); W2(b2)
```

Here, W1(b1) means that transaction T1 writes block b1, etc. This schedule results from running the first half of T1, followed by the first half of T2, the second half of T1, and the second half of T2. This schedule is serializable, because it is equivalent to doing T1 first and then T2. On the other hand, consider the following schedule:

```
W1(b1); W2(b1); W2(b2); W1(b2)
```

This transaction does the first half of T1, all of T2, and then the second half of T1. The result of this schedule is that block b1 contains the values written by T2, but block b2 contains the values written by T1. This result cannot be produced by any serial schedule, and so the schedule is said to be *non-serializable*.

Recall the ACID property of *isolation*, which said that each transaction should execute as if it were the only transaction in the system. A non-serializable schedule does not have this property. Therefore, you are forced to admit that non-serializable schedules are incorrect. In other words, a schedule is correct if and only if it is serializable.

5.4.2 The Lock Table

The database engine is responsible for ensuring that all schedules are serializable. A common technique is to use *locking* to postpone the execution of a transaction. Section 5.4.3 will look at how locking can be used to ensure serializability. This section simply examines how the basic locking mechanism works.

Each block has two kinds of lock—a *shared* lock (or *slock*) and an *exclusive* lock (or *xlock*). If a transaction holds an exclusive lock on a block, then no other transaction is allowed to have any kind of lock on it; if the transaction holds a shared lock on a block, then other transactions are only allowed to have shared locks on it. Note that these restrictions apply only to other transactions. A single transaction is allowed to hold both a shared and exclusive lock on a block.

The *lock table* is the database engine component responsible for granting locks to transactions. The SimpleDB class `LockTable` implements the lock table. Its API appears in Fig. 5.18.

LockTable

```
public void sLock(Block blk);
public void xLock(Block blk);
public void unlock(Block blk);
```

Fig. 5.18 The API for the SimpleDB class `LockTable`

The method sLock requests a shared lock on the specified block. If an exclusive lock already exists on the block, the method waits until the exclusive lock has been released. The method xLock requests an exclusive lock on the block. This method waits until no other transaction has any kind of lock on it. The unlock method releases a lock on the block.

Figure 5.19 presents the class ConcurrencyTest, which demonstrates some interactions between lock requests.

```
public class ConcurrencyTest {
   private static FileMgr fm;
   private static LogMgr lm;
   private static BufferMgr bm;

   public static void main(String[] args) {
      //initialize the database engine
      SimpleDB db = new SimpleDB("concurrencytest", 400, 8);
      fm = db.fileMgr();
      lm = db.logMgr();
      bm = db.bufferMgr();
      A a = new A(); new Thread(a).start();
      B b = new B(); new Thread(b).start();
      C c = new C(); new Thread(c).start();
   }

   static class A implements Runnable {
      public void run() {
         try {
            Transaction txA = new Transaction(fm, lm, bm);
            BlockId blk1 = new BlockId("testfile", 1);
            BlockId blk2 = new BlockId("testfile", 2);
            txA.pin(blk1);
            txA.pin(blk2);
            System.out.println("Tx A: request slock 1");
            txA.getInt(blk1, 0);
            System.out.println("Tx A: receive slock 1");
            Thread.sleep(1000);
            System.out.println("Tx A: request slock 2");
            txA.getInt(blk2, 0);
            System.out.println("Tx A: receive slock 2");
            txA.commit();
         }
         catch(InterruptedException e) {};
      }
   }

   static class B implements Runnable {
      public void run() {
         try {
            Transaction txB = new Transaction(fm, lm, bm);
```

Fig. 5.19 Testing the interaction between lock requests

```
            BlockId blk1 = new BlockId("testfile", 1);
            BlockId blk2 = new BlockId("testfile", 2);
            txB.pin(blk1);
            txB.pin(blk2);
            System.out.println("Tx B: request xlock 2");
            txB.setInt(blk2, 0, 0, false);
            System.out.println("Tx B: receive xlock 2");
            Thread.sleep(1000);
            System.out.println("Tx B: request slock 1");
            txB.getInt(blk1, 0);
            System.out.println("Tx B: receive slock 1");
            txB.commit();
         }
         catch(InterruptedException e) {};
      }
   }

   static class C implements Runnable {
      public void run() {
         try {
            Transaction txC = new Transaction(fm, lm, bm);
            BlockId blk1 = new BlockId("testfile", 1);
            BlockId blk2 = new BlockId("testfile", 2);
            txC.pin(blk1);
            txC.pin(blk2);
            System.out.println("Tx C: request xlock 1");
            txC.setInt(blk1, 0, 0, false);
            System.out.println("Tx C: receive xlock 1");
            Thread.sleep(1000);
            System.out.println("Tx C: request slock 2");
            txC.getInt(blk2, 0);
            System.out.println("Tx C: receive slock 2");
            txC.commit();
         }
         catch(InterruptedException e) {};
      }
   }
}
```

Fig. 5.19 (continued)

The `main` method executes three concurrent threads, corresponding to an object from each of classes A, B, and C. These transactions do not explicitly lock and unlock blocks. Instead, `Transaction`'s `getInt` method obtains an slock, its `setInt` method obtains an xlock, and its `commit` method unlocks all its locks. The sequence of locks and unlocks for each transaction thus looks like this:

```
txA: sLock(blk1); sLock(blk2); unlock(blk1); unlock(blk2)
txB: xLock(blk2); sLock(blk1); unlock(blk1); unlock(blk2)
txC: xLock(blk1); sLock(blk2); unlock(blk1); unlock(blk2)
```

The threads have sleep statements to force the transactions to alternate their lock requests. The following sequence of events occurs:

1. Thread A obtains an slock on blk1.
2. Thread B obtains an xlock on blk2.
3. Thread C cannot get an xlock on blk1, because someone else has a lock on it. Thus thread C waits.
4. Thread A cannot get an slock on blk2, because someone else has an xlock on it. Thus thread A also waits.
5. Thread B can continue. It obtains an slock on block blk1, because nobody currently has an xlock on it. (It doesn't matter that thread C is waiting for an xlock on that block.)
6. Thread B unlocks block blk1, but this does not help either waiting thread.
7. Thread B unlocks block blk2.
8. Thread A can now continue and obtains its slock on blk2.
9. Thread A unlocks block blk1.
10. Thread C finally is able to obtain its xlock on blk1.
11. Threads A and C can continue in any order until they complete.

5.4.3 The Lock Protocol

It is time to tackle the question of how locking can be used to ensure that all schedules are serializable. Consider two transactions having the following histories:

```
T1: R(b1); W(b2)
T2: W(b1); W(b2)
```

What is it that causes their serial schedules to have different results? Transactions T1 and T2 both write to the same block b2, which means that the order of these operations makes a difference—whichever transaction writes last is the "winner." The operations {`W1(b2)`, `W2(b2)`} are said to *conflict*. In general, two operations conflict if the order in which they are executed can produce a different result. If two transactions have conflicting operations, then their serial schedules may have different (but equally correct) results.

This conflict is an example of a *write-write* conflict. A second kind of conflict is a *read-write* conflict. For example, the operations {`R1(b1)`, `W2(b1)`} conflict—if `R1(b1)` executes first, then T1 reads one version of block b1, whereas if `W2(b1)` executes first, then T1 reads a different version of block b1. Note that two read operations cannot ever conflict, nor can operations involving different blocks.

The reason to care about conflicts is because they influence the serializability of a schedule. The order in which conflicting operations are executed in a non-serial schedule determines what the equivalent serial schedule must be. In the above example, if `W2(b1)` executes before `R1(b1)`, then any equivalent serial schedule

1. Before reading a block, acquire a shared lock on it.
2. Before modifying a block, acquire an exclusive lock on it.
3. Release all locks after a commit or rollback.

Fig. 5.20 The lock protocol

must have T2 running before T1. In general, if you consider all operations in T1 that conflict with T2, then either they all must be executed before any conflicting T2 operations or they all must be executed after them. Nonconflicting operations can happen in an arbitrary order.[3]

Locking can be used to avoid write-write and read-write conflicts. In particular, suppose that all transactions use locks according to the protocol of Fig. 5.20.

From this protocol, you can infer two important facts. First, if a transaction gets a shared lock on a block, then no other active transaction will have written to the block (otherwise, some transaction would still have an exclusive lock on the block). Second, if a transaction gets an exclusive lock on a block, then no other active transaction will have accessed the block in any way (otherwise, some transaction would still have a lock on the block). These facts imply that an operation performed by a transaction will never conflict with a previous operation by another active transaction. In other words, if all transactions obey the lock protocol, then:

- The resulting schedule will always be serializable (and hence correct)
- The equivalent serial schedule is determined by the order in which the transactions commit

By forcing transactions to hold their locks until they complete, the lock protocol drastically limits the concurrency in the system. It would be nice if a transaction could release its locks when they are no longer needed, so other transactions wouldn't have to wait as long. However, two serious problems can arise if a transaction releases its locks before it completes: it may no longer be serializable, and other transactions can read its uncommitted changes. These two issues are discussed next.

5.4.3.1 Serializability Problems

Once a transaction unlocks a block, it can no longer lock another block without impacting serializability. To see why, consider a transaction T1 that unlocks block x before locking block y.

```
T1: ... R(x); UL(x); SL(y); R(y); ...
```

[3]Actually, you can construct obscure examples in which certain write-write conflicts can also occur in any order; see Exercise 5.26. Such examples, however, are not practical enough to be worth considering.

Suppose that T1 is interrupted during the time interval between the unlock of x and the slock of y. At this point, T1 is extremely vulnerable, because both x and y are unlocked. Suppose that another transaction T2 jumps in, locks both x and y, writes to them, commits, and releases its locks. The following situation has occurred: T1 must come before T2 in the serial order, because T1 read the version of block x that existed before T2 wrote it. On the other hand, T1 must also come after T2 in the serial order, because T1 will read the version of block y written by T2. Thus, the resulting schedule is non-serializable.

It can be shown that the converse is also true—if a transaction acquires all of its locks before unlocking any of them, the resulting schedule is guaranteed to be serializable (see Exercise 5.27). This variant of the lock protocol is called *two-phase locking*. This name comes from the fact that under this protocol, a transaction has two phases—the phase where it accumulates the locks and the phase where it releases the locks.

Although two-phase locking is theoretically a more general protocol, a database engine cannot easily take advantage of it. Usually by the time a transaction has finished accessing its final block (which is when locks are finally able to be released), it is ready to commit anyway. So the fully general two-phase locking protocol is rarely effective in practice.

5.4.3.2 Reading Uncommitted Data

Another problem with releasing locks early (even with two-phase locking) is that transactions will be able to read uncommitted data. Consider the following partial schedule:

```
... W1(b); UL1(b); SL2(b); R2(b); ...
```

In this schedule, T1 writes to block b and unlocks it; transaction T2 then locks and reads b. If T1 eventually commits, then there is no problem. But suppose that T1 does a rollback. Then T2 will also have to roll back, because its execution is based on changes that no longer exist. And if T2 rolls back, this could cause still other transactions to roll back. This phenomenon is known as *cascading rollback*.

When the database engine lets a transaction read uncommitted data, it enables more concurrency, but it takes the risk that the transaction that wrote the data will not commit. Certainly, rollbacks tend to be infrequent, and cascaded rollbacks should be more so. The question is whether a database engine wants to take *any* risk of possibly rolling back a transaction unnecessarily. Most commercial database systems are not willing to take this risk and therefore always wait until a transaction completes before releasing its exclusive locks.

5.4.4 Deadlock

Although the lock protocol guarantees that schedules will be serializable, it does not guarantee that all transactions will commit. In particular, it is possible for transactions to be *deadlocked*.

Section 4.5.1 gave an example of deadlock in which two client threads were each waiting for the other to release a buffer. A similar possibility exists with locks. A deadlock occurs when there is a cycle of transactions in which the first transaction is waiting for a lock held by the second transaction, the second transaction is waiting for a lock held by the third transaction, and so on, until the last transaction is waiting for a lock held by the first transaction. In such a case, none of the waiting transactions can continue, and all will wait potentially forever. For a simple example, consider the following two histories, in which the transactions write to the same blocks but in different orders:

```
T1: W(b1); W(b2)
T2: W(b2); W(b1)
```

Suppose that T1 first acquires its lock on block b1. There is now a race for the lock on block b2. If T1 gets it first, then T2 will wait, T1 will eventually commit and release its locks, and T2 can continue. No problem. But if T2 gets the lock on block b2 first, then deadlock occurs—T1 is waiting for T2 to unlock block b2, and T2 is waiting for T1 to unlock block b1. Neither transaction can continue.

The concurrency manager can detect a deadlock by keeping a "waits-for" graph. This graph has one node for each transaction and an edge from T1 to T2 if T1 is waiting for a lock that T2 holds; each edge is labeled by the block that the transaction is waiting for. Every time a lock is requested or released, the graph is updated. For example, the waits-for graph corresponding to the above deadlock scenario appears in Fig. 5.21.

It is easy to show that a deadlock exists iff the waits-for graph has a cycle; see Exercise 5.28. When the transaction manager detects the occurrence of a deadlock, it can break it by summarily rolling back any one of the transactions in the cycle. A reasonable strategy is to roll back the transaction whose lock request "caused" the cycle, although other strategies are possible; see Exercise 5.29.

If you consider threads waiting for buffers as well as those waiting for locks, then testing for deadlock gets considerably more complicated. For example, suppose that the buffer pool contains only two buffers, and consider the following scenario:

```
T1: xlock(b1); pin(b4)
T2: pin(b2); pin(b3); xlock(b1)
```

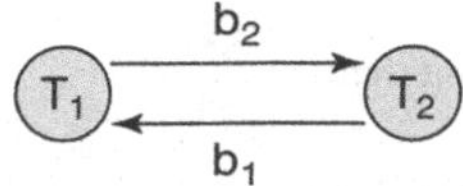

Fig. 5.21 A waits-for graph

Suppose transaction T1 gets interrupted after obtaining the lock on block b1, and then T2 pins blocks b2 and b3. T2 will wind up on the waiting list for xlock(b1), and T1 will wind up on the waiting list for a buffer. There is deadlock, even though the waits-for graph is acyclic.

In order to detect deadlock in such situations, the lock manager must not only keep a waits-for graph, it also needs to know about which transactions are waiting for what buffers. Incorporating this additional consideration into the deadlock detection algorithm turns out to be fairly difficult. Adventurous readers are encouraged to try Exercise 5.37.

The problem with using a waits-for graph to detect deadlock is that the graph is somewhat difficult to maintain and the process of detecting cycles in the graph is time-consuming. Consequently, simpler strategies have been developed to approximate deadlock detection. These strategies are conservative, in the sense that they will always detect a deadlock, but they might also treat a non-deadlock situation as a deadlock. This section considers two such possible strategies; Exercise 5.33 considers another.

The first approximation strategy is called *wait-die*, which is defined in Fig. 5.22. This strategy ensures that no deadlocks can occur, because the waits-for graph will contain only edges from older transactions to newer transactions. But the strategy also treats every potential deadlock as a cause for rollback. For example, suppose transaction T1 is older than T2, and T2 requests a lock currently held by T1. Even though this request may not immediately cause deadlock, there is the potential for it, because at some later point, T1 might request a lock held by T2. Thus the wait-die strategy will preemptively roll back T2.

The second approximation strategy is to use a time limit to detect a possible deadlock. If a transaction has been waiting for some preset amount of time, then the transaction manager will assume that it is deadlocked and will roll it back. See Fig. 5.23.

Regardless of the deadlock detection strategy, the concurrency manager must break the deadlock by rolling back an active transaction. The hope is that by

Suppose T1 requests a lock that conflicts with a lock held by T2.
    If T1 is older than T2 then:
        T1 waits for the lock.
    Otherwise:
        T1 is rolled back (i.e. it "dies").

Fig. 5.22 The wait-die deadlock detection strategy

Suppose T1 requests a lock that conflicts with a lock held by T2.

1. T1 waits for the lock.
2. If T1 stays on the wait list too long then:
    T1 is rolled back.

Fig. 5.23 The time limit deadlock detection strategy

releasing that transaction's locks, the remaining transactions will be able to complete. Once the transaction is rolled back, the concurrency manager throws an exception; in SimpleDB, this exception is called a `LockAbortException`. As with the `BufferAbortException` of Chap. 4, this exception is caught by the JDBC client of the aborted transaction, which then decides how to handle it. For example, the client could choose to simply exit, or it could try to run the transaction again.

5.4.5 File-Level Conflicts and Phantoms

This chapter has so far considered the conflicts that arise from the reading and writing of blocks. Another kind of conflict involves the methods `size` and `append`, which read and write the end-of-file marker. These two methods clearly conflict with each other: Suppose that transaction T1 calls `append` before transaction T2 calls `size`; then T1 must come before T2 in any serial order.

One of the consequences of this conflict is known as the *phantom problem*. Suppose that T2 reads the entire contents of a file repeatedly and calls `size` before each iteration to determine how many blocks to read. Moreover, suppose that after T2 reads the file the first time, transaction T1 appends some additional blocks to the file, fills them with values, and commits. The next time through the file, T2 will see these additional values, in violation of the ACID property of isolation. These additional values are called *phantoms*, because to T2 they have shown up mysteriously.

How can the concurrency manager avoid this conflict? The lock protocol requires T2 to obtain an slock on each block it reads, so that T1 will not be able to write new values to those blocks. However, this approach will not work here, because it would require T2 to slock the new blocks *before* T1 creates them!

The solution is to allow transactions to lock the end-of-file marker. In particular, a transaction needs to xlock the marker in order to call the `append` method, and it needs to slock the marker in order to call the `size` method. In the above scenario, if T1 calls `append` first, then T2 will not be able to determine the file size until T1 completes; conversely, if T2 has already determined the file size, then T1 would be blocked from appending until T2 commits. In either case, phantoms cannot occur.

5.4.6 Multiversion Locking

Transactions in many database applications are read-only. Read-only transactions coexist nicely within the database engine because they share locks and never have to wait for each other. However, they do not get along well with update transactions. Suppose that one update transaction is writing to a block. Then all read-only transactions that want to read that block must wait, not just until the block is written but until the update transaction has completed. Conversely, if an update transaction wants to write a block, it needs to wait until all of the read-only transactions that read the block have completed.

In other words, a lot of waiting is going to occur when read-only and update transactions conflict, regardless of which transaction gets its lock first. Given that this situation is a common one, researchers have developed strategies for reducing this waiting. One such strategy is called *multiversion locking*.

5.4.6.1 The Principle of Multiversion Locking

As its name suggests, multiversion locking works by storing multiple versions of each block. The basic idea is as follows:

- Each version of a block is timestamped with the commit time of the transaction that wrote it.
- When a read-only transaction requests a value from a block, the concurrency manager uses the version of the block that was most recently committed at the time the transaction began.

In other words, a read-only transaction sees a snapshot of the committed data as it would have looked at the time the transaction began. Note the term "committed data." The transaction sees the data written by transactions that committed before it began and does not see the data written by later transactions.

Consider the following example of multiversion locking. Suppose four transactions have the following histories:

```
T1: W(b1); W(b2)
T2: W(b1); W(b2)
T3: R(b1); R(b2)
T4: W(b2)
```

and that they execute according to the following schedule:

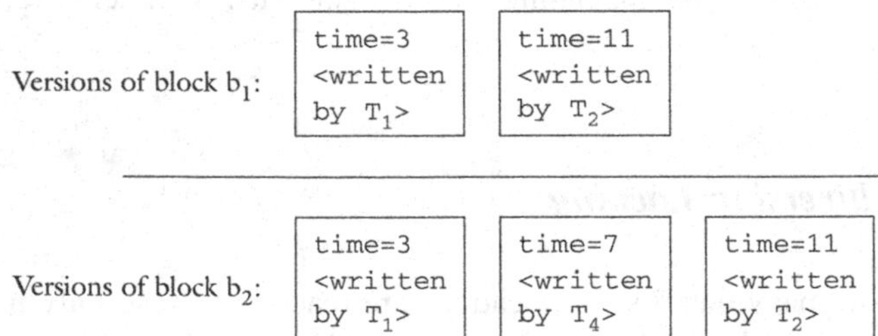

Fig. 5.24 Multiversion concurrency

```
W1(b1); W1(b2); C1; W2(b1); R3(b1); W4(b2); C4; R3(b2); C3; W2(b1); C2
```

This schedule assumes that a transaction begins at its first operation and obtains its locks immediately before they are needed. The operation Ci indicates when transaction Ti commits. The update transactions T1, T2, and T4 follow the lock protocol, as you can verify from the schedule. Transaction T3 is a read-only transaction and does not follow the protocol.

The concurrency manager stores a version of a block for each update transaction that writes to it. Thus, there will be two versions of b1 and three versions of b2, as shown in Fig. 5.24.

The timestamp on each version is the time when its transaction commits, not when the writing occurred. Assume that each operation takes one time unit, so T1 commits at time 3, T4 at time 7, T3 at time 9, and T2 at time 11.

Now consider the read-only transaction T3. It begins at time 5, which means that it should see the values that were committed at that point, namely, the changes made by T1 but not T2 or T4. Thus, it will see the versions of b1 and b2 that were timestamped at time 3. Note that T3 will not see the version of b2 that was timestamped at time 7, even though that version had been committed by the time that the read occurred.

The beauty of multiversion locking is that read-only transactions do not need to obtain locks and thus *never have to wait*. The concurrency manager chooses the appropriate version of a requested block according to the start time of the transaction. An update transaction can be concurrently making changes to the same block, but a read-only transaction will not care because it sees a different version of that block.

Multiversion locking only applies to read-only transactions. Update transactions need to follow the lock protocol, obtaining both slocks and xlocks as appropriate. The reason is every update transaction reads and writes the current version of the data (and never a previous version), and thus conflicts are possible. But remember that these conflicts are between update transactions only and not with the read-only transactions. Thus, assuming that there are relatively few conflicting update transactions, waiting will be much less frequent.

5.4.6.2 Implementing Multiversion Locking

Now that you have seen how multiversion locking should work, let's examine how the concurrency manager does what it needs to do. The basic issue is how to maintain the versions of each block. A straightforward but somewhat difficult approach would be to explicitly save each version in a dedicated "version file." A different approach is to use the log to reconstruct any desired version of a block. Its implementation works as follows.

Each read-only transaction is given a timestamp when it starts. Each update transaction is given a timestamp when it commits. The `commit` method for an update transaction is revised to include the following actions:

- The recovery manager writes the transaction's timestamp as part of its commit log record.
- For each xlock held by the transaction, the concurrency manager pins the block, writes the timestamp to the beginning of the block, and unpins the buffer.

Suppose that a read-only transaction having timestamp t requests a block b. The concurrency manager takes the following steps to reconstruct the appropriate version:

- It copies the current version of block b to a new page.
- It reads the log backwards three times, as follows:
  - *It constructs a list of transactions that committed after time t.* Since transactions commit in timestamp order, the concurrency manager can stop reading the log when it finds a commit record whose timestamp is less than t.
  - *It constructs a list of uncompleted transactions* by looking for log records written by transactions that do not have a commit or rollback record. It can stop reading the log when it encounters a quiescent checkpoint record or the earliest start record of a transaction in a nonquiescent checkpoint record.
  - *It uses the update records to undo values in the copy of b.* When it encounters an update record for b written by a transaction on either of the above lists, it performs an undo. It can stop reading the log when it encounters the start record for the earliest transaction on the lists.
- The modified copy of b is returned to the transaction.

In other words, the concurrency manager reconstructs the version of the block at time t by undoing modifications made by transactions that did not commit before t. This algorithm uses three passes through the log for simplicity. Exercise 5.38 asks you to rewrite the algorithm to make a single pass through the log.

Finally, a transaction needs to specify whether it is read-only or not, since the concurrency manager treats the two types of transaction differently. In JDBC, this specification is performed by the method `setReadOnly` in the `Connection` interface. For example:

```
Connection conn = ... // obtain the connection
conn.setReadOnly(true);
```

The call to `setReadOnly` is considered to be a "hint" to the database system. The system can choose to ignore the call if it does not support multiversion locking.

ISOLATION LEVEL	PROBLEMS	LOCK USAGE	COMMENTS
serializable	none	slocks held to completion, slock on eof marker	the only level that guarantees correctness
repeatable read	phantoms	slocks held to completion, no slock on eof marker	useful for modify-based transactions
read committed	phantoms, values may change	slocks released early, no slock on eof marker	useful for conceptually separable transactions whose updates are "all or nothing"
read uncommitted	phantoms, values may change, dirty reads	no slocks at all	useful for read-only transactions that tolerate inaccurate results

Fig. 5.25 Transaction isolation levels

5.4.7 Transaction Isolation Levels

Enforcing serializability causes a considerable amount of waiting, because the lock protocol requires transactions to hold their locks until they complete. Consequently, if a transaction T1 happens to need just one lock that conflicts with a lock held by T2, then T1 cannot do anything else until T2 completes.

Multiversion locking is very attractive because it allows read-only transactions to execute without locks and therefore without the inconvenience of having to wait. However, the implementation of multiversion locking is somewhat complex and requires additional disk accesses to recreate the versions. Moreover, multiversion locking does not apply to transactions that update the database.

There is another way for a transaction to reduce the amount of time it waits for locks—it can specify that it does not need complete serializability. Chapter 2 examined the four *transaction isolation levels* of JDBC. Figure 5.25 summarizes these levels and their properties.

Chapter 2 related these isolation levels to the various problems that can occur. What is new about Fig. 5.25 is that it also relates these levels to the way that slocks are used. Serializable isolation requires very restrictive shared locking, whereas read-uncommitted isolation does not even use slocks. Clearly, the less restrictive the locking, the less waiting that occurs. But less restrictive locking also introduces more inaccuracies into the results of queries: a transaction may see phantoms, or it may see two different values at a location at different times, or it may see values written by an uncommitted transaction.

I want to stress that these isolation levels apply only to data *reading*. All transactions, regardless of their isolation level, should behave correctly with respect to writing data. They must obtain the appropriate xlocks (including the xlock on the eof marker) and hold them to completion. The reason is that an individual transaction may choose to tolerate inaccuracies when it runs a query, but an inaccurate update poisons the entire database and cannot be tolerated.

How does read uncommitted isolation compare with multiversion locking? Both apply to read-only transactions, and both operate without locks. However, a transaction that uses read uncommitted isolation sees the current value of each block that it reads, regardless of which transaction wrote to it or when. It is not even close to being serializable. On the other hand, a transaction that uses multiversion locking sees the committed contents of the blocks at a single point in time and is serializable.

5.4.8 Data Item Granularity

This chapter has assumed that the concurrency manager locks blocks. But other locking granularities are possible: The concurrency manager could lock values, files, or even the entire database. The unit of locking is called a *concurrency data item*.

The principles of concurrency control are not affected by the granularity of data item used. All of the definitions, protocols, and algorithms in this chapter apply to any data item. The choice of granularity is therefore a practical one, which needs to balance efficiency with flexibility. This section examines some of these trade-offs.

The concurrency manager keeps a lock for each data item. A smaller granularity size is useful because it allows for more concurrency. For example, suppose that two transactions wish to concurrently modify different parts of the same block. These concurrent modifications are possible with value-granularity locking but not with block-granularity locking.

However, a smaller granularity requires more locks. Values tend to make impractically small data items, because they entail an enormous number of locks. At the other extreme, using files as data items would require very few locks but would also significantly impact concurrency—a client would need to xlock the entire file in order to update any portion of it. Using blocks as data items is a reasonable compromise.

As an aside, note that some operating systems (such as MacOS and Windows) use file-granularity locking to implement a primitive form of concurrency control. In particular, an application cannot write to a file without an xlock on the file, and it cannot obtain the xlock if that file is currently being used by another application.

Some concurrency managers support data items at multiple granularities, such as blocks and files. A transaction that plans to access only a few blocks of a file could lock them separately; but if the transaction plans to access all (or most of) the file, it would obtain a single file-granularity lock. This approach blends the flexibility of small-granularity items with the convenience of high-level items.

Another possible granularity is to use *data records* as concurrency data items. Data records are handled by the record manager, which is the topic of the next chapter. SimpleDB is structured so that the concurrency manager does not understand records and therefore cannot lock them. However, some commercial systems (such as Oracle) are built so that the concurrency manager knows about the record manager and can call its methods. In this case, data records would be a reasonable concurrency data item.

ConcurrencyMgr

```
public ConcurrencyMgr(int txnum);
public void sLock(Block blk);
public void xLock(Block blk);
public void release();
```

Fig. 5.26 The API for the SimpleDB concurrency manager

Although data-record granularity appears attractive, it introduces additional problems with phantoms. Since new data records can get inserted into existing blocks, a transaction that reads all records from a block needs a way to keep other transactions from inserting records into that block. The solution is for the concurrency manager to also support a coarser-granularity data item, such as blocks or files. In fact, some commercial systems avoid phantoms by simply forcing a transaction to obtain an xlock on the file before it performs any insertion.

5.4.9 The SimpleDB Concurrency Manager

The SimpleDB concurrency manager is implemented via the class `ConcurrencyMgr` in the package `simpledb.tx.concurrency`. The concurrency manager implements the lock protocol, using block-level granularity. Its API appears in Fig. 5.26.

Each transaction has its own concurrency manager. The methods of the concurrency manager are similar to those of the lock table but are transaction-specific. Each `ConcurrencyMgr` object keeps track of the locks held by its transaction. The methods `sLock` and `xLock` will request a lock from the lock table only if the transaction does not yet have it. The method `release` is called at the end of the transaction to unlock all its locks.

The `ConcurrencyMgr` class makes use of the class `LockTable`, which implements the SimpleDB lock table. The remainder of this section examines the implementation of these two classes.

5.4.9.1 The Class `LockTable`

The code for the class `LockTable` appears in Fig. 5.27. The `LockTable` object holds a `Map` variable called `locks`. This map contains an entry for each block that currently has an assigned lock. The value of an entry will be an `Integer` object; a value of -1 denotes that an exclusive lock is assigned, whereas a positive value denotes the current number of shared locks assigned.

The `sLock` and `xLock` methods work very similarly to the `pin` method of `BufferMgr`. Each method calls the Java `wait` method inside of a loop, which

```
class LockTable {
   private static final long MAX_TIME = 10000; // 10 seconds

   private Map<Block,Integer> locks = new HashMap<Block,Integer>();

   public synchronized void sLock(Block blk) {
      try {
         long timestamp = System.currentTimeMillis();
         while (hasXlock(blk) && !waitingTooLong(timestamp))
            wait(MAX_TIME);
         if (hasXlock(blk))
            throw new LockAbortException();
         int val = getLockVal(blk);  // will not be negative
         locks.put(blk, val+1);
      }
      catch(InterruptedException e) {
         throw new LockAbortException();
      }
   }

   public synchronized void xLock(Block blk) {
      try {
         long timestamp = System.currentTimeMillis();
         while (hasOtherSLocks(blk) && !waitingTooLong(timestamp))
            wait(MAX_TIME);
         if (hasOtherSLocks(blk))
            throw new LockAbortException();
         locks.put(blk, -1);
      }
      catch(InterruptedException e) {
         throw new LockAbortException();
      }
   }

   public synchronized void unlock(Block blk) {
      int val = getLockVal(blk);
      if (val > 1)
         locks.put(blk, val-1);
      else {
         locks.remove(blk);
         notifyAll();
      }
   }

   private boolean hasXlock(Block blk) {
      return getLockVal(blk) < 0;
   }
```

Fig. 5.27 The code for the SimpleDB class `LockTable`

```
   private boolean hasOtherSLocks(Block blk) {
      return getLockVal(blk) > 1;
   }

   private boolean waitingTooLong(long starttime) {
      return System.currentTimeMillis() - starttime > MAX_TIME;
   }

   private int getLockVal(Block blk) {
      Integer ival = locks.get(blk);
      return (ival == null) ? 0 : ival.intValue();
   }
}
```

Fig. 5.27 (continued)

means that the client thread is continually placed on the wait list as long as the loop condition holds. The loop condition for `sLock` calls the method `hasXlock`, which returns `true` if the block has an entry in `locks` with a value of -1. The loop condition for `xLock` calls the method `hasOtherLocks`, which returns `true` if the block has an entry in `locks` with a value greater than 1. The rationale is that the concurrency manager will always obtain an slock on the block before requesting the xlock, and so a value higher than 1 indicates that some other transaction also has a lock on this block.

The `unlock` method either removes the specified lock from the `locks` collection (if it is either an exclusive lock or a shared lock held by only one transaction) or decrements the number of transactions still sharing the lock. If the lock is removed from the collection, the method calls the Java `notifyAll` method, which moves all waiting threads to the ready list for scheduling. The internal Java thread scheduler resumes each thread in some unspecified order. There may be several threads waiting on the same released lock. By the time a thread is resumed, it may discover that the lock it wants is unavailable and will place itself on the wait list again.

This code is not especially efficient about how it manages thread notification. The `notifyAll` method moves *all* waiting threads, which includes threads waiting on other locks. Those threads, when scheduled, will (of course) discover that their lock is still unavailable and will place themselves back on the wait list. On one hand, this strategy will not be too costly if there are relatively few conflicting database threads running concurrently. On the other hand, a database engine ought to be more sophisticated than that. Exercises 5.53–5.54 ask you to improve the wait/notification mechanism.

5.4.9.2 The Class `ConcurrencyMgr`

The code for the class `ConcurrencyMgr` appears in Fig. 5.28. Although there is a concurrency manager for each transaction, they all need to use the same lock table.

```
public class ConcurrencyMgr {
   private static LockTable locktbl = new LockTable();
   private Map<Block,String> locks  = new HashMap<Block,String>();

   public void sLock(Block blk) {
      if (locks.get(blk) == null) {
         locktbl.sLock(blk);
         locks.put(blk, "S");
      }
   }

   public void xLock(Block blk) {
      if (!hasXLock(blk)) {
         sLock(blk);
         locktbl.xLock(blk);
         locks.put(blk, "X");
      }
   }

   public void release() {
      for (Block blk : locks.keySet())
         locktbl.unlock(blk);
      locks.clear();
   }

   private boolean hasXLock(Block blk) {
      String locktype = locks.get(blk);
      return locktype != null && locktype.equals("X");
   }
}
```

Fig. 5.28 The code for the SimpleDB class *ConcurrencyMgr*

This requirement is implemented by having each `ConcurrencyMgr` object share a static `LockTable` variable. The description of the locks held by the transaction is held in the local variable *locks*. This variable holds a map that has an entry for each locked block. The value associated with the entry is either "S" or "X," depending on whether there is an slock or an xlock on that block.

The method `sLock` first checks to see if the transaction already has a lock on the block; if so, there is no need to go to the lock table. Otherwise, it calls the lock table's `sLock` method and waits for the lock to be granted. The method `xLock` need not do anything if the transaction already has an xlock on the block. If not, the method first obtains an slock on the block and then obtains the xlock. (Recall that the lock table's `xLock` method assumes that the transaction already has an slock.) Note that xlocks are "stronger" than slocks, in the sense that a transaction having an xlock on a block also has an implied slock on it.

5.5 Implementing SimpleDB Transactions

Section 5.2 introduced the API for the class `Transaction`. It is now possible to discuss its implementation. The `Transaction` class makes use of the class `BufferList` to manage the buffers it has pinned. Each class is discussed in turn.

The Class `Transaction`
The code for class `Transaction` appears in Fig. 5.29. Each `Transaction` object creates its own recovery manger and concurrency manager. It also creates the object `myBuffers` to manage the currently pinned buffers.

The `commit` and `rollback` methods perform the following activities:

- They unpin any remaining buffers.
- They call the recovery manager to commit (or roll back) the transaction.
- They call the concurrency manager to release its locks.

The methods `getInt` and `getString` first acquire an slock on the specified block from the concurrency manager and then return the requested value from the buffer. The methods `setInt` and `setString` first acquire an xlock from the concurrency manager and then call the corresponding method in the recovery manager to create the appropriate log record and return its LSN. This LSN can then be passed to the buffer's `setModified` method.

The methods `size` and `append` treat the end-of-file marker as a "dummy" block with block number `-1`. The method `size` obtains an slock on the block, and *append* obtains an xlock on the block.

The Class `BufferList`
The class `BufferList` manages the list of currently pinned buffers for a transaction; see Fig. 5.30. A `BufferList` object needs to know two things: which buffer is assigned to a specified block, and how many times each block is pinned. The code uses a map to determine buffers and a list to determine pin counts. The list contains a `BlockId` object as many times as it is pinned; each time the block is unpinned, one instance is removed from the list.

The method `unpinAll` performs the buffer-related activity required when a transaction commits or rolls back—it has the buffer manager flush all buffers modified by the transaction and unpins any still-pinned buffers.

5.6 Chapter Summary

- Data can get lost or corrupted when client programs are able to run indiscriminately. Database engines force client programs to consist of *transactions*.
- A transaction is a group of operations that behaves as a single operation. It satisfies the ACID properties of *atomicity*, *consistency*, *isolation*, and *durability*.
- The *recovery manager* is responsible for ensuring atomicity and durability. It is the portion of the server that reads and processes the log. It has three functions: to

```
public class Transaction {
   private static int nextTxNum = 0;
   private static final int END_OF_FILE = -1;
   private RecoveryMgr    recoveryMgr;
   private ConcurrencyMgr concurMgr;
   private BufferMgr bm;
   private FileMgr fm;
   private int txnum;
   private BufferList mybuffers;

   public Transaction(FileMgr fm, LogMgr lm, BufferMgr bm) {
      this.fm = fm;
      this.bm = bm;
      txnum = nextTxNumber();
      recoveryMgr = new RecoveryMgr(this, txnum, lm, bm);
      concurMgr = new ConcurrencyMgr();
      mybuffers = new BufferList(bm);
   }
   public void commit() {
      recoveryMgr.commit();
      concurMgr.release();
      mybuffers.unpinAll();
      System.out.println("transaction " + txnum + " committed");
   }
   public void rollback() {
      recoveryMgr.rollback();
      concurMgr.release();
      mybuffers.unpinAll();
      System.out.println("transaction " + txnum + " rolled back");
   }
   public void recover() {
      bm.flushAll(txnum);
      recoveryMgr.recover();
   }
   public void pin(BlockId blk) {
      mybuffers.pin(blk);
   }
   public void unpin(BlockId blk) {
      mybuffers.unpin(blk);
   }

   public int getInt(BlockId blk, int offset) {
      concurMgr.sLock(blk);
      Buffer buff = mybuffers.getBuffer(blk);
      return buff.contents().getInt(offset);
   }

   public String getString(BlockId blk, int offset) {
      concurMgr.sLock(blk);
      Buffer buff = mybuffers.getBuffer(blk);
      return buff.contents().getString(offset);
   }
```

Fig. 5.29 The code for the SimpleDB class `Transaction`

```
  public void setInt(BlockId blk, int offset, int val,
                     boolean okToLog) {
     concurMgr.xLock(blk);
     Buffer buff = mybuffers.getBuffer(blk);
     int lsn = -1;
     if (okToLog)
        lsn = recoveryMgr.setInt(buff, offset, val);
     Page p = buff.contents();
     p.setInt(offset, val);
     buff.setModified(txnum, lsn);
  }
  public void setString(BlockId blk, int offset, String val,
                        boolean okToLog) {
     concurMgr.xLock(blk);
     Buffer buff = mybuffers.getBuffer(blk);
     int lsn = -1;
     if (okToLog)
        lsn = recoveryMgr.setString(buff, offset, val);
     Page p = buff.contents();
     p.setString(offset, val);
     buff.setModified(txnum, lsn);
  }
  public int size(String filename) {
     BlockId dummyblk = new BlockId(filename, END_OF_FILE);
     concurMgr.sLock(dummyblk);
     return fm.length(filename);
  }
  public BlockId append(String filename) {
     BlockId dummyblk = new BlockId(filename, END_OF_FILE);
     concurMgr.xLock(dummyblk);
     return fm.append(filename);
  }
  public int blockSize() {
     return fm.blockSize();
  }
  public int availableBuffs() {
     return bm.available();
  }
  private static synchronized int nextTxNumber() {
     nextTxNum++;
     System.out.println("new transaction: " + nextTxNum);
     return nextTxNum;
  }
}
```

Fig. 5.29 (continued)

```
class BufferList {
   private Map<BlockId,Buffer> buffers = new HashMap<>();
   private List<BlockId> pins = new ArrayList<>();
   private BufferMgr bm;

   public BufferList(BufferMgr bm) {
      this.bm = bm;
   }

   Buffer getBuffer(BlockId blk) {
      return buffers.get(blk);
   }

   void pin(BlockId blk) {
      Buffer buff = bm.pin(blk);
      buffers.put(blk, buff);
      pins.add(blk);
   }

   void unpin(BlockId blk) {
      Buffer buff = buffers.get(blk);
      bm.unpin(buff);
      pins.remove(blk);
      if (!pins.contains(blk))
         buffers.remove(blk);
   }

   void unpinAll() {
      for (BlockId blk : pins) {
         Buffer buff = buffers.get(blk);
         bm.unpin(buff);
      }
      buffers.clear();
      pins.clear();
   }
}
```

Fig. 5.30 The code for the SimpleDB class `BufferList`

write log records, to roll back a transaction, and to recover the database after a system crash.

- Each transaction writes a *start record* to the log to denote when it begins, *update records* to indicate the modifications it makes, and a *commit* or *rollback record* to denote when it completes. In addition, the recovery manager can write *checkpoint records* to the log at various times.
- The recovery manager *rolls back* a transaction by reading the log backwards. It uses the transaction's update records to undo the modifications.
- The recovery manager *recovers* the database after a system crash.

- The *undo-redo recovery algorithm* undoes the modifications made by uncommitted transactions and redoes the modifications made by committed transactions.
- The *undo-only recovery algorithm* assumes that modifications made by a committed transaction are flushed to the disk before the transaction commits. Thus, it only needs to undo modifications made by uncommitted transactions.
- The *redo-only recovery algorithm* assumes that modified buffers are not flushed until the transaction commits. This algorithm requires a transaction to keep modified buffers pinned until it completes, but it avoids the need to undo uncommitted transactions.
- The *write-ahead logging* strategy requires that an update log record be forced to disk before the modified data page. Write-ahead logging guarantees that modifications to the database will always be in the log and therefore will always be undoable.
- Checkpoint records are added to the log in order to reduce the portion of the log that the recovery algorithm needs to consider. A *quiescent checkpoint record* can be written when no transactions are currently running; a *nonquiescent checkpoint record* can be written at any time. If undo-redo (or redo-only) recovery is used, then the recovery manager must flush modified buffers to disk before it writes a checkpoint record.
- A recovery manager can choose to log values, records, pages, files, etc. The unit of logging is called a *recovery data item*. The choice of data item involves a tradeoff: A large-granularity data item will require fewer update log records, but each log record will be larger.
- The *concurrency manager* is the portion of the database engine that is responsible for the correct execution of concurrent transactions.
- The sequence of operations performed by the transactions in the engine is called a *schedule*. A schedule is *serializable* if it is equivalent to a serial schedule. Only serializable schedules are correct.
- The concurrency manager uses locking to guarantee that schedules are serializable. In particular, it requires all transactions to follow the *lock protocol*, which states:
  - Before reading a block, acquire a shared lock on it.
  - Before modifying a block, acquire an exclusive lock on it.
  - Release all locks after commit or rollback.
- A *deadlock* can occur if there is a cycle of transactions where each transaction is waiting for a lock held by the next transaction. The concurrency manager can detect deadlock by keeping a *waits-for* graph and checking for cycles.
- The concurrency manager can also use algorithms to approximate deadlock detection. The *wait-die algorithm* forces a transaction to roll back if it needs a lock held by an older transaction. The *time-limit algorithm* forces a transaction to roll back if it has been waiting for a lock longer than expected. Both of these algorithms will remove deadlock when it exists, but might also roll back a transaction unnecessarily.

- While one transaction is examining a file, another transaction might append new blocks to it. The values in those blocks are called *phantoms*. Phantoms are undesirable because they violate serializability. A transaction can avoid phantoms by locking the end-of-file marker.
- The locking needed to enforce serializability significantly reduces concurrency. The *multiversion locking* strategy allows read-only transactions to run without locks (and thus without having to wait). The concurrency manager implements multiversion locking by associating timestamps with each transaction and using those timestamps to reconstruct the version of the blocks as they were at a specified point in time.
- Another way to reduce the waiting time imposed by locking is to remove the requirement of serializability. A transaction can specify that it belongs to one of four *isolation levels*: *serializable*, *repeatable read*, *read committed*, or *read uncommitted*. Each non-serializable isolation level reduces the restrictions on slocks given by the log protocol and results in less waiting as well as increased severity of read problems. Developers who choose non-serializable isolation levels must consider carefully the extent to which inaccurate results will occur and the acceptability of such inaccuracies.
- As with recovery, a concurrency manager can choose to lock values, records, pages, files, etc. The unit of locking is called a *concurrency data item*. The choice of data item involves a trade-off. A large-granularity data item will require fewer locks, but the larger locks will conflict more readily and thus reduce concurrency.

5.7 Suggested Reading

The notion of a transaction is fundamental to many areas of distributed computing, not just database systems. Researchers have developed an extensive set of techniques and algorithms; the ideas in this chapter are the small tip of a very large iceberg. Two excellent books that provide an overview of the field are Bernstein and Newcomer (1997) and Gray and Reuter (1993). A comprehensive treatment of many concurrency control and recovery algorithms appears in Bernstein et al. (1987). A widely adopted recovery algorithm is called ARIES and is described in Mohan et al. (1992).

Oracle's implementation of the serializable isolation level is called *snapshot isolation*, which extends multiversion concurrency control to include updates. Details can be found in Chap. 9 of Ashdown et al. (2019). Note that Oracle calls this isolation level "serializable," although it is subtly different from it. Snapshot isolation is more efficient than the locking protocol, but it does not guarantee serializability. Although most schedules will be serializable, there are certain scenarios in which is can result in non-serializable behavior. The article Fekete et al. (2005) analyzes these scenarios and shows how to modify at-risk applications to guarantee serializability.

Oracle implements undo-redo recovery, but it separates the undo information (i.e., the old, overwritten values) from the redo information (the newly written values). Redo information is stored in a redo log, which is managed similarly to the descriptions in this chapter. However, undo information is not stored in a log file but in special *undo buffers*. The reason is that Oracle uses previous, overwritten values for multiversion concurrency as well as for recovery. Details can be found in Chap. 9 of Ashdown et al. (2019).

It is often useful to think of a transaction as being comprised of several smaller, coordinated transactions. For example, in a *nested transaction*, a parent transaction is able to spawn one or more child subtransactions; when a subtransaction completes, its parent decides what to do. If the subtransaction aborts, the parent could choose to abort all of its children, or it might continue by spawning another transaction to replace the aborted one. The basics of nested transactions can be found in Moss (1985). The article Weikum (1991) defines *multilevel transactions*, which are similar to nested transactions; the difference is that a multilevel transaction uses subtransactions as a way to increase efficiency via parallel execution.

Ashdown, L., et al. (2019). *Oracle database concepts*. Document E96138-01, Oracle Corporation. Retrieved from https://docs.oracle.com/en/database/oracle/oracle-database/19/cncpt/database-concepts.pdf

Bernstein, P., Hadzilacos, V., & Goodman, N. (1987). *Concurrency control and recovery in database systems*. Reading, MA: Addison-Wesley.

Bernstein, P., & Newcomer, E. (1997). *Principles of transaction processing*. San Mateo: Morgan Kaufman.

Fekete, A., Liarokapis, D., O'Neil, E., O'Neil, P., & Shasha, D. (2005). Making snapshot isolation serializable. *ACM Transactions on Database Systems, 30*(2), 492–528.

Gray, J., & Reuter, A. (1993). *Transaction processing: concepts and techniques*. San Mateo: Morgan Kaufman.

Mohan, C., Haderle, D., Lindsay, B., Pirahesh, H., & Schwartz, P. (1992). ARIES: A transaction recovery method supporting fine-granularity locking and partial rollbacks using write-ahead logging. *ACM Transactions on Database Systems, 17* (1), 94–162.

Moss, J. (1985). *Nested transactions: An approach to reliable distributed computing*. Cambridge, MA: MIT Press.

Weikum, G. (1991). Principles and realization strategies of multilevel transaction management. *ACM Transactions on Database Systems, 16*(1), 132–180.

5.8 Exercises

Conceptual Exercises

5.1. Assume that the code of Fig. 5.1 is being run by two concurrent users, but without transactions. Give a scenario in which two seats are reserved but only one sale is recorded.

5.2. Software configuration managers such as Git or Subversion allow a user to commit a series of changes to a file and to roll back a file to a previous state. They also allow multiple users to modify a file concurrently.

(a) What is the notion of a transaction in such systems?
(b) How do such systems ensure serializability?
(c) Would such an approach work for a database system? Explain.

5.3. Consider a JDBC program that performs several unrelated SQL queries but does not modify the database. The programmer decides that since nothing is updated, the concept of a transaction is unimportant; thus, the entire program is run as a single transaction.

(a) Explain why the concept of a transaction *is* important to a read-only program.
(b) What is the problem with running the entire program as a large transaction?
(c) How much overhead is involved in committing a read-only transaction? Does it make sense for the program to commit after every SQL query?

5.4. The recovery manager writes a start record to the log when each transaction begins.

(a) What is the practical benefit of having start records in the log?
(b) Suppose that a database system decides not to write start records to the log. Can the recovery manager still function properly? What capabilities are impacted?

5.5. The SimpleDB `rollback` method writes the rollback log record to disk before it returns. Is this necessary? Is it a good idea?

5.6. Suppose that the recovery manager was modified so that it didn't write rollback log records when it finished. Would there be a problem? Would this be a good idea?

5.7. Consider the undo-only commit algorithm of Fig. 5.7. Explain why it would be incorrect to swap steps 1 and 2 of the algorithm.

5.8. Show that if the system crashes during a rollback or a recovery, then redoing the rollback (or recovery) is still correct.

5.9. Is there any reason to log the changes made to the database during rollback or recovery? Explain.

5.10. A variation on the nonquiescent checkpointing algorithm is to mention only one transaction in the checkpoint log record, namely, the oldest active transaction at the time.

(a) Explain how the recovery algorithm will work.
(b) Compare this strategy with the strategy given in the text. Which is simpler to implement? Which is more efficient?

5.11. What should the rollback method do if it encounters a quiescent checkpoint log record? What if it encounters a nonquiescent log record? Explain.

5.12. The algorithm for nonquiescent checkpointing does not allow new transactions to start while it is writing the checkpoint record. Explain why this restriction is important for correctness.

5.13. Another way to do nonquiescent checkpointing is to write two records to the log. The first record is `<BEGIN_NQCKPT>`, and contains nothing else. The second record is the standard `<NQCKPT ...>` record, which contains the list of active transactions. The first record is written as soon as the recovery manager decides to do a checkpoint. The second record is written later, after the list of active transactions has been created.

(a) Explain why this strategy solves the problem of Exercise 5.12.
(b) Give a revised recovery algorithm that incorporates this strategy.

5.14. Explain why the recovery manager will never encounter more than one quiescent checkpoint record during recovery.

5.15. Give an example showing that the recovery manager could encounter several nonquiescent checkpoint records during recovery. What is the best way for it to handle the nonquiescent checkpoint records it finds after the first one?

5.16. Explain why the recovery manager could not encounter both a nonquiescent and a quiescent checkpoint record during recovery.

5.17. Consider the recovery algorithm of Fig. 5.6. Step 1c doesn't undo a value for transactions that have been rolled back.

(a) Explain why this is a correct thing to do.
(b) Would the algorithm be correct if it did undo those values? Explain.

5.18. When the `rollback` method needs to restore the original contents of a value, it writes the page directly and doesn't request any kind of lock. Can this cause a non-serializable conflict with another transaction? Explain.

5.19. Explain why it is not possible to have a recovery algorithm that combines the techniques of undo-only and redo-only recovery. That is, explain why it is necessary to keep either undo information or redo information.

5.20. Suppose that the recovery manager finds the following records in the log file when the system restarts after a crash.

```
<START, 1>
<START, 2>
<SETSTRING, 2, junk, 33, 0, abc, def>
<SETSTRING, 1, junk, 44, 0, abc, xyz>
<START, 3>
<COMMIT, 2>
<SETSTRING, 3, junk, 33, 0, def, joe>
<START, 4>
<SETSTRING, 4, junk, 55, 0, abc, sue>
<NQCKPT, 1, 3, 4>
<SETSTRING, 4, junk, 55, 0, sue, max>
<START, 5>
<COMMIT, 4>
```

(a) Assuming undo-redo recovery, indicate what changes to the database will be performed.
(b) Assuming undo-only recovery, indicate what changes to the database will be performed.
(c) Is it possible for transaction T1 to have committed, even though it has no commit record in the log?
(d) Is it possible for transaction T1 to have modified a buffer containing block 23?
(e) Is it possible for transaction T1 to have modified block 23 on disk?
(f) Is it possible for transaction T1 to have not modified a buffer containing block 44?

5.21. Is a serial schedule always serializable? Is a serializable schedule always serial? Explain.

5.22. This exercise asks you to examine the need for non-serial schedules.
(a) Suppose that the database is much larger than the size of the buffer pool. Explain why the database system will handle transactions more quickly if it can execute the transactions concurrently.
(b) Conversely, explain why concurrency is less important if the database fits into the buffer pool.

5.23. The *get/set* methods in the SimpleDB class `Transaction` obtain a lock on the specified block. Why don't they unlock the block when they are done?

5.24. Consider Fig. 5.3. Give the history of the transaction if files are the element of concurrency.

5.25. Consider the following two transactions and their histories:

```
T1: W(b1); R(b2); W(b1); R(b3); W(b3); R(b4); W(b2)
T2: R(b2); R(b3); R(b1); W(b3); R(b4); W(b4)
```

(a) Give a serializable non-serial schedule for these transactions.
(b) Add lock and unlock actions to these histories that satisfy the lock protocol.
(c) Give a non-serial schedule corresponding to these locks that deadlocks.
(d) Show that there is no non-deadlocked non-serial serializable schedule for these transactions that obeys the lock protocol.

5.26. Give an example schedule which is serializable but has conflicting write-write operations that do not affect the order in which the transactions commit. (*Hint*: Some of the conflicting operations will not have corresponding read operations.)

5.27. Show that if all transactions obey the two-phase locking protocol, then all schedules are serializable.

5.28. Show that the waits-for graph has a cycle if and only if there is a deadlock.

5.29. Suppose that a transaction manager maintains a waits-for graph in order to accurately detect deadlocks. Section 5.4.4 suggested that the transaction manager roll back the transaction whose request caused the cycle in the graph. Other possibilities are to roll back the oldest transaction in the cycle, the newest transaction in the cycle, the transaction holding the most locks, or the transaction holding the fewest locks. Which possibility makes the most sense to you? Explain.

5.30. Suppose in SimpleDB that transaction T currently has a shared lock on a block and calls `setInt` on it. Give a scenario in which this will cause a deadlock.

5.31. Consider the `ConcurrencyTest` class of Fig. 5.19. Give a schedule that causes deadlock.

5.32. Consider the locking scenario described for Fig. 5.19. Draw the different states of the waits-for graph as locks are requested and released.

5.33. A variant of the *wait-die* protocol is called *wound-wait* and is as follows:

- If T1 has a lower number than T2, then T2 is aborted (i.e., T1 "wounds" T2).
- If T1 has a higher number than T2, then T1 waits for the lock.

The idea is that if an older transaction needs a lock held by a younger one, then it simply kills the younger one and takes the lock.

(a) Show that this protocol prevents deadlock.
(b) Compare the relative benefits of the *wait-die* and *wound-wait* protocols.

5.34. In the *wait-die* deadlock detection protocol, a transaction is aborted if it requests a lock held by an older transaction. Suppose you modified the protocol so that transactions are aborted instead if they request a lock held by a younger transaction. This protocol would also detect deadlocks. How does this revised protocol compare to the original one? Which would you prefer the transaction manager to use? Explain.

5.35. Explain why the lock/unlock methods in class `LockTable` are synchronized. What bad thing could happen if they were not?

5.36. Suppose that a database system uses files as concurrency elements. Explain why phantoms are not possible.

5.37. Give an algorithm for deadlock detection that also handles transactions waiting for buffers.

5.38. Rewrite the algorithm for multiversion locking so that the concurrency manager only makes one pass through the log file.

5.39. The read-committed transaction isolation level purports to reduce a transaction's waiting time by releasing its slocks early. At first glance, it is not obvious why a transaction would wait less by releasing locks that it already has. Explain the advantages of early lock release and give illustrative scenarios.

5.40. The method `nextTransactionNumber` is the only method in `Transaction` that is synchronized. Explain why synchronization is not necessary for the other methods.

5.41. Consider the SimpleDB class `Transaction`.

(a) Can a transaction pin a block without locking it?
(b) Can a transaction lock a block without pinning it?

Programming Exercises

5.42. A SimpleDB transaction acquires an slock on a block whenever a `getInt` or `getString` method is called. Another possibility is for the transaction to acquire the slock when the block is pinned, under the assumption that you don't pin a block unless you intend to look at its contents.

(a) Implement this strategy.
(b) Compare the benefits of this strategy with that of SimpleDB. Which do you prefer and why?

5.43. After recovery, the log is not needed except for archival purposes. Revise the SimpleDB code so that the log file is saved to a separate directory after recovery, and a new empty log file is begun.

5.44. Revise the SimpleDB recovery manager so that it undoes an update record only when necessary.

5.45. Revise SimpleDB so that it uses blocks as the elements of recovery. A possible strategy is to save a copy of a block the first time a transaction modifies it. The copy could be saved in a separate file, and the update log record could hold the block number of the copy. You will also need to write methods that can copy blocks between files.

5.46. Implement a static method in class `Transaction` that performs quiescent checkpointing. Decide how the method will get invoked (e.g., every `N` transactions, every `N` seconds, or manually). You will need to revise `Transaction` as follows:

- Use a static variable to hold all currently active transactions.
- Revise the constructor of `Transaction` to see if a checkpoint is being performed and, if so, to place itself on a wait list until the checkpoint procedure completes.

5.47. Implement nonquiescent checkpointing using the strategy described in the text.

5.48. Suppose a transaction appends a lot of blocks to a file, writes a bunch of values to these blocks, and then rolls back. The new blocks will be restored to their initial condition, but they themselves will not be deleted from the file. Modify SimpleDB so that they will. (*Hint*: You can take advantage of the fact that only one transaction at a time can be appending to a file, which means that the file can be truncated during rollback. You will need to add to the file manager the ability to truncate a file.)

5.49. Log records could also be used for auditing a system as well as recovery. For auditing, the record needs to store the date when the activity occurred, as well as the IP address of the client.

(a) Revise the SimpleDB log records in this way.

(b) Design and implement a class whose methods support common auditing tasks, such as finding when a block was last modified, or what activity occurred by a particular transaction or from a particular IP address.

5.50. Each time the server starts up, transaction numbers begin again at 0. This means that throughout the history of the database, there will be multiple transactions having the same number.

(a) Explain why this non-uniqueness of transaction numbers is not a significant problem.
(b) Revise SimpleDB so that transaction numbers continue from the last time the server was running.

5.51. Revise SimpleDB so that it uses undo-redo recovery.
5.52. Implement deadlock detection in SimpleDB using:

(a) The *wait-die* protocol given in the text
(b) The *wound-wait* protocol given in Exercise 5.33

5.53. Revise the lock table so that it uses individual wait lists for each block. (So `notifyAll` only touches the threads waiting on the same lock.)
5.54. Revise the lock table so that it keeps its own explicit wait list(s) and chooses itself which transactions to notify when a lock becomes available. (i.e., it uses the Java method *notify* instead of `notifyAll`.)
5.55. Revise the SimpleDB concurrency manager so that:

(a) Files are the elements of concurrency.
(b) Values are the elements of concurrency. (*Warning*: You will still need to keep the methods `size` and `append` from causing conflicts.)

5.56. Write test programs:

(a) To verify that the recovery manager works (commit, rollback, and recovery)
(b) To more completely test the lock manager
(c) To test the entire transaction manager

Chapter 6
Record Management

The transaction manager is able to read and write values at specified locations on a disk block. However, it has no idea what values are in a block nor where those values might be located. This responsibility belongs to the record manager. It organizes a file into a collection of records and has methods for iterating through the records and placing values in them. This chapter studies the functionality provided by the record manager and the techniques used to implement that functionality.

6.1 Designing a Record Manager

A record manager must address several issues, such as:

- Should each record be placed entirely within one block?
- Will all of the records in a block be from the same table?
- Is each field representable using a predetermined number of bytes?
- Where should each field value be positioned within its record?

This section discusses these issues and their trade-offs.

6.1.1 Spanned Versus Unspanned Records

Suppose that the record manager needs to insert four 300-byte records into a file, where the block size is 1000 bytes. Three records fit nicely into the first 900 bytes of the block. But what should the record manager do with the fourth record? Figure 6.1 depicts two options.

In Fig. 6.1a, the record manager creates a *spanned record*, that is, a record whose values span two or more blocks. It stores the first 100 bytes of the record in the

E. Sciore, *Database Design and Implementation*, Data-Centric Systems and Applications, https://doi.org/10.1007/978-3-030-33836-7_6

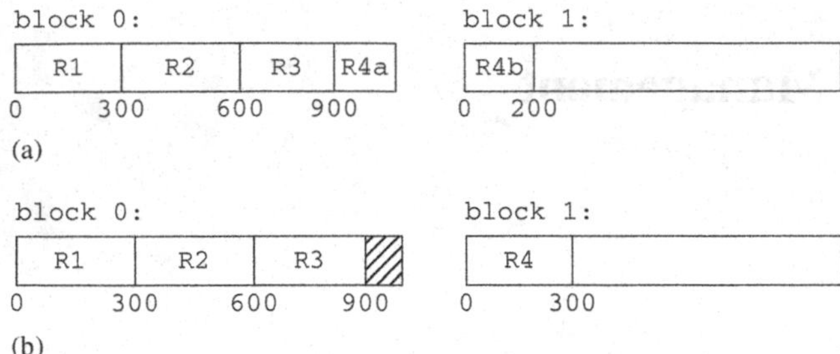

Fig. 6.1 Spanned versus unspanned records. (**a**) Record R4 spans blocks 0 and 1, (**b**) record R4 is stored entirely in block 1

existing block and the next 200 bytes of the record in a new block. In Fig. 6.1b, the record manager stores the entire fourth record in a new block.

The record manager has to decide whether to create spanned records or not. A disadvantage of unspanned records is that they waste disk space. In Fig. 6.1b, 100 bytes (or 10%) of each block is wasted. An even worse case would be if each record contained 501 bytes—then a block could contain only 1 record, and nearly 50% of its space would be wasted. Another disadvantage is that the size of an unspanned record is limited to the block size. If records can be larger than a block, then spanning is necessary.

The main disadvantage of spanned records is that they increase the complexity of record access. Because a spanned record is split among several blocks, multiple block accesses will required to read it. Moreover, the spanned record may need to be reconstructed from these blocks by reading it into a separate area of memory.

6.1.2 Homogeneous Versus Nonhomogeneous Files

A file is *homogeneous* if all its records come from the same table. The record manager must decide whether or not to allow nonhomogeneous files. The trade-off is again one of efficiency versus flexibility.

For example, consider the STUDENT and DEPT tables from Fig. 1.1. A homogeneous implementation would place all STUDENT records in one file and all DEPT records in another file. This placement makes single-table SQL queries easy to answer—the record manager needs to scan only through the blocks of one file. However, multi-table queries become less efficient. Consider a query that joins these two tables, such as "Find the names of students and their major departments." The record manager will have to search back and forth between the blocks of STUDENT records and the blocks of DEPT records (as will be discussed in Chap. 8), looking for matching records. Even if the query could be performed without excess searching (e.g., via an index join of Chap. 12), the disk drive will still have to seek repeatedly as it alternates between reading the STUDENT and DEPT blocks.

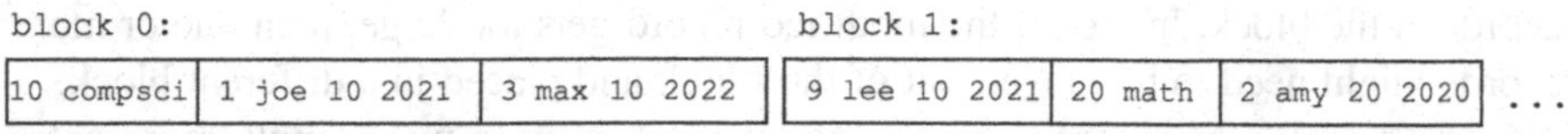

block 0:			block 1:			
10 compsci	1 joe 10 2021	3 max 10 2022	9 lee 10 2021	20 math	2 amy 20 2020	...

Fig. 6.2 Clustered, nonhomogeneous records

A nonhomogeneous organization would store the STUDENT and DEPT records in the same file, with the record for each student stored near the record for its major department. Figure 6.2 depicts the first two blocks of such an organization, assuming three records per block. The file consists of a DEPT record, followed by the STUDENT records having that department as a major. This organization requires fewer block accesses to calculate the join, because the joined records are *clustered* on the same (or a nearby) block.

Clustering improves the efficiency of queries that join the clustered tables because the matching records are stored together. However, clustering will cause single-table queries to become less efficient because the records for each table are spread out over more blocks. Similarly, joins with other tables will also be less efficient. Thus clustering is effective only if the most heavily used queries perform the join encoded by the clustering.[1]

6.1.3 Fixed-Length Versus Variable-Length Fields

Every field in a table has a defined type. Based on that type, the record manager decides whether to implement the field using a *fixed-length* or *variable-length* representation. A fixed-length representation uses exactly the same number of bytes to store each of the field's values, whereas a variable-length representation expands and contracts based on the data value stored.

Most types are naturally fixed-length. For example, both integers and floating-point numbers can be stored as 4-byte binary values. In fact, all numeric and date/time types have natural fixed-length representations. The Java type `String` is the prime example of a type that needs a variable-length representation, because character strings can be arbitrarily long.

Variable-length representations can cause significant complications. Consider, for example, a record sitting in the middle of a block packed with records, and suppose that you modify one of its field values. If the field is fixed-length, then the record will remain the same size, and the field can be modified in place. However, if the field is variable-length, then the record may get larger. In order to make room for the larger record, the record manager may have to rearrange the location of the

[1]In fact, clustering is the fundamental organizational principle behind the early hierarchical database systems, such as IBM's *IMS* system. Databases that are naturally understood hierarchically can be implemented very efficiently in such systems.

records in the block. In fact, if the modified record gets too large, then one or more records might need to be moved out of the block and placed in a different block.

Consequently, the record manager tries its best to use a fixed-length representation whenever possible. For example, a record manager can choose from three different representations of a string field:

- A variable-length representation, in which the record manager allocates the exact amount of space in the record that the string requires
- A fixed-length representation, in which the record manager stores the string in a location outside of the record and keeps a fixed-length reference to that location in the record
- A fixed-length representation, in which the record manager allocates the same amount of space in the record for each string, regardless of its length

These representations are depicted in Fig. 6.3. Part (a) shows three COURSE records, where the `Title` field is implemented using a variable-length representation. These records are space-efficient but have the problems just discussed.

Part (b) shows the same three records, but with the `Title` strings placed in a separate "string area." This area could be a separate file or (if the strings are very large) a directory in which each string is stored in its own file. In either case, the field contains a reference to the string's location in that area. This representation results in records that are both fixed-length and small. Small records are good, because they can be stored in fewer blocks and thus require fewer block accesses. The downside to this representation is that retrieving the string value from a record requires an additional block access.

Part (c) shows two of the records, implemented using a fixed-length `Title` field. This implementation has the advantage that the records are fixed-length and the strings are stored in the record. However, the downside is that some records will be larger than they need to be. If there is a wide difference in string sizes, then this

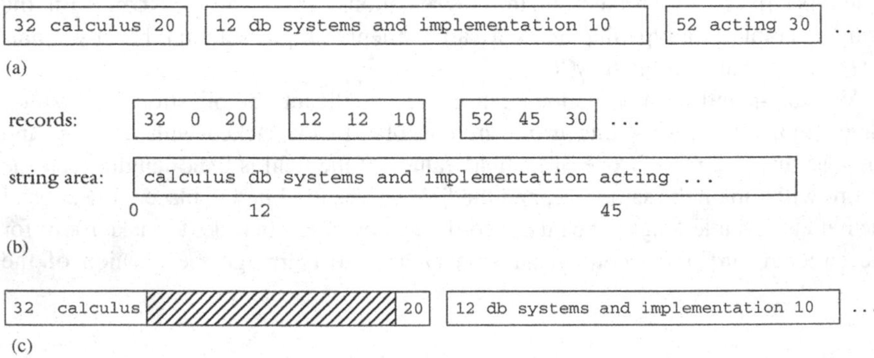

Fig. 6.3 Alternative representations for the `Title` field in COURSE records. (**a**) Allocating exactly as much space as each string needs, (**b**) storing the strings in a separate location. (**c**) allocating the same amount of space for each string

wasted space will be significant, resulting in a larger file and correspondingly more block accesses.

None of these representations are clearly better than the others. As a way to help the record manager choose the proper representation, standard SQL provides three different string datatypes: `char`, `varchar`, and `clob`. The type `char(n)` specifies strings of exactly `n` characters. The types `varchar(n)` and `clob(n)` specify strings of at most `n` characters. Their difference is the expected size of `n`. In `varchar(n)`, `n` is reasonably small, say no more than 4K. On the other hand, the value of `n` in `clob(n)` can be in the giga-character range. (The acronym CLOB stands for "character large object.") For an example of a `clob` field, suppose that the university database adds a field `Syllabus` to its SECTION table, with the idea that the values of this field would contain the text of each section's syllabus. Assuming that syllabi can be no more than 8000 characters, you could reasonably define the field as `clob(8000)`.

Fields of type `char` most naturally correspond to Fig. 6.3c. Since all strings will be the same length, there is no wasted space inside the records, and the fixed-length representation will be most efficient.

Fields of type `varchar(n)` most naturally correspond to Fig. 6.3a. Since `n` will be relatively small, placing the string inside the record will not make the record too large. Moreover, the variance in string sizes means that the fixed-length representation would waste space. Thus, the variable-length representation is the best alternative.

If `n` happens to be small (say, less than 20), then the record manager might choose to implement a `varchar` field using the third representation. The reason is that the wasted space will be insignificant compared to the benefits of a fixed-length representation.

Fields of type `clob` correspond to Fig. 6.3b, because that representation handles large strings the best. By storing the large string outside of the record, the records themselves become smaller and more manageable.

6.1.4 Placing Fields in Records

The record manager determines the structure of its records. For fixed-length records, it determines the location of each field within the record. The most straightforward strategy is to store the fields next to each other. The size of the record then becomes the sum of the sizes of the fields, and the offset of each field is the end of the previous field.

This strategy of tightly packing fields into records is appropriate for Java-based systems (like SimpleDB and Derby) but can cause problems elsewhere. The issue has to do with ensuring that values are aligned properly in memory. In most computers, the machine code to access an integer requires that the integer be stored in a memory location that is a multiple of 4; the integer is said to be *aligned* on a 4-byte boundary. The record manager must therefore ensure that every integer in every page is aligned on a 4-byte boundary. Since OS pages are always aligned on a 2^N-byte boundary for some reasonably large N, the first byte of each page will be properly aligned. Thus, the record manager must simply make sure that the offset of each integer within each page is a multiple of 4. If the previous field ended at a location that is not a multiple of 4, then the record manager must *pad* it with enough bytes so that it does.

For example, consider the STUDENT table, which consists of three integer fields and a `varchar(10)` string field. The integer fields are multiples of 4, so they don't need to be padded. The string field, however, requires 14 bytes (assuming the SimpleDB representation of Sect. 3.5.2); it therefore needs to be padded with 2 additional bytes so that the field following it will be aligned on a multiple of 4.

In general, different types may require different amounts of padding. Double-precision floating point numbers, for example, are usually aligned on an 8-byte boundary, and small integers are usually aligned on a 2-byte boundary. The record manager is responsible for ensuring these alignments. A simple strategy is to position the fields in the order that they were declared, padding each field to ensure the proper alignment of the next field. A more clever strategy is to reorder the fields so that the least amount of padding is required. For example, consider the following SQL table declaration:

```
create table T (A smallint, B double precision, C smallint, D int, E int)
```

Suppose the fields are stored in the order given. Then field A needs to be padded with 6 extra bytes and field C needs to be padded with 2 extra bytes, leading to a record length of 28 bytes; see Fig. 6.4a. On the other hand, if the fields are stored in the order [B, D, A, C, E], then no padding is required, and the record length is only 20 bytes, as shown in Fig. 6.4b.

In addition to padding fields, the record manager must also pad each record. The idea is that each record needs to end on a k-byte boundary, where k is the largest supported alignment, so that every record in a page has the same alignment as the first one. Consider again the field placement of Fig. 6.4a, which has a record length of 28 bytes. Suppose that the first record begins at byte 0 of the block. Then the second record will start at byte 28 of the block, which means that field B of the second record will start at byte 36 of the block, which is the wrong alignment. It is essential that each record begin on an 8-byte boundary. In the example of Fig. 6.4, the records of both part (a) and part (b) need to be padded with 4 additional bytes.

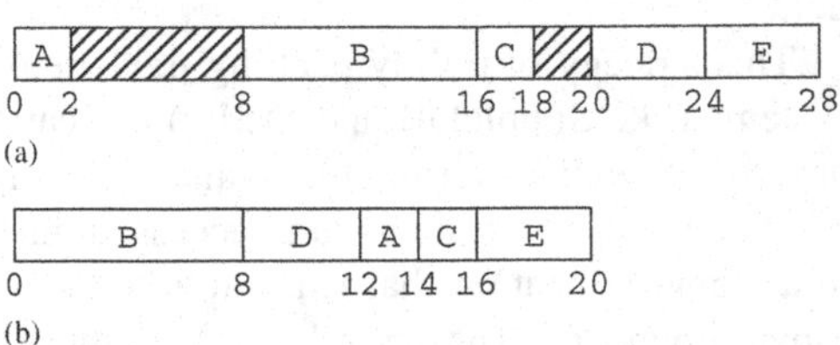

Fig. 6.4 Placing fields in a record to establish alignment. (**a**) A placement that requires padding, (**b**) a placement that needs no padding

A Java program does not need to consider padding because it cannot directly access numeric values in a byte array. For example, the Java method to read an integer from a page is `ByteBuffer.getInt`. This method does not call a machine-code instruction to obtain the integer but instead constructs the integer itself from the 4 specified bytes of the array. This activity is less efficient than a single machine-code instruction, but it avoids alignment issues.

6.2 Implementing a File of Records

The previous section considered the various decisions that the record manager must address. This section considers how these decisions get implemented. It begins with the most straightforward implementation: a file containing homogeneous, unspanned, fixed-length records. It then considers how other design decisions affect this implementation.

6.2.1 A Straightforward Implementation

Suppose you want to create a file of homogeneous, unspanned, fixed-length records. The fact that the records are unspanned means that you can treat the file as a sequence of blocks, where each block contains its own records. The fact that the records are homogeneous and fixed-length means that you can allocate the same amount of space for each record within a block. In other words, you can think of each block as an *array of records*. SimpleDB calls such a block a *record page*.

A record manager can implement record pages as follows. It divides a block into *slots*, where each slot is large enough to hold a record plus one additional byte. The value of this byte is a flag that denotes whether the slot is empty or in use; let's say that a 0 means "empty" and a 1 means "in use."[2]

For example, suppose that the block size is 400 and the record size is 26; then each slot is 27 bytes long, and the block holds 14 slots with 22 bytes of wasted space. Figure 6.5 depicts this situation. This figure shows 4 of the 14 slots; slots 0 and 13 currently contain records, whereas slots 1 and 2 are empty.

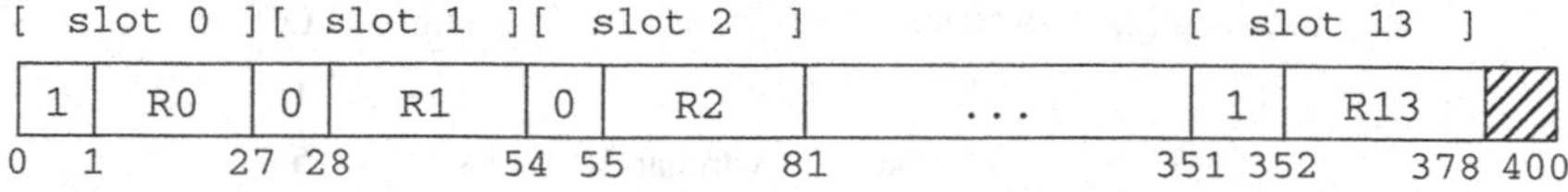

Fig. 6.5 A record page with space for 14 26-byte records

[2]You can improve the space usage by only using a bit to hold each empty/inuse flag. See Exercise 6.7.

The record manager needs to be able to insert, delete, and modify records in a record page. To do so, it uses the following information about the records:

- The size of a slot
- The name, type, length, and offset of each field of a record

These values constitute the record's *layout*. For an example, consider the table STUDENT as defined in Fig. 2.4. A STUDENT record contains three integers plus a ten-character *varchar* field. Assuming the storage strategy of SimpleDB, each integer requires 4 bytes and a ten-character string requires 14 bytes. Let's also assume that padding is not necessary, that `varchar` fields are implemented by allocating fixed space for the largest possible string, and that the empty/inuse flag takes up one byte at the beginning of each slot. Figure 6.6 gives the resulting layout of this table.

Given a layout, the record manager can determine the location of each value within the page. The record in slot `k` begins at location `RL*k`, where `RL` is the record length. The empty/inuse flag for that record is at location `RL*k`, and the value of its field `F` is at location `RL*k+Offset(F)`.

The record manager can process insertions, deletions, modifications, and retrievals quite easily:

- To insert a new record, the record manager examines the empty/inuse flag of each slot until it finds a 0. It then sets the flag to 1 and returns the location of that slot. If all flag values are 1, then the block is full and insertion is not possible.
- To delete a record, the record manager simply sets its empty/inuse flag to 0.
- To modify a field value of a record (or to initialize a field of a new record), the record manager determines the location of that field and writes the value to that location.
- To retrieve the records in the page, the record manager examines the empty/inuse flag of each slot. Each time it finds a 1, it knows that that slot contains an existing record.

The record manager also needs a way to identify a record within a record page. When records are fixed-length, the most straightforward record identifier is its slot number.

Slot Size: 27

Field Information:

Name	Type	Length	Offset
SId	int	4	1
SName	varchar(10)	14	5
GradYear	int	4	19
MajorId	int	4	23

Fig. 6.6 The layout of STUDENT

6.2.2 Implementing Variable-Length Fields

The implementation of fixed-length fields is very straightforward. This section considers how the introduction of variable-length fields affects that implementation.

One issue is that the field offsets in a record are no longer fixed. In particular, the offsets of all fields following a variable-length field will differ from record to record. The only way to determine the offset of those fields is to read the previous field and see where it ends. If the first field in a record is variable-length, then it will be necessary to read the first `n-1` fields of the record in order to determine the offset of the `nth` field. Consequently, the record manager typically places the fixed-length fields at the beginning of each record so that they can be accessed by a precomputed offset. The variable-length fields are placed at the end of the record. The first variable-length field will have a fixed offset, but the remaining ones will not.

Another issue is that modifying a field value can cause a record's length to change. If the new value is larger, then the block contents to the right of the modified value must be shifted to make room. In extreme cases, the shifted records will spill out of the block; this situation must be handled by allocating an *overflow block*.

An overflow block is a new block allocated from an area known as the *overflow area*. Any record that spills out of the original block is removed from that block and added to an overflow block. If many such modifications occur, then a chain of several overflow blocks may be necessary. Each block will contain a reference to the next overflow block on the chain. Conceptually, the original and overflow blocks form a single (large) record page.

For example, consider the COURSE table, and suppose that course titles are saved as variable-length strings. Figure 6.7a depicts a block containing the first three records of the table. (The `Title` field has been moved to the end of the record because the other fields are fixed-length.) Figure 6.7b depicts the result of modifying the title "DbSys" to "Database Systems Implementation." Assuming a block size of 80 bytes, the third record no longer fits in the block, and so it is placed in an overflow block. The original block contains a reference to that overflow block.

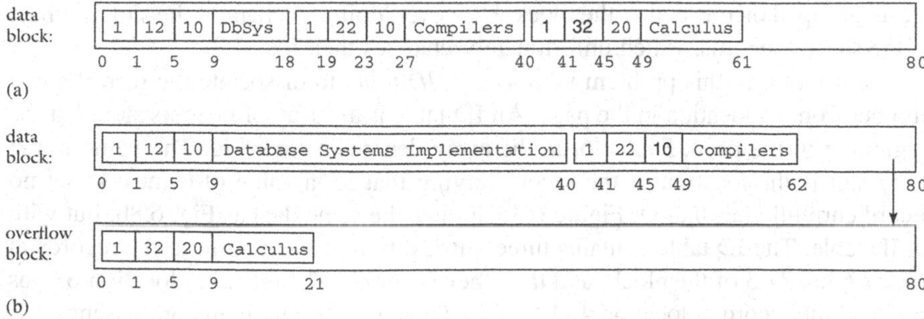

Fig. 6.7 Using an overflow block to implement variable-length records. (**a**) The original block, (**b**) the result of modifying the title of course 12

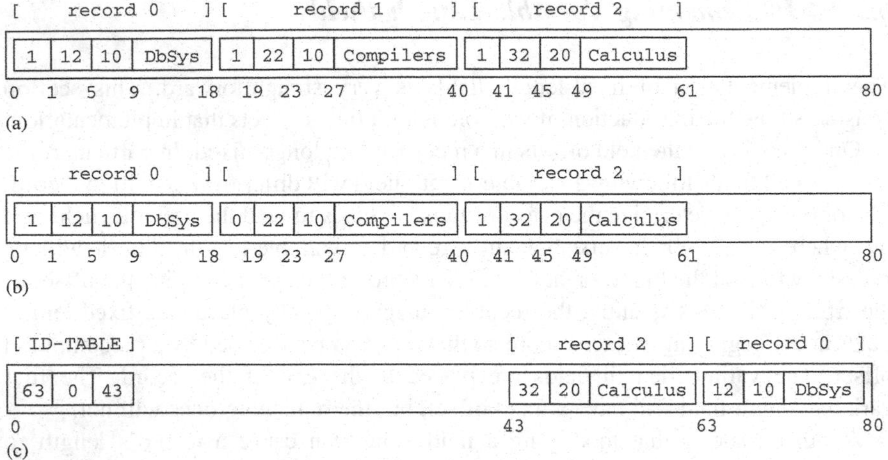

Fig. 6.8 Using an ID table to implement variable-length records. (**a**) The original block, (**b**) the straightforward way to delete record 1, (**c**) using an ID table to delete record 1

A third issue concerns the use of the slot number as a record identifier. It is no longer possible to multiply the slot number by the slot size, as with fixed-length records. The only way to find the beginning of a record having a given id is to read the records starting from the beginning of the block.

The use of the slot number as a record identifier also complicates record insertions. Figure 6.8 illustrates the issue.

Part (a) depicts a block containing the first three COURSE records, the same as in Fig. 6.7a. Deleting the record for course 22 sets the flag to 0 (for "empty") and leaves the record intact, as shown in Part (b). This space is now available for insertion. However, a record can be inserted into the space only if its `Title` field has nine or fewer characters. In general, a new record might not fit into the block even though there are numerous empty spaces left by smaller deleted records. The block is said to be *fragmented*.

A way to reduce this fragmentation is to shift the remaining records so that they are all grouped on one end of the block. However, doing so changes the slot numbers of the shifted records, which unfortunately changes their ids.

The solution to this problem is to use an *ID table* to dissociate the record's slot number from its location in the page. An ID table is an array of integers stored at the beginning of the page. Each slot in the array denotes a record id. The value in the array slot is the location of the record having that id; a value of 0 means that no record currently has that id. Figure 6.8c depicts the same data as Fig. 6.8b, but with an ID table. The ID table contains three entries: two of them point to the records at offsets 63 and 43 of the block, and the other is empty. The record at location 63 has id 0, and the record at location 43 has id 2. There is currently no record having id 1.

The ID table provides a level of indirection that allows the record manager to move records within a block. If the record moves, its entry in the ID table is adjusted correspondingly; if the record is deleted, its entry is set to 0. When a new record is inserted, the record manager finds an available entry in the array and assigns it as the id of the new record. In this way, the ID table allows variable-length records to be moved within a block, while providing each record with a fixed identifier.

The ID table expands as the number of records in the block increases. The size of the array is necessarily open-ended, because a block can hold a varying number of variable-length records. Typically the ID table is placed at one end of the block, and the records are placed at the other end, and they grow toward each other. This situation can be seen in Fig. 6.8c, where the first record in the block is at its far right.

An ID table makes empty/inuse flags unnecessary. A record is in use if an entry of the ID table points to it. Empty records have an id of 0 (and in fact don't even exist). The ID table also enables the record manager to quickly find each record in the block. To move to a record having a particular id, the record manager simply uses the location stored in that entry of the ID table; to move to the next record, the record manager scans the ID table until it finds the next non-zero entry.

6.2.3 Implementing Spanned Records

This section considers how spanned records can be implemented. When records are unspanned, the first record in each block always begins at the same location. With spanned records, this situation is no longer true. Consequently, the record manager must store an integer at the beginning of each block to hold the offset of the first record.

For example, consider Fig. 6.9. The first integer in block 0 is a 4, denoting that the first record R1 begins at offset 4 (i.e., immediately after the integer). Record R2 spans blocks 0 and 1, and so the first record in block 1 is R3, which begins at offset 60. Record R3 continues through block 2 into block 3. Record R4 is the first record in block 3 and begins at offset 30. Note that the first integer of block 2 is 0, denoting the fact that no record begins in that block.

The record manager can choose to split a spanned record in two different ways. The first way is to fill the block as much as possible, splitting it on the block boundary; the remaining bytes are placed into the next block(s) of the file. The second way is to write the record value by value; when the page becomes full, the writing continues on a new page. The first way has the advantage that it wastes absolutely no space but has the disadvantage of splitting a value across blocks. To access the split value, the record manager must reconstruct the value by catenating the bytes from the two blocks.

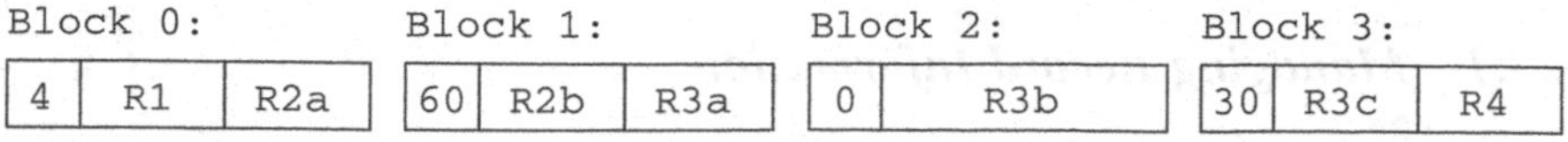

Block 0:

4	R1	R2a

Block 1:

60	R2b	R3a

Block 2:

0	R3b

Block 3:

30	R3c	R4

Fig. 6.9 Implementing spanned records

6.2.4 Implementing Nonhomogeneous Records

If the record manager supports nonhomogeneous records, then it will also need to support variable-length records, because records from different tables need not be the same size. There are two issues related to having nonhomogeneous records in a block:

- The record manager needs to know the layout of each type of record in the block.
- Given a record, the record manager needs to know which table it comes from.

The record manager can address the first issue by keeping an array of layouts, one for each possible table. The record manager can address the second issue by adding an extra value to the beginning of each record; this value, sometimes called a *tag value*, is an index into the layout array, which specifies the table that the record belongs to.

For example, consider again Fig. 6.2, which depicts nonhomogeneous blocks from the DEPT and STUDENT tables. The record manager will keep an array containing the layout information from both of these tables; let's assume that DEPT information is in index 0 of the array and STUDENT information is in index 1. Then the tag value for each record from DEPT will be 0, and the tag value for each STUDENT record will be 1.

The behavior of the record manager does not need much change. When the record manager accesses a record, it determines from the tag value which table information to use. It can then use that table to read or write to any field, the same as in the homogeneous case.

The log records in SimpleDB are an example of nonhomogeneous records. The first value of each log record is an integer that indicates the type of the log record. The recovery manager uses that value to determine how to read the rest of the record.

6.3 SimpleDB Record Pages

The next two sections examine the SimpleDB record manager, which implements the basic record manager of Sect. 6.2.1. This section covers the implementation of record pages, and the next section covers how to implement a file of record pages. Some of the end-of-chapter exercises ask you to modify it to handle other design decisions.

6.3.1 Managing Record Information

The SimpleDB record manager uses the classes *Schema* and *Layout* to manage a record's information. Their API appears in Fig. 6.10.

<u>Schema</u>

```
public Schema();
public void addField(String fldname, int type, int length);
public void addIntField(String fldname);
public void addStringField(String fldname, int length);
public void add(String fldname, Schema sch);
public void addAll(Schema sch);

public List<String> fields();
public boolean hasField(String fldname);
public int type(String fldname);
public int length(String fldname);
```

<u>Layout</u>

```
public Layout(Schema schema);
public Layout(Schema schema, Map<String,Integer> offsets,
                             int slotSize);

public Schema schema();
public int offset(String fldname);
public int slotSize();
```

Fig. 6.10 The API for SimpleDB record information

A `Schema` object holds a record's *schema*, that is, the name and type of each field, and the length of each string field. This information corresponds to what a user would specify when creating a table and contains no physical information. For example, the length of a string is the maximum number of characters allowed, not its size in bytes.

A schema can be thought of as a list of triples of the form [fieldname, type, length]. The class `Schema` contains five methods to add a triple to the list. The method `addField` adds a triple explicitly. The methods `addIntField`, `addStringField`, `add`, and `addAll` are convenience methods; the first two of these methods calculate the triple, and the last two copy triples from an existing schema. The class also has accessor methods to retrieve the collection of field names, determine if a specified field is in the collection, and retrieve the type and length of a specified field.

The class `Layout` additionally contains the physical information about a record. It calculates field and slot sizes, and the field offsets within the slot. The class has two constructors, corresponding to the two reasons for creating a `Layout` object. The first constructor is called when a table is created; it calculates the layout information based on the given schema. The second constructor is called after the table has been created; the client simply provides the previously-calculated values.

The code fragment in Fig. 6.11 illustrates the use of these two classes. The first part of the code creates a schema containing the three fields of the COURSE table

```
Schema sch = new Schema();
sch.addIntField("cid");
sch.addStringField("title", 20);
sch.addIntField("deptid");
Layout layout = new Layout(sch);

for (String fldname : layout.schema().fields()) {
   int offset = layout.offset(fldname);
   System.out.println(fldname + " has offset " + offset);
}
```

Fig. 6.11 Specifying the structure of COURSE records

and then creates a `Layout` object from it. The second part of the code prints the name and offset of each field.

6.3.2 Implementing the Schema and Layout

The code for the class `Schema` is straightforward and appears in Fig. 6.12. Internally, the class stores the triples in a map keyed on the field name. The object associated with the field name belongs to the private class `FieldInfo`, which encapsulates the length and type of the field.

Types are denoted by the constants `INTEGER` and `VARCHAR`, as defined in the JDBC class `Types`. The length of a field is only meaningful for string fields; the method `addIntField` gives integers a length value of 0, but this value is irrelevant as it will never be accessed.

The code for `Layout` appears in Fig. 6.13. The first constructor positions the fields in the order they appear in the schema. It determines the length of each field in bytes, calculates the slot size as the sum of the field lengths, adding four bytes for an integer-sized empty/inuse flag. It assigns the flag to be at offset 0 of the slot, and assigns the offset of each field to be the location at which the previous field ends (i.e., with no padding).

6.3.3 Managing the Records in a Page

The class `RecordPage` manages the records within a page. Its API appears in Fig. 6.14.

The methods `nextAfter` and `insertAfter` search the page for desired records. The `nextAfter` method returns the first used slot that follows the specified slot, skipping over any empty slots. A negative return value indicates that all remaining slots are empty. The method `insertAfter` looks for the first empty slot following the specified slot. If an empty slot is found, the method sets its flag to `USED` and returns the slot number. Otherwise, the method returns −1.

```
public class Schema {
   private List<String> fields = new ArrayList<>();
   private Map<String,FieldInfo> info = new HashMap<>();

   public void addField(String fldname, int type, int length) {
      fields.add(fldname);
      info.put(fldname, new FieldInfo(type, length));
   }

   public void addIntField(String fldname) {
      addField(fldname, INTEGER, 0);
   }

   public void addStringField(String fldname, int length) {
      addField(fldname, VARCHAR, length);
   }

   public void add(String fldname, Schema sch) {
      int type   = sch.type(fldname);
      int length = sch.length(fldname);
      addField(fldname, type, length);
   }

   public void addAll(Schema sch) {
      for (String fldname : sch.fields())
      add(fldname, sch);
   }

   public List<String> fields() {
      return fields;
   }

   public boolean hasField(String fldname) {
      return fields.contains(fldname);
   }

   public int type(String fldname) {
      return info.get(fldname).type;
   }

   public int length(String fldname) {
      return info.get(fldname).length;
   }

   class FieldInfo {
      int type, length;
      public FieldInfo(int type, int length) {
         this.type = type;
         this.length = length;
      }
   }
}
```

Fig. 6.12 The code for SimpleDB class Schema

```
public class Layout {
   private Schema schema;
   private Map<String,Integer> offsets;
   private int slotsize;

   public Layout(Schema schema) {
      this.schema = schema;
      offsets = new HashMap<>();
      int pos = Integer.BYTES; // space for the empty/inuse flag
      for (String fldname : schema.fields()) {
         offsets.put(fldname, pos);
         pos += lengthInBytes(fldname);
      }
      slotsize = pos;
   }

   public Layout(Schema schema, Map<String,Integer> offsets,
                                     int slotsize) {
      this.schema    = schema;
      this.offsets   = offsets;
      this.slotsize  = slotsize;
   }

   public Schema schema() {
      return schema;
   }

   public int offset(String fldname) {
      return offsets.get(fldname);
   }

   public int slotSize() {
      return slotsize;
   }

   private int lengthInBytes(String fldname) {
      int fldtype = schema.type(fldname);
      if (fldtype == INTEGER)
         return Integer.BYTES;
      else // fldtype == VARCHAR
         return Page.maxLength(schema.length(fldname));
   }
}
```

Fig. 6.13 The code for the SimpleDB class `Layout`

The `get/set` methods access the value of a specified field in the specified record. The `delete` method sets the record's flag to `EMPTY`. The `format` method gives default values to all record slots in the page. It sets each empty/inuse flag to `EMPTY`, all integers to 0, and all strings to `""`.

<u>*RecordPage*</u>

```
public RecordPage(Transaction tx, BlockId blk, Layout layout);
public BlockId block();

public int     getInt    (int slot, String fldname);
public String  getString(int slot, String fldname);
public void    setInt    (int slot, String fldname, int val);
public void    setString(int slot, String fldname, String val);
public void    format();
public void    delete(int slot);

public int     nextAfter(int slot);
public int     insertAfter(int slot);
```

Fig. 6.14 The API for SimpleDB record pages

The class `RecordTest` illustrates the use of the `RecordPage` methods; its code appears in Fig. 6.15. It defines a record schema having two fields: an integer field `A` and a string field `B`. It then creates a `RecordPage` object for a new block and formats it. The `for` loop uses the `insertAfter` method to fill the page with random-valued records. (Each `A`-value is a random number between 0 and 49, and the `B`-values are a string version of that number.) The two `while` loops use the `nextAfter` method to search the page. The first loop deletes selected records, and the second loop prints the contents of the remaining records.

6.3.4 Implementing Record Pages

SimpleDB implements the slotted-page structure of Fig. 6.5. The only difference is that the empty/inuse flags are implemented as 4-byte integers instead of single bytes (the reason being that SimpleDB doesn't support byte-sized values). The code for the class `RecordPage` appears in Fig. 6.16.

The private method `offset` uses the slot size to calculate the starting location of a record slot. The `get/set` methods calculate the location of their specified field by adding the offset of the field to the offset of the record. The methods `nextAfter` and `insertAfter` call the private method `searchAfter` to find a slot having the specified flag `USED` or `EMPTY`, respectively. Method `searchAfter` repeatedly increments the specified slot until it either finds a slot having the specified flag or it runs out of slots. The `delete` method sets the flag of the specified slot to `EMPTY`, and `insertAfter` sets the flag of the found slot to `USED`.

```
public class RecordTest {
   public static void main(String[] args) throws Exception {
      SimpleDB db = new SimpleDB("recordtest", 400, 8);
      Transaction tx = db.newTx();
      Schema sch = new Schema();
      sch.addIntField("A");
      sch.addStringField("B", 9);
      Layout layout = new Layout(sch);
      for (String fldname : layout.schema().fields()) {
         int offset = layout.offset(fldname);
         System.out.println(fldname + " has offset " + offset);
      }
      BlockId blk = tx.append("testfile");
      tx.pin(blk);
      RecordPage rp = new RecordPage(tx, blk, layout);
      rp.format();
      System.out.println("Filling the page with random records.");
      int slot = rp.insertAfter(-1);
      while (slot >= 0) {
         int n = (int) Math.round(Math.random() * 50);
         rp.setInt(slot, "A", n);
         rp.setString(slot, "B", "rec"+n);
         System.out.println("inserting into slot " + slot + ": {"
                              + n + ", " + "rec"+n + "}");
         slot = rp.insertAfter(slot);
      }
      System.out.println("Deleted these records with A-values < 25.");
      int count = 0;
      slot = rp.nextAfter(-1);
      while (slot >= 0) {
         int a = rp.getInt(slot, "A");
         String b = rp.getString(slot, "B");
         if (a < 25) {
            count++;
            System.out.println("slot " + slot + ": {"
                                 + a + ", " + b + "}");
            rp.delete(slot);
         }
         slot = rp.nextAfter(slot);
      }
      System.out.println(count + " values under 25 were deleted.\n");
      System.out.println("Here are the remaining records.");
      slot = rp.nextAfter(-1);
      while (slot >= 0) {
         int a = rp.getInt(slot, "A");
         String b = rp.getString(slot, "B");
         System.out.println("slot " + slot + ": {"
                              + a + ", " + b + "}");
         slot = rp.nextAfter(slot);
      }
      tx.unpin(blk);
      tx.commit();
   }
}
```

Fig. 6.15 Testing the RecordPage class

```
public class RecordPage {
   public static final int EMPTY = 0, USED = 1;
   private Transaction tx;
   private BlockId blk;
   private Layout layout;
   public RecordPage(Transaction tx, BlockId blk, Layout layout) {
      this.tx = tx;
      this.blk = blk;
      this.layout = layout;
      tx.pin(blk);
   }
   public int getInt(int slot, String fldname) {
      int fldpos = offset(slot) + layout.offset(fldname);
      return tx.getInt(blk, fldpos);
   }
   public String getString(int slot, String fldname) {
      int fldpos = offset(slot) + layout.offset(fldname);
      return tx.getString(blk, fldpos);
   }
   public void setInt(int slot, String fldname, int val) {
      int fldpos = offset(slot) + layout.offset(fldname);
      tx.setInt(blk, fldpos, val, true);
   }
   public void setString(int slot, String fldname, String val) {
      int fldpos = offset(slot) + layout.offset(fldname);
      tx.setString(blk, fldpos, val, true);
   }
   public void delete(int slot) {
      setFlag(slot, EMPTY);
   }
   public void format() {
      int slot = 0;
      while (isValidSlot(slot)) {
         tx.setInt(blk, offset(slot), EMPTY, false);
         Schema sch = layout.schema();
         for (String fldname : sch.fields()) {
            int fldpos = offset(slot) + layout.offset(fldname);
            if (sch.type(fldname) == INTEGER)
               tx.setInt(blk, fldpos, 0, false);
            else
               tx.setString(blk, fldpos, "", false);
         }
         slot++;
      }
   }
```

Fig. 6.16 The code for the SimpleDB class RecordPage

```
   public int nextAfter(int slot) {
      return searchAfter(slot, USED);
   }
   public int insertAfter(int slot) {
      int newslot = searchAfter(slot, EMPTY);
      if (newslot >= 0)
         setFlag(newslot, USED);
      return newslot;
   }
   public BlockId block() {
      return blk;
   }
   // Private auxiliary methods
   private void setFlag(int slot, int flag) {
      tx.setInt(blk, offset(slot), flag, true);
   }
   private int searchAfter(int slot, int flag) {
      slot++;
      while (isValidSlot(slot)) {
         if (tx.getInt(blk, offset(slot)) == flag)
            return slot;
         slot++;
      }
      return -1;
   }
   private boolean isValidSlot(int slot) {
      return offset(slot+1) <= tx.blockSize();
   }
   private int offset(int slot) {
      return slot * layout.slotSize();
   }
}
```

Fig. 6.16 (continued)

6.4 SimpleDB Table Scans

A record page manages a block of records. This section examines *table scans*, which store arbitrarily many records in multiple blocks of a file.

6.4.1 *Table Scans*

The `TableScan` class manages the records in a table. Its API is given in Fig. 6.17.

A `TableScan` object keeps track of a *current record*, and its methods change the current record and access its contents. The method `beforeFirst` positions the current record before the first record of the file, and `next` positions the current record at the next record in the file. If the current block has no more records, then

```
TableScan
   public TableScan(Transaction tx, String tblname,
                                    Layout layout);

   public void    close();
   public boolean hasField(String fldname);

   // methods that establish the current record
   public void    beforeFirst();
   public boolean next();
   public void    moveToRid(RID r);
   public void    insert();

   // methods that access the current record
   public int     getInt(String fldname);
   public String  getString(String fldname);
   public void    setInt(String fldname, int val);
   public void    setString(String fldname, String val);
   public RID     currentRid();
   public void    delete();

RID
   public RID(int blknum, int slot);
   public int     blockNumber();
   public int     slot();
```

Fig. 6.17 The API for SimpleDB table scans

`next` will read succeeding blocks in the file until another record is found. If no more records can be found, then the call to `next` returns `false`.

The `get/set` and `delete` methods apply to the current record. The `insert` method inserts a new record somewhere in the file, starting with the current record's block. Unlike the insertion method of `RecordPage`, this insertion method always succeeds; if it cannot find a place to insert the record in the existing blocks of the file, it appends a new block to the file and inserts the record there.

Each record in a file can be identified by a pair of values: its block number in the file and its slot within the block. These two values are known as a *record identifier* (or *rid*). The class `RID` implements these record identifiers. Its class constructor saves the two values; the accessor methods `blockNumber` and `slot` retrieves them.

The `TableScan` class contains two methods that interact with rids. The method `moveToRid` positions the current record at the specified rid, and the method `currentRid` returns the rid of the current record.

The `TableScan` class provides a level of abstraction significantly different from the other classes you have seen so far. That is, the methods of `Page`, `Buffer`, `Transaction`, and `RecordPage` all apply to a particular block. The `TableScan` class, on the other hand, hides the block structure from its clients. In general, a client will not know (or care) which block is currently being accessed.

```
public class TableScanTest {
   public static void main(String[] args) throws Exception {
      SimpleDB db = new SimpleDB("tabletest", 400, 8);
      Transaction tx = db.newTx();
      Schema sch = new Schema();
      sch.addIntField("A");
      sch.addStringField("B", 9);
      Layout layout = new Layout(sch);
      for (String fldname : layout.schema().fields()) {
         int offset = layout.offset(fldname);
         System.out.println(fldname + " has offset " + offset);
      }
      TableScan ts = new TableScan(tx, "T", layout);
      System.out.println("Filling the table with 50 random records.");
      ts.beforeFirst();
      for (int i=0; i<50;  i++) {
         ts.insert();
         int n = (int) Math.round(Math.random() * 50);
         ts.setInt("A", n);
         ts.setString("B", "rec"+n);
         System.out.println("inserting into slot " + ts.getRid() + ": {"
                            + n + ", " + "rec"+n + "}");
      }
      System.out.println("Deleting records with A-values < 25.");
      int count = 0;
      ts.beforeFirst();
      while (ts.next()) {
         int a = ts.getInt("A");
         String b = ts.getString("B");
         if (a < 25) {
            count++;
            System.out.println("slot " + ts.getRid() + ": {"
                               + a + ", " + b + "}");
            ts.delete();
         }
      }
      System.out.println(count + " values under 10 were deleted.\n");
      System.out.println("Here are the remaining records.");
      ts.beforeFirst();
      while (ts.next()) {
         int a = ts.getInt("A");
         String b = ts.getString("B");
         System.out.println("slot " + ts.getRid() +
                            ": {" + a + ", " + b + "}");
      }
      ts.close();
      tx.commit();
   }
}
```

Fig. 6.18 Testing the table scan

The class `TableScanTest` in Fig. 6.18 illustrates the use of table scans. The code is similar to `RecordTest`, except that it inserts 50 records into the file. The calls to `ts.insert` will allocate as many new blocks as necessary to hold the records. In this case, three blocks will be allocated (at 18 records per block). However, the code has no idea that this is happening. If you run this code multiple times, you will observe that another 50 records are inserted into the file and that they fill in the slots abandoned by the previously deleted records.

6.4.2 Implementing Table Scans

The code for class `TableScan` appears in Fig. 6.19. A `TableScan` object holds the record page for its current block. The `get/set/delete` methods simply call the corresponding method of the record page. The private method `moveToBlock` is called when the current block changes; that method closes the current record page and opens another one for the specified block, positioned before the its first slot.

The algorithm for the `next` method is as follows:

1. Move to the next record in the current record page.
2. If there are no more records in that page, then move to the next block of the file and get its next record.
3. Continue until either a next record is found or the end of the file is encountered.

It is possible for multiple blocks of a file to be empty (see Exercise 6.2), so a call to `next` may need to loop through several blocks.

The `insert` method tries to insert a new record starting after the current record. If the current block is full, then it moves to the next one and continues until it finds an empty slot. If all blocks are full, then it appends a new block to the file and inserts the record there.

`TableScan` implements the interface `UpdateScan` (and also `Scan`, by extension). These interfaces are central to the execution of queries and will be discussed in Chap. 8. The methods `getVal` and `setVal` are also discussed in Chap. 8. They get and set objects of type `Constant`. A constant is an abstraction of a value type (such as `int` or `String`) and makes it easier to express a query without having to know the type of a given field.

`RID` objects are simply a combination of two integers: a block number and a slot number. The code for the class `RID` is therefore straightforward and appears in Fig. 6.20.

```
public class TableScan implements UpdateScan {
   private Transaction tx;
   private Layout layout;
   private RecordPage rp;
   private String filename;
   private int currentslot;
   public TableScan(Transaction tx, String tblname, Layout layout) {
      this.tx = tx;
      this.layout = layout;
      filename = tblname + ".tbl";
      if (tx.size(filename) == 0)
         moveToNewBlock();
      else
         moveToBlock(0);
   }
   // Methods that implement Scan
   public void close() {
      if (rp != null)
         tx.unpin(rp.block());
   }
   public void beforeFirst() {
      moveToBlock(0);
   }
   public boolean next() {
      currentslot = rp.nextAfter(currentslot);
      while (currentslot < 0) {
         if (atLastBlock())
            return false;
         moveToBlock(rp.block().number()+1);
         currentslot = rp.nextAfter(currentslot);
      }
      return true;
   }
   public int getInt(String fldname) {
      return rp.getInt(currentslot, fldname);
   }
   public String getString(String fldname) {
      return rp.getString(currentslot, fldname);
   }
   public Constant getVal(String fldname) {
      if (layout.schema().type(fldname) == INTEGER)
         return new IntConstant(getInt(fldname));
      else
         return new StringConstant(getString(fldname));
   }
   public boolean hasField(String fldname) {
      return layout.schema().hasField(fldname);
   }
   // Methods that implement UpdateScan
   public void setInt(String fldname, int val) {
```

Fig. 6.19 The code for the SimpleDB class `TableScan`

```
      rp.setInt(currentslot, fldname, val);
   }
   public void setString(String fldname, String val) {
      rp.setString(currentslot, fldname, val);
   }
   public void setVal(String fldname, Constant val) {
      if (layout.schema().type(fldname) == INTEGER)
         setInt(fldname, (Integer)val.asJavaVal());
      else
         setString(fldname, (String)val.asJavaVal());
   }
   public void insert() {
      currentslot = rp.insertAfter(currentslot);
      while (currentslot < 0) {
         if (atLastBlock())
            moveToNewBlock();
         else
            moveToBlock(rp.block().number()+1);
         currentslot = rp.insertAfter(currentslot);
      }
   }
   public void delete() {
      rp.delete(currentslot);
   }
   public void moveToRid(RID rid) {
      close();
      BlockId blk = new BlockId(filename, rid.blockNumber());
      rp = new RecordPage(tx, blk, layout);
      currentslot = rid.slot();
   }
   public RID getRid() {
      return new RID(rp.block().number(), currentslot);
   }
   // Private auxiliary methods
   private void moveToBlock(int blknum) {
      close();
      BlockId blk = new BlockId(filename, blknum);
      rp = new RecordPage(tx, blk, layout);
      currentslot = -1;
   }
   private void moveToNewBlock() {
      close();
      BlockId blk = tx.append(filename);
      rp = new RecordPage(tx, blk, layout);
      rp.format();
      currentslot = -1;
   }
   private boolean atLastBlock() {
      return rp.block().number() == tx.size(filename) - 1;
   }
}
```

Fig. 6.19 (continued)

```
public class RID {
    private int blknum;
    private int slot;

    public RID(int blknum, int slot) {
        this.blknum = blknum;
        this.slot   = slot;
    }

    public int blockNumber() {
        return blknum;
    }

    public int slot() {
        return slot;
    }

    public boolean equals(Object obj) {
        RID r = (RID) obj;
        return blknum == r.blknum && slot==r.slot;
    }

    public String toString() {
        return "[" + blknum + ", " + slot + "]";
    }
}
```

Fig. 6.20 The code for the SimpleDB class `RID`

6.5 Chapter Summary

- The record manager is the portion of the database system that stores records in a file. It has three basic responsibilities:
  - Placing fields within records
  - Placing records within blocks
  - Providing access to the records in a file

There are several issues that must be addressed when designing a record manager.

- One issue is whether to support *variable-length fields*. Fixed-length records can be implemented easily, because fields can be updated in place. Updating a variable-length field can cause records to spill out of a block and be placed into an *overflow block*.
- SQL has three different string types: `char`, `varchar`, and `clob`.
  - The `char` type is most naturally implemented using a fixed-length representation.
  - The `varchar` type is most naturally implemented using a variable-length representation.
  - The `clob` type is implemented most naturally using a fixed-length representation that stores the string in an auxiliary file.

- A common implementation technique for variable-length records is to use an *ID table*. Each entry in the table points to a record in the page. A record can move around in a page by just changing its entry in the ID table.
- A second issue is whether to create *spanned records*. Spanned records are useful because they do not waste space and allow for large records, but they are more complicated to implement.
- A third issue is whether to allow *nonhomogeneous records* in a file. Nonhomogeneous records allow related records to be *clustered* on a page. Clustering can lead to very efficient joins but tend to make other queries more expensive. The record manager can implement nonhomogeneous records by storing a *tag field* at the beginning of each record; the tag denotes the table that the record belongs to.
- A fourth issue is how to determine the offset of each field within a record. The record manager may need to pad the fields so that they are *aligned* on appropriate byte boundaries. A field in a fixed-length record has the same offset for each record. It may be necessary to search a variable-length record for the beginning of its fields.

6.6 Suggested Reading

The ideas and techniques in this chapter have been present in relational databases from the very beginning. Section 3.3 of Stonebraker et al. (1976) describes the approach taken by the first version of INGRES; this approach uses the variation of the ID table described in Sect. 6.2.2. Section 3 of Astrahan et al. (1976) describes the page structure for the early System R database system (which later became IBM's DB2 product), which stored records nonhomogeneously. Both articles discuss a broad range of implementation ideas and are well worth reading in their entirety. A more detailed discussion of these techniques, together with a C-based implementation of an example record manager, appears in Chap. 14 of Gray and Reuter (1993).

The strategy of storing each record contiguously in a page is not necessarily best. The article Ailamaki et al. (2002) advocates breaking up the records on a page and placing the values for each field together. Although this record organization doesn't change the number of disk accesses performed by the record manager, it significantly improves the performance of the CPU because its data cache is utilized more effectively. The article Stonebraker et al. (2005) goes even farther, proposing that tables should be organized by field values, that is, all of the record values for each field should be stored together. The article shows how field-based storage can be more compact than record-based storage, which can lead to more efficient queries.

An implementation strategy for very large records is described in Carey et al. (1986).

Ailamaki, A., DeWitt, D., & Hill, M. (2002). Data page layouts for relational databases on deep memory hierarchies. *VLDB Journal, 11*(3), 198–215.

Astrahan, M., Blasgen, M., Chamberlin, D., Eswaren, K., Gray, J., Griffiths, P., King, W., Lorie, R., McJones, P., Mehl, J., Putzolu, G., Traiger, I., Wade, B., &

Watson, V. (1976). System R: Relational approach to database management. *ACM Transactions on Database Systems, 1*(2), 97–137.

Carey, M., DeWitt, D., Richardson, J., & Shekita, E. (1986). Object and file management in the EXODUS extendable database system. In *Proceedings of the VLDB Conference* (pp. 91–100).

Gray, J., & Reuter, A. (1993). *Transaction processing: concepts and techniques*. San Mateo, CA: Morgan Kaufman.

Stonebraker, M., Abadi, D., Batkin, A., Chen, X., Cherniack, M., Ferreira, M., Lau, E., Lin, A., Madden, S., O'Neil, E., O'Neil, P., Rasin, A., Tran, N., & Zdonik, S. (2005). C-Store: A column-oriented DBMS. In *Proceedings of the VLDB Conference* (pp. 553–564).

Stonebraker, M., Kreps, P., Wong, E., & Held, G. (1976). The design and implementation of INGRES. *ACM Transactions on Database Systems, 1*(3), 189–222.

6.7 Exercises

Conceptual Problems

6.1. Assume that the block size is 400 bytes and that records cannot span blocks. Calculate the maximum number of records that can fit in a SimpleDB record page and the amount of wasted space in the page for each of the following slot sizes: 10 bytes, 20 bytes, 50 bytes, and 100 bytes.

6.2. Explain how the file for a table can contain blocks having no records.

6.3. Consider each table in the university database (except STUDENT).

(a) Give the layout for that table, as in Fig. 6.6. (You can use the `varchar` declarations in the demo client files or assume that all string fields are defined as `varchar(20)`.)

(b) Draw a picture of the record page(s) (as in Fig. 6.5) for each table, using the records of Fig. 1.1. As in Fig. 6.5, assume that the empty/full flag is a single byte long. Also assume a fixed-length implementation of string fields.

(c) Do part (b), but assume a variable-length implementation of string fields. Use Fig. 6.8c as a model.

(d) Revise your pictures from parts (b) and (c) to show the state of the pages after their second record has been deleted.

6.4. Another way to deal with very large strings is to not store them in the database. Instead, you could place the strings in an OS file and store the name of the file in the database. This strategy would eliminate the need for the `clob` type. Give several reasons why this strategy is not particularly good.

6.5. Suppose that you want to insert a record into a block that contains an overflow block, as in Fig. 6.7b. Is it a good idea to save the record in the overflow block? Explain.

6.6. Here is another way to implement variable-length records. Each block has two areas: a sequence of fixed-length slots (as in SimpleDB) and a place where variable-length values are stored. A record is stored in a slot. Its fixed-length values are stored with the record, and its variable-length values are stored in the value area. The record will contain the block offset where the value is located. For example, the records in Fig. 6.8a could be stored like this:

```
[   slot 0    ] [   slot 1    ] [   slot 2    ]          value area
| 1 | 12 | 10 | 71 | 1 | 22 | 10 | 58 | 1 | 32 | 20 | 46 |   Calculus Compilers DbSys   |
0  1    5    9   13  14   18   22  26  27   31   35   39     46        58       71   80
```

(a) Explain what should happen when a variable-length value gets modified. Do you need an overflow block? If so, what should it look like?
(b) Compare this storage strategy with that of ID tables. Explain the comparative benefits of each.
(c) Which implementation strategy do you prefer? Why?

6.7. Using a byte for each empty/inuse flag wastes space, since only a bit is needed. An alternative implementation strategy is to store the empty/inuse bits for each slot in a bit array at the beginning of the block. This bit array could be implemented as one or more 4-byte integers.

(a) Compare this bit array with the ID table of Fig. 6.8c.
(b) Suppose that the block size is 4K and records are assumed to be at least 15 bytes. How many integers are needed to store the bit array?
(c) Describe an algorithm for finding an empty slot to insert a new record.
(d) Describe an algorithm for finding the next non-empty record in a block.

Programming Problems

6.8. Revise the class `RecordPage` so that its block is not pinned by the constructor but instead is pinned at the beginning of each `get/set` method. Similarly, the block is unpinned at the end of each `get/set` method, thereby eliminating the need for a `close` method. Do you think this is better than the SimpleDB implementation? Explain.

6.9. Revise the record manager so that `varchar` fields have a variable-length implementation.

6.10. SimpleDB only knows how to read files in the forward direction.

(a) Revise the classes `TableScan` and `RecordPage` to support a `previous` method, as well as the method `afterLast`, which positions the current record to be after the last record in the file (or page).
(b) Revise the `TableScanTest` program to print its records in reverse order.

6.11. Revise the record manager so that records are spanned.

6.12. Revise the class `Layout` to pad string fields so that their size is always a multiple of 4.

6.13. Revise the SimpleDB record manager to handle null field values. Since it is unreasonable to use a particular integer or string value to denote a `null`, you should use flags to specify which values are null. In particular, suppose that a record contains `N` fields. Then you can store `N` additional bits with each record, such that the value of the `ith` bit is 1 iff the value of the `ith` field is null. Assuming that `N<32`, the empty/inuse integer can be used for this purpose. Bit 0 of this integer denotes empty/inuse, as before. But now the other bits hold null-value information. You should make the following revisions to the code:

- Modify `Layout` so that it has a method `bitLocation(fldname)`, which returns the position in the flag where the field's null information bit is located.
- Modify `RecordPage` and `TableScan` to have two additional public methods: a void method `setNull(fldname)`, which stores a 1 in the appropriate bit of the flag, and a boolean method `isNull(fldname)`, which returns `true` if the null-bit for the specified field of the current record is 1.
- Modify the `format` method of `RecordPage` to explicitly set of the fields of the new record to non-null.
- Modify the `setString` and `setInt` methods to set the specified field to non-null.

6.14. Suppose that `setString` is called with a string that is longer than is specified in the schema.

(a) Explain what kinds of things can go wrong and when they will be detected.

(b) Fix the SimpleDB code so that the error is detected and handled appropriately.

Chapter 7
Metadata Management

The previous chapter examined how the record manager stores records in files. As you saw, however, a file is useless by itself; the record manager also needs to know the records' layout in order to "decode" the contents of each block. The layout is an example of *metadata*. This chapter examines the kinds of metadata supported by a database engine, their purpose and functionality, and the ways that the engine stores metadata in the database.

7.1 The Metadata Manager

Metadata is data that describes a database. A database engine maintains a wide variety of metadata. For example:

- *Table* metadata describes the structure of the table's records, such as the length, type, and offset of each field. The layout used by the record manager is an example of this kind of metadata.
- *View* metadata describes the properties of each view, such as its definition and creator. This metadata helps the planner handle queries that mention views.
- *Index* metadata describes the indexes that have been defined on the table (to be discussed in Chap. 12). The planner uses this metadata to see if a query can be evaluated using an index.
- *Statistical* metadata describes the size of each table and the distribution of its field values. The query optimizer uses this metadata to estimate the cost of a query.

The metadata for the first three categories is generated when a table, view, or index is created. Statistical metadata is generated each time the database is updated.

The *metadata manager* is the component of the database engine that stores and retrieves its metadata. The SimpleDB metadata manager is comprised of four separate managers, corresponding to each of the four metadata types. The remaining sections of this chapter cover these managers in detail.

E. Sciore, *Database Design and Implementation*, Data-Centric Systems and Applications, https://doi.org/10.1007/978-3-030-33836-7_7

7.2 Table Metadata

The SimpleDB class *TableMgr* manages table data. Its API, shown in Fig. 7.1, consists of a constructor and two methods. The constructor is called once, during system startup. The method `createTable` takes the table's name and schema as arguments; the method calculates the record offsets and saves it all in the catalog. The method `getLayout` goes to the catalog, extracts the metadata for the specified table, and returns a `Layout` object containing the metadata.

The class `TableMgrTest` in Fig. 7.2 demonstrates these methods. It first defines a schema containing an integer field named "A" and a string field named

TableMgr

```
   public TableMgr(boolean isnew, Transaction tx);
   public void createTable(String tblname, Schema sch,
                                         Transaction tx);
   public Layout getLayout(String tblname, Transactcion tx);
```

Fig. 7.1 The API for the SimpleDB table manager

```
public class TableMgrTest {
   public static void main(String[] args) throws Exception {
      SimpleDB db = new SimpleDB("tblmgrtest", 400, 8);
      Transaction tx = db.newTx();
      TableMgr tm = new TableMgr(true, tx);

      Schema sch = new Schema();
      sch.addIntField("A");
      sch.addStringField("B", 9);
      tm.createTable("MyTable", sch, tx);

      Layout layout = tm.getLayout("MyTable", tx);
      int size = layout.slotSize();
      Schema sch2 = layout.schema();
      System.out.println("MyTable has slot size " + size);
      System.out.println("Its fields are:");
      for (String fldname : sch2.fields()) {
         String type;
         if (sch2.type(fldname) == INTEGER)
            type = "int";
         else {
            int strlen = sch2.length(fldname);
            type = "varchar(" + strlen + ")";
         }
         System.out.println(fldname + ": " + type);
      }
      tx.commit();
   }
}
```

Fig. 7.2 Using the table manager methods

"B." It then calls `createTable` to create a table named "MyTable" having this schema. The code then calls `getLayout` to retrieve the calculated layout.

The metadata manager saves its metadata in the part of the database called the *catalog*. But how does it implement the catalog? The most common strategy is for the database engine to store catalog information in database tables. SimpleDB uses two tables to hold its table metadata: the table `tblcat` stores metadata specific to each table, and the table `fldcat` stores metadata specific to each field of each table. These tables have the following fields:

```
tblcat(TblName, SlotSize)
fldcat(TblName, FldName, Type, Length, Offset)
```

There is one record in `tblcat` for each database table and one record in `fldcat` for each field of each table. The `SlotSize` field gives the length of the slot in bytes, as calculated by `Layout`. The `Length` field gives the length of the field in characters, as specified in its table's schema. For an example, the catalog tables corresponding to the university database of Fig. 1.1 are shown in Fig. 7.3. Note how the table's layout information has been "flattened" into a series of `fldcat` records. The `Type` values in table `fldcat` contain the values 4 and 12; these values are the codes for types `INTEGER` and `VARCHAR` that are defined in the JDBC class `Types`.

Catalog tables can be accessed the same as any user-created table. For example, the SQL query of Fig. 7.4 retrieves the names and length of all fields in the STUDENT table.[1]

The catalog tables even contain records describing their own metadata. These records are not shown in Fig. 7.3. Instead, Exercise 7.1 asks you to determine them. Figure 7.5 shows the code for the class `CatalogTest`, which prints the record length of each table and the offset of each field. If you run the code, you will see that the metadata for the catalog tables is also printed.

Figure 7.6 gives the code for `TableMgr`. The constructor creates the schemas for the catalog tables `tblcat` and `fldcat` and calculates their `Layout` objects. If the database is new, it also creates the two catalog tables.

The `createTable` method uses a table scan to insert records into the catalog. It inserts one record into `tblcat` for the table and one record into `fldcat` for each field of the table.

The `getLayout` method opens table scans on the two catalog tables and scans them for records corresponding to the specified table name. It then constructs the requested `Layout` object from those records.

---

[1]Note that the constant "student" is in lower case, even though the table was defined in upper case. The reason is that all table and field names in SimpleDB are stored in lower case, and constants in SQL statements are case-sensitive.

tblcat	TblName	SlotSize
	student	30
	dept	20
	course	36
	section	28
	enroll	22

fldcat	TblName	FldName	Type	Length	Offset
	student	sid	4	0	4
	student	sname	12	10	8
	student	majorid	4	0	22
	student	gradyear	4	0	26
	dept	did	4	0	4
	dept	dname	12	8	8
	course	cid	4	0	4
	course	title	12	20	8
	course	deptid	4	0	32
	section	sectid	4	0	4
	section	courseid	4	0	8
	section	prof	12	8	12
	section	year	4	0	24
	enroll	eid	4	0	4
	enroll	studentid	4	0	8
	enroll	sectionid	4	0	12
	enroll	grade	12	2	16

Fig. 7.3 Catalog tables for the university database

```
select FldName, Length
from fldcat
where TblName = 'student'
```

Fig. 7.4 An SQL query to retrieve metadata

```
public class CatalogTest {
   public static void main(String[] args) throws Exception {
      SimpleDB db = new SimpleDB("catalogtest", 400, 8);
      Transaction tx = db.newTx();
      TableMgr tm = new TableMgr(true, tx);

      Schema sch = new Schema();
      sch.addIntField("A");
      sch.addStringField("B", 9);
      tm.createTable("MyTable", sch, tx);

      System.out.println("All tables and their lengths:");
      Layout layout = tm.getLayout("tblcat", tx);
      TableScan ts = new TableScan(tx, "tblcat", layout);
      while (ts.next()) {
         String tname = ts.getString("tblname");
         int size     = ts.getInt("slotsize");
         System.out.println(tname + " " + size);
      }
      ts.close();

      System.out.println("All fields and their offsets:");
      layout = tm.getLayout("fldcat", tx);
      ts = new TableScan(tx, "fldcat", layout);
      while (ts.next()) {
         String tname = ts.getString("tblname");
         String fname = ts.getString("fldname");
         int offset   = ts.getInt("offset");
         System.out.println(tname + " " + fname + " " + offset);
      }
      ts.close();
   }
}
```

Fig. 7.5 Using table scans to read the catalog tables

7.3 View Metadata

A *view* is a table whose records are computed dynamically from a query. That query is called the *definition* of the view and is specified when the view is created. The metadata manager stores the definition of each newly created view and retrieves its definition when requested.

The SimpleDB class `ViewMgr` handles this responsibility. The class stores view definitions in the catalog table `viewcat`, one record per view. The table has the following fields:

```
viewcat(ViewName, ViewDef)
```

```
public class TableMgr {
   public static final int MAX_NAME = 16; // table or field name
   private Layout tcatLayout, fcatLayout;

   public TableMgr(boolean isNew, Transaction tx) {
      Schema tcatSchema = new Schema();
      tcatSchema.addStringField("tblname", MAX_NAME);
      tcatSchema.addIntField("slotsize");
      tcatLayout = new Layout(tcatSchema);

      Schema fcatSchema = new Schema();
      fcatSchema.addStringField("tblname", MAX_NAME);
      fcatSchema.addStringField("fldname", MAX_NAME);
      fcatSchema.addIntField("type");
      fcatSchema.addIntField("length");
      fcatSchema.addIntField("offset");
      fcatLayout = new Layout(fcatSchema);

      if (isNew) {
         createTable("tblcat", tcatSchema, tx);
         createTable("fldcat", fcatSchema, tx);
      }
   }
   public void createTable(String tblname, Schema sch,
                           Transaction tx) {
      Layout layout = new Layout(sch);
      // insert one record into tblcat
      TableScan tcat = new TableScan(tx, "tblcat", tcatLayout);
      tcat.insert();
      tcat.setString("tblname", tblname);
      tcat.setInt("slotsize", layout.slotSize());
      tcat.close();
      // insert a record into fldcat for each field
      TableScan fcat = new TableScan(tx, "fldcat", fcatLayout);
      for (String fldname : sch.fields()) {
         fcat.insert();
         fcat.setString("tblname", tblname);
         fcat.setString("fldname", fldname);
         fcat.setInt   ("type",   sch.type(fldname));
         fcat.setInt   ("length", sch.length(fldname));
         fcat.setInt   ("offset", layout.offset(fldname));
      }
      fcat.close();
   }
   public Layout getLayout(String tblname, Transaction tx) {
      int size = -1;
      TableScan tcat = new TableScan(tx, "tblcat", tcatLayout);
      while(tcat.next())
         if(tcat.getString("tblname").equals(tblname)) {
            size = tcat.getInt("slotsize");
            break;
         }
      tcat.close();
```

Fig. 7.6 The code for the SimpleDB class `TableMgr`

```
      Schema sch = new Schema();
      Map<String,Integer> offsets = new HashMap<String,Integer>();
      TableScan fcat = new TableScan(tx, "fldcat", fcatLayout);
      while(fcat.next())
         if(fcat.getString("tblname").equals(tblname)) {
            String fldname = fcat.getString("fldname");
            int fldtype    = fcat.getInt("type");
            int fldlen     = fcat.getInt("length");
            int offset     = fcat.getInt("offset");
            offsets.put(fldname, offset);
            sch.addField(fldname, fldtype, fldlen);
         }

      fcat.close();
      return new Layout(sch, offsets, size);
   }
}
```

Fig. 7.6 (continued)

The code for `ViewMgr` appears in Fig. 7.7. Its constructor is called during system startup and creates the `viewcat` table if the database is new. The methods `createView` and `getViewDef` both use a table scan to access the catalog table—`createView` inserts a record into the table, and `getViewDef` iterates through the table looking for the record corresponding to the specified view name.

View definitions are stored as `varchar` strings, which means that there is a relatively small limit on the length of a view definition. The current limit of 100 characters is, of course, completely unrealistic, as a view definition could be thousands of characters long. A better choice would be to implement the `ViewDef` field as a `clob` type, such as `clob(9999)`.

7.4 Statistical Metadata

Another form of metadata managed by a database system is the statistical information about each table in the database, such as how many records it has and the distribution of their field values. These statistics are used by the query planner to estimate costs. Experience has shown that a good set of statistics can significantly improve the execution time of queries. Consequently, commercial metadata managers tend to maintain detailed, comprehensive statistics, such as value and range histograms for each field in each table and correlation information between fields in different tables.

For simplicity, this section considers only the following three kinds of statistical information:

- The number of blocks used by each table T
- The number of records in each table T
- For each field F of table T, the number of distinct F-values in T

```
class ViewMgr {
   private static final int MAX_VIEWDEF = 100; // max view def chars
   TableMgr tblMgr;

   public ViewMgr(boolean isNew, TableMgr tblMgr, Transaction tx) {
      this.tblMgr = tblMgr;
      if (isNew) {
         Schema sch = new Schema();
         sch.addStringField("viewname", TableMgr.MAX_NAME);
         sch.addStringField("viewdef", MAX_VIEWDEF);
         tblMgr.createTable("viewcat", sch, tx);
      }
   }

   public void createView(String vname, String vdef,
                          Transaction tx) {
      Layout layout = tblMgr.getLayout("viewcat", tx);
      TableScan ts = new TableScan(tx, "viewcat", layout);
      ts.setString("viewname", vname);
      ts.setString("viewdef", vdef);
      ts.close();
   }

   public String getViewDef(String vname, Transaction tx) {
      String result = null;
      Layout layout = tblMgr.getLayout("viewcat", tx);
      TableScan ts = new TableScan(tx, "viewcat", layout);
      while (ts.next())
         if (ts.getString("viewname").equals(vname)) {
            result = ts.getString("viewdef");
            break;
         }
      ts.close();
      return result;
   }
}
```

Fig. 7.7 The code for the SimpleDB class `ViewMgr`

These statistics are denoted by *B(T)*, *R(T)*, and *V(T,F)* respectively.

Figure 7.8 gives some example statistics for the university database. The values correspond to a university that admits about 900 students per year and offers about 500 sections per year; the university has kept this information for the last 50 years. The values in Fig. 7.8 try to be realistic and do not necessarily correspond to values that might be calculated from Fig. 1.1. Instead, the figures assume that 10 STUDENT records fit per block, 20 DEPT records per block, and so on.

Look at the V(T,F) values for the STUDENT table. The fact that `SId` is a key of STUDENT means that V(STUDENT, `SId`) = 45,000. The assignment V(STUDENT, `SName`) = 44,960 means that 40 of the 45,000 students have duplicate names. The assignment V(STUDENT, `GradYear`) = 50 means that at least one student graduated in each of the last 50 years. And the assignment V(STUDENT,

T	B(T)	R(T)	V(T,F)
STUDENT	4,500	45,000	45,000 for F=SId 44,960 for F=SName 50 for F=GradYear 40 for F=MajorId
DEPT	2	40	40 for F=DId, DName
COURSE	25	500	500 for F=CId, Title 40 for F=DeptId
SECTION	2,500	25,000	25,000 for F=SectId 500 for F=CourseId 250 for F=Prof 50 for F=YearOffered
ENROLL	50,000	1,500,000	1,500,000 for F=EId 25,000 for F=SectionId 45,000 for F=StudentId 14 for F=Grade

Fig. 7.8 Example statistics about the university database

StatMgr
```
public StatMgr(TableMgr tm, Transaction tx);
public StatInfo getStatInfo(String tblname, Layout lo,
                            Transaction tx);
```
StatInfo
```
public int blocksAccessed();
public int recordsOutput();
public int distinctValues(String fldname);
```

Fig. 7.9 The API for SimpleDB table statistics

`MajorId`) = 40 means that each of the 40 departments has had at least one major at some point.

The SimpleDB class `StatMgr` manages this statistical information. The database engine holds one `StatMgr` object. This object has a method `getStatInfo`, which returns a `StatInfo` object for a specified table. The `StatInfo` object holds the statistics for that table and has methods `blocksAccessed`, `recordsOutput`, and `distinctValues`, which, respectively, implement the statistical functions B(T), R(T), and V(T,F). The API for these classes appears in Fig. 7.9.

```
SimpleDB db = ...
Transaction tx = db.newTx();
TableMgr tblmgr = ...
StatMgr  statmgr = new StatMgr(tblmgr, tx);
Layout layout = tblmgr.getLayout("student", tx);
StatInfo si = statmgr.getStatInfo("student", layout, tx);
System.out.println(si.blocksAccessed() + " " +
                   si.recordsOutput()   + " " +
                   si.distinctValues("majorid"));
tx.commit();
```

Fig. 7.10 Obtaining and printing statistics about a table

The code fragment in Fig. 7.10 illustrates a typical use of these methods. This code obtains the statistics for the STUDENT table and prints the value of B(STUDENT), R(STUDENT), and V(STUDENT, `MajorId`).

A database engine can manage statistical metadata in one of two ways. One way is to store the information in the database catalog, updating it whenever the database changes. The other is to store the information in memory, calculating it when the engine is initialized.

The first approach corresponds to creating two new catalog tables, called `tblstats` and fldstats, having the following fields:

```
tblstats(TblName, NumBlocks, NumRecords)
fldstats(TblName, FldName, NumValues)
```

The `tblstats` table would have one record for each table T, containing the values for B(T) and R(T). The `fldstats` table would have one record for each field F of each table T, containing the value for V(T,F). The problem with this approach is the cost of keeping the statistics up to date. Every call to `insert`, `delete`, `setInt`, and `setString` would potentially need to update these tables. Additional disk accesses would be required to write the modified pages to disk. Moreover, concurrency would be reduced—every update to table T would xlock the blocks containing T's statistical records, which would force the transactions that need to read T's statistics (as well as the statistics of the other tables having records on the same pages) to wait.

One viable solution to this problem is to let transactions read the statistics without obtaining slocks, as in the read-uncommitted isolation level of Sect. 5.4.7. The loss of accuracy is tolerable because the database system uses these statistics to compare the estimated execution times of query plans. The statistics therefore do not need to be accurate, as long as the estimates they produce are reasonable.

The second implementation strategy is to forget about catalog tables and to store the statistics directly in memory. The statistical data is relatively small and should fit easily in main memory. The only problem is that the statistics will need to be computed from scratch each time the server starts. This calculation requires a scan of each table in the database to count the number of records, blocks, and values seen.

If the database is not too large, this computation will not delay the system startup too much.

This main-memory strategy has two options for dealing with database updates. The first option is for each update to the database to update the statistics, as before. The second option is to leave the statistics un-updated but to recalculate them, from scratch, every so often. This second option relies again on the fact that accurate statistical information is not necessary, and so it is tolerable to let the statistics get a bit out of date before refreshing them.

SimpleDB adopts the second option of the second approach. The class `StatMgr` keeps a variable, called `tableStats`, which holds cost information for each table. The class has a public method `statInfo` that returns the cost values for a specified table, and private methods `refreshStatistics` and `refreshTableStats` that recalculate the cost values. The code for the class appears in Fig. 7.11.

The class `StatMgr` keeps a counter that is incremented each time `statInfo` is called. If the counter reaches a particular value (here, 100), then `refreshStatistics` is called to recalculate the cost values for all tables. If `statInfo` is called on a table for which there are no known values, then `refreshTableStats` is called to calculate the statistics for that table.

The code for `refreshStatistics` loops through the `tblcat` table. The body of the loop extracts the name of a table and calls `refreshTableStats` to calculate the statistics for that table. The `refreshTableStats` method loops through the contents of that table, counting records, and calls `size` to determine the number of blocks used. For simplicity, the method does not count field values. Instead, the `StatInfo` object makes a wild guess at the number of distinct values for a field, based on the number of records in its table.

The code for class `StatInfo` appears in Fig. 7.12. Note that `distinctValues` does not use the field value passed into it, because it naïvely assumes that approximately 1/3 of the values of any field are distinct. Needless to say, this assumption is pretty bad. Exercise 7.12 asks you to rectify the situation.

7.5 Index Metadata

The metadata for an index consists of its name, the name of the table it is indexing, and the list of its indexed fields. The *index manager* is the system component that stores and retrieves this metadata. The SimpleDB index manager consists of two classes, `IndexMgr` and `IndexInfo`. Their API appears in Fig. 7.13.

An index's metadata consists of its name, the name of the table being indexed, and the field it is indexed on. The `IndexMgr` method `createIndex` stores this metadata in the catalog. The `getIndexInfo` method retrieves the metadata for all indexes on a specified table. In particular, it returns a map of `Indexinfo` objects, keyed by the indexed field. The map's `keyset` method tells you the fields of the table having an available index. The `IndexInfo` methods provide statistical information about a chosen index, similar to the class `StatInfo`. The method

```
class StatMgr {
   private TableMgr tblMgr;
   private Map<String,StatInfo> tablestats;
   private int numcalls;

   public StatMgr(TableMgr tblMgr, Transaction tx) {
      this.tblMgr = tblMgr;
      refreshStatistics(tx);
   }

   public synchronized StatInfo getStatInfo(String tblname,
                                   Layout layout, Transaction tx) {
      numcalls++;
      if (numcalls > 100)
         refreshStatistics(tx);
      StatInfo si = tablestats.get(tblname);
      if (si == null) {
         si = calcTableStats(tblname, layout, tx);
         tablestats.put(tblname, si);
      }
      return si;
   }

   private synchronized void refreshStatistics(Transaction tx) {
      tablestats = new HashMap<String,StatInfo>();
      numcalls = 0;
      Layout tcatlayout = tblMgr.getLayout("tblcat", tx);
      TableScan tcat = new TableScan(tx, "tblcat", tcatlayout);
      while(tcat.next()) {
         String tblname = tcat.getString("tblname");
         Layout layout = tblMgr.getLayout(tblname, tx);
         StatInfo si = calcTableStats(tblname, layout, tx);
         tablestats.put(tblname, si);
      }
      tcat.close();
   }

   private synchronized StatInfo calcTableStats(String tblname,
                        Layout layout, Transaction tx) {
      int numRecs = 0;
      int numblocks = 0;
      TableScan ts = new TableScan(tx, tblname, layout);
      while (ts.next()) {
         numRecs++;
         numblocks = ts.getRid().blockNumber() + 1;
      }
      ts.close();
      return new StatInfo(numblocks, numRecs);
   }
}
```

Fig. 7.11 The code for the SimpleDB class `StatMgr`

```
public class StatInfo {
   private int numBlocks;
   private int numRecs;

   public StatInfo(int numblocks, int numrecs) {
      this.numBlocks = numblocks;
      this.numRecs   = numrecs;
   }

   public int blocksAccessed() {
      return numBlocks;
   }

   public int recordsOutput() {
      return numRecs;
   }

   public int distinctValues(String fldname) {
      return 1 + (numRecs / 3);  // This is wildly inaccurate.
   }
}
```

Fig. 7.12 The code for the SimpleDB class `StatInfo`

IndexMgr

```
public IndexMgr(boolean isnew, TableMgr tmgr, StatMgr smgr,
                                               Transaction tx);
public createIndex(String iname, String tname, String fname,
                                               Transaction tx);
public Map(String,IndexInfo> getIndexInfo(String tblname,
                                               Transaction tx);
```

IndexInfo

```
public IndexInfo(String iname, String tname, String fname,
                                               Transaction tx);
public int blocksAccessed();
public int recordsOutput();
public int distinctValues(String fldname);
public Index open();
```

Fig. 7.13 The API for SimpleDB index metadata

`blocksAccessed` returns the number of block accesses required to search the index (not the size of the index). Methods `recordsOutput` and `distinctValues` return the number of records in the index and the number of distinct values of the indexed field, which are the same values as in the indexed table.

An `IndexInfo` object also has the method `open`, which returns the `Index` object for the index. The class `Index` contains methods to search the index, and is discussed in Chap. 12.

```
SimpleDB db = ...
Transaction tx = db.newTx();
TableMgr tblmgr = ...
StatMgr  statmgr = new StatMgr(tblmgr, tx);
IndexMgr idxmgr = new IndexMgr(true, tblmgr, statmgr, tx);
idxmgr.createIndex("sidIdx", "student", "sid");
idxmgr.createIndex("snameIdx", "student", "sname");

Map<String,IndexInfo> indexes = idxmgr.getIndexInfo("student", tx);
for (String fldname : indexes.keySet()) {
   IndexInfo ii = indexes.get(fldname);
   System.out.println(fldname + "\t" + ii.blocksAccessed(fldname));
}
```

Fig. 7.14 Using the SimpleDB index manager

The code fragment of Fig. 7.14 illustrates the use of these methods. The code creates two indexes on the STUDENT table. It then retrieves their metadata, printing the name and search cost of each one.

Figure 7.15 gives the code for `IndexMgr`. It stores index metadata in the catalog table `idxcat`. This table has one record for each index and three fields: the name of the index, the name of the table being indexed, and the name of the indexed field.

The constructor is called during system startup and creates the catalog table if the database is new. The code for methods `createIndex` and `getIndexInfo` is straightforward. Both methods open a table scan on the catalog table. The method `createIndex` inserts a new record into the table. The method `getIndexInfo` searches the table for those records having the specified table name and inserts them into the map.

The code for the class `IndexInfo` appears in Fig. 7.16. The constructor receives the name of the index and the indexed field, as well as variables holding the layout and statistical metadata of its associated table. This metadata allows the `IndexInfo` object to construct the schema for the index record and to estimate the size of the index file.

The method `open` opens the index by passing the index name and schema to the `HashIndex` constructor. The class `HashIndex` implements a static hashed index and is discussed in Chap. 12. To use B-Tree indexing instead, replace this constructor with the commented-out one. The method `blocksAccessed` estimates the search cost of the index. It first uses the index's `Layout` information to determine the length of each index record and estimate the records per block (RPB) of the index and the size of the index file. Then it calls the index-specific method `searchCost` to calculate the number of block accesses for that index type. The method `recordsOutput` estimates the number of index records matching a search key. And the method `distinctValues` returns the same value as in the indexed table.

```
public class IndexMgr {
   private Layout layout;
   private TableMgr tblmgr;
   private StatMgr statmgr;

   public IndexMgr(boolean isnew, TableMgr tblmgr, StatMgr statmgr,
         Transaction tx) {
      if (isnew) {
         Schema sch = new Schema();
         sch.addStringField("indexname", MAX_NAME);
         sch.addStringField("tablename", MAX_NAME);
         sch.addStringField("fieldname", MAX_NAME);
         tblmgr.createTable("idxcat", sch, tx);
      }
      this.tblmgr = tblmgr;
      this.statmgr = statmgr;
      layout = tblmgr.getLayout("idxcat", tx);
   }

   public void createIndex(String idxname, String tblname,
                           String fldname,Transaction tx) {
      TableScan ts = new TableScan(tx, "idxcat", layout);
      ts.insert();
      ts.setString("indexname", idxname);
      ts.setString("tablename", tblname);
      ts.setString("fieldname", fldname);
      ts.close();
   }

   public Map<String,IndexInfo> getIndexInfo(String tblname,
                                             Transaction tx) {
      Map<String,IndexInfo> result = new HashMap<String,IndexInfo>();
      TableScan ts = new TableScan(tx, "idxcat", layout);
      while (ts.next())
         if (ts.getString("tablename").equals(tblname)) {
         String idxname = ts.getString("indexname");
         String fldname = ts.getString("fieldname");
         Layout tblLayout = tblmgr.getLayout(tblname, tx);
         StatInfo tblsi = statmgr.getStatInfo(tblname, tbllayout, tx);
         IndexInfo ii = new IndexInfo(idxname, fldname,
                                  tblLayout.schema(),tx, tblsi);
         result.put(fldname, ii);
      }
      ts.close();
      return result;
   }
}
```

Fig. 7.15 The code for the SimpleDB index manager

```
public class IndexInfo {
   private String idxname, fldname;
   private Transaction tx;
   private Schema tblSchema;
   private Layout idxLayout;
   private StatInfo si;

   public IndexInfo(String idxname, String fldname, Schema tblSchema,
                    Transaction tx, StatInfo si) {
      this.idxname = idxname;
      this.fldname = fldname;
      this.tx = tx;
      this.idxLayout = createIdxLayout();
      this.si = si;
   }

   public Index open() {
      Schema sch = schema();
      return new HashIndex(tx, idxname, idxLayout);
//    return new BTreeIndex(tx, idxname, idxLayout);
   }

   public int blocksAccessed() {
      int rpb = tx.blockSize() / idxLayout.slotSize();
      int numblocks = si.recordsOutput() / rpb;
      return HashIndex.searchCost(numblocks, rpb);
//    return BTreeIndex.searchCost(numblocks, rpb);
   }

   public int recordsOutput() {
      return si.recordsOutput() / si.distinctValues(fldname);
   }

   public int distinctValues(String fname) {
      return fldname.equals(fname) ? 1 : si.distinctValues(fldname);
   }

   private Layout createIdxLayout() {
      Schema sch = new Schema();
      sch.addIntField("block");
      sch.addIntField("id");
      if (layout.schema().type(fldname) == INTEGER)
         sch.addIntField("dataval");
      else {
         int fldlen = layout.schema().length(fldname);
         sch.addStringField("dataval", fldlen);
      }
      return new Layout(sch);
   }
}
```

Fig. 7.16 The code for the SimpleDB class `IndexInfo`

MetadataMgr
```
public void createTable(String tblname, Schema sch,
                                        Transaction tx);
public Layout getLayout(String tblname, Transaction tx);

public void createView(String viewname, String viewdef,
                                        Transaction tx);
public String getViewDef(String viewname, Transaction tx);

public void createIndex(String idxname, String tblname,
                        String fldname, Transaction tx);
public Map<String,IndexInfo> getIndexinfo(String tblname,
                                          Transaction tx);
public StatInfo getStatInfo(String tblname, Layout layout,
                                            Transaction tx);
```

Fig. 7.17 The API for the SimpleDB metadata manager

7.6 Implementing the Metadata Manager

SimpleDB simplifies the client interface to the metadata manager by hiding the four separate manager classes `TableMgr`, `ViewMgr`, `StatMgr`, and `IndexMgr`. Instead, clients use the class `MetadataMgr` as the single place to obtain metadata. The code for `MetadataMgr` API appears in Fig. 7.17.

This API contains two methods for each type of metadata—one method generates and saves the metadata, and the other method retrieves it. The only exception is for statistical metadata, whose generation method is called internally and is thus private.

Figure 7.18 gives the code for the class `MetadataMgrTest`, which illustrates the use of these methods.

Part 1 illustrates table metadata. It creates the table MyTable and prints its layout, as in Fig. 7.2. Part 2 illustrates the statistics manager. It inserts several records into MyTable and prints the resulting table statistics. Part 3 illustrates the view manager, creating a view and retrieving the view definition. Part 4 illustrates the index manager. It creates an index on fields A and B and prints the properties of each index.

The class `MetadataMgr` is known as a *façade class*. Its constructor creates the four manager objects and saves them in private variables. Its methods replicate the public methods of the individual managers. When a client calls a method on the metadata manager, that method calls the appropriate local manager to do the work. Its code appears in Fig. 7.19.

All test programs so far in this book have called the three-argument SimpleDB constructor. That constructor uses the provided block size and buffer pool size to customize the system's `FileMgr`, `LogMgr`, and `BufferMgr` objects. Its purpose is to help debug the low levels of the system and does not create a `MetadataMgr` object.

```
public class MetadataMgrTest {
   public static void main(String[] args) throws Exception {
      SimpleDB db = new SimpleDB("metadatamgrtest", 400, 8);
      Transaction tx = db.newTx();
      MetadataMgr mdm = new MetadataMgr(true, tx);

      Schema sch = new Schema();
      sch.addIntField("A");
      sch.addStringField("B", 9);

      // Part 1: Table Metadata
      mdm.createTable("MyTable", sch, tx);
      Layout layout = mdm.getLayout("MyTable", tx);
      int size = layout.slotSize();
      Schema sch2 = layout.schema();
      System.out.println("MyTable has slot size " + size);
      System.out.println("Its fields are:");
      for (String fldname : sch2.fields()) {
         String type;
         if (sch2.type(fldname) == INTEGER)
            type = "int";
         else {
            int strlen = sch2.length(fldname);
            type = "varchar(" + strlen + ")";
         }
         System.out.println(fldname + ": " + type);
      }

      // Part 2: Statistics Metadata
      TableScan ts = new TableScan(tx, "MyTable", layout);
      for (int i=0; i<50; i++) {
         ts.insert();
         int n = (int) Math.round(Math.random() * 50);
         ts.setInt("A", n);
         ts.setString("B", "rec"+n);
      }
      StatInfo si = mdm.getStatInfo("MyTable", layout, tx);
      System.out.println("B(MyTable) = " + si.blocksAccessed());
      System.out.println("R(MyTable) = " + si.recordsOutput());
      System.out.println("V(MyTable,A) = " + si.distinctValues("A"));
      System.out.println("V(MyTable,B) = " + si.distinctValues("B"));

      // Part 3: View Metadata
      String viewdef = "select B from MyTable where A = 1";
      mdm.createView("viewA", viewdef, tx);
      String v = mdm.getViewDef("viewA", tx);
      System.out.println("View def = " + v);

      // Part 4: Index Metadata
      mdm.createIndex("indexA", "MyTable", "A", tx);
      mdm.createIndex("indexB", "MyTable", "B", tx);
      Map<String,IndexInfo> idxmap = mdm.getIndexInfo("MyTable", tx);
```

Fig. 7.18 Testing the MetadataMgr methods

```
        IndexInfo ii = idxmap.get("A");
        System.out.println("B(indexA) = " + ii.blocksAccessed());
        System.out.println("R(indexA) = " + ii.recordsOutput());
        System.out.println("V(indexA,A) = " + ii.distinctValues("A"));
        System.out.println("V(indexA,B) = " + ii.distinctValues("B"));

        ii = idxmap.get("B");
        System.out.println("B(indexB) = " + ii.blocksAccessed());
        System.out.println("R(indexB) = " + ii.recordsOutput());
        System.out.println("V(indexB,A) = " + ii.distinctValues("A"));
        System.out.println("V(indexB,B) = " + ii.distinctValues("B"));
        tx.commit();
    }
}
```

Fig. 7.18 (continued)

SimpleDB has another constructor that has one argument, the database name. This constructor is used for non-debug situations. It first creates the file, log, and buffer managers using default values. It then calls the recovery manager to recover the database (in case recovery is needed) and creates the metadata manager (which, if the database is new, includes creating the catalog files). The code for the two `SimpleDB` constructors appears in Fig. 7.20.

With this one-argument constructor, the code for `MetadataMgrTest` in Fig. 7.18 can be rewritten more simply, as shown in Fig. 7.21.

7.7 Chapter Summary

- *Metadata* is the information about a database, apart from its contents. The *metadata manager* is the portion of the database system that stores and retrieves its metadata.
- Database metadata in SimpleDB falls into four categories:
  - *Table* metadata describes the structure of the table's records, such as the length, type, and offset of each field.
  - *View* metadata describes the properties of each view, such as its definition and creator.
  - *Index* metadata describes the indexes that have been defined on the table.
  - *Statistical* metadata describes the size of each table and the distribution of its field values.
- The metadata manager saves its metadata in the *system catalog*. The catalog is often implemented as tables in the database, called *catalog tables*. Catalog tables can be queried the same as any other table in the database.

```
public class MetadataMgr {
   private static TableMgr  tblmgr;
   private static ViewMgr   viewmgr;
   private static StatMgr   statmgr;
   private static IndexMgr  idxmgr;

   public MetadataMgr(boolean isnew, Transaction tx) {
      tblmgr  = new TableMgr(isnew, tx);
      viewmgr = new ViewMgr(isnew, tblmgr, tx);
      statmgr = new StatMgr(tblmgr, tx);
      idxmgr  = new IndexMgr(isnew, tblmgr, statmgr, tx);
   }

   public void createTable(String tblname, Schema sch,
                           Transaction tx) {
      tblmgr.createTable(tblname, sch, tx);
   }

   public Layout getLayout(String tblname, Transaction tx) {
      return tblmgr.getLayout(tblname, tx);
   }

   public void createView(String viewname, String viewdef,
                          Transaction tx) {
      viewmgr.createView(viewname, viewdef, tx);
   }

   public String getViewDef(String viewname, Transaction tx) {
      return viewmgr.getViewDef(viewname, tx);
   }

   public void createIndex(String idxname, String tblname,
                           String fldname, Transaction tx) {
      idxmgr.createIndex(idxname, tblname, fldname, tx);
   }

   public Map<String,IndexInfo> getIndexInfo(String tblname,
                                             Transaction tx)
      {return idxmgr.getIndexInfo(tblname, tx);
   }

   public StatInfo getStatInfo(String tblname, Layout layout,
                                                Transaction tx)
      {return statmgr.getStatInfo(tblname, layout, tx);
   }
}
```

Fig. 7.19 The code for the SimpleDB class `MetadataMgr`

```
public SimpleDB(String dirname, int blocksize, int buffsize) {
   String homedir = System.getProperty(HOME_DIR);
   File dbDirectory = new File(homedir, dirname);
   fm = new FileMgr(dbDirectory, blocksize);
   lm = new LogMgr(fm, LOG_FILE);
   bm = new BufferMgr(fm, lm, buffsize);
}

public SimpleDB(String dirname) {
   this(dirname, BLOCK_SIZE, BUFFER_SIZE);
   Transaction tx = new Transaction(fm, lm, bm);
   boolean isnew = fm.isNew();
   if (isnew)
      System.out.println("creating new database");
   else {
      System.out.println("recovering existing database");
      tx.recover();
   }
   mdm = new MetadataMgr(isnew, tx);
   tx.commit();
}
```

Fig. 7.20 The two SimpleDB constructors

```
public class MetadataMgrTest {
   public static void main(String[] args) throws Exception {
      SimpleDB db = new SimpleDB("metadatamgrtest");
      MetadataMgr mdm = db.mdMgr();
      Transaction tx = db.newTx();
      ...
}
```

Fig. 7.21 Using the one-argument SimpleDB constructor

- Table metadata can be stored in two catalog tables—one table stores table information (such as the slot size), and the other table stores field information (such as the name, length, and type of each field).
- View metadata consists primarily of the view definition and can be saved in its own catalog table. The view definition will be an arbitrarily long string, so a variable-length representation is appropriate.
- Statistical metadata holds information about the size and value distribution of each table in the database. Commercial database systems tend to maintain detailed, comprehensive statistics, such as value and range histograms for each field in each table, and correlation information between fields in different tables.
- A basic set of statistics consists of three functions:
  - B(T) returns the number of blocks used by table T.
  - R(T) returns the number of records in table T.
  - V(T,F) returns the number of distinct F-values in T.

- Statistics can be stored in catalog tables, or they can be calculated from scratch each time the database restarts. The former option avoids the long startup time but can slow down the execution of transactions.
- Index metadata holds information on the name of each index, the table it is indexed on, and the indexed fields.

7.8 Suggested Reading

The catalog tables used in SimpleDB are about as small as possible and similar to those used in the early INGRES system (Stonebraker et al. 1976). On the other side of the spectrum, Oracle currently has such an extensive catalog that a 60-page book has been written to describe it (Kreines 2003).

Standard SQL defines a standard set of views that provide access to the database metadata. These views are called the *information schema* of the database. There are over 50 defined view tables, which expand upon the metadata described in this chapter. For example, there are views to display information on triggers, assertions, constraints, user-defined types, and so on. There are also several views that hold information about privileges and roles. The idea is that each database system can store this metadata any way that it chooses, but it is obligated to provide a standard interface to this metadata. Details can be found in Chap. 16 of Gulutzan and Pelzer (1999).

Accurate and detailed statistical metadata is critical for good query planning. The approach taken in this chapter is crude, and commercial systems use much more sophisticated techniques. The article Gibbons et al. (2002) describes the use of histograms and shows how they can be maintained efficiently in the face of frequent updates. Histogram information can be determined in various ways, one of the more interesting being via wavelet techniques (Matias et al. 1998). It is even possible to collect statistics on previously run queries, which can then be used to plan related queries (Bruno and Chaudhuri 2004).

Bruno, N., & Chaudhuri, S. (2004). Conditional selectivity for statistics on query expressions. In *Proceedings of the ACM SIGMOD Conference* (pp. 311–322).

Gibbons, P., Matias, Y., & Poosala, V. (2002). Fast incremental maintenance of incremental histograms. *ACM Transactions on Database Systems, 27*(3), 261–298.

Gulutzan, P., & Pelzer, T. (1999). *SQL-99 complete, really*. Lawrence, KA: R&D Books.

Kreines, D. (2003). *Oracle data dictionary pocket reference*. Sebastopol, CA: O'Reilly.

Matias, Y., Vitter, J., & Wang, M. (1998). Wavelet-based histograms for selectivity estimation. In *Proceedings of the ACM SIGMOD Conference* (pp. 448–459).

Stonebraker, M., Kreps, P., Wong, E., & Held, G. (1976). The design and implementation of INGRES. *ACM Transactions on Database Systems, 1*(3), 189–222.

7.9 Exercises

Conceptual Exercises

7.1. Give the `tblcat` and `fldcat` records that SimpleDB creates for the `tblcat` and `fldcat` tables. (*Hint*: Examine the code for `TableMgr`.)

7.2. Suppose that the only thing transaction T1 does is create table X, and the only thing transaction T2 does is create table Y.

(a) What possible concurrent schedules can these transactions have?
(b) Could T1 and T2 ever deadlock? Explain.

7.3. Standard SQL also allows a client to add a new field to an existing table. Give a good algorithm to implement this functionality.

Programming Exercises

7.4. Standard SQL allows a client to remove a field from an existing table. Suppose that this functionality is implemented in a method of `TableMgr` called `removeField`.

(a) One way to implement this method is to simply modify the field's record in `fldcat` to have a blank fieldname. Write the code for this method.
(b) In part (a), none of the table's records are changed. What happens to their deleted field values? Why can't they ever be accessed?
(c) Another way to implement this method is to remove the field's record from `fldcat` and modify all of the existing data records in the table. This is considerably more work than in (a). Is it ever worth it? Explain the trade-offs.

7.5. In the SimpleDB catalog tables, the field `tblname` of `tblcat` is its key, and the field `tblname` of `fldcat` is the corresponding foreign key. Another way to implement these tables would be to use an artificial key (say, `tblId`) for `tblcat`, with a corresponding foreign key in `fldcat` (say, named `tableId`).

(a) Implement this design in SimpleDB.
(b) Is this design better than the original one? (Does it save space? Does it save block accesses?)

7.6. Suppose that SimpleDB crashes while the catalog tables for a new database are being created.

(a) Describe what will occur when the database is recovered after system restart. What problem arises?
(b) Revise the SimpleDB code to fix this problem.

7.7. Write SimpleDB clients to do each of the following tasks, by querying the `tblcat` and `fldcat` tables directly:

(a) Print the names and fields of all tables in the database (e.g., in the form of "T(A, B)").
(b) Reconstruct and print the text of the SQL `create table` statement used to create a particular table (e.g., in the form of "create table T (A integer, B varchar(7))").

7.8. What happens when the method `getLayout` is called with a nonexistent table name? Revise the code so that `null` is returned instead.
7.9. What problem can occur when a client creates a table with the same name as a table already in the catalog? Revise the code to prevent this from happening.
7.10. Revise `TableMgr` to have the method `dropTable`, which removes the table from the database. Do you need to modify the file manager also?
7.11. Revise the SimpleDB code so that statistics are stored in the catalog tables and updated each time the database is changed.
7.12. Revise the SimpleDB code so that V(T, F) is computed for each table T and field F. (*Hint*: Keeping track of the count of each field can be memory-intensive, as the number of distinct values may be unbounded. A reasonable idea is to count values for a portion of the table and extrapolate. For example, one might count how many records are required to read 1000 different values.)
7.13. Suppose that a client creates a table, inserts some records into it, and then does a rollback.

(a) What happens to the table's metadata in the catalog?
(b) What happens to the file containing the data? Explain what problem could occur if a client subsequently creates a table with the same name but a different schema.
(c) Fix the SimpleDB code so that this problem is solved.

7.14. Modify the index manager so that it also saves the type of the index in the catalog. Assume that there are two types of index, in classes `BTreeIndex` and `HashIndex`. The class constructor and static method `searchCost` have the same arguments in each of these classes.
7.15. The SimpleDB index manager uses the table `idxcat` to hold index information. Another design possibility is to keep index information in the catalog table `fldcat`.

(a) Compare the two possibilities. What are the advantages of each way?
(b) Implement this alternative way.

Chapter 8
Query Processing

The next three chapters examine how database engines execute SQL queries. The issue is that an SQL query specifies what data to return but not how to get it. The solution is for the engine to implement a set of data-retrieval operators, known as *relational algebra*. The engine can translate an SQL query to a relational algebra query which can then be executed. This chapter introduces relational algebra queries and their implementation. The following two chapters will examine the translation of SQL into relational algebra.

8.1 Relational Algebra

Relational algebra consists of a set of *operators*. Each operator performs one specialized task, taking one or more tables as input and producing one output table. Complex queries can be constructed by composing these operators in various ways.

The SimpleDB version of SQL can be implemented using three operators:

- *select*, whose output table has the same columns as its input table but with some rows removed
- *project*, whose output table has the same rows as its input table but with some columns removed
- *product*, whose output table consists of all possible combinations of records from its two input tables

These operators are examined in the following subsections.

E. Sciore, *Database Design and Implementation*, Data-Centric Systems and Applications, https://doi.org/10.1007/978-3-030-33836-7_8

8.1.1 Select

The *select* operator takes two arguments: an input table and a predicate. The output table consists of the input records that satisfy the predicate. A select query always returns a table having the same schema as the input table but with a subset of the records.

For example, query Q1 returns a table listing those students who graduated in 2019.

```
Q1 = select(STUDENT, GradYear=2019)
```

A predicate can be any boolean combination of terms and corresponds to a `where` clause in SQL. For example, query Q2 finds those students who graduated in 2019 and whose major was either in department 10 or 20.

```
Q2 = select(STUDENT, GradYear=2019 and (MajorId=10 or MajorId=20))
```

The output table of one query can be the input to another query. For example, queries Q3 and Q4 are each equivalent to Q2:

```
Q3 = select(select(STUDENT, GradYear=2019), MajorId=10 or MajorId=20)

Q4 = select(Q1, MajorId=10 or MajorId=20)
```

In Q3, the first argument of the outermost query is another query, identical to Q1, which finds the students who graduated in 2019. The outer query retrieves, from those records, the students in department 10 or 20. Query Q4 is similar, except that it uses the name of Q1 in place of its definition.

A relational algebra query can be expressed pictorially, as a *query tree*. A query tree contains a node for each table and operator mentioned in the query. The table nodes are the leaves of the tree, and the operator nodes are non-leaves. An operator node has a child for each of its input tables. For example, the query tree for Q3 appears in Fig. 8.1.

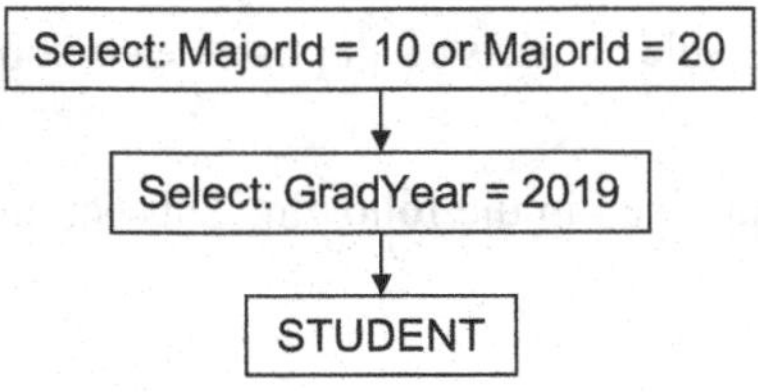

Fig. 8.1 A query tree for Q3

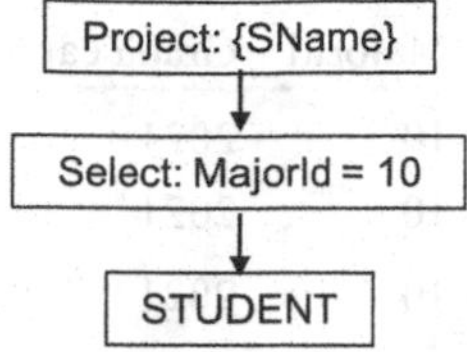

Fig. 8.2 A query tree for Q6

8.1.2 Project

The *project* operator takes two arguments: an input table and a set of field names. The output table has the same records as the input table, but its schema contains only those specified fields. For example, query Q5 returns the name and graduation year of all students:

```
Q5 = project(STUDENT, {SName, GradYear})
```

A query can be composed of both project and select operators. Query Q6 returns a table listing the name of all students majoring in department 10:

```
Q6 = project(select(STUDENT, MajorId=10), {SName})
```

The query tree for Q6 appears in Fig. 8.2.

The output table of a project query may have duplicate records. For example, if there are three students named "pat" having major 10, then the output of Q6 will contain "pat" three times.

Not all compositions of operators are meaningful. For example, consider the query you get by inverting Q6:

```
Q7 = select(project(STUDENT, {SName}), MajorId=10) // Not legal!
```

This query does not make sense, because the output table of the inner query does not contain a `MajorId` field to select on.

8.1.3 Product

The select and project operators act upon a single table. The *product* operator makes it possible to combine and compare information from multiple tables. This operator takes two input tables as arguments. Its output table consists of all combinations of records from the input tables, and its schema consists of the union of the fields in the input schemas. The input tables must have disjoint field names so that the output table will not have two fields with the same name.

Q8	SId	SName	MajorId	GradYear	DId	DName
	1	joe	10	2021	10	compsci
	1	joe	10	2021	20	math
	1	joe	10	2021	30	drama
	2	amy	20	2020	10	compsci
	2	amy	20	2020	20	math
	2	amy	20	2020	30	drama
	3	max	10	2022	10	compsci
	3	max	10	2022	20	math
	3	max	10	2022	30	drama
	4	sue	20	2022	10	compsci
	4	sue	20	2022	20	math
	4	sue	20	2022	30	drama
	5	bob	30	2020	10	compsci
	5	bob	30	2020	20	math
	5	bob	30	2020	30	drama
	6	kim	20	2020	10	compsci
	6	kim	20	2020	20	math
	6	kim	20	2020	30	drama
	7	art	30	2021	10	compsci
	7	art	30	2021	20	math
	7	art	30	2021	30	drama
	8	pat	20	2019	10	compsci
	8	pat	20	2019	20	math
	8	pat	20	2019	30	drama
	9	lee	10	2021	10	compsci
	9	lee	10	2021	20	math
	9	lee	10	2021	30	drama

Fig. 8.3 The output of query Q8

Query Q8 returns the product of the STUDENT and DEPT tables:

```
Q8 = product(STUDENT, DEPT)
```

The university database of Fig. 1.1 showed nine records in STUDENT and three records in DEPT. Figure 8.3 depicts the output of Q8 given those input tables. The

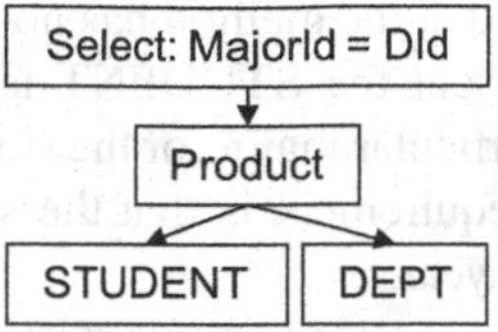

Fig. 8.4 The query tree for Q9

output table contains 27 records, 1 record for each pairing of a student record with a department record. In general, if there are `N` records in STUDENT and `M` records in DEPT, then the output table will contain `N*M` records (which, by the way, is the reason why the operator is called "product").

Query Q8 is not especially meaningful, as it does not take into consideration the major of each student. This meaning can be expressed in a selection predicate, as shown in query Q9 and Fig. 8.4:

```
Q9 = select(product(STUDENT, DEPT), MajorId=Did)
```

The output table for this query contains only the combinations of records from STUDENT and DEPT that satisfy the predicate. Thus out of the 27 possible combinations, the only combinations that will remain are those for which the student's major ID is the same as the department's ID—in other words, the result table will consist of students and their major departments. Instead of 27 records, the output table now has 9 records.

8.2 Scans

A *scan* is an object that represents the output of a relational algebra query. Scans in SimpleDB implement the interface `Scan`; see Fig. 8.5. The `Scan` methods are a subset of the `TableScan` methods, and they have the same behavior. This correspondence should not be surprising—the output of a query is a table, and so it is natural for queries and tables to be accessed the same way.

For an example, consider the method `printNameAndGradYear` in Fig. 8.6. This method iterates through its scan, printing the values of the fields `sname` and `gradyear` for each record.

```
public interface Scan {
   public void      beforeFirst();
   public boolean   next();
   public int       getInt(String fldname);
   public String    getString(String fldname);
   public Constant  getVal(String fldname);
   public boolean   hasField(String fldname);
   public void      close();
}
```

Fig. 8.5 The SimpleDB `Scan` interface

The point of this example is that the method has no idea what query (or table) the scan represents. It could represent the STUDENT table, or perhaps a query that selects the students having a particular major, or the students who took a course with Professor Einstein. The only requirement is that the scan's output table contains a student name and a graduation year.

A `Scan` object corresponds to a node in a query tree. SimpleDB contains a `Scan` class for each relational operator. Objects from those classes constitute the internal nodes of the query tree, and `TableScan` objects denote the leaves of the tree. Figure 8.7 shows the scan constructors for tables and the three basic operators supported by SimpleDB.

The `SelectScan` constructor takes two arguments: an underlying scan and a predicate. The underlying scan is the input to the select operator. Since `Scan` is an interface, the `SelectScan` object does not know if its input is a stored table or the output of another query. This situation corresponds to the fact that the input to a relational operator can be any table or query.

The selection predicate passed into the `SelectScan` constructor is of type `Predicate`. Section 8.6 discusses the details of how SimpleDB handles predicates; until then, I shall remain somewhat vague on the issue.

Query trees are built by composing scans. There will be a scan for each node of the tree. For example, Fig. 8.8 gives the SimpleDB code for the query tree of Fig. 8.2 (omitting the details on the selection predicate). The `Scan` variables `s1`, `s2`, and `s3` each correspond to a node in the query tree. The tree is built bottom-up: First the table scan is created, then the select scan, and finally the project scan. Variable `s3` holds the final query tree. The while-loop traverses `s3`, printing each student name.

Figure 8.9 gives the SimpleDB code corresponding to the query tree of Fig. 8.4. The code contains four scans because the query tree has four nodes. Variable `s4` holds the final query tree. Note how the while-loop is nearly identical to the previous

```
public static void printNameAndGradyear(Scan s) {
   s.beforeFirst();
   while (s.next()) {
      String sname  = s.getString("sname");
      String gradyr = s.getInt("gradyear");
      System.out.println(sname + "\t" + gradyr);
   }
   s.close();
}
```

Fig. 8.6 Printing the name and graduation year of a scan's records

Scan

```
  public TableScan(Transaction tx, String filename, Layout layout);
  public SelectScan(Scan s, Predicate pred);
  public ProjectScan(Scan s, List<String> fldlist);
  public ProductScan(Scan s1, Scan s2);
```

Fig. 8.7 The API of the SimpleDB constructors that implement `Scan`

```
Transaction tx  = db.newTx();
MetadataMgr mdm = db.MetadataMgr();

// the STUDENT node
Layout layout = mdm.getLayout("student", tx);
Scan s1 = new TableScan(tx, "student", layout);

// the Select node
Predicate pred = new Predicate(. . .); // majorid=10
Scan s2 = new SelectScan(s1, pred);

// the Project node
List<String> c = Arrays.asList("sname");
Scan s3 = new ProjectScan(s2, c);

while (s3.next())
   System.out.println(s3.getString("sname"));
s3.close();
```

Fig. 8.8 Representing Fig. 8.2 as a scan

```
Transaction tx = db.newTx();
MetadataMgr mdm = db.MetadataMgr();

// the STUDENT node
Layout layout1 = mdm.getLayout("student", tx);
Scan s1 = new TableScan(tx, "student", layout1);

// the DEPT node
Layout layout2 = mdm.getLayout("dept", tx);
Scan s2 = new TableScan(tx, "dept", layout2);

// the Product node
Scan s3 = new ProductScan(s1, s2);

// the Select node
Predicate pred = new Predicate(. . .); //majorid=did
Scan s4 = new SelectScan(s3, pred);

while (s4.next())
   System.out.println(s4.getString("sname")
                    + ", " + s4.getString("gradyear")
                    + ", " + s4.getString("dname") );
s4.close();
```

Fig. 8.9 Representing Fig. 8.4 as a scan

one. In the interest of saving space, the loop only prints three field values for each output record, but it can easily be modified to include all six field values.

Finally, note that the `close` method gets called only on the outermost scan of a query tree. Closing a scan automatically closes its underlying scans.

8.3 Update Scans

A query defines a virtual table. The `Scan` interface has methods that allow clients to read from this virtual table but not update it. Not all scans can be meaningfully updated. A scan is *updatable* if every output record `r` in the scan has a corresponding record `r′` in an underlying database table. In this case, an update to `r` is defined as an update to `r′`.

Updatable scans support the interface `UpdateScan`; see Fig. 8.10. The first five methods of the interface are basic modification operations. The other two methods involve the identifier of the stored record underlying the scan's current record. The `getRid` method returns this identifier, and `moveToRid` positions the scan at the specified stored record.

The only two classes in SimpleDB that implement `UpdateScan` are `TableScan` and `SelectScan`. As an example of their use, consider Fig. 8.11. Part (a) shows an SQL statement that changes the grade of every student who took section 53, and part (b) gives the code that implements this statement. The code first creates a select scan of all enrollment records for section 53; it then iterates through the scan, changing the grade of each record.

Variable `s2` calls the method `setString`, so it must be declared as an update scan. On the other hand, the first argument to the `SelectScan` constructor is a scan, which means that it need not be declared as an update scan. Instead, the code for `s2`'s `setString` method will cast its underlying scan (i.e., `s1`) to an update scan; if that scan is not updatable, a `ClassCastException` will be thrown.

```
public interface UpdateScan extends Scan {
   public void setInt(String fldname, int val);
   public void setString(String fldname, String val);
   public void setVal(String fldname, Constant val);
   public void insert();
   public void delete();

   public RID  getRid();
   public void moveToRid(RID rid);
}
```

Fig. 8.10 The SimpleDB `UpdateScan` interface

```
update ENROLL
set Grade = 'C' where SectionId = 53
```

(a)

```
Transaction tx  = db.newTx();
MetadataMgr mdm = db.MetadataMgr();

Layout layout = mdm.getLayout("enroll", tx);
Scan s1 = new TableScan(tx, "enroll", layout);

Predicate pred = new Predicate(. . .); // SectionId=53
UpdateScan s2  = new SelectScan(s1, pred);

while (s2.next())
   s2.setString("grade", "C");
s2.close();
```

(b)

Fig. 8.11 Representing an SQL update statement as an update scan. (**a**) An SQL statement to modify the grades of students in section 53, (**b**) the SimpleDB code corresponding to the statement

8.4 Implementing Scans

The SimpleDB engine contains four `Scan` classes: the class `TableScan` and a class for the operators select, project, and product. Chapter 6 examined `TableScan`. The following subsections discuss the three operator classes.

8.4.1 Select Scans

The code for `SelectScan` appears in Fig. 8.12. The constructor holds the scan of its underlying input table. A scan's current record is the same as the current record of its underlying scan, which means that most methods can be implemented by simply calling the corresponding method of that scan.

The only nontrivial method is `next`. The job of this method is to establish a new current record. The code loops through the underlying scan, looking for a record that satisfies the predicate. If such a record is found then it becomes the current record, and the method returns `true`. If there is no such record then the `while` loop will complete, and the method will return `false`.

Select scans are updatable. The `UpdateScan` methods assume that the underlying scan is also updatable; in particular, they assume that they can cast the underlying scan to `UpdateScan` without causing a `ClassCastException`. Since the scans created by the SimpleDB update planner only involve table scans and select scans, an occurrence of such an exception should not occur.

```
public class SelectScan implements UpdateScan {
   private Scan s;
   private Predicate pred;

   public SelectScan(Scan s, Predicate pred) {
      this.s = s;
      this.pred = pred;
   }

   // Scan methods

   public void beforeFirst() {
      s.beforeFirst();
   }

   public boolean next() {
      while (s.next())
         if (pred.isSatisfied(s))
            return true;
      return false;
   }

   public int getInt(String fldname) {
      return s.getInt(fldname);
   }

   public String getString(String fldname) {
      return s.getString(fldname);
   }

   public Constant getVal(String fldname) {
      return s.getVal(fldname);
   }

   public boolean hasField(String fldname) {
      return s.hasField(fldname);
   }

   public void close() {
      s.close();
   }

   // UpdateScan methods

   public void setInt(String fldname, int val) {
      UpdateScan us = (UpdateScan) s;
      us.setInt(fldname, val);
   }
```

Fig. 8.12 The code for the SimpleDB class `SelectScan`

```
   public void setString(String fldname, String val) {
      UpdateScan us = (UpdateScan) s;
      us.setString(fldname, val);
   }

   public void setVal(String fldname, Constant val) {
      UpdateScan us = (UpdateScan) s;
      us.setVal(fldname, val);
   }

   public void delete() {
      UpdateScan us = (UpdateScan) s;
      us.delete();
   }

   public void insert() {
      UpdateScan us = (UpdateScan) s;
      us.insert();
   }

   public RID getRid() {
      UpdateScan us = (UpdateScan) s;
      return us.getRid();
   }

   public void moveToRid(RID rid) {
      UpdateScan us = (UpdateScan) s;
      us.moveToRid(rid);
   }
}
```

Fig. 8.12 (continued)

8.4.2 Project Scans

The code for `ProjectScan` appears in Fig. 8.13. The list of output fields is passed into the constructor and is used to implement the method `hasField`. The other methods simply forward their requests to the corresponding method of the underlying scan. The `getVal`, `getInt`, and `getString` methods check to see if the specified fieldname is in the field list; if not, an exception is generated.

The class `ProjectScan` does not implement `UpdateScan`, even though projections are updatable. Exercise 8.12 asks you to complete the implementation.

8.4.3 Product Scans

The code for `ProductScan` appears in Fig. 8.14. A product scan needs to be able to iterate through all possible combinations of records from its underlying scans `s1`

```
public class ProjectScan implements Scan {
   private Scan s;
   private Collection<String> fieldlist;

   public ProjectScan(Scan s, List<String> fieldlist) {
      this.s = s;
      this.fieldlist = fieldlist;
   }

   public void beforeFirst() {
      s.beforeFirst();
   }

   public boolean next() {
      return s.next();
   }

   public int getInt(String fldname) {
      if (hasField(fldname))
         return s.getInt(fldname);
      else
         throw new RuntimeException("field not found.");
   }

   public String getString(String fldname) {
      if (hasField(fldname))
         return s.getString(fldname);
      else
         throw new RuntimeException("field not found.");
   }

   public Constant getVal(String fldname) {
      if (hasField(fldname))
         return s.getVal(fldname);
      else
         throw new RuntimeException("field not found.");
   }

   public boolean hasField(String fldname) {
      return fieldlist.contains(fldname);
   }

   public void close() {
      s.close();
   }
}
```

Fig. 8.13 The code for the SimpleDB class `ProjectScan`

```
public class ProductScan implements Scan {
  private Scan s1, s2;
  public ProductScan(Scan s1, Scan s2) {
     this.s1 = s1;
     this.s2 = s2;
     s1.next();
  }
  public void beforeFirst() {
     s1.beforeFirst();
     s1.next();
     s2.beforeFirst();
  }
  public boolean next() {
     if (s2.next())
        return true;
     else {
        s2.beforeFirst();
        return s2.next() && s1.next();
     }
  }
  public int getInt(String fldname) {
     if (s1.hasField(fldname))
        return s1.getInt(fldname);
     else
        return s2.getInt(fldname);
  }
  public String getString(String fldname) {
     if (s1.hasField(fldname))
        return s1.getString(fldname);
     else
        return s2.getString(fldname);
  }
  public Constant getVal(String fldname) {
     if (s1.hasField(fldname))
        return s1.getVal(fldname);
     else
        return s2.getVal(fldname);
  }
  public boolean hasField(String fldname) {
     return s1.hasField(fldname) || s2.hasField(fldname);
  }
  public void close() {
     s1.close();
     s2.close();
  }
}
```

Fig. 8.14 The code for the SimpleDB class ProductScan

and `s2`. It does so by starting at the first record of `s1` and iterating through each record of `s2`, then moving to the second record of `s1` and iterating through `s2`, etc. Conceptually, it is like having a nested loop with the outer loop iterating `s1` and the inner loop iterating `s2`.

The method `next` implements this "nested loops" idea as follows. Each call to `next` moves to the next record of `s2`. If `s2` has such a record, then it can return `true`. If not, then the iteration of `s2` is complete, so the method moves to the next record of `s1` and the first record of `s2`. If this is possible, then it returns `true`; if there are no more records of `s1`, then the scan is complete and `next` returns `false`.

The `getVal`, `getInt`, and `getString` methods simply access the field of the appropriate underlying scan. Each method checks to see if the specified field is in scan `s1`. If so, then it accesses the field using `s1`; otherwise, it accesses the field using `s2`.

8.5 Pipelined Query Processing

The implementations of these three relational algebra operators have two characteristics in common:

- They generate their output records one at a time, as needed.
- They do not save their output records, nor do they save any intermediate computation.

Such implementations are called *pipelined*. This section analyzes pipelined implementations and their properties.

Consider a `TableScan` object. It holds a record page, which holds a buffer, which holds a page containing the current record. The current record is just a location in that page. The record doesn't need to be removed from its page; if a client requests the value of a field, then the record manager simply extracts that value from the page and sends it back to the client. Each call to `next` positions the table scan at its next record, which may cause it to hold a different record page.

Now consider a `SelectScan` object. Each call to its `next` method repeatedly calls `next` on its underlying scan until the current record of the underlying scan satisfies the predicate. But of course, there is no actual "current record"—if the underlying scan is a table scan, then the current record is just a location in the page held by the table scan. And if the underlying scan is another kind of scan (such as the product scan in Figs. 8.4 and 8.9), then the values of the current record are determined from the current records of the table scans that are in that node's subtree.

Each time a pipelined scan processes another call to `next`, it starts its search from where it left off. As a result, the scan requests only as many records as its needs from its underlying scan to determine the next output record.

A pipelined scan does not keep track of the records it has selected. Consequently, if the client asks for the records a second time, the scan will need to perform the entire search all over again.

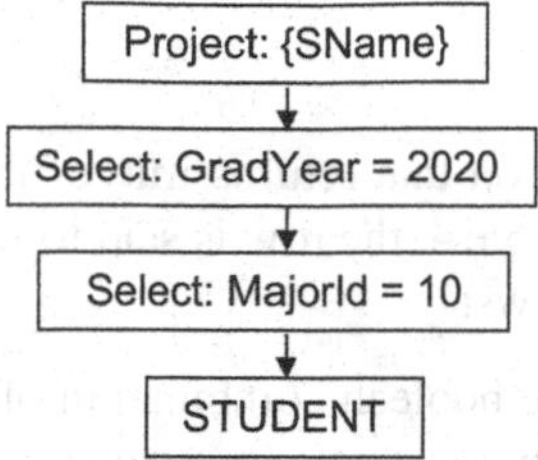

Fig. 8.15 A query tree containing multiple select nodes

The term "pipelined" refers to the flow of the method calls down the query tree and the flow of result values back up the tree. For example, consider a call to the method `getInt`. Each node in the tree passes that call down to one of its child nodes until a leaf node is reached. That leaf node (which is a table scan) extracts the desired value from its page and returns the value back up the tree. Or consider a call to the method `next`. Each node makes one or more calls to `next` (and possibly `beforeFirst`, in the case of a product node) on its child nodes until it is satisfied that its children contain the contents of the next record. It then returns success to its parent node (or failure, if no such record exists).

Pipelined implementations can be exceptionally efficient. For example, consider the query tree of Fig. 8.15, which retrieves the names of the students graduating in 2020 with major 10.

The project and select nodes in this tree incur no additional block accesses to the STUDENT table beyond those needed for the table scan. To see why, first consider the project node. Each call to `next` on that node will simply call `next` on its child node and pass back the return value of that node. In other words, the project node doesn't change the number of block accesses performed by the rest of the query.

Now consider the select nodes. A call to `next` on the outer select node will call `next` on the inner select node. The inner node will repeatedly call `next` on its child until the current record satisfies the predicate "MajorId = 10." The inner select node then returns `true`, and the outer select node examines the current record. If its grad year is not 2020, then the outer node will call `next` on the inner node again and await another current record. The only way for the outer select node to return `true` is if that record satisfies both predicates. This process continues each time the outer node calls `next`, with the underlying table scan continually moving to its next record until both predicates are satisfied. When the table scan recognizes that there are no more STUDENT records, its `next` method will return `false`, and the value of `false` will propagate up the tree. In other words, STUDENT is scanned only once, which is exactly the same as if the query had executed just a table scan. It follows that the select nodes in this query are cost-free.

Although pipelined implementations are very efficient in these cases, there are other cases when they are not so good. Once such case is when a select node is on the right side of a product node, where it will get executed multiple times. Instead of performing the selection over and over, it may be better to use an implementation that materializes the output records and stores them in a temporary table. Such implementations are the topic of Chap. 13.

8.6 Predicates

A predicate specifies a condition that returns true or false for each row of a given scan. If the condition returns `true`, the row is said to *satisfy* the predicate. An SQL predicate is structured as follows:

- A *predicate* is a term or the boolean combination of terms.
- A *term* is a comparison between two expressions.
- An *expression* consists of operations on constants and field names.
- A *constant* is a value from a predetermined set of types, such as integers and strings.

For example, consider the following predicate in standard SQL:

```
( GradYear>2021 or MOD(GradYear,4)=0 ) and MajorId=DId
```

This predicate consists of three terms (shown in bold). The first two terms compare the field name `GradYear` (or a function of `GradYear`) against a constant, and the third term compares two field names. Each term contains two expressions. For example, the second term contains the expressions `MOD(GradYear,4)` and `0`.

SimpleDB greatly simplifies the allowable constants, expressions, terms, and predicates. A SimpleDB constant can only be an integer or string, an expression can only be a constant or a field name, a term can compare expressions only for equality, and a predicate can create only conjuncts of terms. Exercises 8.7–8.9 ask you to extend SimpleDB predicates to be more expressive.

Consider the following predicate:

```
SName = 'joe' and MajorId = DId
```

The code fragment of Fig. 8.16 shows how to create this predicate in SimpleDB. Note how the predicate is created inside out, starting with the constant and expressions, then the terms, and finally the predicates.

Figure 8.17 gives the code for the class `Constant`. Each `Constant` object contains an `Integer` variable and a `String` variable. Only one of these variables will be non-null, depending on which constructor was called. The methods `equals`, `compareTo`, `hasCode`, and `toString` use whichever variable is non-null.

The code for the class `Expression` appears in Fig. 8.18. It also has two constructors, one for a constant expression and one for a field name expression. Each constructor assigns a value to its associated variable. The method `isFieldName` provides a convenient way to determine if the expression denotes a field name or not. The method `evaluate` returns the value of the expression with respect to a scan's current output record. If the expression is a constant, then the scan is irrelevant, and the method simply returns the constant. If the expression is a field,

```
Expression lhs1 = new Expression("SName");
Constant c = new Constant("joe");
Expression rhs1 = new Expression(c);
Term t1 = new Term(lhs1, rhs1);

Expression lhs2 = new Expression("MajorId");
Expression rhs2 = new Expression("DId");
Term t2 = new Term(lhs2, rhs2);

Predicate pred1 = new Predicate(t1);
Predicate pred2 = new Predicate(t2);
pred1.conjoinWith(pred2);
```

Fig. 8.16 SimpleDB code to create a predicate

then the method returns the field's value from the scan. The `appliesTo` method is used by the query planner to determine the scope of the expression.

Terms in SimpleDB are implemented by the interface `Term`, whose code appears in Fig. 8.19. Its constructor takes two arguments, which denote the left-side and right-side expressions. The most important method is `isSatisfied`, which returns true if both expressions evaluate to the same value in the given scan. The remaining methods help the query planner determine the effect and scope of the term. For example, the method `reductionFactor` determines the expected number of records that will satisfy the predicate and will be discussed in more detail in Chap. 10. The methods `equatesWithConstant` and `equatesWithField` help the query planner decide when to use indexing and will be discussed in Chap. 15.

The code for class `Predicate` appears in Fig. 8.20. A predicate is implemented as a list of terms, and a predicate responds to its methods by calling the corresponding methods on each of its terms. The class has two constructors. One constructor has no arguments and creates a predicate having no terms. Such a predicate is always satisfied and corresponds to the predicate *true*. The other constructor creates a predicate having a single term. The method `conjoinWith` adds the terms from the argument predicate to the specified predicate.

8.7 Chapter Summary

- A relational algebra query is composed of *operators*. Each operator performs one specialized task. The composition of the operators in a query can be written as a *query tree*.
- The chapter describes the three operators that are useful for understanding and translating the SimpleDB version of SQL. They are:
  - *select*, whose output table has the same columns as its input table but with some rows removed

```
public class Constant implements Comparable<Constant> {
   private Integer ival = null;
   private String  sval = null;

   public Constant(Integer ival) {
      this.ival = ival;
   }

   public Constant(String sval) {
      this.sval = sval;
   }

   public int asInt() {
      return ival;
   }

   public String asString() {
      return sval;
   }

   public boolean equals(Object obj) {
      Constant c = (Constant) obj;
      return (ival != null) ? ival.equals(c.ival)
                            : sval.equals(c.sval);
   }

   public int compareTo(Constant c) {
      return (ival!=null) ? ival.compareTo(c.ival)
                          : sval.compareTo(c.sval);
   }

   public int hashCode() {
      return (ival != null) ? ival.hashCode() : sval.hashCode();
   }

   public String toString() {
      return (ival != null) ? ival.toString() : sval.toString();
   }
}
```

Fig. 8.17 The class Constant

  - *project*, whose output table has the same rows as its input table but with some columns removed
  - *product*, whose output table consists of all possible combinations of records from its two input tables

- A s*can* is an object that represents a relational algebra query tree. Each relational operator has a corresponding class that implements the Scan interface; objects

```
public class Expression {
   private Constant val = null;
   private String fldname = null;

   public Expression(Constant val) {
      this.val = val;
   }
   public Expression(String fldname) {
      this.fldname = fldname;
   }

   public boolean isFieldName() {
      return fldname != null;
   }

   public Constant asConstant() {
      return val;
   }

   public String asFieldName() {
      return fldname;
   }

   public Constant evaluate(Scan s) {
      return (val != null) ? val : s.getVal(fldname);
   }

   public boolean appliesTo(Schema sch) {
      return (val != null) ? true : sch.hasField(fldname);
   }

   public String toString() {
      return (val != null) ? val.toString() : fldname;
   }
}
```

Fig. 8.18 The class `Expression`

from those classes constitute the internal nodes of the query tree. There is also a scan class for tables, whose objects constitute the leaves of the tree.

- The `Scan` methods are essentially the same as in `TableScan`. Clients iterate through a scan, moving from one output record to the next and retrieving field values. The scan manages the implementation of the query, by moving appropriately through record files and comparing values.
- A scan is *updatable* if every record `r` in the scan has a corresponding record `r′` in some underlying database table. In this case, an update to virtual record `r` is defined as an update to stored record `r′`.
- The methods of each scan class implement the intent of that operator. For example:

```
public class Term {
   private Expression lhs, rhs;

   public Term(Expression lhs, Expression rhs) {
      this.lhs = lhs;
      this.rhs = rhs;
   }

   public boolean isSatisfied(Scan s) {
      Constant lhsval = lhs.evaluate(s);
      Constant rhsval = rhs.evaluate(s);
      return rhsval.equals(lhsval);
   }

   public boolean appliesTo(Schema sch) {
      return lhs.appliesTo(sch) && rhs.appliesTo(sch);
   }

   public int reductionFactor(Plan p) {
      String lhsName, rhsName;
      if (lhs.isFieldName() && rhs.isFieldName()) {
         lhsName = lhs.asFieldName();
         rhsName = rhs.asFieldName();
         return Math.max(p.distinctValues(lhsName),
                         p.distinctValues(rhsName));
      }
      if (lhs.isFieldName()) {
         lhsName = lhs.asFieldName();
         return p.distinctValues(lhsName);
      }
      if (rhs.isFieldName()) {
         rhsName = rhs.asFieldName();
         return p.distinctValues(rhsName);
      }
      // otherwise, the term equates constants
      if (lhs.asConstant().equals(rhs.asConstant()))
         return 1;
      else
         return Integer.MAX_VALUE;
   }

   public Constant equatesWithConstant(String fldname) {
      if (lhs.isFieldName() &&
          lhs.asFieldName().equals(fldname) &&
          !rhs.isFieldName())
         return rhs.asConstant();
      else if (rhs.isFieldName() &&
               rhs.asFieldName().equals(fldname) &&
               !lhs.isFieldName())
         return lhs.asConstant();
      else
         return null;
   }
```

Fig. 8.19 The code for the SimpleDB class `Term`

```
    public String equatesWithField(String fldname) {
       if (lhs.isFieldName() &&
           lhs.asFieldName().equals(fldname) &&
           rhs.isFieldName())
          return rhs.asFieldName();
       else if (rhs.isFieldName() &&
                rhs.asFieldName().equals(fldname) &&
                lhs.isFieldName())
          return lhs.asFieldName();
       else
          return null;
    }

    public String toString() {
       return lhs.toString() + "=" + rhs.toString();
    }
}
```

Fig. 8.19 (continued)

  - A select scan checks each record in its underlying scan and returns only those that satisfy its predicate.
  - A product scan returns a record for every combination of records from its two underlying scans.
  - A table scan opens a record file for the specified table, which pins buffers and obtains locks as necessary.

- These scan implementations are called *pipelined* implementations. A pipelined implementation does not try to read ahead, cache, sort, or otherwise preprocess its data.
- A pipelined implementation does not construct output records. Each leaf in the query tree is a table scan, containing a buffer that holds the current record of that table. The "current record" of the operation is determined from the records in each buffer. Requests to get field values are directed down the tree to the appropriate table scan; results are returned from table scans back up to the root.
- Scans that use pipelined implementations operate on a need-to-know basis. Each scan will request only as many records from its children as it needs to determine its next record.

8.8 Suggested Reading

Relational algebra is defined in nearly every introductory database text, although each text tends to have its own syntax. A detailed presentation of relational algebra and its expressive power can be found in Atzeni and DeAntonellis (1992). That book also introduces *relational calculus*, which is a query language based on predicate logic. The interesting thing about relational calculus is that it can be extended to

```
public class Predicate {
   private List<Term> terms = new ArrayList<Term>();

   public Predicate() {}

   public Predicate(Term t) {
      terms.add(t);
   }

   public void conjoinWith(Predicate pred) {
      terms.addAll(pred.terms);
   }

   public boolean isSatisfied(Scan s) {
      for (Term t : terms)
         if (!t.isSatisfied(s))
         return false;
      return true;
   }

   public int reductionFactor(Plan p) {
      int factor = 1;
      for (Term t : terms)
         factor *= t.reductionFactor(p);
      return factor;
   }

   public Predicate selectSubPred(Schema sch) {
      Predicate result = new Predicate();
      for (Term t : terms)
         if (t.appliesTo(sch))
         result.terms.add(t);
      if (result.terms.size() == 0)
         return null;
      else
         return result;
   }

   public Predicate joinSubPred(Schema sch1, Schema sch2) {
      Predicate result = new Predicate();
      Schema newsch = new Schema();
      newsch.addAll(sch1);
      newsch.addAll(sch2);
      for (Term t : terms)
         if (!t.appliesTo(sch1)  &&
             !t.appliesTo(sch2) &&
             t.appliesTo(newsch))
         result.terms.add(t);
      if (result.terms.size() == 0)
         return null;
```

Fig. 8.20 The code for the SimpleDB class *Predicate*

```
      else
         return result;
   }

   public Constant equatesWithConstant(String fldname) {
      for (Term t : terms) {
         Constant c = t.equatesWithConstant(fldname);
         if (c != null)
            return c;
      }
      return null;
   }

   public String equatesWithField(String fldname) {
      for (Term t : terms) {
         String s = t.equatesWithField(fldname);
         if (s != null)
            return s;
      }
      return null;
   }

   public String toString() {
      Iterator<Term> iter = terms.iterator();
      if (!iter.hasNext())
         return "";
      String result = iter.next().toString();
      while (iter.hasNext())
         result += " and " + iter.next().toString();
      return result;
   }
}
```

Fig. 8.20 (continued)

allow recursive queries (i.e., queries in which the output table is also mentioned in the query definition). Recursive relational calculus is called *datalog* and is related to the Prolog programming language. A discussion of datalog and its expressive power also appears in Atzeni and DeAntonellis (1992).

The topic of pipelined query processing is a small piece of the query-processing puzzle, which also includes the topics of later chapters. The article Graefe (1993) contains comprehensive information about query-processing techniques; Section 1 has a large discussion of scans and pipelined processing. The article Chaudhuri (1998) discusses query trees, in addition to statistical gathering and optimization.

Atzeni, P., & DeAntonellis, V. (1992). *Relational database theory*. Upper Saddle River, NJ: Prentice-Hall.

Chaudhuri, S. (1998). An overview of query optimization in relational systems. In *Proceedings of the ACM Principles of Database Systems Conference* (pp. 34–43).
Graefe, G. (1993). Query evaluation techniques for large databases. *ACM Computing Surveys, 25*(2), 73–170.

8.9 Exercises

Conceptual Exercises

8.1. What is the output of a product operation if either one of its inputs is empty?

8.2. Implement the following query as a scan, using Fig. 8.9 as a template.

```
select sname, dname, grade
from STUDENT, DEPT, ENROLL, SECTION
where SId=StudentId and SectId=SectionId and DId=MajorId
and YearOffered=2020
```

8.3. Consider the code of Fig. 8.9.

(a) What locks will the transaction need to obtain in order to execute this code?
(b) For each of these locks, give a scenario that would cause the code to wait for that lock.

8.4. Consider the code for `ProductScan`.

(a) What problem can occur when the first underlying scan has no records? How should the code be fixed?
(b) Explain why no problems occur when the second underlying scan has no records.

8.5. Suppose you want to find all pairs of students by taking the product of STUDENT with itself.

(a) One way is to create a table scan on STUDENT and use it twice in the product, as in the following code fragment:

```
Layout layout = mdm.getLayout("student", tx);
Scan s1 = new TableScan(tx, "student", layout);
Scan s2 = new ProductScan(s1, s1);
```

Explain why this will produce incorrect (and strange) behavior when the scan is executed.
(b) A better way is to create two different table scans on STUDENT and create a product scan on them. This returns all combinations of STUDENT records but has a problem. What is it?

Programming Exercises

8.6. The `getVal`, `getInt`, and `getString` methods in `ProjectScan` check that their argument field names are valid. None of the other scan classes do this. For each of the other scan classes:

(a) Say what problem will occur (and in what method) if those methods are called with an invalid field.
(b) Fix the SimpleDB code so that an appropriate exception is thrown.

8.7. Currently, SimpleDB supports only integer and string constants.

(a) Revise SimpleDB to have other kinds of constant, such as short integers, byte arrays, and dates.
(b) Exercise 3.17 asked you to modify the class `Page` to have get/set methods for types such as short integers, dates, etc. If you have done this exercise, add similar `get/set` methods to `Scan` and `UpdateScan` (and their various implementation classes), as well as to the record manager, the transaction manager, and the buffer manager. Then modify the methods `getVal` and `setVal` appropriately.

8.8. Revise expressions to handle arithmetic operators on integers.
8.9. Revise the class `Term` to handle the comparison operators $<$ and $>$.
8.10. Revise the class `Predicate` to handle arbitrary combinations of the boolean connectives `and`, `or` and `not`.
8.11. In Exercise 6.13, you extended the SimpleDB record manager to handle database null values. Now extend the query processor to handle nulls. In particular:

- Modify the class `Constant` appropriately.
- Modify the methods `getVal` and `setVal` in `TableScan` so that they recognize null values and handle them appropriately.
- Determine which of the various `Expression`, `Term`, and `Predicate` classes need to be modified to handle null constants.

8.12. Revise the class `ProjectScan` to be an update scan.
8.13. Exercise 6.10 asked you to write methods `previous` and `afterLast` for class `TableScan`.

(a) Modify SimpleDB so that all scans have these methods.
(b) Write a program to test your code. Note that you will not be able to test your changes on the SimpleDB engine unless you also extend its implementation of JDBC. See Exercise 11.5.

8.14. The *rename* operator takes three arguments: an input table, the name of a field from the table, and a new field name. The output table is identical to the input table, except that the specified field has been renamed. For example, the following query renames the field `SName` to `StudentName`:

```
rename(STUDENT, SName, StudentName)
```

Write a class `RenameScan` to implement this operator. This class will be needed in Exercise 10.13.

8.15. The *extend* operator takes three arguments: an input table, an expression, and a new field name. The output table is identical to the input table, except that it also contains a new field whose value is determined by the expression. For example, the following query extends STUDENT with a new field (called `JuniorYear`) that calculates the year when the student was a junior:

```
extend(STUDENT, GradYear-1, JuniorYear)
```

Write a class `ExtendScan` to implement this operator. This class will be needed in Exercise 10.14.

8.16. The *union* relational operator takes two arguments, both of which are tables. Its output table contains those records that appear somewhere in the input tables. A union query requires that both underlying tables have the same schema; the output table will also have that schema. Write a class `UnionScan` to implement this operator. This class will be needed in Exercise 10.15.

8.17. The *semijoin* operator takes three arguments: two tables and a predicate. It returns the records in the first table that have a "matching" record in the second table. For example, the following query returns those departments that have at least one student major:

```
semijoin(DEPT, STUDENT, Did=MajorId)
```

Analogously, the *antijoin* operator returns the records in the first table that have no matching records. For example, the following query returns departments having no student majors:

```
antijoin(DEPT, STUDENT, Did=MajorId)
```

Write the classes `SemijoinScan` and `AntijoinScan` to implement these operators. These classes will be needed in Exercise 10.16.

Chapter 9
Parsing

A JDBC client submits an SQL statement to the database engine as a string. The engine must extract from this string the information needed to create a query tree. This extraction process has two stages: a syntax-based stage, known as parsing, and a semantics-based stage, known as planning. This chapter covers parsing. Planning is covered in Chap. 10.

9.1 Syntax Versus Semantics

The *syntax* of a language is a set of rules that describe the strings that could possibly be meaningful statements. For example, consider the following string:

```
select from tables T1 and T2 where b - 3
```

There are several reasons why this string is not syntactically legal:

- The `select` clause must contain something.
- The identifier `tables` is not a keyword and will be treated as a table name.
- Table names need to be separated by commas, not the keyword `and`.
- The string "*b – 3*" does not denote a predicate.

Each one of these problems causes this string to be completely meaningless as an SQL statement. There is no way that the engine could ever figure out how to execute it, regardless of what the identifiers `tables`, `T1`, `T2`, and `b` happen to denote.

The *semantics* of a language specifies the actual meaning of a syntactically correct string. Consider the following syntactically legal string:

```
select a from x, z where b = 3
```


E. Sciore, *Database Design and Implementation*, Data-Centric Systems and Applications, https://doi.org/10.1007/978-3-030-33836-7_9

You can infer that this statement is a query that requests one field (named `a`) from two tables (named `x` and `z`) and has predicate $b = 3$. Thus, the statement is possibly meaningful.

Whether the statement is actually meaningful depends on *semantic information* about `x`, `z`, `a`, and `b`. In particular, `x` and `z` must be names of tables such that these tables contain a field named `a` and a numeric field named `b`. This semantic information can be determined from the database's metadata. The parser knows nothing about metadata and thus cannot evaluate the meaningfulness of an SQL statement. Instead, the responsibility for examining the metadata belongs to the planner and will be discussed in Chap. 10.

9.2 Lexical Analysis

The first task of the parser is to split the input string into "chunks" called *tokens*. The portion of the parser that performs this task is called the *lexical analyzer*.

Each token has a *type* and a *value*. The SimpleDB lexical analyzer supports five token types:

- Single-character *delimiters*, such as the comma
- *Integer constants*, such as `123`
- *String constants*, such as `'joe'`
- *Keywords*, such as `select`, `from`, and `where`
- *Identifiers*, such as `STUDENT`, `x`, and `glop34a`

Whitespace characters (spaces, tabs, and newlines) are generally not part of tokens; the only exception is inside of string constants. The purpose of whitespace is to enhance readability and separate tokens from each other.

Consider again the previous SQL statement:

```
select a from x, z where b = 3
```

The lexical analyzer creates ten tokens for it, shown in Fig. 9.1.

Conceptually, the behavior of a lexical analyzer is straightforward—it reads the input string one character at a time, stopping when it determines that the next token has been read. The complexity of a lexical analyzer is in direct proportion to the set of token types: the more token types to look for, the more complex the implementation.

Java supplies two different built-in *tokenizers* (their term for lexical analyzers): one in class `StringTokenizer` and one in class `StreamTokenizer`. The string tokenizer is simpler to use, but it only supports two kinds of token: delimiters and words (which are the substrings between delimiters). This is not appropriate for SQL, in particular because the string tokenizer does not understand numbers or quoted strings. On the other hand, the stream tokenizer has an extensive set of token types, including support for all five types used by SimpleDB.

TYPE	VALUE
keyword	select
identifier	a
keyword	from
identifier	x
delimiter	,
identifier	z
keyword	where
identifier	b
delimiter	=
intconstant	3

Fig. 9.1 Tokens produced by the lexical analyzer

Figure 9.2 gives the code for the class `TokenizerTest`, which illustrates the use of `StreamTokenizer`. The code tokenizes a given line of input and prints the type and value of each token.

The call `tok.ordinaryChar('.')` tells the tokenizer to interpret a period as a delimiter. (Even though periods are not used in SimpleDB, it is important to identify them as delimiters to keep them from being accepted as part of an identifier.) Conversely, the call `tok.wordChars('_', '_')` tells the tokenizer to interpret underscores as part of identifiers. The call `tok.lowerCaseMode(true)` tells the tokenizer to convert all string tokens (but not quoted strings) to lower case, which lets SQL be case insensitive for keywords and identifiers.

The method `nextToken` positions the tokenizer at the next token in the stream; a return value of `TT_EOF` indicates that there are no more tokens. The tokenizer's public variable `ttype` holds the type of the current token. The value `TT_NUMBER` indicates a numeric constant, `TT_WORD` denotes an identifier or keyword, and the integer representation of a single quote denotes a string constant. The type of a single-character delimiter token is the integer representation of that character.

9.3 The SimpleDB Lexical Analyzer

The `SteamTokenizer` class is a general-purpose lexical analyzer, but it can be awkward to use. The SimpleDB class `Lexer` provides an easier way for the parser to access the token stream. There are two kinds of methods that the parser can call: methods that ask about the current token and methods that tell the lexical analyzer to "eat" the current token, returning its value and moving to the next token. Each token type has a corresponding pair of methods. The API for these ten methods appear in Fig. 9.3.

The first five methods return information about the current token. The method `matchDelim` returns `true` if the current token is a delimiter having the specified

```
public class TokenizerTest {
   private static Collection<String> keywords =
         Arrays.asList("select", "from", "where", "and", "insert",
                    "into", "values", "delete", "update", "set",
                    "create", "table","int", "varchar", "view", "as",
                    "index", "on");

   public static void main(String[] args) throws IOException {
      String s = getStringFromUser();
      StreamTokenizer tok = new StreamTokenizer(new StringReader(s));
      tok.ordinaryChar('.');
      tok.wordChars('_', '_');
      tok.lowerCaseMode(true); //convert ids and keywords to
                                         lower case
      while (tok.nextToken() != TT_EOF)
         printCurrentToken(tok);
   }
  private static String getStringFromUser() {
     System.out.println("Enter tokens:");
     Scanner sc = new Scanner(System.in);
     String s = sc.nextLine();
     sc.close();
     return s;
  }
  private static void printCurrentToken(StreamTokenizer tok)
                                            throws IOException {
     if (tok.ttype == TT_NUMBER)
        System.out.println("IntConstant " + (int)tok.nval);
     else if (tok.ttype == TT_WORD) {
        String word = tok.sval;
        if (keywords.contains(word))
           System.out.println("Keyword " + word);
        else
           System.out.println("Id " + word);
     }
     else if (tok.ttype == '\'')
        System.out.println("StringConstant " + tok.sval);
     else
        System.out.println("Delimiter " + (char)tok.ttype);
  }
}
```

Fig. 9.2 The class *TokenizerTest*

value. Similarly, `matchKeyword` returns `true` if the current token is a keyword having the specified value. The other three `matchXXX` methods return `true` if the current token is of the proper type.

The last five methods "eat" the current token. Each method calls its corresponding `matchXXX` method. If that method returns `false`, then an exception is thrown; otherwise, the next token becomes current. In addition, the methods `eatIntConstant`, `eatStringConstant`, and `eatId` return the value of the current token.

Lexer

```
public boolean matchDelim(char d);
public boolean matchIntConstant();
public boolean matchStringConstant();
public boolean matchKeyword(String w);
public boolean matchId();

public void    eatDelim(char d);
public int     eatIntConstant();
public String  eatStringConstant();
public void    eatKeyword(String w);
public String  eatId();
```

Fig. 9.3 The API for the SimpleDB lexical analyzer

The class `LexerTest` in Fig. 9.4 illustrates the use of these methods. The code reads lines of input. It expects each line to be of the form "A = c" or "c = A," where A is an identifier and c is an int constant. An input line in any other form generates an exception.

The code for `Lexer` appears in Fig. 9.5. Its constructor sets up the stream tokenizer. The methods `eatIntConstant`, `eatStringConstant`, and `eatId` return the value of the current token. The method `initKeywords` constructs a collection of the keywords used in SimpleDB's version of SQL.

```
public class LexerTest {
   public static void main(String[] args) {
      String x = "";
      int y = 0;
      Scanner sc = new Scanner(System.in);
      while (sc.hasNext()) {
         String s = sc.nextLine();
         Lexer lex = new Lexer(s);
         if (lex.matchId()) {
            x = lex.eatId();
            lex.eatDelim('=');
            y = lex.eatIntConstant();
         }
         else {
            y = lex.eatIntConstant();
            lex.eatDelim('=');
            x = lex.eatId();
         }
         System.out.println(x + " equals " + y);
      }
      sc.close();
   }
}
```

Fig. 9.4 The class `LexerTest`

```
public class Lexer {
   private Collection<String> keywords;
   private StreamTokenizer tok;

   public Lexer(String s) {
      initKeywords();
      tok = new StreamTokenizer(new StringReader(s));
      tok.ordinaryChar('.');
      tok.wordChars('_', '_');
      tok.lowerCaseMode(true);
      nextToken();
   }

//Methods to check the status of the current token

   public boolean matchDelim(char d) {
      return d == (char)tok.ttype;
   }

   public boolean matchIntConstant() {
      return tok.ttype == StreamTokenizer.TT_NUMBER;
   }

   public boolean matchStringConstant() {
      return '\'' == (char)tok.ttype;
   }

   public boolean matchKeyword(String w) {
     return tok.ttype == StreamTokenizer.TT_WORD &&
                         tok.sval.equals(w);
   }

   public boolean matchId() {
     return tok.ttype == StreamTokenizer.TT_WORD &&
                         !keywords.contains(tok.sval);
   }

//Methods to "eat" the current token

   public void eatDelim(char d) {
      if (!matchDelim(d))
         throw new BadSyntaxException();
      nextToken();
   }

   public int eatIntConstant() {
      if (!matchIntConstant())
         throw new BadSyntaxException();
      int i = (int) tok.nval;
      nextToken();
      return i;
   }
```

Fig. 9.5 The code for the SimpleDB class *Lexer*

```
   public String eatStringConstant() {
      if (!matchStringConstant())
         throw new BadSyntaxException();
      String s = tok.sval;
      nextToken();
      return s;
   }

   public void eatKeyword(String w) {
      if (!matchKeyword(w))
         throw new BadSyntaxException();
      nextToken();
   }

   public String eatId() {
      if (!matchId())
         throw new BadSyntaxException();
      String s = tok.sval;
      nextToken();
      return s;
   }

   private void nextToken() {
      try {
         tok.nextToken();
      }
      catch(IOException e) {
         throw new BadSyntaxException();
      }
   }

   private void initKeywords() {
      keywords = Arrays.asList("select", "from", "where", "and",
                    "insert","into", "values", "delete", "update",
                          "set", "create", "table", "varchar",
                          "int", "view", "as", "index", "on");
   }
}
```

Fig. 9.5 (continued)

The `StreamTokenizer` method `nextToken` throws an `IOException`. The `Lexer` method `nextToken` transforms this exception to a `BadSyntaxException`, which is passed back to the client (and turned into an `SQLException`, as will be described in Chap. 11).

9.4 Grammars

A *grammar* is a set of rules that describe how tokens can be legally combined. The following is an example of a grammar rule:

```
<Field> := IdTok
```

The left side of a grammar rule specifies a *syntactic category*. A syntactic category denotes a particular concept in the language. In the above rule, *<Field>* denotes the concept of a field name. The right side of a grammar rule is a pattern that specifies the set of strings that belong to the syntactic category. In the above rule, the pattern is simply `IdTok`, which matches any identifier token. Thus, <Field> contains the set of strings corresponding to identifiers.

Each syntactic category can be thought of as its own mini-language. For example, "SName" and "Glop" are members of <Field>. Remember that the identifiers need not be meaningful—they just need to be identifiers. So "Glop" is a perfectly good member of <Field>, even in the SimpleDB university database. However, "select" would not be a member of <Field>, because it is a keyword token, not an identifier token.

The pattern on the right side of a grammar rule can contain references to both tokens and syntactic categories. Tokens that have well-known values (i.e., keywords and delimiters) appear explicitly. Other tokens (identifiers, integer constants, and string constants) are written as `IdTok`, `IntTok`, and `StrTok` respectively. Three meta-characters ('[', ']', and '|') are used as punctuation; these characters are not delimiters in the language, so they can be used to help express patterns. To illustrate, consider the following four additional grammar rules:

```
<Constant>   := StrTok | IntTok
<Expression> := <Field> | <Constant>
<Term>       := <Expression> = <Expression>
<Predicate>  := <Term> [ AND <Predicate> ]
```

The first rule defines the category <Constant>, which stands for any constant—string or integer. The meta-character '|' means "or." Thus, the category <Constant> matches either string tokens or integer tokens, and its contents (as a language) will contain all string constants as well as all integer constants.

The second rule defines the category <Expression>, which denotes operator-free expressions. The rule specifies that an expression is either a field or a constant.

The third rule defines the category <Term>, which denotes simple equality terms between expressions (as in the SimpleDB class `Term`). For example, the following strings belong to <Term>:

```
DeptId = DId
'math' = DName
```

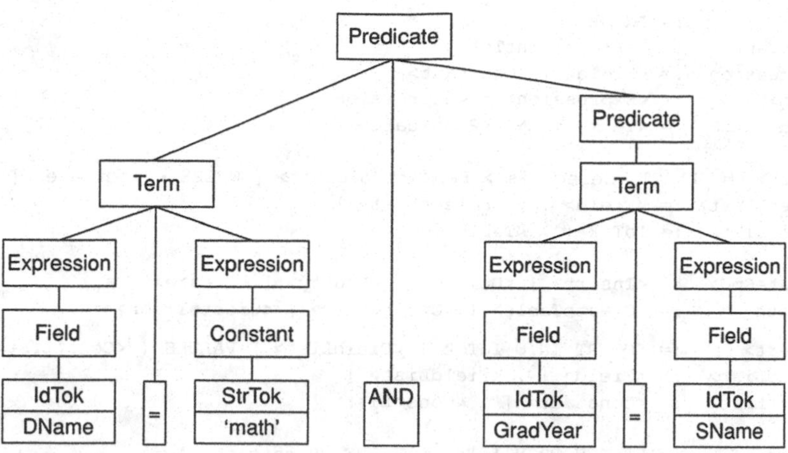

Fig. 9.6 A parse tree for the string DName = 'math' AND GradYear = SName

```
SName  = 123
65     = 'abc'
```

Recall that the parser does not check for type consistency; thus the last two strings are syntactically correct even though they are semantically incorrect.

The fourth rule defines the category <Predicate>, which stands for a boolean combination of terms, similar to the SimpleDB class `Predicate`. The meta-characters '[' and ']' denote something optional. Thus, the right side of the rule matches any sequence of tokens that is either a <Term>, or a <Term> followed by an AND keyword token followed (recursively) by another <Predicate>. For example, the following strings belong to <Predicate>:

```
DName = 'math'
Id = 3 AND DName = 'math'
MajorId = DId AND Id = 3 AND DName = 'math'
```

The first string is of the form *<Term>*. The second two strings are of the form *<Term> AND <Predicate>*.

If a string belongs to a particular syntactic category, you can draw a *parse tree* to depict why. A parse tree has syntactic categories as its internal nodes and tokens as its leaf nodes. The children of a category node correspond to the application of a grammar rule. For example, Fig. 9.6 contains the parse tree for the following string:

```
DName = 'math' AND GradYear = SName
```

In this figure, the tree's leaf nodes appear along the bottom of the tree, to make it easier to read the input string. Starting from the root node, this tree asserts that the entire string is a <Predicate> because "`DName='math'`" is a <Term> and "`GradYear=SName`" is a <Predicate>. You can expand each of the subtrees similarly. For example, "`DName='math'`" is a <Term> because both "`DName`" and "`'math'`" belong to <Expression>.

```
<Field>       := IdTok
<Constant>    := StrTok | IntTok
<Expression> := <Field> | <Constant>
<Term>        := <Expression> = <Expression>
<Predicate>   := <Term> [ AND <Predicate> ]

<Query> := SELECT <SelectList> FROM <TableList> [ WHERE <Predicate> ]
<SelectList> := <Field> [ , <SelectList> ]
<TableList>  := IdTok [ , <TableList> ]

<UpdateCmd>  := <Insert> | <Delete> | <Modify> | <Create>
<Create>     := <CreateTable> | <CreateView> | <CreateIndex>

<Insert>     := INSERT INTO IdTok ( <FieldList> ) VALUES ( <ConstList> )
<FieldList>  := <Field> [ , <FieldList> ]
<ConstList>  := <Constant> [ , <ConstList> ]

<Delete>     := DELETE FROM IdTok [ WHERE <Predicate> ]

<Modify> := UPDATE IdTok SET <Field> = <Expression> [ WHERE <Predicate> ]

<CreateTable> := CREATE TABLE IdTok ( <FieldDefs> )
<FieldDefs>   := <FieldDef> [ , <FieldDefs> ]
<FieldDef>    := IdTok <TypeDef>
<TypeDef>     := INT | VARCHAR ( IntTok )

<CreateView>  := CREATE VIEW IdTok AS <Query>

<CreateIndex> := CREATE INDEX IdTok ON IdTok ( <Field> )
```

Fig. 9.7 The grammar for the SimpleDB subset of SQL

Figure 9.7 lists the entire grammar for the subset of SQL supported by SimpleDB. The grammar rules are divided into nine sections: one section for common constructs such as predicates, expressions, and fields; one section for queries; and seven sections for the various kinds of update statement.

Lists of items appear frequently in SQL. In a query, for example, the `select` clause contains a comma-separated list of fields, the `from` clause contains a comma-separated list of identifiers, and the `where` clause contains an AND-separated list of terms. Each list is specified in the grammar using the same recursive technique that you saw for <Predicate>. Also note how the "option-bracket" notation is used in the rules for <Query>, <Delete>, and <Modify>, to allow them to have optional `where` clauses.

I mentioned that the parser cannot enforce type compatibility because it cannot know the types of the identifiers it sees. The parser also cannot enforce compatible list sizes. For example, an SQL `insert` statement must mention the same number of values as field names, but the grammar rule for <Insert> requires only that the string have a <FieldList> and a <ConstList>. The planner must be responsible for verifying that these lists are the same size (and are type compatible).[1]

9.5 Recursive-Descent Parsers

A parse tree can be thought of as a proof that a given string is syntactically legal. But how do you determine the parse tree? How can a database engine determine if a string is syntactically legal?

Programming-language researchers have developed numerous *parsing algorithms* for this purpose. The complexity of a parsing algorithm is usually in proportion to the complexity of the grammars it can support. Fortunately for us, our SQL grammar is about as simple as you can get, and so it can use the simplest possible parsing algorithm, known as *recursive descent*.

In a basic recursive-descent parser, each syntactic category is implemented by a `void` method. A call to this method will "eat" those tokens that comprise the parse tree for that category and return. The method throws an exception when the tokens do not correspond to a parse tree for that category.

Consider the first five grammar rules from Fig. 9.7, which form the subset of SQL corresponding to predicates. A Java class corresponding to this grammar appears in Fig. 9.8.

Consider the method `field`, which makes one call to the lexical analyzer (and ignores any return values). If the next token is an identifier, then the call returns successfully and that token will be eaten. If not, then the method throws the exception back to the caller. Similarly, consider the method `term`. Its first call to `expression` eats the tokens corresponding to a single SQL expression, its call to `eatDelim` eats the equals-sign token, and its second call to `expression` eats the tokens corresponding to another SQL expression. If any of these method calls did not find the tokens it expected, it would throw an exception, which the `term` method would pass on to its caller.

Grammar rules that contain alternatives are implemented using `if` statements. The condition of the `if` statement looks at the current token in order to decide what to do. For a trivial example, consider the method `constant`. If the current token is a string constant then the method eats it; otherwise, the method tries to eat an integer constant. If the current token is neither a string constant nor an integer constant, then the call to `lex.eatIntConstant` will generate the exception. For a less trivial example, consider the method `expression`. Here the method knows that if the

[1]This situation is certainly not desirable; in fact, it would be really nice to have a grammar in which equal list sizes are enforced. However, one can use automata theory to prove that no such grammar is possible.

```
public class PredParser {

   private Lexer lex;

   public PredParser(String s) {
      lex = new Lexer(s);
   }

   public void field() {
      lex.eatId();
   }

   public void constant() {
      if (lex.matchStringConstant())
         lex.eatStringConstant();
      else
         lex.eatIntConstant();
   }

   public void expression() {
      if (lex.matchId())
         field();
      else
         constant();
   }

   public void term() {
      expression();
      lex.eatDelim('=');
      expression();
   }

   public void predicate() {
      term();
      if (lex.matchKeyword("and")) {
         lex.keyword("and");
         predicate();
      }
   }
}
```

Fig. 9.8 The code for a simplified recursive-descent parser for predicates

current token is an identifier then it must look for a field; otherwise it must look for a constant.[2]

The method `predicate` illustrates how a recursive rule is implemented. It first calls the method `term` and then checks to see if the current token is the keyword AND. If so, it eats the AND-token and calls itself recursively. If the current token is not an AND, then it knows it has seen the last term in the list and returns. Consequently, a call to `predicate` will eat as many tokens as it can from the token stream—if it sees an AND-token it keeps going, even if it has already seen a valid predicate.

The interesting thing about recursive-descent parsing is that the sequence of method calls determines the parse tree for the input string. Exercise 9.4 asks you to modify the code of each method to print its name, appropriately indented; the result will resemble a sideways parse tree.

9.6 Adding Actions to the Parser

The basic recursive-descent parsing algorithm returns normally when the input string is syntactically valid. Although this behavior is somewhat interesting, it is not especially useful. To that end, the basic parser needs to be modified to return

[2]This example also demonstrates the limitations of recursive-descent parsing. If a grammar rule has two alternatives that both require the same first token, then there would be no way to know which alternative to take and recursive descent will not work. In fact, you may have noticed that the grammar of Fig. 9.7 has this very problem. Exercise 9.3 addresses the issue.

information that the planner needs. This modification is called adding *actions* to the parser.

In general, an SQL parser should extract information such as table names, field names, predicates, and constants from the SQL statement. What gets extracted depends on the kind of SQL statement it is.

- *For a query*: a list of field names (from the `select` clause), a collection of table names (from the `from` clause), and a predicate (from the `where` clause)
- *For an insertion*: a table name, a list of field names, and a list of values
- *For a deletion*: a table name and a predicate
- *For a modification*: a table name, the name of the field to be modified, an expression denoting the new field value, and a predicate
- *For a table creation*: a table name and its schema
- *For a view creation*: a table name and its definition
- *For index creation*: an index name, a table name, and the name of the indexed field

This information can be extracted from the token stream via the return values of the `Lexer` methods. Thus, the strategy for modifying each parser method is straightforward: Get the return values from calls to `eatId`, `eatStringConstant`, and `eatIntConstant`, assemble them into an appropriate object, and return the object to the method's caller.

Figure 9.9 gives the code for the class `Parser`, whose methods implement the grammar of Fig. 9.7. The following subsections examine this code in detail.

9.6.1 Parsing Predicates and Expressions

The heart of the parser deals with the five grammar rules that define predicates and expressions, because they are used to parse several different kinds of SQL statement. Those methods in `Parser` are the same as in `PredParser` (in Fig. 9.8), except that they now contain actions and return values. In particular, the method `field` grabs the fieldname from the current token and returns it. The methods `constant`, `expression`, `term`, and `predicate` are similar, returning a `Constant` object, an `Expression` object, a `Term` object, and a `Predicate` object.

9.6.2 Parsing Queries

The method `query` implements the syntactic category <Query>. As the parser parses a query, it acquires the three items needed by the planner—the field names, the table names, and the predicate—and saves them in a `QueryData` object. The class `QueryData` makes these values available via its methods `fields`, `tables`, and `pred`; see Fig. 9.10. The class also has a method `toString`, which re-creates the query string. This method will be needed when processing view definitions.

```
public class Parser {
   private Lexer lex;

   public Parser(String s) {
      lex = new Lexer(s);
   }

// Methods for parsing predicates and their components

   public String field() {
      return lex.eatId();
   }

   public Constant constant() {
      if (lex.matchStringConstant())
         return new Constant(lex.eatStringConstant());
      else
         return new Constant(lex.eatIntConstant());
   }

   public Expression expression() {
      if (lex.matchId())
         return new Expression(field());
      else
         return new Expression(constant());
   }

   public Term term() {
      Expression lhs = expression();
      lex.eatDelim('=');
      Expression rhs = expression();
      return new Term(lhs, rhs);
   }

   public Predicate predicate() {
      Predicate pred = new Predicate(term());
      if (lex.matchKeyword("and")) {
         lex.eatKeyword("and");
         pred.conjoinWith(predicate());
      }
      return pred;
   }

// Methods for parsing queries

   public QueryData query() {
      lex.eatKeyword("select");
      List<String> fields = selectList();
      lex.eatKeyword("from");
      Collection<String> tables = tableList();
      Predicate pred = new Predicate();
      if (lex.matchKeyword("where")) {
         lex.eatKeyword("where");
         pred = predicate();
      }
      return new QueryData(fields, tables, pred);
```

Fig. 9.9 The code for the SimpleDB class *Parser*

```
   }
   private List<String> selectList() {
      List<String> L = new ArrayList<String>();
      L.add(field());
      if (lex.matchDelim(',')) {
         lex.eatDelim(',');
         L.addAll(selectList());
      }
      return L;
   }
   private Collection<String> tableList() {
      Collection<String> L = new ArrayList<String>();
      L.add(lex.eatId());
      if (lex.matchDelim(',')) {
         lex.eatDelim(',');
         L.addAll(tableList());
      }
      return L;
   }
// Methods for parsing the various update commands
   public Object updateCmd() {
      if (lex.matchKeyword("insert"))
         return insert();
      else if (lex.matchKeyword("delete"))
         return delete();
      else if (lex.matchKeyword("update"))
         return modify();
      else
         return create();
   }
   private Object create() {
      lex.eatKeyword("create");
      if (lex.matchKeyword("table"))
         return createTable();
      else if (lex.matchKeyword("view"))
         return createView();
      else
         return createIndex();
   }
// Method for parsing delete commands
   public DeleteData delete() {
      lex.eatKeyword("delete");
      lex.eatKeyword("from");
      String tblname = lex.eatId();
      Predicate pred = new Predicate();
      if (lex.matchKeyword("where")) {
         lex.eatKeyword("where");
         pred = predicate();
      }
      return new DeleteData(tblname, pred);
   }
```

Fig. 9.9 (continued)

```
// Methods for parsing insert commands
   public InsertData insert() {
      lex.eatKeyword("insert");
      lex.eatKeyword("into");
      String tblname = lex.eatId();
      lex.eatDelim('(');
      List<String> flds = fieldList();
      lex.eatDelim(')');
      lex.eatKeyword("values");
      lex.eatDelim('(');
      List<Constant> vals = constList();
      lex.eatDelim(')');
      return new InsertData(tblname, flds, vals);
   }
   private List<String> fieldList() {
      List<String> L = new ArrayList<String>();
      L.add(field());
      if (lex.matchDelim(',')) {
         lex.eatDelim(',');
         L.addAll(fieldList());
      }
      return L;
   }
   private List<Constant> constList() {
      List<Constant> L = new ArrayList<Constant>();
      L.add(constant());
      if (lex.matchDelim(',')) {
         lex.eatDelim(',');
         L.addAll(constList());
      }
      return L;
   }
// Method for parsing modify commands
   public ModifyData modify() {
      lex.eatKeyword("update");
      String tblname = lex.eatId();
      lex.eatKeyword("set");
      String fldname = field();
      lex.eatDelim('=');
      Expression newval = expression();
      Predicate pred = new Predicate();
      if (lex.matchKeyword("where")) {
         lex.eatKeyword("where");
         pred = predicate();
      }
      return new ModifyData(tblname, fldname, newval, pred);
   }
// Method for parsing create table commands
   public CreateTableData createTable() {
      lex.eatKeyword("table");
      String tblname = lex.eatId();
      lex.eatDelim('(');
      Schema sch = fieldDefs();
```

Fig. 9.9 (continued)

```
      lex.eatDelim(')');
      return new CreateTableData(tblname, sch);
   }
   private Schema fieldDefs() {
      Schema schema = fieldDef();
      if (lex.matchDelim(',')) {
         lex.eatDelim(',');
         Schema schema2 = fieldDefs();
         schema.addAll(schema2);
      }
      return schema;
   }
   private Schema fieldDef() {
      String fldname = field();
      return fieldType(fldname);
   }
   private Schema fieldType(String fldname) {
      Schema schema = new Schema();
      if (lex.matchKeyword("int")) {
         lex.eatKeyword("int");
         schema.addIntField(fldname);
      }
      else {
         lex.eatKeyword("varchar");
         lex.eatDelim('(');
         int strLen = lex.eatIntConstant();
         lex.eatDelim(')');
         schema.addStringField(fldname, strLen);
      }
      return schema;
   }
// Method for parsing create view commands
   public CreateViewData createView() {
      lex.eatKeyword("view");
      String viewname = lex.eatId();
      lex.eatKeyword("as");
      QueryData qd = query();
      return new CreateViewData(viewname, qd);
   }
//  Method for parsing create index commands
   public CreateIndexData createIndex() {
      lex.eatKeyword("index");
      String idxname = lex.eatId();
      lex.eatKeyword("on");
      String tblname = lex.eatId();
      lex.eatDelim('(');
      String fldname = field();
      lex.eatDelim(')');
      return new CreateIndexData(idxname, tblname, fldname);
   }
}
```

Fig. 9.9 (continued)

```
public class QueryData {
   private List<String> fields;
   private Collection<String> tables;
   private Predicate pred;

   public QueryData(List<String> fields, Collection<String> tables,
                    Predicate pred) {
      this.fields = fields;
      this.tables = tables;
      this.pred   = pred;
   }
   public List<String> fields() {
      return fields;
   }
   public Collection<String> tables() {
      return tables;
   }

   public Predicate pred() {
      return pred;
   }
   public String toString() {
      String result = "select ";
      for (String fldname : fields)
         result += fldname + ", ";
      result = result.substring(0, result.length()-2); //zap final comma
      result += " from ";
      for (String tblname : tables)
         result += tblname + ", ";
      result = result.substring(0, result.length()-2); //zap final comma
      String predstring = pred.toString();
      if (!predstring.equals(""))
         result += " where " + predstring;
      return result;
   }
}
```

Fig. 9.10 The code for the SimpleDB class `QueryData`

9.6.3 Parsing Updates

The parser method `updateCmd` implements the syntactic category <UpdateCmd>, which denotes the union of the various SQL update statements. This method will be called during the execution of the JDBC method `executeUpdate`, to determine the kind of update the command denotes. The method uses the initial tokens of the string to identify the command, and then dispatches to the particular parser method for that command. Each update method has a different return type, because each one extracts different information from its command string; thus, the method `updateCmd` returns a value of type `Object`.

```
public class InsertData {
   private String tblname;
   private List<String> flds;
   private List<Constant> vals;

   public InsertData(String tblname, List<String> flds,
                     List<Constant> vals) {
      this.tblname = tblname;
      this.flds = flds;
      this.vals = vals;
   }

   public String tableName() {
      return tblname;
   }

   public List<String> fields() {
      return flds;
   }

   public List<Constant> vals() {
      return vals;
   }
}
```

Fig. 9.11 The code for the SimpleDB class `InsertData`

9.6.4 Parsing Insertions

The parser method `insert` implements the syntactic category <Insert>. This method extracts three items: the table name, the field list, and the value list. The class `InsertData`, shown in Fig. 9.11, holds these values and makes them available via accessor methods.

9.6.5 Parsing Deletions

Deletion statements are handled by the method `delete`. The method returns an object of class `DeleteData`; see Fig. 9.12. The class constructor stores the table name and predicate from the specified deletion statement and provides methods `tableName` and `pred` to access them.

9.6.6 Parsing Modifications

Modification statements are handled by the method `modify`. The method returns an object of class `ModifyData`, as shown in Fig. 9.13. This class is very similar to that

```
public class DeleteData {
   private String tblname;
   private Predicate pred;

   public DeleteData(String tblname, Predicate pred) {
      this.tblname = tblname;
      this.pred = pred;
   }

   public String tableName() {
      return tblname;
   }

   public Predicate pred() {
      return pred;
   }
}
```

Fig. 9.12 The code for the SimpleDB class `DeleteData`

```
public class ModifyData {
   private String tblname;
   private String fldname;
   private Expression newval;
   private Predicate pred;

   public ModifyData(String tblname, String fldname,
                     Expression newval, Predicate pred) {
      this.tblname = tblname;
      this.fldname = fldname;
      this.newval = newval;
      this.pred = pred;
   }

   public String tableName() {
      return tblname;
   }

   public String targetField() {
      return fldname;
   }

   public Expression newValue() {
      return newval;
   }

   public Predicate pred() {
      return pred;
   }
}
```

Fig. 9.13 The code for the SimpleDB class `ModifyData`

of DeleteData. The difference is that this class also holds the assignment information: the fieldname of the left-hand side of the assignment and the expression of the right-hand side of the assignment. The additional methods targetField and newValue return this information.

9.6.7 Parsing Table, View, and Index Creation

The syntactic category <Create> specifies the three SQL creation statements supported by SimpleDB. Table creation statements are handled by the syntactic category <CreateTable> and its method createTable. The methods fieldDef and fieldType extract the information of one field and save it in its own Schema object. The method fieldDefs then adds this schema to the table's schema. The table name and schema are returned inside a CreateTableData object, whose code appears in Fig. 9.14.

View creation statements are handled by the method createView. The method extracts the name and definition of the view and returns them in an object of type CreateViewData; see Fig. 9.15. The handling of the view definition is unusual. It needs to be parsed as a <Query>, in order to detect badly formed view definitions. However, the metadata manager doesn't want to save the parsed representation of the definition; it wants the actual query string. Consequently, the CreateViewData constructor re-creates the view definition by calling toString on the returned QueryData object. In effect, the toString method "unparses" the query.

An index is a data structure that the database system uses to improve query efficiency; indexes are the topic of Chap. 12. The createIndex parser method extracts the index name, table name, and field name and saves them in a CreateIndexData object; see Fig. 9.16.

```
public class CreateTableData {
   private String tblname;
   private Schema sch;

   public CreateTableData(String tblname, Schema sch) {
      this.tblname = tblname;
      this.sch = sch;
   }

   public String tableName() {
      return tblname;
   }

   public Schema newSchema() {
      return sch;
   }
}
```

Fig. 9.14 The code for the SimpleDB class CreateTableData

```
public class CreateViewData {
    private String viewname;
    private QueryData qrydata;

    public CreateViewData(String viewname, QueryData qrydata) {
       this.viewname = viewname;
       this.qrydata = qrydata;
    }

    public String viewName() {
       return viewname;
    }

    public String viewDef() {
       return qrydata.toString();
    }
}
```

Fig. 9.15 The code for the SimpleDB class `CreateViewData`

```
public class CreateIndexData {
   private String idxname, tblname, fldname;

   public CreateIndexData(String idxname, String tblname,
                          String fldname) {
      this.idxname = idxname;
      this.tblname = tblname;
      this.fldname = fldname;
   }

   public String indexName() {
      return idxname;
   }

   public String tableName() {
      return tblname;
   }

   public String fieldName() {
      return fldname;
   }
}
```

Fig. 9.16 The code for the SimpleDB class `CreateIndexData`

9.7 Chapter Summary

- The *syntax* of a language is a set of rules that describe the strings that could possibly be meaningful statements.

- The *parser* is responsible for ensuring that its input string is syntactically correct.
- The *lexical analyzer* is the portion of the parser that splits the input string into a series of *tokens*.
- Each token has a *type* and a *value*. The SimpleDB lexical analyzer supports five token types:
  - Single-character *delimiters*, such as the comma
  - *Integer constants*, such as `123`
  - *String constants*, such as `'joe'`
  - *Keywords*, such as `select`, `from`, and `where`
  - *Identifiers*, such as `STUDENT`, `x`, and `glop34a`
- Each token type has two methods: methods that ask about the current token and methods that tell the lexical analyzer to "eat" the current token, returning its value and moving to the next token.
- A *grammar* is a set of rules that describe how tokens can be legally combined.
  - The left side of a grammar rule specifies its *syntactic category*. A syntactic category denotes a particular concept in the language.
  - The right side of a grammar rule specifies the *contents* of that category, which is the set of strings that satisfy the rule.
- A *parse tree* has syntactic categories as its internal nodes and tokens as its leaf nodes. The children of a category node correspond to the application of a grammar rule. A string is in a syntactic category iff it has a parse tree having that category as its root.
- A *parsing algorithm* constructs a parse tree from a syntactically legal string. The complexity of the parsing algorithm is usually in proportion to the complexity of the grammars it can support. A simple parsing algorithm is known as *recursive descent*.
- A recursive-descent parser has a method for each grammar rule. Each method calls the methods corresponding to the items in the right side of the rule.
- Each method in a recursive-descent parser extracts the values of the tokens it reads and returns them. An SQL parser should extract information such as table names, field names, predicates, and constants from the SQL statement. What gets extracted depends on the kind of SQL statement it is:
  - *For a query*: a collection of field names (from the `select` clause), a collection of table names (from the `from` clause), and a predicate (from the `where` clause)
  - *For an insertion*: a table name, a list of field names, and a list of values
  - *For a deletion*: a table name and a predicate
  - *For a modification*: a table name, the name of the field to be modified, an expression denoting the new field value, and a predicate
  - *For a table creation*: a table name and its schema
  - *For a view creation*: a table name and its definition
  - *For index creation*: an index name, a table name, and the name of the indexed field

9.8 Suggested Reading

The area of lexical analysis and parsing has received a tremendous amount of attention, going back over 60 years. The book (Scott, 2000) gives an excellent introduction to the various algorithms in current use. Numerous SQL parsers are available over the web, such as Zql (zql.sourceforge.net). An SQL grammar can be found in the appendix of Date and Darwen (2004). A copy of the SQL-92 standard, which describes SQL and its grammar, is at the URL www.contrib.andrew.cmu.edu/~shadow/sql/sql1992.txt. If you have never looked at a standards document, you should check this out just for the experience.

Date, C., & Darwen, H. (2004). *A guide to the SQL standard* (4th ed.). Boston, MA: Addison Wesley.

Scott, M. (2000). *Programming language pragmatics*. San Francisco, CA: Morgan Kaufman.

9.9 Exercises

Conceptual Problems

9.1. Draw a parse tree for the following SQL statements.

```
(a) select a from x where b = 3
(b) select a, b from x,y,z
(c) delete from x where a = b and c = 0
(d) update x set a = b where c = 3
(e) insert into x (a,b,c) values (3, 'glop', 4)
(f) create table x ( a varchar(3), b int, c varchar(2))
```

9.2. For each of the following strings, state where the exception will be generated when it is parsed and why. Then execute each query from a JDBC client and see what happens.

```
(a) select from x
(b) select x x from x
(c) select x from y z
(d) select a from where b=3
(e) select a from y where b -=3
(f) select a from y where
```

9.3. The parser method `create` does not correspond to the SQL grammar of Fig. 9.7.

(a) Explain why the grammar rule for <Create> is too ambiguous to be used for recursive-descent parsing.

(b) Revise the grammar so that it corresponds to how the `create` method actually works.

Programming Problems

9.4. Revise each parser method corresponding to a recursive rule so that it uses a while-loop instead of recursion.

9.5. Revise the class `PredParser` (from Fig. 9.8) to print the parse tree resulting from the sequence of method calls.

9.6. Exercise 8.8 asked you to modify expressions to handle arithmetic.

(a) Revise the SQL grammar similarly.
(b) Revise the SimpleDB parser to implement the grammar changes.
(c) Write a JDBC client to test the server. For example, write a program to execute an SQL query that increments the graduation year of all students having major 30.

9.7. Exercise 8.9 asked you to modify terms.

(a) Revise the SQL grammar similarly.
(b) Revise the SimpleDB parser to implement the grammar changes.
(c) Write a JDBC client to test the server. For example, write a program to execute an SQL query that retrieves the names of all students who graduated before 2010.

9.8. Exercise 8.10 asked you to modify predicates.

(a) Revise the SQL grammar similarly.
(b) Revise the SimpleDB parser to implement the grammar changes.
(c) Write a JDBC client to test the server. For example, write a program to execute an SQL query that retrieves the names of all students having majors 10 or 20.

9.9. SimpleDB also does not allow parentheses in its predicates.

(a) Revise the SQL grammar appropriately (either with or without having done Exercise 9.8).
(b) Revise the SimpleDB parser to implement the grammar changes.
(c) Write a JDBC client to test out your changes.

9.10. Join predicates can be specified in standard SQL by means of the JOIN keyword in the from clause. For example, the following two queries are equivalent:

```
select SName, DName
from STUDENT, DEPT
where MajorId = Did and GradYear = 2020
```

```
select SName, DName
from STUDENT join DEPT on MajorId = Did
where GradYear = 2020
```

(a) Revise the SQL lexical analyzer to include the keywords "join" and "on."
(b) Revise the SQL grammar to handle explicit joins.
(c) Revise the SimpleDB parser to implement your grammar changes. Add the join predicate to the predicate you get from the where clause.
(d) Write a JDBC program that tests out your changes.

9.11. In standard SQL, a table can have an associated *range variable*. Field references from that table are prefixed by that range variable. For example, the following query is equivalent to either of the queries from Exercise 9.10:

```
select s.SName, d.DName
from STUDENT s, DEPT d
where s.MajorId = d.Did and s.GradYear = 2020
```

(a) Revise the SimpleDB grammar to allow for this feature.
(b) Revise the SimpleDB parser to implement your grammar changes. You will also have to modify the information returned by the parser. Note that you will not be able to test your changes on the SimpleDB server unless you also extend the planner; see Exercise 10.13.

9.12. The keyword `AS` can be used in standard SQL to extend the output table with computed values. For example:

```
select SName, GradYear-1 as JuniorYear from STUDENT
```

(a) Revise the SimpleDB grammar to allow an optional AS expression after any fields in the select clause.
(b) Revise the SimpleDB lexical analyzer and parser to implement your grammar changes. How should the parser make this additional information available? Note that you will not be able to test your changes on the SimpleDB server unless you also extend the planner; see Exercise 10.14.

9.13. The keyword `UNION` can be used in standard SQL to combine the output tables of two queries. For example:

```
select SName from STUDENT where MajorId = 10
union
select SName from STUDENT where MajorId = 20
```

(a) Revise the SimpleDB grammar to allow a query to be the union of two other queries.
(b) Revise the SimpleDB lexical analyzer and parser to implement your grammar changes. Note that you will not be able to test your changes on

the SimpleDB server unless you also extend the planner; see Exercise 10.15.

9.14. Standard SQL supports nested queries in the `where` clause. For example,

```
select SName from STUDENT
where MajorId in select Did from DEPT where DName = 'math'
```

(a) Revise the SimpleDB grammar to allow a term to be of the form "*fieldname op query,*" where *op* is either "in" or "not in."

(b) Revise the SimpleDB lexical analyzer and parser to implement your grammar changes. Note that you will not be able to test your changes on the SimpleDB server unless you also extend the planner; see Exercise 10.16.

9.15. In standard SQL, the "*" character can be used in the `select` clause to denote all fields of a table. If SQL supports range variables (as in Exercise 9.11), then the "*" can likewise be prefixed by a range variable.

(a) Revise the SimpleDB grammar to allow "*" to appear in queries.

(b) Revise the SimpleDB parser to implement your grammar changes. Note that you will not be able to test your changes on the SimpleDB server unless you also extend the planner; see Exercise 10.17.

9.16. In Standard SQL, one can insert records into a table via the following variant on the insert statement:

```
insert into MATHSTUDENT(SId, SName)
select SId, SName
from STUDENT, DEPT
where MajorId = DId and DName = 'math'
```

That is, the records returned by the select statement are inserted into the specified table. (The above statement assumes that an empty *MATHSTUDENT* table has already been created.)

(a) Revise the SimpleDB SQL grammar to handle this form of insertion.

(b) Revise the SimpleDB parser code to implement your grammar. Note that you will not be able to run JDBC queries until you also modify the planner; see Exercise 10.18.

9.17. Exercise 8.7 asked you to create new types of constant.

(a) Modify the SimpleDB SQL grammar to allow these types to be used in a create table statement.

(b) Do you need to introduce new constant literals? If so, modify the <Constant> syntactic category.

(c) Revise the SimpleDB parser code to implement your grammar.

9.18. Exercise 8.11 asked you to implement null values. This exercise asks you to revise SQL to understand nulls.

(a) Revise the SimpleDB grammar to accept the keyword `null` as a constant.
(b) Revise the SimpleDB parser to implement the grammar change from part (a).
(c) In standard SQL, a term can be of the form `GradYear is null`, which returns true if the expression `GradYear` is a null value. The two keywords `is null` are treated as a single operator having one argument. Revise the SimpleDB grammar to have this new operator.
(d) Revise the SimpleDB parser and the class `Term` to implement the grammar changes from part (c).
(e) Write a program in JDBC to test your code. Your program can set values to `null` (or use an unassigned value of a newly inserted record) and then execute a query that involves `is null`. Note that your program will not be able to print null values until you modify the SimpleDB implementation of JDBC; see Exercise 11.6.

9.19. The open-source software package *javacc* (see the URL *javacc.github.io/javacc*) builds parsers from grammar specifications. Use javacc to create a parser for the SimpleDB grammar. Then replace the existing parser with your new one.

9.20. The class `Parser` contains a method for each syntactic category in the grammar. Our simplified SQL grammar is small, and so the class is manageable. However, a full-featured grammar would cause the class to be significantly larger. An alternative implementation strategy is to put each syntactic category in its own class. The constructor of the class would perform the parsing for that category. The class would also have methods that returned the values extracted from the parsed tokens. This strategy creates a large number of classes, each of which is relatively small. Rewrite the SimpleDB parser using this strategy.

Chapter 10
Planning

During the first step of query processing, the parser extracts the relevant data from an SQL statement. The next step is to turn that data into a relational algebra query tree. This step is called *planning*. This chapter examines the basic planning process. It examines what the planner needs to do to verify that an SQL statement is semantically meaningful and looks at two rudimentary plan-construction algorithms.

An SQL statement can have many equivalent query trees, often with wildly different costs. A database system that hopes to be commercially viable must have a planning algorithm that finds efficient plans. Chapter 15 addresses the difficult topic of creating optimal plans.

10.1 Verification

The first responsibility of a planner is to determine whether a given SQL statement is actually meaningful. The planner needs to verify the following things about the statement:

- The mentioned tables and fields actually exist in the catalog.
- The mentioned fields are not ambiguous.
- The actions on fields are type-correct.
- All constants are the correct size and type for their fields.

All of the information required to perform this verification can be found by examining the schemas of the mentioned tables. For example, the absence of a schema indicates that the mentioned table does not exist. Similarly, the absence of a field in any of the schemas indicates that the field does not exist, and its presence in multiple schemas indicates the possibility of ambiguity.

E. Sciore, *Database Design and Implementation*, Data-Centric Systems and Applications, https://doi.org/10.1007/978-3-030-33836-7_10

The planner should also determine type correctness of predicates, modification assignments, and inserted values by examining the type and length of each mentioned field. For a predicate, the arguments to each operator in an expression must be of compatible types, as must the expressions in each term. A modification assigns an expression to a field; both of these types must be compatible. And for an insertion statement, the type of each inserted value must be compatible with the type of its associated field.

A SimpleDB planner can obtain the necessary table schemas via the `getLayout` method of the metadata manager. However, the planner currently does not perform any explicit verification. Exercises 10.4–10.8 ask you to rectify this situation.

10.2 The Cost of Evaluating a Query Tree

The second responsibility of a planner is to construct a relational algebra query tree for the query. One complication is that an SQL query can be implemented by several different query trees, each having its own execution time. The planner is responsible for choosing the most efficient one.

But how can the planner calculate the efficiency of a query tree? Recall that the most important contributor to the running time of a query is the number of blocks it accesses. The *cost of a query tree* is therefore defined as the number of block accesses required to completely iterate through the query's scan.

The cost of a scan can be calculated by recursively calculating the cost of its children and then applying a cost formula based on the type of scan. Figure 10.1 gives formulas for three cost functions. Each relational operator has its own formulas for these functions. The cost functions are:

s	B(s)	R(s)	V(s,F)
TableScan(T)	B(T)	R(T)	V(T,F)
SelectScan(s1,A=c)	B(s1)	R(s1)/V(s1,A)	1 if F = A V(s1,F) if F ≠ A
SelectScan(s1,A=B)	B(s1)	R(s1) / max{V(s1,A),V(s1,B)}	min{V(s1,A), V(s1,B)} if F = A,B V(s1,F) if F ≠ A,B
ProjectScan(s1,L)	B(s1)	R(s1)	V(s1,F)
ProductScan(s1,s2)	B(s1) + R(s1)*B(s2)	R(s1)*R(s2)	V(s1,F) if F is in s1 V(s2,F) if F is in s2

Fig. 10.1 The cost formulas for scans

B(s) = the number of block accesses required to construct the output of scan s.
R(s) = the number of records in the output of scan s.
V(s, F) = the number of different F-values in the output of scan s.

These functions are analogous to the `blocksAccessed`, `recordsOutput`, and `distinctValues` methods of the statistics manager. The difference is that they apply to scans instead of tables.

A quick examination of Fig. 10.1 shows the interrelationship among the three cost functions. Given a scan s, the planner wants to calculate B(s). But if s is the product of two tables, then the value of B(s) depends on the number of blocks of the two tables as well as the number of records in its left-side scan. And if the left-side scan involves a select operator, then the number of its records depends on the number of distinct values of the fields mentioned in the predicate. In other words, the planner needs all three functions.

The following subsections derive the cost functions shown in Fig. 10.1 and give an example of how they can be used to calculate the cost of a query tree.

10.2.1 The Cost of a Table Scan

Each table scan in a query holds its current record page, which holds a buffer, which pins a page. When the records in that page have been read, its buffer is unpinned and a record page for the next block in the file takes its place. Thus, a single pass through the table scan will access each block exactly once, pinning a single buffer at a time.

Therefore, when s is a table scan, the values for B(s), R(s), and V(s, F) are the number of blocks, records, and distinct values in the underlying table.

10.2.2 The Cost of a Select Scan

A select scan s has a single underlying scan; call it s1. Each call to method `next` will cause the select scan to make one or more calls to `s1.next`; the method will return `false` when the call to `s1.next` returns `false`. Each call to `getInt`, `getString`, or `getVal` simply requests the field value from s1 and requires no block accesses. Thus, iterating though a select scan requires exactly the same number of block accesses as its underlying scan. That is:

```
B(s) = B(s1)
```

The calculation of R(s) and V(s, F) depends on the selection predicate. As an example, I shall analyze the common cases where the selection predicate equates a field either to a constant or to another field.

Selection on a Constant

Suppose that the predicate is of the form A=c for some field A. Assuming that the values in A are equally distributed, there will be R(s1)/V(s1, A) records that match the predicate. That is:

```
R(s) = R(s1) / V(s1, A)
```

The equal-distribution assumption also implies that the values of the other fields are still equally distributed in the output. That is:

```
V(s, A) = 1
V(s, F) = V(s1, F) for all other fields F
```

Selection on a Field

Now suppose that the predicate is of the form A=B for fields A and B. In this case, it is reasonable to assume that the values in fields A and B are somehow related. In particular, assume that if there are more B-values than A-values (i.e., *V(s1, A) < V(s1, B)*), then every A-value appears somewhere in B; and if there are more A-values than B-values, the opposite is true. (This assumption is certainly true in the typical case that A and B have a key-foreign key relationship.) So suppose that there are more B-values than A-values, and consider any record in s1. Its A-value has a 1/V(s1, B) chance of matching with its B-value. Similarly, if there are more A-values than B-values, then its B-value has a 1/V(s1, A) chance of matching its A-value. Thus:

```
R(s) = R(s1) / max{V(s1, A), V(s1, B)}
```

The equal-distribution assumption also implies that the each A-value will be equally likely to match with a B-value. Thus, we have:

```
V(s, F) = min(V(s1, A), V(s1, B)} for F = A or B
V(s, F) = V(s1, F) for all fields F other than A or B
```

10.2.3 The Cost of a Project Scan

As with select scans, a project scan has a single underlying scan (called s1) and requires no additional block accesses beyond those required by its underlying scan. Moreover, a projection operation does not change the number of records, nor does it change the values of any records. Thus:

```
B(s) = B(s1)
R(s) = R(s1)
V(s, F) = V(s1, F) for all fields F
```

10.2.4 The Cost of a Product Scan

A product scan has two underlying scans, s1 and s2. Its output consists of all combinations of records from s1 and s2. As the scan is traversed, the underlying scan s1 will be traversed once, and the underlying scan s2 will be traversed once for each record of s1. The following formulas follow:

```
B(s) = B(s1) + (R(s1)*B(s2))
R(s) = R(s1) * R(s2)
V(s, F) = V(s1, F) or V(s2, F), depending on which schema F belongs to
```

It is extremely interesting and important to realize that the formula for B(s) is not symmetric with respect to s1 and s2. That is, the statement

```
Scan s3 = new ProductScan(s1, s2);
```

can result in a different number of block accesses than the logically equivalent statement

```
Scan s3 = new ProductScan(s2, s1);
```

How different can it be? Define

```
RPB(s) = R(s) / B(s)
```

That is, RPB(s) denotes the "records per block" of scan s—the average number of output records that result from each block access of s. The above formula can then be rewritten as follows:

```
B(s) = B(s1) + (RPB(s1)*B(s1)*B(s2))
```

The dominating term is `RPB(s1)*B(s1)*B(s2)`. If you compare this term with the term you get by swapping `s1` with `s2`, you can see that the cost of the product scan will usually be lowest when `s1` is the underlying scan with the lowest RPB.

For example, suppose that `s1` is a table scan of STUDENT and `s2` is a table scan of DEPT. Since STUDENT records are larger than DEPT records, more DEPT records fit in a block, which means that STUDENT has a smaller RPB than DEPT. The above analysis shows that the fewest number of disk accesses occur when the scan for STUDENT is first.

10.2.5 A Concrete Example

Consider a query that returns the names of those students majoring in math. Figure 10.2a depicts a query tree for that query, and Fig. 10.2b gives SimpleDB code for the corresponding scan.

Figure 10.3 calculates the cost of each scan in Fig. 10.2b, using the statistical metadata from Fig. 7.8. The entries for `s1` and `s2` simply duplicate the statistics for STUDENT and DEPT in Fig. 7.8. The entry for `s3` says that the selection on `DName` returns 1 record but requires searching both blocks of DEPT to find it. Scan `s4` returns all combinations of the 45,000 STUDENT records with the 1 selected record; the output is 45,000 records. However, the operation requires 94,500 block accesses, because the single math-department record must be found 45,000 times and each time requires a 2-block scan of DEPT. (The other 4500 block accesses come from the single scan of STUDENT.) The selection on `MajorId` in scan `s5` reduces the output to 1125 records (45,000 students/40 departments) but does not change the

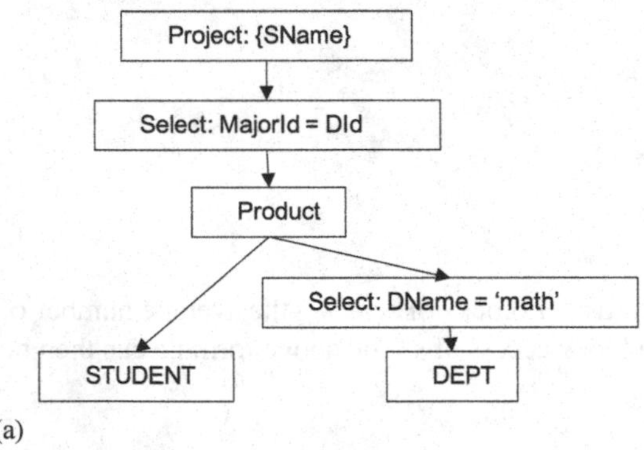

(a)

```
SimpleDB db = new SimpleDB("studentdb");
Transaction tx = db.newTx();
MetadataMgr mdm = db.mdMgr();
Layout slayout = mdm.getLayout("student", tx);
Layout dlayout = mdm.getLayout("dept", tx);
Scan s1 = new TableScan(tx, "student", slayout);
Scan s2 = new TableScan(tx, "dept", dlayout);
Predicate pred1 = new Predicate(. . .); //dname='math'
Scan s3 = new SelectScan(s2, pred1);
Scan s4 = new ProductScan(s1, s3);
Predicate pred2 = new Predicate(. . .); //majorid=did
Scan s5 = new SelectScan(s4, pred2);
List<String> fields = Arrays.asList("sname");
Scan s6 = new ProjectScan(s5, fields);
```

(b)

Fig. 10.2 Finding the names of students majoring in math. (**a**) The query tree, (**b**) the corresponding SimpleDB scan

s	B(s)	R(s)	V(s,F)
s1	4,500	45,000	45,000 for F=SId 44,960 for F=SName 50 for F=GradYear 40 for F=MajorId
s2	2	40	40 for F=DId, DName
s3	2	1	1 for F=DId, DName
s4	94,500	45,000	45,000 for F=SId 44,960 for F=SName 50 for F=GradYear 40 for F=MajorId 1 for F=DId, DName
s5	94,500	1,125	1,125 for F=SId 1,124 for F=SName 50 for F=GradYear 1 for F=MajorId, DId, DName
s6	94,500	1,125	1,124 for F=SName

Fig. 10.3 The cost of the scans in Fig. 10.2

number of block accesses required. And of course, the projection doesn't change anything.

It may seem strange that the database system recomputes the math-department record 45,000 times and at considerable cost; however, this is the nature of pipelined query processing. (In fact, this is a situation where the non-pipelined implementations of Chap. 13 are useful.)

Looking at the RPB figures for STUDENT and s3, you can see that RPB(STUDENT) = 10 and RPB(s3) = 0.5. Since products are fastest when the scan with the smaller RPB is on the left side, a more efficient strategy would be to define s4 as follows:

```
s4 = new ProductScan(s3, STUDENT)
```

Exercise 10.3 asks you to show that in this case, the operation would have required only 4502 block accesses. The difference is due primarily to the fact that the selection is now computed only once.

10.3 Plans

The SimpleDB object that calculates the cost of a query tree is called a *plan*. Plans implement the interface `Plan`, whose code appears in Fig. 10.4.

This interface supports the methods `blocksAccessed`, `recordsOutput`, and `distinctValues`, which calculate the values B(s), R(s), and V(s, F) for the query. The method `schema` returns the schema of the output table. The query planner can use this schema to verify type correctness and to look for ways to optimize the plan. Finally, every plan has the method `open`, which creates its corresponding scan.

Plans and scans are conceptually similar, in that they both denote a query tree. The difference is that a plan accesses the metadata of the tables in the query, whereas a scan accesses their data. When you submit an SQL query, the database planner may create several plans for the query and use their metadata to choose the most efficient one. It then uses that plan's `open` method to create the desired scan.

A plan is constructed similarly to a scan. There is a `Plan` class for each relational algebra operator, plus the class `TablePlan` for handling stored tables. For example, the code of Fig. 10.5 retrieves the names of those students majoring in math, the same query as in Fig. 10.2. The only difference is that Fig. 10.5 constructs the query tree using plans, converting the final plan to a scan.

```
public interface Plan {
   public Scan   open();
   public int    blocksAccessed();
   public int    recordsOutput();
   public int    distinctValues(String fldname);
   public Schema schema();
}
```

Fig. 10.4 The SimpleDB `Plan` interface

```
SimpleDB db = new SimpleDB("studentdb");
MetadataMgr mdm = db.mdMgr();
Transaction tx = db.newTx();
Plan p1 = new TablePlan(tx, "student", mdm);
Plan p2 = new TablePlan(tx, "dept", mdm);
Predicate pred1 = new Predicate(. . .); //dname='math'
Plan p3 = new SelectPlan(p2, pred1);
Plan p4 = new ProductPlan(p1, p3);
Predicate pred2 = new Predicate(. . .); //majorid=did
Plan p5 = new SelectPlan(p4, pred2);
List<String> fields = Arrays.asList("sname");
Plan p6 = new ProjectPlan(p5, fields);
Scan s = p6.open();
```

Fig. 10.5 Using plans to create a query

```
public class TablePlan implements Plan {
   private Transaction tx;
   private String tblname;
   private Layout layout;
   private StatInfo si;

   public TablePlan(Transaction tx, String tblname, MetadataMgr md) {
      this.tx = tx;
      this.tblname = tblname;
      layout = md.getLayout(tblname, tx);
      si = md.getStatInfo(tblname, layout, tx);
   }

   public Scan open() {
      return new TableScan(tx, tblname, layout);
   }

   public int blocksAccessed() {
      return si.blocksAccessed();
   }

   public int recordsOutput() {
      return si.recordsOutput();
   }

   public int distinctValues(String fldname) {
      return si.distinctValues(fldname);
   }

   public Schema schema() {
      return layout.schema();
   }
}
```

Fig. 10.6 The code for the SimpleDB class `TablePlan`

Figures 10.6, 10.7, 10.8, 10.9, and 10.10 give the code for classes `TablePlan`, `SelectPlan`, `ProjectPlan`, and `ProductPlan`. Class `TablePlan` obtains its cost estimates directly from the metadata manager. The other classes use the formulas of the previous section to compute their estimates.

Cost estimation for select plans is more complex than for the other operators, because the estimates depend on the predicate. A predicate, therefore, has methods `reductionFactor` and `equatesWithConstant` for use by the select plan. Method `reductionFactor` is used by `recordsAccessed` to calculate the extent to which the predicate reduces the size of the input table. Method `equatesWithConstant` is used by `distinctValues` to determine whether the predicate equates the specified field with a constant.

The constructors of `ProjectPlan` and `ProductPlan` create their schemas from the schemas of their underlying plans. The `ProjectPlan` schema is created

```
public class SelectPlan implements Plan {
   private Plan p;
   private Predicate pred;

   public SelectPlan(Plan p, Predicate pred) {
      this.p = p;
      this.pred = pred;
   }

   public Scan open() {
      Scan s = p.open();
      return new SelectScan(s, pred);
   }

   public int blocksAccessed() {
      return p.blocksAccessed();
   }

   public int recordsOutput() {
      return p.recordsOutput() / pred.reductionFactor(p);
   }

   public int distinctValues(String fldname) {
      if (pred.equatesWithConstant(fldname) != null)
         return 1;
      else {
         String fldname2 = pred.equatesWithField(fldname);
         if (fldname2 != null)
            return Math.min(p.distinctValues(fldname),
                            p.distinctValues(fldname2));
         else
            return p.distinctValues(fldname);
      }
   }

   public Schema schema() {
      return p.schema();
   }
}
```

Fig. 10.7 The code for the SimpleDB class `SelectPlan`

by looking up each field of the underlying field list and adding that information to the new schema. The `ProductPlan` schema is the union of the underlying schemas.

The `open` method for each of these plan classes is straightforward. In general, constructing a scan from a plan has two steps: First, the method recursively constructs a scan for each underlying plan. Second, it passes those scans into the `Scan` constructor for the operator.

```
public class ProjectPlan implements Plan {
   private Plan p;
   private Schema schema = new Schema();

   public ProjectPlan(Plan p, List<String> fieldlist) {
      this.p = p;
      for (String fldname : fieldlist)
         schema.add(fldname, p.schema());
   }

   public Scan open() {
      Scan s = p.open();
      return new ProjectScan(s, schema.fields());
   }

   public int blocksAccessed() {
      return p.blocksAccessed();
   }

   public int recordsOutput() {
      return p.recordsOutput();
   }

   public int distinctValues(String fldname) {
      return p.distinctValues(fldname);
   }

   public Schema schema() {
      return schema;
   }
}
```

Fig. 10.8 The code for the SimpleDB class `ProjectPlan`

10.4 Query Planning

Recall that the parser takes an SQL query string as input and returns a `QueryData` object as output. This section tackles the problem of how to construct a plan from that `QueryData` object.

10.4.1 The SimpleDB Query Planning Algorithm

SimpleDB supports a simplified subset of SQL that contains no computation, no sorting, no grouping, no nesting, and no renaming. Consequently, all of its SQL queries can be implemented by a query tree that uses only the three operators select, project, and product. An algorithm for creating such a plan appears in Fig. 10.10.

```
public class ProductPlan implements Plan {
   private Plan p1, p2;
   private Schema schema = new Schema();

   public ProductPlan(Plan p1, Plan p2) {
      this.p1 = p1;
      this.p2 = p2;
      schema.addAll(p1.schema());
      schema.addAll(p2.schema());
   }

   public Scan open() {
      Scan s1 = p1.open();
      Scan s2 = p2.open();
      return new ProductScan(s1, s2);
   }

   public int blocksAccessed() {
      return p1.blocksAccessed()
          + (p1.recordsOutput() * p2.blocksAccessed());
   }

   public int recordsOutput() {
      return p1.recordsOutput() * p2.recordsOutput();
   }

   public int distinctValues(String fldname) {
      if (p1.schema().hasField(fldname))
         return p1.distinctValues(fldname);
      else
         return p2.distinctValues(fldname);
   }

   public Schema schema() {
      return schema;
   }
}
```

Fig. 10.9 The code for the SimpleDB class `ProductPlan`

1. Construct a plan for each table T in the `from` clause.
   a) If T is a stored table, then the plan is a table plan for T.
   b) If T is a view, the plan is the result of calling this algorithm recursively on T's definition.
2. Take the product of these table plans, in the order given.
3. Select on the predicate in the `where` clause.
4. Project on the fields in the `select` clause.

Fig. 10.10 The basic query planning algorithm for the SimpleDB subset of SQL

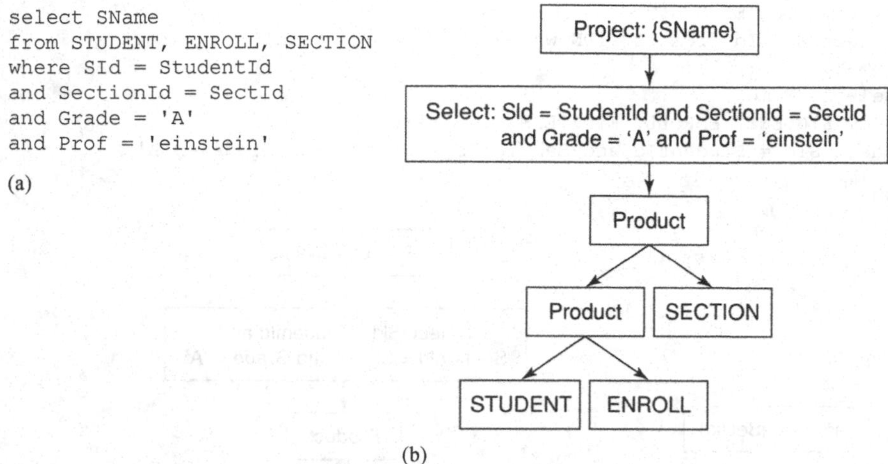

Fig. 10.11 Applying the basic query planning algorithm to an SQL query

For an example of this query planning algorithm, consider Fig. 10.11. Part (a) gives an SQL query that retrieves the name of students who received an "A" with Professor Einstein. Part (b) is the query tree produced by the algorithm.

Figure 10.12 illustrates the query planning algorithm for an equivalent query that uses a view. Part (a) gives the view definition and the query, part (b) depicts the query tree for the view, and part (c) depicts the tree for the entire query.

Note how the final tree consists of the product of the two tables and the view tree, followed by a selection and a projection. This final tree is equivalent to, but somewhat different from, the tree of Fig. 10.11b. In particular, part of the original selection predicate has been "pushed" down the tree, and there is an intermediate projection. The query optimization techniques of Chap. 15 take advantage of such equivalences.

10.4.2 Implementing the Query Planning Algorithm

The SimpleDB class `BasicQueryPlanner` implements the basic query planning algorithm; its code appears in Fig. 10.13. Each of the four steps in the code implements the corresponding step in that algorithm.

The basic query planning algorithm is rigid and naïve. It generates the product plans in the order returned by the method `QueryData.tables`. Note that this order is completely arbitrary—any other ordering of the tables would produce an equivalent scan. The performance of this algorithm will therefore be erratic (and

```
create view EINSTEIN as
select SectId from SECTION where Prof = 'einstein'

select SName
from STUDENT, ENROLL, EINSTEIN
where SId = StudentId and SectionId = SectId and Grade = 'A'
```

(a)

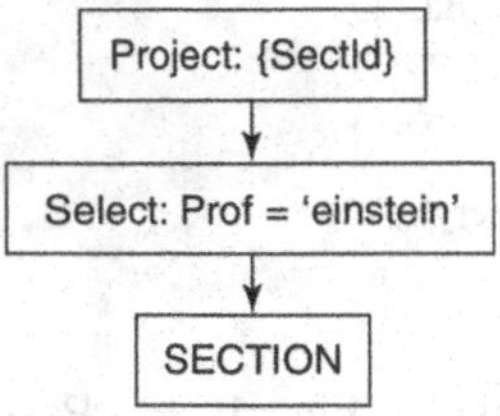

Project: {SectId}
Select: Prof = 'einstein'
SECTION

(b)

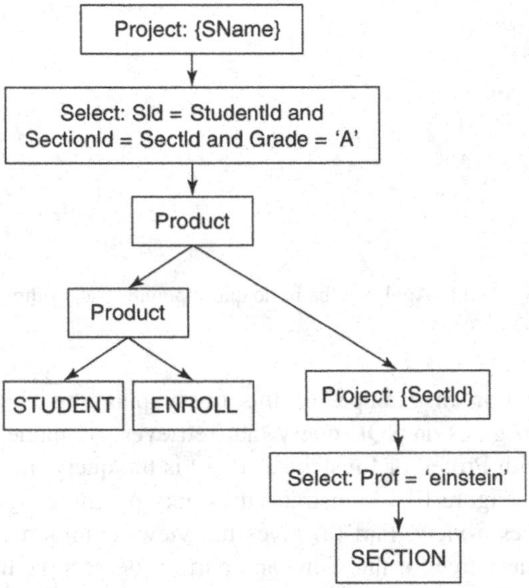

Project: {SName}
Select: SId = StudentId and SectionId = SectId and Grade = 'A'
Product
Product
STUDENT
ENROLL
Project: {SectId}
Select: Prof = 'einstein'
SECTION

(c)

Fig. 10.12 Applying the basic query planning algorithm in the presence of views. (**a**) The SQL query, (**b**) the tree for the view, (**c**) the tree for the entire query

often poor) because it doesn't use the plan metadata to help determine the order of the product plans.

Figure 10.14 shows a small improvement to the planning algorithm. It still considers the tables in the same order, but it now creates two product plans for each table—one where it is on the left side of the product, and one where it is on the right side—and keeps the plan having smallest cost.

This algorithm is better than the basic planning algorithm, but it still depends too much on the order of the tables in the query. The planning algorithms in commercial database systems are much more sophisticated. They not only analyze the cost of many equivalent plans; they also implement additional relational operations that can be applied in special circumstances. Their goal is to choose the most efficient plan

```
public class BasicQueryPlanner implements QueryPlanner {
   private MetadataMgr mdm;

   public BasicQueryPlanner(MetadataMgr mdm) {
      this.mdm = mdm;
   }

   public Plan createPlan(QueryData data, Transaction tx) {
      //Step 1: Create a plan for each mentioned table or view.
      List<Plan> plans = new ArrayList<Plan>();
      for (String tblname : data.tables()) {
         String viewdef = mdm.getViewDef(tblname, tx);
         if (viewdef != null) { // Recursively plan the view.
            Parser parser = new Parser(viewdef);
            QueryData viewdata = parser.query();
            plans.add(createPlan(viewdata, tx));
         }
         else
            plans.add(new TablePlan(tblname, tx, mdm));
      }
      //Step 2: Create the product of all table plans
      Plan p = plans.remove(0);
      for (Plan nextplan : plans)
         p = new ProductPlan(p, nextplan);

      //Step 3: Add a selection plan for the predicate
      p = new SelectPlan(p, data.pred());

      //Step 4: Project on the field names
      return new ProjectPlan(p, data.fields());
   }
}
```

Fig. 10.13 The code for the SimpleDB class `BasicQueryPlanner`

(and thereby be more desirable than their competition). These techniques are the subject of Chaps. 12, 13, 14, and 15.

10.5 Update Planning

This section examines how a planner should process update statements. The SimpleDB class `BasicUpdatePlanner` provides a straightforward implementation of an update planner; its code appears in Fig. 10.15. This class contains one method for each kind of update. These methods are discussed in the following subsections.

```
public class BetterQueryPlanner implements QueryPlanner {
   ...
   public Plan createPlan(QueryData data, Transaction tx) {
      ...
      //Step 2: Create the product of all table plans
      // At each step, choose the plan having smallest cost
      Plan p = plans.remove(0);
      for (Plan nextplan : plans) {
         Plan p1 = new ProductPlan(nextplan, p);
         Plan p2 = new ProductPlan(p, nextplan);
         p = (p1.blocksAccessed() < p2.blocksAccessed() ? p1 : p2;
      }
      ...
   }
}
```

Fig. 10.14 The code for the SimpleDB class `BetterQueryPlanner`

10.5.1 Delete and Modify Planning

The scan for a delete (or modify) statement is a select scan that retrieves those records to be deleted (or modified). For example, consider the following modification statement:

```
update STUDENT
set MajorId = 20
where MajorId = 30 and GradYear = 2020
```

and the following deletion statement:

```
delete from STUDENT
where MajorId = 30 and GradYear = 2020
```

These statements have the same scan, namely, all students in department 30 graduating in 2020. The methods `executeDelete` and `executeModify` create and iterate through this scan, performing the appropriate action on each of its records. In the case of the modification statement, each record is modified; in the case of the deletion statement, each record is deleted.

Looking at the code, you can see that both methods create the same plan, which is similar to the plan created by the query planner (except that the query planner would also add a project plan). Both methods also open the scan and iterate through it in the same way. The `executeDelete` method calls `delete` on each record in the scan, whereas `executeModify` performs a `setVal` operation on the modified field of each record in the scan. Both methods also keep a count of the affected records, which is returned to the caller.

```
public class BasicUpdatePlanner implements UpdatePlanner {
   private MetadataMgr mdm;
   public BasicUpdatePlanner(MetadataMgr mdm) {
      this.mdm = mdm;
   }
   public int executeDelete(DeleteData data, Transaction tx) {
      Plan p = new TablePlan(data.tableName(), tx, mdm);
      p = new SelectPlan(p, data.pred());
      UpdateScan us = (UpdateScan) p.open();
      int count = 0;
      while(us.next()) {
         us.delete();
         count++;
      }
      us.close();
      return count;
   }
   public int executeModify(ModifyData data, Transaction tx) {
      Plan p = new TablePlan(data.tableName(), tx, mdm);
      p = new SelectPlan(p, data.pred());
      UpdateScan us = (UpdateScan) p.open();
      int count = 0;
      while(us.next()) {
         Constant val = data.newValue().evaluate(us);
         us.setVal(data.targetField(), val);
         count++;
      }
      us.close();
      return count;
   }
   public int executeInsert(InsertData data, Transaction tx) {
      Plan p = new TablePlan(data.tableName(), tx, mdm);
      UpdateScan us = (UpdateScan) p.open();
      us.insert();
      Iterator<Constant> iter = data.vals().iterator();
      for (String fldname : data.fields()) {
         Constant val = iter.next();
         us.setVal(fldname, val);
      }
      us.close();
      return 1;
   }
   public int executeCreateTable(CreateTableData data, Transaction tx) {
      mdm.createTable(data.tableName(), data.newSchema(), tx);
      return 0;
   }
   public int executeCreateView(CreateViewData data, Transaction tx) {
      mdm.createView(data.viewName(), data.viewDef(), tx);
      return 0;
   }
   public int executeCreateIndex(CreateIndexData data, Transaction tx) {
      mdm.createIndex(data.indexName(), data.tableName(),
                      data.fieldName(), tx);
      return 0;
   }
}
```

Fig. 10.15 The code for the SimpleDB class `BasicUpdatePlanner`

10.5.2 Insert Planning

The scan corresponding to an insert statement is simply a table scan of the underlying table. The `executeInsert` method begins by inserting a new record into this scan. It then iterates through the `fields` and `vals` lists in parallel, calling `setInt` or `setString` to modify the value of each specified field of the record. The method returns a 1, denoting that one record was inserted.

10.5.3 Planning for Table, View, and Index Creation

The codes for the methods `executeCreateTable`, `executeCreateView`, and `executeCreateIndex` are different from the others, because they don't require accessing any data records and thus do not require a scan. They simply call the metadata methods `createTable`, `createView`, and `createIndex`, using the appropriate information from the parser; they return 0 to indicate that no records were affected.

10.6 The SimpleDB Planner

The planner is the component of the database engine that transforms an SQL statement into a plan. The SimpleDB planner is implemented by the class `Planner`, whose API appears in Fig. 10.16.

The first argument of both methods is a string representation of an SQL statement. The method `createQueryPlan` creates and returns a plan for the input query string. The method `executeUpdate` creates a plan for the input string, executes it, and returns the number of affected records (the same as the `executeUpdate` method in JDBC).

A client can obtain a `Planner` object by calling the static method `planner` in the class `SimpleDB`. Figure 10.17 contains code for the class `PlannerTest`, which illustrates the use of the planner. Part 1 of the code illustrates the processing of an SQL query. The query string is passed into the planner's `createQueryPlan` method, and a plan is returned. Opening that plan returns a scan, whose records are then accessed and printed. Part 2 of the code illustrates an SQL update command.

<u>*Planner*</u>

```
public Plan createQueryPlan(String query, Transaction tx);
public int  executeUpdate(String cmd, Transaction tx);
```

Fig. 10.16 The API for the SimpleDB planner

```
public class PlannerTest {
   public static void main(String[] args) {
      SimpleDB db = new SimpleDB("studentdb");
      Planner planner = db.planner();
      Transaction tx  = db.newTx();

      // part 1: Process a query
      String qry = "select sname, gradyear from student";
      Plan p = planner.createQueryPlan(qry, tx);
      Scan s = p.open();
      while (s.next())
         System.out.println(s.getString("sname") + " " +
               s.getInt("gradyear"));
      s.close();

      // part 2: Process an update command
      String cmd = "delete from STUDENT where MajorId = 30";
      int num = planner.executeUpdate(cmd, tx);
      System.out.println(num + " students were deleted");

      tx.commit();
   }
}
```

Fig. 10.17 The class `PlannerTest`

1. *Parse the SQL statement.* The method calls the parser, passing it the input string; the parser returns an object containing the data from the SQL statement. For example, the parser returns a `QueryData` object for a query, an `InsertData` object for an insert statement, and so on.
2. *Verify the SQL statement.* The method examines the `QueryData` (or `InsertData`, etc.) object to determine if it is semantically meaningful.
3. *Create a plan for the SQL statement.* The method uses a planning algorithm to determine a query tree corresponding to the statement, and to create a plan corresponding to that tree.

4a. *Return the plan* (for the `createQueryPlan` method).

4b. *Execute the plan* (for the `executeUpdate` method). The method creates a scan by opening the plan; then it iterates through the scan, making the appropriate update for each record in the scan and returning the number of records affected.

Fig. 10.18 The steps taken by the two planner methods

The command string is passed into the planner's `executeUpdate` method, which performs all of the necessary work.

The SimpleDB planner has two methods: one to handle queries and one to handle updates. These methods both process their input quite similarly; Fig. 10.18 lists the steps they take. In particular, both methods perform steps 1–3. The methods differ primarily in what they do with the plan that they create. The method `createQueryPlan` simply returns its plan, whereas `executeUpdate` opens and executes its plan.

```
public class Planner {
   private QueryPlanner  qplanner;
   private UpdatePlanner uplanner;

   public Planner(QueryPlanner qplanner, UpdatePlanner uplanner) {
      this.qplanner = qplanner;
      this.uplanner = uplanner;
   }

   public Plan createQueryPlan(String cmd, Transaction tx) {
      Parser parser = new Parser(cmd);
      QueryData data = parser.query();
      // code to verify the query should be here...
      return qplanner.createPlan(data, tx);
   }

   public int executeUpdate(String cmd, Transaction tx) {
      Parser parser = new Parser(cmd);
      Object obj = parser.updateCmd();
      // code to verify the update command should be here ...
      if (obj instanceof InsertData)
         return uplanner.executeInsert((InsertData)obj, tx);
      else if (obj instanceof DeleteData)
         return uplanner.executeDelete((DeleteData)obj, tx);
      else if (obj instanceof ModifyData)
         return uplanner.executeModify((ModifyData)obj, tx);
      else if (obj instanceof CreateTableData)
         return uplanner.executeCreateTable((CreateTableData)obj, tx);
      else if (obj instanceof CreateViewData)
         return uplanner.executeCreateView((CreateViewData)obj, tx);
      else if (obj instanceof CreateIndexData)
         return uplanner.executeCreateIndex((CreateIndexData)obj, tx);
      else
         return 0;  // this option should never occur
   }
}
```

Fig. 10.19 The code for the SimpleDB class `Planner`

Figure 10.19 gives the SimpleDB code for the `Planner` class. The methods are a straightforward implementation of Fig. 10.18. The method `createQueryPlan` creates a parser for its input SQL query, calls the parser method `query` to parse the string, verifies the returned `QueryData` object (at least, the method ought to), and returns the plan generated by the query planner. The method `executeUpdate` is similar: it parses the update string, verifies the object returned by the parser, and calls the appropriate update planner method to perform the execution.

The object returned by the update parser will be of type `InsertData`, `DeleteData`, etc., according to what kind of update statement was submitted. The `executeUpdate` code checks this type in order to determine which planner method to call.

The `Planner` object depends on its query planner and update planner to do the actual planning. These objects are passed into the `Planner` constructor, which allows you to configure the planner with different planning algorithms. For example, Chap. 15 develops a fancy query planner called `HeuristicQueryPlanner`; you can use this planner instead of `BasicQueryPlanner` if you want, simply by passing a `HeuristicQueryPlanner` object into the `Planner` constructor.

The code uses Java interfaces to obtain this plug-and-play capability. The arguments to the `Planner` constructor belong to the interfaces `QueryPlanner` and `UpdatePlanner`, whose code appears in Fig. 10.20. The `BasicQueryPlanner` and `BasicUpdatePlanner` classes implement these interfaces, as do the more sophisticated query and update planners in Chap. 15.

`Planner` objects are created by the constructor to the `SimpleDB` class. The constructor creates a new basic query planner and a new basic update planner and passes them to the `Planner` constructor, as shown in Fig. 10.21. To reconfigure the engine to use a different query planner, you just need to modify the `SimpleDB` constructor so that it creates different `QueryPlanner` and `UpdatePlanner` objects.

```
public interface QueryPlanner {
   public Plan createPlan(QueryData data, Transaction tx);
}

public interface UpdatePlanner {
   public int executeInsert(InsertData data, Transaction tx);
   public int executeDelete(DeleteData data, Transaction tx);
   public int executeModify(ModifyData data, Transaction tx);
   public int executeCreateTable(CreateTableData data,
                                          Transaction tx);
   public int executeCreateView(CreateViewData data,
                                          Transaction tx);
   public int executeCreateIndex(CreateIndexData data,
                                          Transaction tx);
}
```

Fig. 10.20 The code for the SimpleDB `QueryPlanner` and `UpdatePlanner` interfaces

```
public SimpleDB(String dirname) {
   ...
   mdm = new MetadataMgr(isnew, tx);
   QueryPlanner qp = new BasicQueryPlanner(mdm);
   UpdatePlanner up = new BasicUpdatePlanner(mdm);
   planner = new Planner(qp, up);
   ...
}
```

Fig. 10.21 The `SimpleDB` code that creates its planner

10.7 Chapter Summary

- In order to construct the most cost-effective scan for a given query, the database system needs to estimate the number of block accesses required to iterate through a scan. The following estimation functions are defined for a scan s:
  - B(s) denotes the number of block accesses required to iterate through s.
  - R(s) denotes the number of records output by s.
  - V(s,F) denotes the number of distinct F-values in the output of s.
- If s is a table scan, then these functions are equivalent to the statistical metadata for the table. Otherwise, each operator has a formula for computing the function based on the values of the functions on its input scans.
- An SQL query may have several equivalent query trees, with each tree corresponding to a different scan. The database planner is responsible for creating the scan having the lowest estimated cost. In order to do so, the planner may need to construct several query trees and compare their costs. It will create a scan only for the tree having lowest cost.
- A query tree constructed for the purpose of cost comparison is called a *plan*. Plans and scans are conceptually similar, in that they both denote a query tree. The difference is that a plan has methods for estimating costs; it accesses the database's metadata, but not the actual data. Creating a plan does not incur any disk accesses. The planner creates multiple plans and compares their costs. It then chooses the plan having the lowest cost and opens a plan from it.
- The *planner* is the database engine component that transforms an SQL statement into a plan.
- In addition, the planner *verifies* the statement is semantically meaningful, by checking that:
  - The mentioned tables and fields actually exist in the catalog
  - The mentioned fields are not ambiguous
  - The actions on fields are type-correct
  - All constants are the correct size and type for their fields
- The *basic query planning algorithm* creates a rudimentary plan, as follows:
  1. Construct a plan for each table T in the `from` clause.
     (a) If T is a stored table, then the plan is a table plan for T.
     (b) If T is a view, then the plan is the result of calling this algorithm recursively on the definition of T.
  2. Take the product of the tables in the `from` clause, in the order given.
  3. Select on the predicate in the `where` clause.
  4. Project on the fields in the `select` clause.

- The basic query planning algorithm generates a naïve and often inefficient plan. The planning algorithms in commercial database systems perform extensive analysis of the various equivalent plans, which will be described in Chap. 15.
- Delete and modify statements are treated similarly. The planner creates a select plan that retrieves those records to be deleted (or modified). The methods `executeDelete` and `executeModify` open the plan and iterate through the resulting scan, performing the appropriate action on each of its records. In the case of the modify statement, each record is modified; in the case of the delete statement, each record is deleted.
- The plan for an insert statement is a table plan for the underlying table. The `executeInsert` method opens the plan and inserts a new record into that resulting scan.
- The plans for the creation statements do not need to create plans, because they do not access any data. Instead, the methods call the appropriate metadata method to perform the creation.

10.8 Suggested Reading

The planner in this chapter understands only a small subset of SQL, and I have touched only briefly on planning issues for the more complex constructs. The article (Kim, 1982) describes the problems with nested queries and proposes some solutions. The article (Chaudhuri, 1998) discusses strategies for the more difficult aspects of SQL, including outer joins and nested queries.

Chaudhuri, S. (1998). An overview of query optimization in relational systems. In *Proceedings of the ACM Principles of Database Systems Conference* (pp. 34–43).

Kim, W. (1982). On optimizing an SQL-like nested query. *ACM Transactions on Database Systems, 7*(3), 443–469.

10.9 Exercises

Conceptual Exercises

10.1. Consider the following relational algebra query:

```
T1 = select(DEPT, DName='math')
T2 = select(STUDENT, GradYear=2018)
product(T1, T2)
```

Using the same assumptions as in Sect. 10.2:

(a) Calculate the number of disk accesses required to execute the operation.
(b) Calculate the number of disk accesses required to execute the operation if the arguments to *product* are exchanged.

10.2. Calculate B(s), R(s), and V(s, F) for the queries of Figs. 10.11 and 10.12.

10.3. Show that if the arguments to the product operation in Sect. 10.2.5 were swapped, then the entire operation would require 4502 block accesses.

10.4. Section 10.2.4 stated that the product of STUDENT and DEPT is more efficient when STUDENT is the outer scan. Using the statistics of Fig. 7.8, calculate the number of block accesses the product would require.

10.5. For each of the following SQL statements, draw a picture of the plan that would be generated by the basic planner of this chapter.

(a)
```
select SName, Grade
from STUDENT, COURSE, ENROLL, SECTION
where SId = StudentId and SectId = SectionId
and CourseId = CId and Title = 'Calculus'
```
(b)
```
select SName
from STUDENT, ENROLL
where MajorId = 10 and SId = StudentId and Grade = 'C'
```

10.6. For each of the queries in Exercise 10.5, explain what things the planner must check to verify its correctness.

10.7. For each of the following update statements, explain what things the planner must check to verify its correctness.

(a)
```
insert into STUDENT(SId, SName, GradYear, MajorId)
values(120, 'abigail', 2012, 30)
```
(b)
```
delete from STUDENT
where MajorId = 10 and SID in (select StudentId
                               from ENROLL
                               where Grade = 'F')
```
(c)
```
update STUDENT
set GradYear = GradYear + 3
where MajorId in (select DId from DEPT
                  where DName = 'drama')
```

Programming Exercises

10.8. The SimpleDB planner does not verify that table names are meaningful.

(a) What problem will occur when a nonexistent table is mentioned in a query?

(b) Fix the `Planner` class to verify table names. Throw a `BadSyntaxException` if the table is nonexistent.

10.9. The SimpleDB planner does not verify that field names exist and are unique.

(a) What problem will occur when a nonexistent field name is mentioned in a query?

(b) What problem will occur when tables having common field names are mentioned in a query?

(c) Fix the code to perform the appropriate verification.

10.10. The SimpleDB planner does not type-check predicates.

(a) What problem will occur if a predicate in an SQL statement is not type-correct?

(b) Fix the code to perform the appropriate verification.

10.11. The SimpleDB update planner doesn't check that string constants are the right size and type for the specified fields in an insert statement, nor does it verify that the size of the constant and field lists are the same. Fix the code appropriately.

10.12. The SimpleDB update planner doesn't verify that the assignment of a new value to the specified field in a modify statement is type-correct. Fix the code appropriately.

10.13. Exercise 9.11 asked you to modify the parser to allow range variables, and Exercise 8.14 asked you to implement the class `RenameScan`. Range variables can be implemented by using renaming—first the planner renames each table field by adding the range variable as a prefix; then it adds the product, select, and project operators; and then it renames the fields back to their non-prefixed names.

(a) Write a class `RenamePlan`.

(b) Revise the basic query planner to perform this renaming.

(c) Write a JDBC program to test out your code. In particular, write a JDBC program that performs a self-join, such as finding the students having the same major as Joe.

10.14. Exercise 9.12 asked you to modify the parser to allow the `AS` keyword in the select clause, and Exercise 8.15 asked you to implement the class `ExtendScan`.

(a) Write the class `ExtendPlan`.

(b) Revise the basic query planner to add `ExtendPlan` objects into the query plan. They should appear after the product plans but before the project plan.

(c) Write a JDBC program to test out your code.

10.15. Exercise 9.13 asked you to modify the parser to allow the `UNION` keyword, and Exercise 8.16 asked you to implement the class `UnionScan`.

(a) Write a class `UnionPlan`.

(b) Revise the basic query planner to add `UnionPlan` objects into the query plan. They should appear after the *project* plan.

(c) Write a JDBC program to test out your code.

10.16. Exercise 9.14 asked you to modify the parser to allow nested queries, and Exercise 8.17 asked you to implement the classes `SemijoinScan` and `AntijoinScan`.

(a) Write the classes `SemijoinPlan` and `AntijoinPlan`.
(b) Revise the basic query planner to add these objects for these classes into the query plan. They should appear after the product plans but before the extend plans.
(c) Write a JDBC program to test out your code.

10.17. Exercise 9.15 asked you to modify the parser to allow "*" to appear in a query's select clause.

(a) Revise the planner appropriately.
(b) Write a JDBC client to test out your code.

10.18. Exercise 9.16 asked you to modify the SimpleDB parser to handle a new kind of insert statement.

(a) Revise the planner appropriately.
(b) Write a JDBC client to test out your code.

10.19. The basic update planner inserts its new record starting from the beginning of the table.

(a) Design and implement a modification to the planner that efficiently inserts from the end of the table or perhaps from the end of the previous insertion.
(b) Compare the benefits of the two strategies. Which do you prefer?

10.20. The SimpleDB basic update planner assumes that the table mentioned in an update command is a stored table. Standard SQL also allows the table to be the name of a view, provided that the view is updatable.

(a) Revise the update planner so that views can be updated. The planner doesn't need to check for non-updatable views. It should just try to perform the update and throw an exception if something goes wrong. Note that you will need to modify `ProjectScan` to implement `UpdateScan` interface, as in Exercise 8.12.
(b) Explain what the planner would have to do to verify that the view definition was updatable.

10.21. The SimpleDB basic update planner deals with view definitions by "unparsing" the query and saving the query string in the catalog. The basic query planner then has to reparse the view definition each time it is used in a query. An alternative approach is for the create-view planner to save the parsed version of the query data in the catalog, which can then be retrieved by the query planner.

(a) Implement this strategy. (*Hint*: Use object-serialization in Java. Serialize the `QueryData` object, and use a `StringWriter` to encode the object as a string. The metadata method `getViewDef` can then reverse the process, reconstructing the `QueryData` object from the stored string.)
(b) How does this implementation compare to the approach taken in SimpleDB?

10.22. Revise the SimpleDB server so that whenever a query is executed, the query and its corresponding plan are printed in the console window; this information will provide interesting insight into how the server is processing the query. There are two tasks required:

(a) Revise all of the classes that implement the `Plan` interface so that they implement the method `toString`. This method should return a well-formatted string representation of the plan, similar to a relational algebra query.
(b) Revise the method `executeQuery` (in class `simpledb.jdbc.network.RemoteStatementImpl` and `simpledb.jdbc.embedded.EmbeddedStatement`) so that it prints its input query and the string from part (a) in the server's console window.

Chapter 11
JDBC Interfaces

This chapter examines how to build JDBC interfaces for a database engine. Writing an embedded interface is relatively straightforward—you simply need to write each JDBC class using corresponding classes from the engine. Writing a server-based interface also requires the development of additional code to implement the server and handle the JDBC requests. This chapter shows how the use of Java RMI can simplify this additional code.

11.1 The SimpleDB API

Chapter 2 introduced JDBC as the standard interface for connecting to database engines and contained several example JDBC clients. Subsequent chapters, however, did not use JDBC. Instead, those chapters contained test programs that illustrated different features of the SimpleDB engine. Nevertheless, these test programs are also database clients; they just happen to access the SimpleDB engine using the SimpleDB API instead of the JDBC API.

The SimpleDB API consists of the public classes of SimpleDB (such as `SimpleDB`, `Transaction`, `BufferMgr`, `Scan`, and so on) and their public methods. This API is far more extensive than JDBC and can access the low-level details of the engine. This low-level access allows application programs to customize the functionality provided by the engine. For example, the test code of Chap. 4 circumvented the transaction manager to access the log and buffer managers directly.

Such low-level access comes at a price. The application writer must have an intimate knowledge of the target engine's API, and porting the application to a different engine (or to use a server-based connection) would require rewriting it to conform to a different API. The purpose of JDBC is to provide a standard API that, apart from minor configuration specifications, is the same for any database engine and configuration mode.

E. Sciore, *Database Design and Implementation*, Data-Centric Systems and Applications, https://doi.org/10.1007/978-3-030-33836-7_11

```
Driver d = new EmbeddedDriver();
Connection conn = d.connect("studentdb", null);

Statement stmt = conn.createStatement();
String qry = "select sname, gradyear from student";
ResultSet rs = stmt.executeQuery(qry);

while (rs.next())
   System.out.println(rs.getString("sname") + " "
                    + rs.getInt("gradyear"));
rs.close();
```

(a)

```
SimpleDB db = new SimpleDB("studentdb");
Transaction tx = db.newTx();

Planner planner = db.planner();
String qry = "select sname, gradyear from student";
Plan p = planner.createQueryPlan(qry, tx);
Scan s = p.open();

while (s.next())
   System.out.println(s.getString("sname") + " "
                    + s.getInt("gradyear"));
s.close();
```

(b)

Fig. 11.1 Two ways to access the database engine. (**a**) Using the JDBC API, (**b**) using the SimpleDB API

JDBC Interface	SimpleDB Class
Driver	SimpleDB
Connection	Transaction
Statement	Planner, Plan
ResultSet	Scan
ResultSetMetaData	Schema

Fig. 11.2 The correspondence between JDBC interfaces and SimpleDB classes

To implement the JDBC API in SimpleDB, it suffices to observe the correspondence between the two APIs. For example, consider Fig. 11.1. Part (a) contains a JDBC application that queries the database, prints its result set, and closes it. Part (b) gives the corresponding application using the SimpleDB API. The code creates a new transaction, calls the planner to get a plan for an SQL query, opens the plan to get a scan, iterates through the scan, and closes it.

The code in Fig. 11.1b uses five classes from SimpleDB: `SimpleDB`, `Transaction`, `Planner`, `Plan`, and `Scan`. The JDBC code uses the interfaces

Driver, Connection, Statement, and ResultSet. Figure 11.2 shows the correspondence between these constructs.

The constructs in each row of Fig. 11.2 share a common purpose. For example, both Connection and Transaction manage the current transaction, the classes Statement and Planner process SQL statements, and ResultSet and Scan iterate through the result of a query. This correspondence is the key to implementing a JDBC API for SimpleDB.

11.2 Embedded JDBC

The package simpledb.jdbc.embedded contains a class for each of the JDBC interfaces. The code for the class EmbeddedDriver appears in Fig. 11.3.

The class has an empty constructor. Its only method, connect, creates a new SimpleDB object for the specified database, passes it to the EmbeddedConnection constructor, and returns that new object. Note that the JDBC Driver interface forces the method to declare that it can throw an SQLException, even though it won't.

The JDBC Driver interface actually has more methods than just connect, although none are relevant to SimpleDB. To ensure that EmbeddedDriver can implement Driver, it extends the class DriverAdapter, which does implement those methods. The code for DriverAdapter appears in Fig. 11.4.

DriverAdapter implements all the Driver methods by either returning a default value or by throwing an exception. The EmbeddedDriver class overrides the method that SimpleDB cares about (namely, connect) and uses the DriverAdapter implementations of the other methods.

Figure 11.5 contains the code for the class EmbeddedConnection. This class manages transactions. Most of the work is performed by the Transaction object currentTx. For example, the commit method calls currentTx.commit and then creates a new transaction to be the new value of currentTx. The method createStatement passes a Planner object to the EmbeddedStatement constructor, as well as a reference to itself.

EmbeddedConnection does not implement Connection directly but instead extends ConnectionAdapter. The code for ConnectionAdapter provides default implementations of all the Connection methods and is omitted here.

```
public class EmbeddedDriver extends DriverAdapter {
   public EmbeddedConnection connect(String dbname, Properties p)
                                        throws SQLException {
      SimpleDB db = new SimpleDB(dbname);
      return new EmbeddedConnection(db);
   }
}
```

Fig. 11.3 The class EmbeddedDriver

```
public abstract class DriverAdapter implements Driver {
   public boolean acceptsURL(String url) throws SQLException {
      throw new SQLException("operation not implemented");
   }

   public Connection connect(String url, Properties info)
                                             throws SQLException {
      throw new SQLException("operation not implemented");
   }

   public int getMajorVersion() {
      return 0;
   }

   public int getMinorVersion() {
      return 0;
   }

   public DriverPropertyInfo[] getPropertyInfo(String url,
                                                 Properties info) {
      return null;
   }

   public boolean jdbcCompliant() {
      return false;
   }

   public Logger getParentLogger()
         throws SQLFeatureNotSupportedException {
      throw new SQLFeatureNotSupportedException("op not implemented");
   }
}
```

Fig. 11.4 The class `DriverAdapter`

The code for `EmbeddedStatement` appears in Fig. 11.6. The class is responsible for executing SQL statements. The method `executeQuery` obtains a plan from the planner and passes the plan to a new `RemoteResultSet` object for execution. The method `executeUpdate` simply calls the planner's corresponding method.

These two methods are also responsible for implementing the JDBC autocommit semantics. If the SQL statement executes correctly, then it must get committed. The method `executeUpdate` tells the connection to commit the current transaction as soon as the update statement has completed. On the other hand, the method `executeQuery` cannot immediately commit because its result set is still in use. Instead, the `Connection` object is sent to the `EmbeddedResultSet` object so that its `close` method can commit the transaction.

If something goes wrong during the execution of an SQL statement then the planner code will throw a runtime exception. These two methods will catch this exception, roll back the transaction, and throw an SQL exception.

```
class EmbeddedConnection extends ConnectionAdapter {
   private SimpleDB db;
   private Transaction currentTx;
   private Planner planner;

   public EmbeddedConnection(SimpleDB db) {
      this.db = db;
      currentTx = db.newTx();
      planner = db.planner();
   }

   public EmbeddedStatement createStatement() throws SQLException {
      return new EmbeddedStatement(this, planner);
   }

   public void close() throws SQLException {
      commit();
   }

   public void commit() throws SQLException {
      currentTx.commit();
      currentTx = db.newTx();
   }

   public void rollback() throws SQLException {
      currentTx.rollback();
      currentTx = db.newTx();
   }

   Transaction getTransaction() {
      return currentTx;
   }
}
```

Fig. 11.5 The class `EmbeddedConnection`

The class `EmbeddedResultSet` contains methods for executing a query plan; its code appears in Fig. 11.7. Its constructor opens the `Plan` object given to it and saves the resulting scan. The methods `next`, `getInt`, `getString`, and `close` simply call their corresponding scan methods. The method `close` also commits the current transaction, as required by the JDBC autocommit semantics. The `EmbeddedResultSet` class obtains a `Schema` object from its plan. The `getMetaData` method passes this `Schema` object to the `EmbeddedMetaData` constructor.

The `EmbeddedMetaData` class contains the `Schema` object that was passed into its constructor; its code appears in Fig. 11.8. The class `Schema` contains analogous methods to those in the `ResultSetMetaData` interface; the difference is that the `ResultSetMetaData` methods refer to fields by column number, whereas the `Schema` methods refer to fields by name. The code for `EmbeddedMetaData` therefore involves translating the method calls from one way to the other.

```
class EmbeddedStatement extends StatementAdapter {
   private EmbeddedConnection conn;
   private Planner planner;

   public EmbeddedStatement(EmbeddedConnection conn,
                                          Planner planner) {
      this.conn = conn;
      this.planner = planner;
   }

   public EmbeddedResultSet executeQuery(String qry)
                                          throws SQLException {
      try {
         Transaction tx = conn.getTransaction();
         Plan pln = planner.createQueryPlan(qry, tx);
         return new EmbeddedResultSet(pln, conn);
      }
      catch(RuntimeException e) {
         conn.rollback();
         throw new SQLException(e);
      }
   }

   public int executeUpdate(String cmd) throws SQLException {
      try {
         Transaction tx = conn.getTransaction();
         int result = planner.executeUpdate(cmd, tx);
         conn.commit();
         return result;
      }
      catch(RuntimeException e) {
         conn.rollback();
         throw new SQLException(e);
      }
   }

   public void close() throws SQLException {
   }
}
```

Fig. 11.6 The class `EmbeddedStatement`

11.3 Remote Method Invocation

The rest of this chapter addresses the issue of how to implement a server-based JDBC interface. The hardest part of implementing server-based JDBC is writing code for the server. Fortunately, the Java library contains classes that do most of the work; these classes are known as *Remote Method Invocation* (or *RMI*). This section introduces RMI. The next section shows how to use it to write a server-based JDBC interface.

```
public class EmbeddedResultSet extends ResultSetAdapter {
   private Scan s;
   private Schema sch;
   private EmbeddedConnection conn;

   public EmbeddedResultSet(Plan plan, EmbeddedConnection conn)
                                                   throws SQLException {
      s = plan.open();
      sch = plan.schema();
      this.conn = conn;
   }

   public boolean next() throws SQLException {
      try {
         return s.next();
      }
      catch(RuntimeException e) {
         conn.rollback();
         throw new SQLException(e);
      }
   }

   public int getInt(String fldname) throws SQLException {
      try {
         fldname = fldname.toLowerCase(); // for case-insensitivity
         return s.getInt(fldname);
      }
      catch(RuntimeException e) {
         conn.rollback();
         throw new SQLException(e);
      }
   }

   public String getString(String fldname) throws SQLException {
      try {
         fldname = fldname.toLowerCase(); // for case-insensitivity
         return s.getString(fldname);
      }
      catch(RuntimeException e) {
         conn.rollback();
         throw new SQLException(e);
      }
   }
   public ResultSetMetaData getMetaData() throws SQLException {
      return new EmbeddedMetaData(sch);
   }
   public void close() throws SQLException {
      s.close();
      conn.commit();
   }
}
```

Fig. 11.7 The class `EmbeddedResultSet`

```
public class EmbeddedMetaData extends ResultSetMetaDataAdapter {
   private Schema sch;

   public EmbeddedMetaData(Schema sch) {
      this.sch = sch;
   }

   public int getColumnCount() throws SQLException {
      return sch.fields().size();
   }

   public String getColumnName(int column) throws SQLException {
      return sch.fields().get(column-1);
   }

   public int getColumnType(int column) throws SQLException {
      String fldname = getColumnName(column);
      return sch.type(fldname);
   }

   public int getColumnDisplaySize(int column) throws SQLException {
      String fldname = getColumnName(column);
      int fldtype = sch.type(fldname);
      int fldlength = (fldtype == INTEGER) ? 6 : sch.length(fldname);
      return Math.max(fldname.length(), fldlength) + 1;
   }
}
```

Fig. 11.8 The class EmbeddedMetaData

11.3.1 Remote Interfaces

RMI makes it possible for Java program on one machine (the *client*) to interact with objects that live on another machine (the *server*). To use RMI, you must define one or more interfaces that extend the Java interface Remote; these are called its *remote interfaces*. You also need to write an implementation class for each interface; these classes will live on the server and are called *remote implementation classes*. RMI will automatically create corresponding implementation classes that live on the client; these are called *stub* classes. When the client calls a method from a stub object, the method call is sent across the network to the server and executed there by the corresponding remote implementation object; the result is then sent back to the stub object on the client. In short, a remote method is called by the client (using the stub object) but executed on the server (using the remote implementation object).

SimpleDB implements five remote interfaces in its package simpledb.jdbc.network: RemoteDriver, RemoteConnection, RemoteStatement, RemoteResultSet, and RemoteMetaData; their code appears in Fig. 11.9. These remote interfaces mirror their corresponding JDBC interfaces, with two differences:

```
public interface RemoteDriver extends Remote {
   public RemoteConnection connect() throws RemoteException;
}

public interface RemoteConnection extends Remote {
   public RemoteStatement createStatement() throws RemoteException;
   public void            close()           throws RemoteException;
}

public interface RemoteStatement extends Remote {
   public RemoteResultSet executeQuery(String qry) throws RemoteException;
   public int            executeUpdate(String cmd) throws RemoteException;
}

public interface RemoteResultSet extends Remote {
   public boolean        next()                    throws RemoteException;
   public int            getInt(String fldname)    throws RemoteException;
   public String         getString(String fldname) throws RemoteException;
   public RemoteMetaData getMetaData()             throws RemoteException;
   public void           close()                   throws RemoteException;
}

public interface RemoteMetaData extends Remote {
   public int getColumnCount()                 throws RemoteException;
   public String getColumnName(int column)     throws RemoteException;
   public int getColumnType(int column)        throws RemoteException;
   public int getColumnDisplaySize(int column) throws RemoteException;
}
```

Fig. 11.9 The SimpleDB remote interfaces

```
RemoteDriver rdvr = ...
RemoteConnection rconn = rdvr.connect();
RemoteStatement  rstmt = rconn.createStatement();
```

Fig. 11.10 Accessing remote interfaces from the client

- They only implement the basic JDBC methods shown in Fig. 2.1.
- They throw a `RemoteException` (as required by RMI) instead of an `SQLException` (as required by JDBC).

To get a feel for how RMI works, consider the client-side code fragment of Fig. 11.10. Each of the variables in the code fragment denotes a remote interface. However, because the code fragment is on the client, you know that the actual objects held by these variables are from the stub classes. The fragment doesn't show how variable `rdvr` obtains its stub; it does so via the RMI registry, which will be discussed in Sect. 11.3.2.

Consider the call to `rdvr.connect`. The stub implements its `connect` method by sending a request over the network to its corresponding `RemoteDriver` implementation object on the server. This remote implementation object executes its `connect` method on the server, which will cause a new

RemoteConnection implementation object to be created on the server. A stub for this new remote object is sent back to the client, which stores it as the value of variable rconn.

Now consider the call to rconn.createStatement. The stub object sends a request to its corresponding RemoteConnection implementation object on the server. This remote object executes its createStatement method. A RemoteStatement implementation object gets created on the server, and its stub is returned to the client.

11.3.2 The RMI Registry

Each client-side stub object contains a reference to its corresponding server-side remote implementation object. A client, once it has a stub object, is able to interact with the server through this object, and that interaction may create other stub objects for the client to use. But the question remains—how does a client get its first stub? RMI solves this problem by means of a program called the *rmi registry*. A server publishes stub objects in the RMI registry, and clients retrieve the stub objects from it.

The SimpleDB server publishes just one object, of type RemoteDriver. The publishing is performed by the following three lines of code from the simpledb.server.StartServer program:

```
Registry reg = LocateRegistry.createRegistry(1099);
RemoteDriver d = new RemoteDriverImpl();
reg.rebind("simpledb", d);
```

The method createRegistry starts the RMI registry on the local machine, using the specified port. (The convention is to use port 1099.) The method call reg.rebind creates a stub for the remote implementation object d, saves it in the rmi registry, and makes it available to clients under the name "simpledb."

A client can request a stub from the registry by calling the method lookup on the registry. In SimpleDB, this request is made via the following lines in the NetworkDriver class:

```
String host = url.replace("jdbc:simpledb://", "");
Registry reg = LocateRegistry.getRegistry(host, 1099);
RemoteDriver rdvr = (RemoteDriver) reg.lookup("simpledb");
```

The method getRegistry returns a reference to the RMI registry on the specified host and port. The call to reg.lookup goes to the RMI registry, retrieves the stub from it named "simpledb," and returns it to the caller.

11.3.3 Thread Issues

When building a large Java program, it is always a good idea to be very clear about what threads exist at any point. In a server-based execution of SimpleDB, there will be two sets of threads: the threads on the client machines and the threads on the server machine.

Each client has its own thread on its machine. This thread continues throughout the execution of the client; all of a client's stub objects are called from this thread. On the other hand, each remote object on the server executes in its own separate thread. A server-side remote object can be thought of as a "mini-server," which sits waiting for its stub to connect to it. When a connection is made, the remote object performs the requested work, sends the return value back to the client, and waits patiently for another connection. The `RemoteDriver` object created by `simpledb.server.Startup` runs in a thread that can be thought of as the "database server" thread.

Whenever a client makes a remote method call, the client thread waits while the corresponding server thread runs, and resumes when the server thread returns a value. Similarly, the server-side thread will be dormant until one of its methods is called and will resume its dormancy when the method completes. Thus, only one of these client and server threads will be doing anything at any given time. Informally, it seems as if the client's thread as actually moving back and forth between the client and server as remote calls are made. Although this image can help you visualize the flow of control in a client-server application, it is also important to understand what is really happening.

One way to distinguish between the client-side and server-side threads is to print something. A call to `System.out.println` will show up on the client machine when called from a client thread and on the server machine when called from a server thread.

11.4 Implementing the Remote Interfaces

The implementation of each remote interface requires two classes: the stub class and the remote implementation class. By convention, the name of the remote implementation class is its interface name appended with the suffix "Impl." You never need to know the name of the stub classes.

Fortunately, the communication between server-side objects and their stubs is the same for all remote interfaces, which means that all communication code can be provided by the RMI library classes. The programmer only needs to supply the code specific to each particular interface. In other words, the programmer does not need to write the stub classes at all and writes only the portions of the remote implementation classes that specify what the server does for each method call.

```
public class RemoteDriverImpl extends    UnicastRemoteObject
                              implements RemoteDriver {

   public RemoteDriverImpl() throws RemoteException {
   }

   public RemoteConnection connect() throws RemoteException {
      return new RemoteConnectionImpl();
   }
}
```

Fig. 11.11 The SimpleDB class RemoteDriverImpl

The class RemoteDriverImpl is the entry point into the SimpleDB server; its code appears in Fig. 11.11. There will be only one RemoteDriverImpl object created, by the simpledb.server.Startup bootstrap class, and its stub is the only object published in the RMI registry. Each time its connect method is called (via the stub), it creates a new RemoteConectionImpl remote object on the server and runs it in a new thread. RMI transparently creates the corresponding RemoteConnection stub object and returns it to the client.

Note how this code is concerned only with server-side objects. In particular, it contains no network code or references to its associated stub object, and when it needs to create a new remote object, it only creates the remote implementation object (and not the stub object). The RMI class UnicastRemoteObject contains all of the code needed to perform these other tasks.

The functionality of RemoteDriverImpl is essentially the same as EmbeddedDriver of Fig. 11.3. It differs only in that its connect method has no arguments. The reason for this difference is that a SimpleDB embedded driver can choose the database to connect to, whereas the server-based driver must connect to the database associated with the remote *SimpleDB* object.

In general, the functionality of each JDBC remote implementation class is equivalent to the corresponding embedded JDBC class. For another example, consider the class RemoteConnectionImpl, whose code appears in Fig. 11.12. Note the close correspondence with the EmbeddedConnection code of Fig. 11.5. The code for the classes RemoteStatementImpl, RemoteResultsetImpl, and RemoteMetaDataImpl correspond similarly to their embedded equivalents and are omitted.

11.5 Implementing the JDBC Interfaces

SimpleDB's implementation of the RMI remote classes provides all of the features required by the JDBC interfaces in java.sql, except two: The RMI methods do not throw SQL exceptions, and they do not implement all of the methods in the interface. That is, you have viable classes that implement interfaces RemoteDriver, RemoteConnection, etc., but what you really need are

```
class RemoteConnectionImpl extends UnicastRemoteObject
                           implements RemoteConnection {
   private SimpleDB db;
   private Transaction currentTx;
   private Planner planner;

   RemoteConnectionImpl(SimpleDB db) throws RemoteException {
      this.db = db;
      currentTx = db.newTx();
      planner = db.planner();
   }

   public RemoteStatement createStatement() throws RemoteException {
      return new RemoteStatementImpl(this, planner);
   }

   public void close() throws RemoteException {
      currentTx.commit();
   }

   Transaction getTransaction() {
      return currentTx;
   }

   void commit() {
      currentTx.commit();
      currentTx = db.newTx();
   }

   void rollback() {
      currentTx.rollback();
      currentTx = db.newTx();
   }
}
```

Fig. 11.12 The SimpleDB class `RemoteConnectionImpl`

classes that implement `Driver`, `Connection`, etc. This is a common problem in object-oriented programming, and the solution is to implement the required classes as client-side *wrappers* of their corresponding stub objects.

To see how the wrapping works, consider the class `NetworkDriver`, whose code appears in Fig. 11.13. Its `connect` method must return an object of type `Connection`, which in this case will be a `NetworkConnection` object. To do so, it first obtains a `RemoteDriver` stub from the RMI registry. It then calls the stub's `connect` method to obtain a `RemoteConnection` stub. The desired `NetworkConnection` object is created by passing the `RemoteConnection` stub into its constructor.

The code for the other JDBC interfaces is similar. For an example, Fig. 11.14 gives the code for `NetworkConnection`. Its constructor takes a

```
public class NetworkDriver extends DriverAdapter {
   public Connection connect(String url, Properties prop)
                                 throws SQLException {
      try {
         String host = url.replace("jdbc:simpledb://", "");
         Registry reg = LocateRegistry.getRegistry(host, 1099);
         RemoteDriver rdvr = (RemoteDriver) reg.lookup("simpledb");
         RemoteConnection rconn = rdvr.connect();
         return new NetworkConnection(rconn);
      }
      catch (Exception e) {
         throw new SQLException(e);
      }
   }
}
```

Fig. 11.13 The code for the SimpleDB class `NetworkDriver`

```
public class NetworkConnection extends ConnectionAdapter {
   private RemoteConnection rconn;

   public NetworkConnection(RemoteConnection c) {
      rconn = c;
   }

   public Statement createStatement() throws SQLException {
      try {
         RemoteStatement rstmt = rconn.createStatement();
         return new NetworkStatement(rstmt);
      }
      catch(Exception e) {
         throw new SQLException(e);
      }
   }
   public void close() throws SQLException {
      try {
         rconn.close();
      }
      catch(Exception e) {
         throw new SQLException(e);
      }
   }
}
```

Fig. 11.14 The code for the SimpleDB class `NetworkConnection`

`RemoteConnection` object, which it uses to implement its methods. The code for `createStatement` passes the newly created `RemoteStatement` object to the `NetworkStatement` constructor and returns that object. In these classes, whenever a stub object throws a `RemoteException`, that exception is caught and translated to an `SQLException`.

11.6 Chapter Summary

- There are two ways that an application program can access a database: via an embedded connection and via a server-based connection. SimpleDB, like most database engines, implements the JDBC API for both types of connection.
- The SimpleDB embedded JDBC connection takes advantage of the fact that each JDBC interface has a corresponding SimpleDB class.
- SimpleDB implements a server-based connection via the Java *Remote Method Invocation* (*RMI*) mechanism. Each JDBC interface has a corresponding RMI remote interface. Their primary difference is that they throw `RemoteException` (as required by RMI) instead of `SQLException` (as required by JDBC).
- Each server-side remote implementation object executes in its own thread, waiting for a stub to contact it. The SimpleDB startup code creates a remote implementation object of type `RemoteDriver` and stores a stub to it in the *RMI registry*. When a JDBC client wants a connection to the database system, it obtains the stub from the registry and calls its `connect` method.
- The `connect` method is typical of RMI remote methods. It creates a new `RemoteConnectionImpl` object on the server machine, which runs in its own thread. The method then returns a stub to this object back to the JDBC client. The client can call `Connection` methods on the stub, which cause the corresponding methods to be executed by the server-side implementation object.
- Server-based JDBC clients do not use remote stubs directly, because they implement the remote interfaces instead of the JDBC interfaces. Instead, the client-side objects *wrap* their corresponding stub objects.

11.7 Suggested Reading

There are numerous books dedicated to explaining RMI, such as Grosso (2001). In addition, Oracle's RMI tutorial is at https://docs.oracle.com/javase/tutorial/rmi/index.html.

The driver implementation used by SimpleDB is technically known as a "Type 4" driver. The online article Nanda (2002) describes and compares the four different driver types. The companion online article Nanda et al. (2002) leads you through the construction of an analogous Type 3 driver.

Grosso, W. (2001). *Java RMI*. Sebastopol, CA: O'Reilly.

Nanda, N. (2002). *Drivers in the wild*. JavaWorld. Retrieved from www.javaworld.com/javaworld/jw-07-2000/jw-0707-jdbc.html

Nanda, N., & Kumar, S. (2002). *Create your own Type 3 JDBC driver*. JavaWorld. Retrieved from www.javaworld.com/javaworld/jw-05-2002/jw-0517-jdbcdriver.html

11.8 Exercises

Conceptual Exercises

11.1. Trace the code of the server-based demo client StudentMajor.java, using the code from the classes in `simpledb.jdbc.network`. What server-side objects get created? What client-side objects get created? What threads get created?

11.2. The `RemoteStatementImpl` methods `executeQuery` and `executeUpdate` require a transaction. A `RemoteStatementImpl` object gets its transaction by calling `rconn.getTransaction()` each time `executeQuery` or `executeUpdate` is called. A simpler strategy would be to just pass the transaction to each `RemoteStatementImpl` object when it was created, via its constructor. However, this would be a very bad idea. Give a scenario in which something incorrect could happen.

11.3. We know that remote implementation objects live on the server. But are the remote implementation classes needed by the client? Are the remote interfaces needed by the client? Create a client configuration that contains the SimpleDB folders `sql` and `remote`. What class files can you remove from these folders without causing the client to break? Explain your results.

Programming Exercises

11.4. Revise the SimpleDB JDBC classes so that they implement the following methods of `ResultSet`. Do it for both the embedded and server-based implementations.

(a) The method `beforeFirst`, which repositions the result set to before the first record (i.e., to its original state). Use the fact that scans have a `beforeFirst` method which does the same thing.

(b) The method `absolute(int n)`, which positions the result set to the `nth` record. (Scans do not have a corresponding `absolute` method.)

11.5. Exercise 8.13 asked you to implement the scan methods `afterLast` and `previous`.

(a) Modify the `ResultSet` implementation to contain these methods.

(b) Test your code by modifying the demo JDBC client class `SimpleIJ` to print its output tables in reverse order.

11.6. Exercise 9.18 asked you to implement null values in SimpleDB. The JDBC `getInt` and `getString` methods do not return null values. A JDBC client can determine if the most recently retrieved value was null only by using the `wasNull` method of `ResultSet`, as was explained in Exercise 2.8.

(a) Modify the `ResultSet` implementation to contain this method.

(b) Write a JDBC program to test your code.

11.7. The JDBC `Statement` interface contains a method `close`, which closes any result set for that statement that may still be open. Implement this method.

11.8. Standard JDBC specifies that the method `Connection.close` should close all of its statements (as in Exercise 11.7). Implement this feature.

11.9. Standard JDBC specifies that a connection is automatically closed when a `Connection` object is garbage collected (e.g., when a client program completes). This ability is important, as it allows the database system to release resources that were abandoned by forgetful clients. Use the `finalizer` construct in Java to implement this feature.

11.10. SimpleDB implements autocommit mode, in which the system automatically decides when to commit a transaction. Standard JDBC allows the client to turn off autocommit mode and to commit and rollback its transactions explicitly. The JDBC `Connection` interface has a method `setAutoCommit(boolean ac)`, which allows a client to turn auto-commit mode on or off, a method `getAutoCommit`, which returns the current auto-commit status, and the methods `commit` and `rollback`. Implement these methods.

11.11. The SimpleDB server allows anyone to connect to it. Modify class `NetworkDriver` so that its `connect` method authenticates users. The method should extract a username and password from the `Properties` object passed into it. The method should then compare them against the contents of a server-side text file and throw an exception if there is no match. Assume that new usernames and passwords are added (or dropped) by simply editing the file on the server.

11.12. Modify `RemoteConnectionImpl` so that it only allows a limited number of connections at a time. What should the system do if there are no available connections left when a client tries to connect?

11.13. Recall from Sect. 2.2.4 that JDBC contains an interface `PreparedStatement`, which separates the planning stage of a query from the execution of its scan. A query can be planned once and executed multiple times, perhaps with different values for some of its constants. Consider the following code fragment:

```
String qry = "select SName from STUDENT where MajorId = ?";
PreparedStatement ps = conn.prepareStatement(qry);
ps.setInt(1, 20);
ResultSet rs = ps.executeQuery();
```

The "?" character in the query denotes an unknown constant, whose value will be assigned prior to execution. A query can have multiple unknown constants. The method `setInt` (or `setString`) assigns a value to the ith unknown constant.

(a) Suppose that the prepared query contains no unknown constants. Then the `PreparedStatement` constructor obtains the plan from the planner, and the `executeQuery` method passes the plan to the `ResultSet` constructor. Implement this special case, which involves changes to the `jdbc` packages, but no changes to the parser or planner.

(b) Now revise your implementation so that it handles unknown constants. The parser must be changed to recognize the "?" characters. The planner must be able to obtain a list of the unknown constants from the parser; those constants can then be assigned values via `setInt` and `setString` methods.

11.14. Suppose you start up a JDBC client program; however, it takes too long to finish, so you cancel it using <CTRL-C>.

(a) What impact does this have on the other JDBC clients running on the server?
(b) When and how will the server notice that your JDBC client program is no longer running? What will it do when it finds out?
(c) What is the best way for the server to handle this kind of situation?
(d) Design and implement your answer to (c).

11.15. Write a Java class `Shutdown` whose main method gracefully shuts down the server. That is, existing connections are allowed to complete, but no new connections should be made. When there are no more transactions running, the code should write a quiescent checkpoint record to the log and write an "ok to shut down" message on the console. (Hint: The easiest way to shut down is to remove the `SimpleDB` object from the RMI registry. Also, remember that this method will execute in a different JVM from the server. You therefore will need to modify the server somehow so that it recognizes that `Shutdown` has been called.)

Chapter 12
Indexing

When querying a table, a user is often interested in only some of its records, such as the records having a specified value of some field. An *index* is a file that allows the database engine to locate such records quickly, without having to search through the entire table. This chapter considers three common ways to implement an index: static hashing, extendable hashing, and B-trees. It then develops new relational algebra operations that take advantage of indexes.

12.1 The Value of Indexing

This book has so far assumed that the records in a table have no particular organization. However, an appropriate table organization can significantly improve the efficiency of some queries. For a good example of the issues, consider the white pages of a paper telephone book.

A telephone book is essentially a large table, whose records list the name, address, and phone number of each subscriber. This table is sorted by subscriber's last name and then by first name. Suppose that you want to retrieve the phone number for a particular person. The best strategy is to use the fact that the records are sorted by name. For example, you can do a binary search to locate the phone number by examining at most $\log_2 N$ listings, where N is the total number of listings. This is exceptionally quick. (For example, suppose that $N = 1{,}000{,}000$. Then $\log_2 N < 20$, which means that you never need to examine more than 20 listings to find someone in a phonebook of a million people.)

Although a telephone book is great for retrieving listings by subscriber name, it is not very good for other kinds of retrieval, such as finding the subscriber who has a particular phone number or lives at a particular address. The only way to get that information from the telephone book is to examine every single one of its listings. Such a search can be quite slow.

E. Sciore, *Database Design and Implementation*, Data-Centric Systems and Applications, https://doi.org/10.1007/978-3-030-33836-7_12

If you want an efficient way to look up subscribers given a phone number, then you need a telephone book that is sorted by phone number (otherwise known as a “reverse telephone book”). Of course, this telephone book is useful only if you know the telephone number. If you have a reverse telephone book and want to know the telephone number of a particular subscriber, then you would again have to examine every single one of the book’s listings.

This discussion illustrates an obvious but critical fact about table organization: *A table can be organized only one way at a time*. If you want retrievals to be fast given either a phone number or a subscriber name, then you need two separate copies of the telephone book, each having a different organization. And if you also wanted fast retrieval of a phone number given an address, you would need a third copy of the telephone book, organized by address.

This principle also applies to database tables. If you want to be able to efficiently find the records in a table having a particular field value, you need a version of the table organized by that field. Database engines address this need by supporting *indexes*. A table can have one or more indexes, each defined on a separate field. Each index acts as a version of the table organized on its field. For example, an index on STUDENT’s `MajorId` field will make it easy to find STUDENT records having a given major.

Specifically, an index is a file of *index records*. The index file has one index record for each record in the associated table. Each index record has two values: the record identifier of its associated record and the value of the specified field of that record. SimpleDB calls these fields the index record’s *datarid* and *dataval*. Figure 12.1 depicts the STUDENT table and two indexes for it—one on the field `SId`

Fig. 12.1 The indexes SID_IDX and MAJOR_IDX

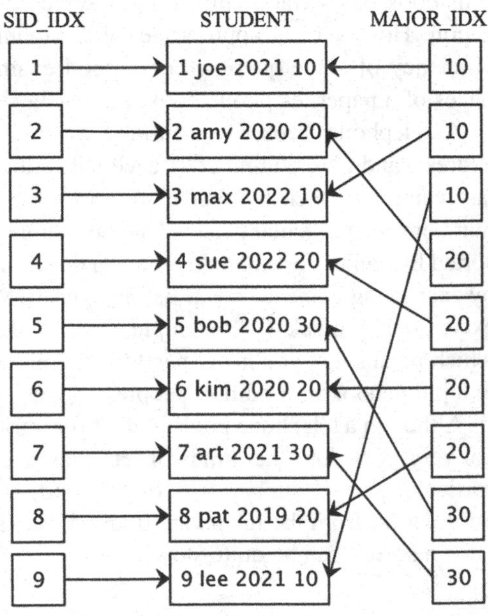

and the other on the field `MajorId`. Each box denotes a record. The dataval for an index record appears within its box, and the datarid appears as an arrow to the associated STUDENT record.

The engine organizes the records in an index file according to their datavals. Sections 12.3–12.5 will examine some sophisticated record organizations. For now, Fig. 12.1 simply assumes that the index records are sorted by their datavals. This sorted organization can be used as follows.

Suppose you want to find the STUDENT record whose `Sid`-value is 6. You first do a binary search on SID_IDX to find the index record whose dataval is 6; then you follow its datarid to locate the associated STUDENT record (which turns out to be the record for Kim).

Suppose instead that you want to find the STUDENT records whose `MajorId`-value is 20. You first do a binary search on MAJOR_IDX to find the first index record whose dataval is 20. Note that because of sorting, the other three index records having dataval 20 will appear consecutively after it in the file. Iterate through these four index records; for each one, follow its datarid to locate the associated STUDENT record.

How efficient is this use of indexes? Without indexes, the best you can do for either query is to perform a sequential search of STUDENT. Recall the statistics of Fig. 7.8, which stated that there are 45,000 STUDENT records that fit 10 per block. Thus, the sequential scan of STUDENT could require 4500 block accesses.

The cost of using the SID_IDX index can be estimated as follows. The index will have 45,000 records, which means that a binary search of the index would require examining at most 16 index records (since `log₂(45,000)` $<$ `16`); in the worst case, each of these index records will be in a different block. It takes one more block access to use the datarid of the chosen index record to access the desired STUDENT record, resulting in 17 total block accesses—a considerable savings over the sequential scan.

The cost of using the MAJOR_IDX index can be calculated as follows. The statistics of Fig. 7.8 stated that there are 40 departments, which means that each department will have about 1125 majors; consequently, MAJOR_IDX will have about 1125 records for each dataval. Index records are small, so let's assume that they fit 100 per block; thus, the 1125 index records will fit in 12 blocks. Again, a binary search on the index requires 16 block accesses to find the first index record. Since all index records having the same dataval are consecutive in the file, iterating through these 1125 index records will require 12 block accesses. Thus the query requires 16 + 12 = 28 block accesses of MAJOR_IDX. That's very efficient. The issue, however, is the number of STUDENT blocks that need to be accessed. When each of the 1125 index records follows its datarid, it will independently request a block of STUDENT. The result is that the query makes 1125 block accesses of STUDENT and 1125 + 28 = 1153 total block accesses. Although this is considerably more accesses than SID_IDX needed, using MAJOR_IDX is still about four times faster than doing a sequential search.

Now suppose that there were only 9 departments instead of 40. Then each department would have 5000 majors, which means that MAJOR_IDX would have about 5000 index records for each dataval. Consider what happens when you execute the previous query. There would now be 5000 MAJOR_IDX records attempting to get their associated STUDENT record, meaning that there would be 5000 independent block reads of STUDENT! That is, using the index would result in more block accesses than there are blocks in STUDENT. In this case, using the index would be worse than simply scanning the STUDENT table directly. The index would be completely useless.

These observations can be summarized in the following rule: *The usefulness of an index on field A is proportional to the number of different A-values in the table.* This rule implies that an index is most useful when its indexed field is a key of the table (such as SID_IDX), because every record has a different key value. Conversely, the rule also implies that an index will be useless if the number of different A-values is less than the number of records per block (see Exercise 12.15).

12.2 SimpleDB Indexes

The previous section illustrated the ways that an index gets used: you can search the index for the first record having a specified dataval; you can find all subsequent index records having that dataval; and you can extract the datarid from a given index record. The SimpleDB interface `Index` formalizes these operations. Its code appears in Fig. 12.2.

These methods are similar to methods in `TableScan`—a client can position the index at the beginning and move through its records, can retrieve the contents of the current index record, and can insert and delete index records. However, because indexes are used in well-known, specific ways, the methods in `Index` are more specific than those in `TableScan`.

In particular, a SimpleDB client always searches an index by providing a value (called the *search key*) and retrieving the index records having a matching dataval. The method `beforeFirst` takes this search key as its argument. Subsequent calls to `next` move the index to the next record whose dataval equals the search key and return `false` if no more such records exist.

Moreover, an index does not need general-purpose `getInt` and `getString` methods, because all index records have the same two fields. Moreover, a client never needs to retrieve a record's dataval, because it will always be the search key.

```
public interface Index {
   public void    beforeFirst(Constant searchkey);
   public boolean next();
   public RID     getDataRid();
   public void    insert(Constant dataval, RID datarid);
   public void    delete(Constant dataval, RID datarid);
   public void    close();
}
```

Fig. 12.2 The code for the SimpleDB `Index` interface

Thus, the only retrieval method it needs is `getDataRid`, which returns the datarid of the current index record.

The class `IndexRetrievalTest` provides an example of index use; see Fig. 12.3. The code opens the index on `MajorId` for students having major 20, retrieves the corresponding STUDENT records, and prints their names.

Note that the code uses a table scan to retrieve the STUDENT records, even though the table is not really "scanned." Instead, the code calls the table scan's `moveToRid` method to position the scan at the desired record.

The API of the index-related metadata classes appeared in Fig. 7.13. In particular, the `getIndexInfo` method in `IndexMgr` returns a map containing `IndexInfo` metadata for all available indexes of the specified table. You obtain the desired `Index` object by selecting the appropriate `IndexInfo` object from the map and calling its `open` method.

The class `IndexUpdateTest` in Fig. 12.4 illustrates how the database engine deals with updates to a table. The code performs two tasks. The first task inserts a new record into STUDENT; the second task deletes a record from STUDENT. The code must deal with the insertion by inserting a corresponding record in each index

```
public class IndexRetrievalTest {
   public static void main(String[] args) {
      SimpleDB db = new SimpleDB("studentdb");
      Transaction tx = db.newTx();
      MetadataMgr mdm = db.mdMgr();

      // Open an scan on the data table.
      Plan studentplan = new TablePlan(tx, "student", mdm);
      Scan studentscan = studentplan.open();

      // Open the index on MajorId.
      Map<String,IndexInfo> indexes = mdm.getIndexInfo("student", tx);
      IndexInfo ii = indexes.get("majorid");
      Index idx = ii.open();

      // Retrieve all index records having a dataval of 20.
      idx.beforeFirst(new Constant(20));
      while (idx.next()) {
         // Use the datarid to go to the corresponding STUDENT record.
         RID datarid = idx.getDataRid();
         studentscan.moveToRid(datarid);
         System.out.println(studentscan.getString("sname"));
      }

      // Close the index and the data table.
      idx.close();
      studentscan.close();
      tx.commit();
   }
}
```

Fig. 12.3 Using an index in SimpleDB

```
public class IndexUpdateTest {
   public static void main(String[] args) {
      SimpleDB db = new SimpleDB("studentdb");
      Transaction tx = db.newTx();
      MetadataMgr mdm = db.mdMgr();
      Plan studentplan = new TablePlan(tx, "student", mdm);
      UpdateScan studentscan = (UpdateScan) studentplan.open();

      // Create a map containing all indexes for STUDENT.
      Map<String,Index> indexes = new HashMap<>();
      Map<String,IndexInfo> idxinfo = mdm.getIndexInfo("student", tx);
      for (String fldname : idxinfo.keySet()) {
         Index idx = idxinfo.get(fldname).open();
         indexes.put(fldname, idx);
      }

      // Task 1: Insert a new STUDENT record for Sam.
      //    First, insert the record into STUDENT.
      studentscan.insert();
      studentscan.setInt("sid", 11);
      studentscan.setString("sname", "sam");
      studentscan.setInt("gradyear", 2023);
      studentscan.setInt("majorid",  30);
      //    Then insert a record into each of the indexes.
      RID datarid = studentscan.getRid();
      for (String fldname : indexes.keySet()) {
         Constant dataval = studentscan.getVal(fldname);
         Index idx = indexes.get(fldname);
         idx.insert(dataval, datarid);
      }

      // Task 2: Find and delete Joe's record.
      studentscan.beforeFirst();
      while (studentscan.next()) {
         if (studentscan.getString("sname").equals("joe")) {
            // First, delete the index records for Joe.
            RID joeRid = studentscan.getRid();
            for (String fldname : indexes.keySet()) {
               Constant dataval = studentscan.getVal(fldname);
               Index idx = indexes.get(fldname);
               idx.delete(dataval, joeRid);
            }
            // Then delete Joe's record in STUDENT.
            studentscan.delete();
            break;
         }
      }

      // Print the records to verify the updates.
```

Fig. 12.4 Updating indexes to reflect changes to data records

```
      studentscan.beforeFirst();
      while (studentscan.next()) {
         System.out.println(studentscan.getString("sname") + " "
                              + studentscan.getInt("sid"));
      }
      studentscan.close();
      for (Index idx : indexes.values())
         idx.close();
      tx.commit();
      }
}
```

Fig. 12.4 (continued)

for STUDENT, and similarly for the deletion. Note how the code begins by opening all of the indexes for STUDENT and saving them in a map. The code can then loop through this map each time it needs to do something to each index.

The code of Figs. 12.3 and 12.4 manipulate indexes without knowing (or caring) how they are actually implemented. The only requirement is that the indexes implement the `Index` interface. Section 12.1 assumed a simple index implementation that used sorted indexes and binary search. Such an implementation is not used in practice, because it does not take advantage of the block structure of the index file. Sections 12.3–12.5 examine three better implementations—two strategies based on hashing and one based on sorted trees.

12.3 Static Hash Indexes

Static hashing is probably the simplest way to implement an index. Although it is not the most efficient strategy, it is easy to understand and illustrates the principles most clearly. Thus it is a good place to begin.

12.3.1 Static Hashing

A static hashed index uses a fixed number `N` of *buckets*, numbered from 0 to `N-1`. The index also uses a *hash function*, which maps values to buckets. Each index record is assigned to the bucket resulting from hashing its dataval. A static hashed index works as follows:

- To store an index record, put it into the bucket assigned by the hash function.
- To find an index record, hash the search key and examine that bucket.
- To delete an index record, first find it (as above), and then delete it from the bucket.

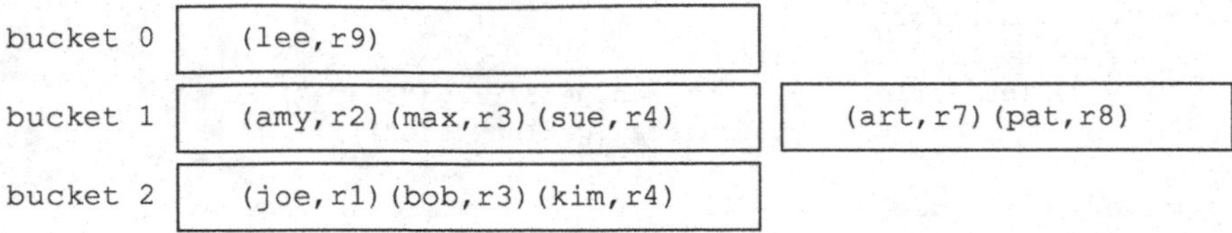

Fig. 12.5 A static hash index with three buckets

The search cost of a hashed index is inversely proportional to the number of buckets it has. If an index contains B blocks and has N buckets, then each bucket contains about B/N blocks, and so searching a bucket requires about B/N block accesses.

For example, consider an index on SName. Suppose for simplicity that N = 3 and that the hash function maps a string s to the number of letters in s (mod N) that come earlier in the alphabet than "m."[1] Assume also that three index records fit into a block. Figure 12.5 depicts the contents of the three index buckets. The figure uses ri to denote the rid of the ith STUDENT record.

Suppose now that you want to find the datarid of all students named "sue." You hash the string "sue" to get bucket 1 and search that bucket. The search requires two block accesses. Similarly, since "ron" hashes to bucket 0, it takes just one block access to determine that there are no students named "ron."

This example uses ridiculously small values for the block size and number of buckets. For a more realistic sample calculation, assume that the index uses 1024 buckets, which means (assuming that the records hash evenly among the buckets) that:

- An index of up to 1024 blocks can be searched in only one disk access
- An index of up to 2048 blocks can be searched in only two disk accesses

and so on. To give some perspective to these numbers, note that an index record on SName requires 22 bytes (14 bytes for the *varchar(10)* dataval, and 8 bytes for the datarid); so if you add 1 byte per record to hold the empty/inuse flag, then 178 index records will fit into a 4K block. An index size of 2048 blocks therefore corresponds to a data file of about 364,544 records. That is a lot of records to be able to search in only two disk accesses!

12.3.2 Implementing Static Hashing

Static hashing in SimpleDB is implemented in the class HashIndex, whose code appears in Fig. 12.6.

[1]This is a remarkably bad hash function, but it helps make the example interesting.

```
public class HashIndex implements Index {
   public static int NUM_BUCKETS = 100;
   private Transaction tx;
   private String idxname;
   private Layout layout;
   private Constant searchkey = null;
   private TableScan ts = null;

   public HashIndex(Transaction tx, String idxname, Layout layout) {
      this.tx = tx;
      this.idxname = idxname;
      this.layout = layout;
   }

   public void beforeFirst(Constant searchkey) {
      close();
      this.searchkey = searchkey;
      int bucket = searchkey.hashCode() % NUM_BUCKETS;
      String tblname = idxname + bucket;
      ts = new TableScan(tx, tblname, layout);
   }

   public boolean next() {
      while (ts.next())
         if (ts.getVal("dataval").equals(searchkey))
            return true;
      return false;
   }

   public RID getDataRid() {
      int blknum = ts.getInt("block");
      int id = ts.getInt("id");
      return new RID(blknum, id);
   }

   public void insert(Constant val, RID rid) {
      beforeFirst(val);
      ts.insert();
      ts.setInt("block", rid.blockNumber());
      ts.setInt("id", rid.slot());
      ts.setVal("dataval", val);
   }

   public void delete(Constant val, RID rid) {
      beforeFirst(val);
      while(next())
         if (getDataRid().equals(rid)) {
            ts.delete();
            return;
         }
   }
```

Fig. 12.6 The code for the SimpleDB class HashIndex

```
    public void close() {
       if (ts != null)
          ts.close();
    }

    public static int searchCost(int numblocks, int rpb){
       return numblocks / HashIndex.NUM_BUCKETS;
    }
}
```

Fig. 12.6 (continued)

This class stores each bucket in a separate table, whose name is the catenation of the index name and the bucket number. For example, the table for bucket #35 of index SID_INDEX is named "*SID_INDEX35*." The method `beforeFirst` hashes the search key and opens a table scan for the resulting bucket. Method `next` starts from the current position in the scan and reads records until one is found having the search key; if no such record is found, the method returns `false`. The datarid of an index record is stored as two integers, in fields `block` and `id`. Method `getDataRid` reads these two values from the current record and constructs the rid; the method `insert` does the opposite.

In addition to implementing the methods for the `Index` interface, the class `HashIndex` implements a static method `searchCost`. This method is called by `IndexInfo.blocksAccessed`, as was shown in Fig. 7.15. The `IndexInfo` object passes in two arguments to the `searchCost` method: the number of blocks in the index and the number of index records per block. It does so because it does not know how the indexes compute their costs. In the case of static indexing, the search cost depends only on the index size, and thus the RPB value is ignored.

12.4 Extendable Hash Indexes

The search cost of a static hash index is inversely proportional to the number of buckets—the more buckets you use, the fewer blocks in each bucket. The best possible situation would be to have enough buckets so that each bucket would be exactly one block long.

If an index always stayed the same size, then it would be easy to calculate this ideal number of buckets. But in practice, indexes grow as new records are inserted into the database. So how to decide how many buckets to use? Suppose that you choose the buckets based on the current index size. The problem is that as the index grows, each bucket will eventually wind up containing many blocks. But if you choose a larger number of buckets based on future needs, then the currently empty and nearly empty buckets will create a lot of wasted space until the index grows into it.

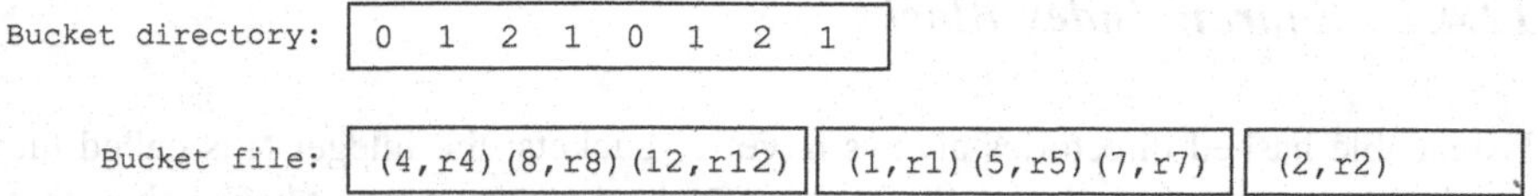

Fig. 12.7 An extendable hash index on the field SId of STUDENT

A strategy known as *extendable hashing* solves this problem by using a very large number of buckets, guaranteeing that each bucket will never be more than one block long.[2] Extendable hashing deals with the problem of wasted space by allowing multiple buckets to share the same block. The idea is that even though there are a lot of buckets, they all share a small number of blocks, so there is very little wasted space. It's a very clever idea.

The sharing of blocks by buckets is achieved by means of two files: the *bucket file* and the *bucket directory*. The bucket file contains the index blocks. The bucket directory maps buckets to blocks. The directory can be thought of as an array of integers, one integer for each bucket. Call this array Dir. If an index record hashes to bucket b, then that record will be stored in block Dir[b] of the bucket file.

For an example, Fig. 12.7 depicts the possible contents of an extendable hash index on field SId of STUDENT, assuming (for the sake of readability) that:

- Three index records fit into a block.
- Eight buckets are used.
- The hash function h(x) = x mod 8.
- The STUDENT table contains seven records, having ID 1, 2, 4, 5, 7, 8, and 12.

As before, ri denotes the rid of the ith STUDENT record.

Note how the bucket directory Dir is used. The fact that Dir[0] = 0 and Dir[4] = 0 means that records hashing to 0 (such as r8) or 4 (such as r4 and r12) will be placed in block 0. Similarly, records hashing to 1, 3, 5, or 7 will be placed in block 1, and records hashing to 2 or 6 will be placed in block 2. Thus, this bucket directory allows the index records to be stored in three blocks, instead of eight.

Of course, there are many ways to set up the bucket directory to share the buckets among three blocks. The directory shown in Fig. 12.7 has a particular logic behind it, which will be discussed next.

[2]An exception must be made when too many records have exactly the same dataval. Since those records will always hash to the same block, there will be no way a hashing strategy could spread them across several buckets. In this case, the bucket would have as many blocks as needed to hold those records.

12.4.1 Sharing Index Blocks

Extendable hashed directories always have 2^{M} buckets; the integer M is called the *maximum depth* of the index. A directory of 2^{M} buckets can support hash values that are M bits long. The example of Fig. 12.7 used M = 3. In practice, M = 32 is a reasonable choice because integer values have 32 bits.

Initially, an empty bucket file will contain a single block, and all directory entries will point to this block. In other words, this block is shared by all of the buckets. Any new index record will be inserted into this block.

Every block in the bucket file has a *local depth*. A local depth of L means that the hash value of every record in the block has the same rightmost L bits. The first block of the file initially has a local depth of 0, because its records can have arbitrary hash values.

Suppose that a record is inserted into the index but does not fit into its assigned block. Then that block *splits*, that is, another block is allocated in the bucket file, and the records in the full block are distributed among itself and the new block. The redistribution algorithm is based on the local depth of the block. Since all records in the block currently have the same rightmost L bits of their hash value, the algorithm considers the rightmost (L + 1)st bit: all records having a 0 are kept in the original block, and all records having a 1 are transferred to the new block. Note that the records in each of these two blocks now have L + 1 bits in common. That is, the local depth of each block has been increased by 1.

When a block splits, the bucket directory must be adjusted. Let b be the hash value of the newly inserted index record, that is, b is the number of a bucket. Suppose that the rightmost L bits of b are $b_L \ldots b_2 b_1$. Then it can be shown (see Exercise 12.10) that the bucket numbers having these rightmost L bits (which includes b) all point to the block that just split. Thus the directory must be modified so that every slot whose rightmost L + 1 bits are $1b_L \ldots b_2 b_1$ points to the new block.

For example, suppose that bucket 17 currently maps to a block B having local depth 2. Since 17 in binary is 1001, its rightmost 2 bits are 01. It follows that all buckets whose rightmost two bits are 01 map to B, such as 1, 5, 9, 13, 17, and 21. Now, suppose that block B is full and needs to split. The system allocates a new block B′ and sets the local depth of both B and B′ to 3. It then adjusts the bucket directory. Those buckets whose rightmost 3 bits are 001 continue to map to block B (i.e., their directory entries stay unchanged). But those buckets whose rightmost 3 bits are 101 are changed to map to B′. That is, buckets 1, 9, 17, 25, and so on will continue to map to B, whereas buckets 5, 13, 21, 29, and so on will now map to B′.

Figure 12.8 gives the algorithm for inserting a record into an extendable hash index. For an example, consider again an extendable hash index on Sid. Assume that the bucket directory has 2^{10} buckets (i.e., the maximum depth is 10) and that the hash function maps each integer n to n%1024. Initially, the bucket file consists of one block, and all directory entries point to that block. The situation is depicted in Fig. 12.9a.

1. Hash the record's dataval to get bucket b.
2. Find B = Dir[b]. Let L be the local depth of block B.
3a. If the record fits into B, insert it and return.
3b. If the record does not fit in B:

- Allocate a new block B′ in the bucket file.
- Set the local depth of both B and B′ to be L+1.
- Adjust the bucket directory so that all buckets having the rightmost L+1 bits $1b_L\ldots b_2b_1$ will point to B′.
- Re-insert each record from B into the index. (These records will hash either to B or to B′.)
- Try again to insert the new record into the index.

Fig. 12.8 The algorithm for inserting a records into an extendable hash index

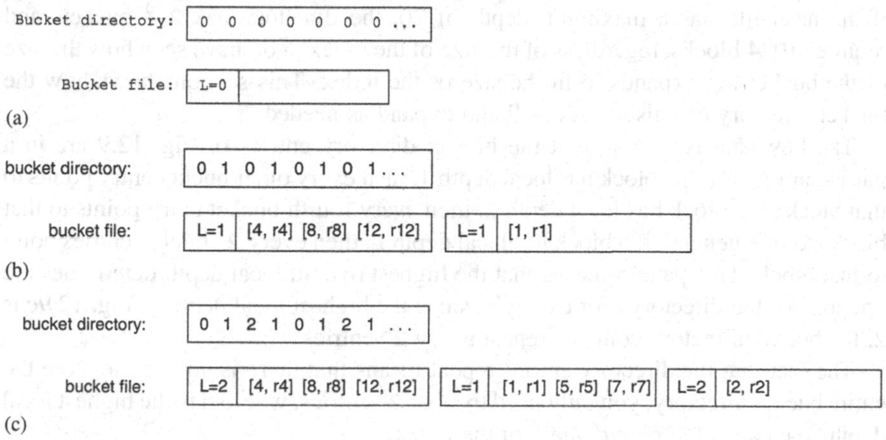

Fig. 12.9 Inserting records into an extendable hash index. **(a)** An index containing one block, **(b)** after the first split, **(c)** after the second split

Suppose now that you insert index records for students 4, 8, 1, and 12. The first three insertions go to block 0, but the fourth one causes a split. This split causes the following events to occur: A new block is allocated, the local depths are increased from 0 to 1, the directory entries are adjusted, the records in block 0 are re-inserted, and the record for employee 12 is inserted. The result is shown in Fig. 12.9b. Note that the odd entries in the bucket directory now point to the new block. The index is now such that all records having an even hash value (i.e., a rightmost bit of 0) are in block 0 of the bucket file, and all odd-value records (i.e., a rightmost bit of 1) are in block 1.

Next, insert index records for employees 5, 7, and 2. The first two records fit into block 1, but the third one causes block 0 to split again. The result is shown in Fig. 12.9c. Block 0 of the bucket file now contains all index records whose hash value ends in 00, and block 2 contains all records whose hash value ends in 10. Block 1 still contains all records whose hash value ends in 1.

One problem with any hashing strategy is that records are not guaranteed to be distributed evenly. When a block splits, all of its records may rehash to the same block; if the new record also hashes to that block, then it still will not fit into the block, and the block must be split again. If the local depth ever equals the maximum depth, then no more splitting is possible, and an overflow block must be created to hold the index records.

12.4.2 Compacting the Bucket Directory

Our examination of extendable hashing still needs to address the size of the bucket directory. A hash file having a maximum depth of 10 requires a directory of 2^{10} buckets and can be stored in one block, assuming a block size of 4K bytes. However, if the hash file has a maximum depth of 20, the directory has 2^{20} buckets and requires 1024 blocks, regardless of the size of the index. You have seen how the size of the bucket file expands to fit the size of the index. This section shows how the bucket directory can also start small and expand as needed.

The key idea is to note that the bucket directory entries of Fig. 12.9 are in a particular pattern. If a block has local depth 1, then every other bucket entry points to that block. If a block has local depth 2, then every fourth bucket entry points to that block. And in general, if a block has local depth L, then every 2^L bucket entries point to that block. This pattern means that the highest overall local depth determines the "period" of the directory. For example, since the highest local depth in Fig. 12.9c is 2, the bucket directory contents repeat every 2^2 entries.

The fact that the directory entries repeat means that there is no need to store the entire bucket directory; you only need to store 2^d entries, where d is the highest local depth. We call d the *global depth* of the index.

The algorithm for searching an index needs a slight modification to accommodate this change to the bucket directory. In particular, after the search key is hashed, the algorithm only uses the rightmost d bits of the hash value to determine the bucket directory entry.

The algorithm for inserting a new index record also needs modification. As with search, the record's dataval is hashed, and the rightmost *d* bits of the hash value determines the directory entry where the index record is inserted. If the block splits, then the algorithm proceeds as usual. The only exception is when the split causes the local depth of the block to become larger than the current global depth of the index. In this case, the global depth must be incremented before the records can be rehashed.

Incrementing the global depth means doubling the size of the bucket directory. Doubling the directory is remarkably easy—since the directory entries repeat, the second half of the doubled directory is identical to the first half. Once this doubling has occurred, the splitting process can continue. To illustrate the algorithm, reconsider the example of Fig. 12.9. The initial index will have global depth 0, which means that the bucket directory will have a single entry, pointing to block 0. The insertion of records for 4, 8, and 1 keep the global depth at 0.

Because the global depth is 0, only the rightmost 0 bits of the hash value are used to determine the directory entry; in other words, entry 0 is always used regardless of the hash value. When the record for 12 is inserted, however, the split causes the local depth of block 0 to increase, which means that the global depth of the index must also increase, and the bucket directory doubles from one to two entries. Initially both entries point to block 0; then all entries whose rightmost bit is `1` are adjusted to point to the new block. The resulting directory has a global depth of 1 and entries `Dir[0]` = `0` and `Dir[1]` = `1`.

Now that the global depth is 1, the insertion of records 5 and 7 use the rightmost 1 bits of the hash value, which is 1 in both cases. Thus bucket `Dir[1]` is used, and both records are inserted into block 1. The split that occurs after record 2 is inserted causes the local depth of block 0 to increase to 2, which means the global depth must also increase. Doubling the directory increases it to four entries, which initially are: 0 1 0 1. The entries having rightmost bits `10` are then adjusted to point to the new block, leading to a directory whose entries are: 0 1 2 1.

Extendable hashing does not work well when the index contains more records with the same dataval than can fit in a block. In this case, no amount of splitting can help, and the bucket directory will expand fully to its maximum size even though there are relatively few records in the index. To avoid this problem, the insertion algorithm must be modified to check for this situation and create a chain of overflow blocks for that bucket without splitting the block.

12.5 B-Tree Indexes

The previous two indexing strategies were based on hashing. We now consider a way to use sorting. The basic idea is to sort the index records by their datavals.

12.5.1 How to Improve a Dictionary

If you think about it, a sorted index file is a lot like a dictionary. An index file is a sequence of index records, each of which contains a dataval and a datarid. A dictionary is a sequence of entries, each of which contains a word and a definition. When you use a dictionary, you want to find the definitions of a word as quickly as possible. When you use an index file, you want to find the datarids of a dataval as quickly as possible. Figure 12.10 summarizes this correspondence.

The close correspondence between dictionaries and sorted indexes means that it should be possible to apply an understanding of dictionaries to the problem of implementing a sorted index. Let's see.

The dictionary on my desk has about 1000 pages. Each page has a *heading*, which lists the first and last word on that page. When I am looking for a word, the heading

	Dictionary	Sorted Index File
ENTRY:	[word, definition]. A word can have more than one definition.	[dataval, datarid]. A dataval can have more than one datarid.
USAGE:	Find the definitions of a given word.	Find the datarids for a given dataval.

Fig. 12.10 The correspondence between a dictionary and a sorted index file

TABLE OF CONTENTS Page i

Word Range	Page
a–ability	1
abject–abscissa	2
abscond–academic	3
…	

(a)

GUIDE TO THE TABLE OF CONTENTS

Word Range	Page
a–bouquet	i
bourbon–couple	ii
couplet–exclude	iii
…	

(b)

Fig. 12.11 An improved table of contents for a dictionary. (**a**) A row for each page, (**b**) a row for each table of contents page

helps me find the correct page—I only need to look at the headings, not the contents of the pages. Once I locate the correct page, I then search it to find my word.

The dictionary also has a table of contents, listing the page where the words beginning with each letter begin. However, I never use the table of contents because its information isn't especially useful. What I would really like is for the table of contents to contain a row for each page header, as in Fig. 12.11a. This table of contents is a real improvement because I no longer have to flip through the pages; all of the header information is in one place.

A 1000-page dictionary will have 1000 headers. Assuming that 100 headers fit on a page, then the table of contents will be 10 pages long. Searching through 10 pages is a lot better than searching through 1000, but it is still too much work. What I need is something that will help me search the table of contents, as in Fig. 12.11b. The "Guide to the Table of Contents" lists the header information for each page in the table of contents. The guide will thus contain ten headers and will easily fit on a single page.

With this setup, I could find any word in my dictionary by looking at exactly three pages:

- The guide page tells me which page in the table of contents to use.
- That table of contents page tells me which word-content page to use.
- I then search that word-content page to find my word.

If I try this strategy with a very large dictionary (say, over 10,000 pages), then its table of contents will be over 100 pages long, and the guide will be over 1 page long.

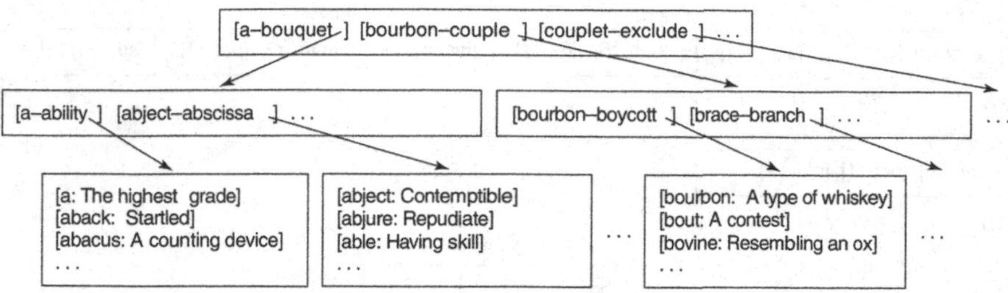

Fig. 12.12 The improved dictionary, represented as a tree

In this case, I could construct a "guide to the guide" page, which would keep me from having to search the guide. In this case, finding a word requires looking at four pages.

Looking at the two parts of Fig. 12.11, you can see that the table of contents and its guide have exactly the same structure. Let's call these pages the *directory* of the dictionary. The table of contents is the level-0 directory, the guide is the level-1 directory, the guide to the guide is the level-2 directory, and so on.

This improved dictionary has the following structure:

- There are numerous word-content pages, in sorted order.
- Each level-0 directory page contains the header for several word-content pages.
- Each level-($N+1$) directory page contains the header for several level-N directory pages.
- There is a single directory page at the highest level.

This structure can be depicted as a tree of pages, with the highest-level directory page as its root and the word-content pages as its leaves. Figure 12.12 depicts this tree.

12.5.2 The B-Tree Directory

The concept of a tree-structured directory can also be applied to sorted indexes. The index records will be stored in an index file. The level-0 directory will have a record for each block of the index file. These directory records will be of the form [dataval, block#], where *dataval* is the dataval of the first index record in the block, and *block#* is the block number of that block.

For example, Fig. 12.13a depicts the index file for a sorted index on the field `SName` of STUDENT. This index file consists of three blocks, with each block containing an unspecified number of records. Figure 12.13b depicts the level-0-directory for this index file. The directory consists of three records, one for each index block.

If the records in the directory are sorted by their dataval, then the range of values in each index block can be determined by comparing adjacent directory entries. For

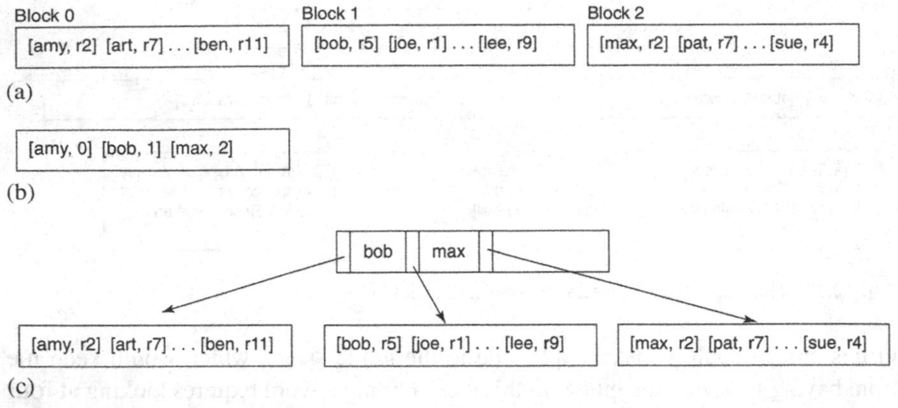

Fig. 12.13 A B-tree index for `Sname`. (**a**) The sorted index file, (**b**) the sorted level-0 directory, (**c**) the tree representation of the index and its directory

example, the three records in the directory of Fig. 12.13b denote the following information:

- Block 0 of the index file contains index records whose datavals range from "amy" up to (but not including) "bob."
- Block 1 contains index records ranging from "bob" up to (but not including) "max."
- Block 2 contains index records ranging from "max" to the end.

In general, the dataval in the first directory record is not interesting and is usually replaced by a special value (such as `null`), denoting "everything from the beginning."

A directory and its index blocks are usually represented graphically as a tree, as shown in Fig. 12.13c. That tree is an example of a *B-tree*.[3] Note how you can obtain the actual directory records by pairing each arrow with the dataval preceding it. The dataval corresponding to the leftmost arrow is omitted in the tree representation, because it is not needed.

Given a dataval v, the directory can be used to find the index records having that dataval or to insert a new index record for that dataval. The algorithms appear in Fig. 12.14.

There are two points to note about these algorithms. The first point is that steps 1 and 2 of these algorithms are identical. In other words, the insertion algorithm will insert an index record into the same block where the search algorithm will look for it—which is, of course, exactly what ought to happen. The second point is that each

[3]Historically, two slightly different versions of B-tree were developed. The version we are using is actually known as a *B+ tree*, because it was developed second; the first version, which I won't consider, preempted the *B-tree* designation. However, because the second version is by far more common in practice, I shall use the simpler (although slightly incorrect) term to denote it.

1. Search the directory block to find the directory record whose range of datavals contains v.
2. Read the index block pointed to by that directory record.
3. Examine the contents of this block to find the desired index records.

(a)

1. Search the directory block to find the directory record whose range of datavals contains v.
2. Read the index block pointed to by that directory record.
3. Insert the new index record into this block.

(b)

Fig. 12.14 Algorithms to find and insert index records into the tree of Fig. 12.13. (**a**) Finding the index records having a specified dataval v, (**b**) inserting a new index record having a specified dataval v

algorithm identifies a single index block where the desired records belong; thus, all index records having the same dataval must be in the same block.

The B-tree of Fig. 12.13 is very simple because the index is so small. As it gets larger, the algorithm must deal with the following three complications:

- The directory may be several blocks long.
- A newly inserted index record may not fit into the block where it needs to go.
- There may be many index records having the same dataval.

These issues are addressed in the following subsections.

12.5.3 A Directory Tree

Continuing the example of Fig. 12.13, suppose that many more new employees have been inserted into the database, so that the index file now contains eight blocks. If you assume (for sake of example) that at most three directory records fit into a block, then the B-tree directory will need at least three blocks. One idea might be to place these directory blocks into a file and scan them sequentially; however, such a scan would not be very efficient. A better idea corresponds to what I did with the improved dictionary: The B-tree needs a "guide" to the level-0 directory.

That is, there are now two levels of directory blocks. Level 0 contains those blocks that point to the index blocks. Level 1 contains a block that points to the level 0 blocks. Pictorially, the B-tree might look like the tree of Fig. 12.15. You search this index by starting at the level-1 block. Suppose, for example, that the search key is "jim." The search key lies between "eli" and "lee," and so you follow the middle arrow and search the level-0 block containing "joe." The search key is less than "joe," and so you follow the left arrow and look in the index block containing "eli." All index records for "jim" (if any) will be in this block.

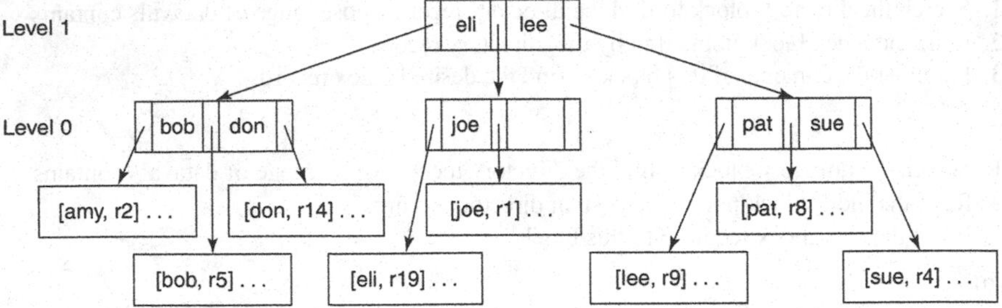

Fig. 12.15 A B-tree having two directory levels

In general, whenever a level contains more than one directory block, there will be directory blocks at the next higher level that point to them. Eventually the highest level will contain a single block. This block is called the *root* of the B-tree.

At this point, you should stop to make sure you are able to traverse a B-tree yourself. Using Fig. 12.15, choose several names and convince yourself that you can find the index block containing each name. There should be no ambiguity—given a dataval, there is exactly one index block where index records containing that dataval must be.

Also note the distribution of names in the directory records of the B-tree. For example, the value "eli" in the level-one node means that "eli" is the first name in the subtree pointed to by the middle arrow, which means that it is the first record of the first index block pointed to by the level-0 directory block. So even though "eli" does not appear explicitly in that level-0 block, it manages to make an appearance in the level-1 block. In fact, it turns out that the first dataval of each index block (except the very first block) appears exactly once in some directory block at some level of the B-tree.

A search of a B-tree requires accessing one directory block at each level, plus one index block. Thus the search cost is equal to the number of directory levels plus 1. To see the practical impact of this formula, consider the example at the end of Sect. 12.3.1, which calculated the search costs for a static hash index on `SName` using 4K-byte blocks. As before, each index record will be 22 bytes, with 178 index records fitting into a block. Each directory record is 18 bytes (14 bytes for the dataval and 4 bytes for the block number), so 227 directory records will fit in a block. Thus:

- A 0-level B-tree, which can be searched using 2 disk accesses, can hold up to $227 \times 178 = 40{,}406$ index records.
- A 1-level B-tree, which can be searched using 3 disk accesses, can hold up to $227 \times 227 \times 178 = 9{,}172{,}162$ index records.
- A 2-level B-tree, which can be searched using 4 disk accesses, can hold up to $227 \times 227 \times 227 \times 178 = 2{,}082{,}080{,}774$ index records.

In other words, B-tree indexes are exceptionally efficient. Any desired data record can be retrieved in no more than five disk accesses, unless its table is unusually large.[4] If a commercial database system implements only one indexing strategy, it almost certainly uses a B-tree.

12.5.4 Inserting Records

If you want to insert a new index record, then the algorithm of Fig. 12.14b implies that there is exactly one index block where it can be inserted. What do you do if that block has no more room? As with extendable hashing, the solution is to *split* the block. Splitting an index block entails the following activities:

- Allocate a new block in the index file.
- Move the high-valued half of the index records into this new block.
- Create a directory record for the new block.
- Insert this new directory record into the same level-0 directory block that pointed to the original index block.

For example, suppose that all index blocks of Fig. 12.15 are full. To insert the new index record (hal, r55), the algorithm follows the B-tree directory and determines that the record belongs in the index block that contains "eli." It therefore splits this block, moving the upper half of its records into the new block. Suppose the new block is block 8 of the index file, and its first record is (jim, r48). The directory record (jim, 8) will get inserted into the level-0 directory block. The resulting subtree appears in Fig. 12.16.

In this case, there was room in the level-0 block for the new directory record. If there is no room, then that directory block also needs to split. For example, return to Fig. 12.15 and suppose that an index record (zoe, r56) is inserted. This record will cause the rightmost index block to split—suppose that the new block is number 9 and its first dataval is "tom." Then (tom, 9) is inserted into the rightmost level-0 directory block. However, there is no room in that level-0 block, and so it also splits. Two directory records stay in the original block, and two move to the new block (which is, say, block 4 of the directory file). The resulting directory and index blocks appear in Fig. 12.17. Note that the directory record for "sue" still exists but is not visible in the picture because it is the first record of its block.

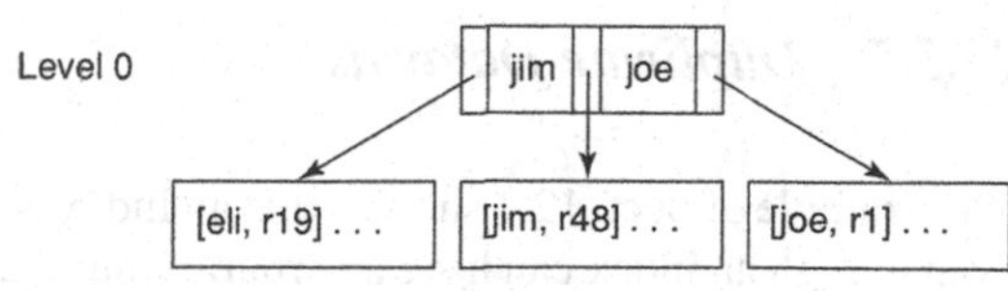

Fig. 12.16 The effect of splitting an index block

[4]And if you consider buffering, things look even better. If the index is used often, then the root block and many of the blocks in the level below it will probably already be in buffers, so it is likely that even fewer disk accesses will be required.

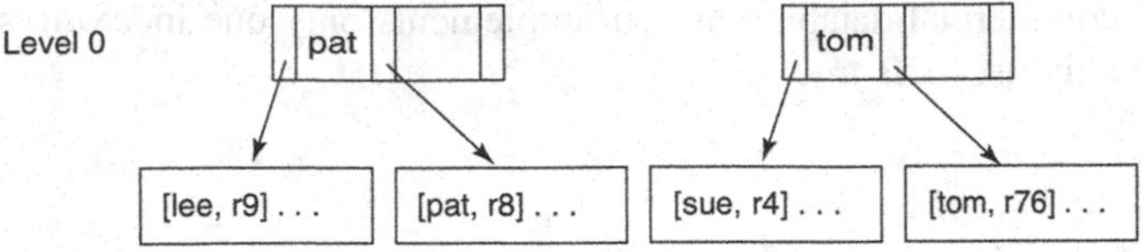

Fig. 12.17 Splitting a directory block

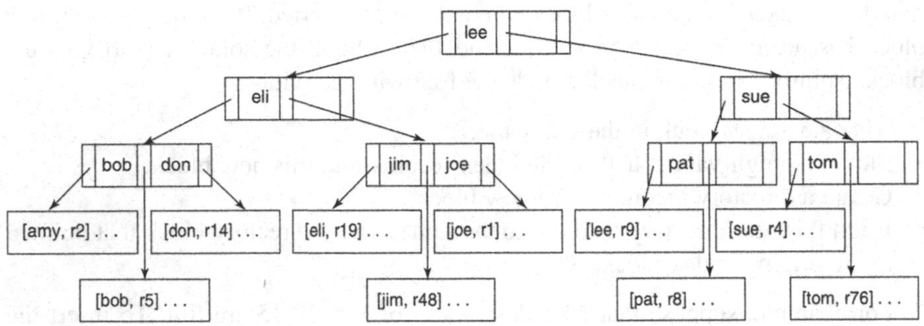

Fig. 12.18 Splitting the root of the B-tree

You are not done. The new level-0 block requires inserting a record into a level-1 directory block, and so the same record-insertion process happens recursively. The new directory record to be inserted is (sue, 4). The value "sue" is used because it is the smallest dataval in the subtree of the new directory block. This recursive insertion of directory records continues up the B-tree. If the root block splits, then a new root block is created, and the B-tree gains an additional level. This is exactly what happens in Fig. 12.17. The level-1 block has no room, and so it also splits, creating a new level-1 block and a new level-2 block to be the root. The resulting B-tree appears in Fig. 12.18.

Note that splitting a block turns a full block into two half-full blocks. In general, the capacity of a B-tree will range from 50% to 100%.

12.5.5 Duplicate Datavals

The example of Sect. 12.1 showed that an index is useful only when it is selective. So even though an index can have an arbitrary number of records with the same dataval, in practice there will not be that many and most likely not enough to fill multiple blocks. Nevertheless, a B-tree must be able to handle such cases.

To see what the issues are, suppose that there are several records for the dataval "ron" in Fig. 12.18. Note that all of those records must be in the same leaf block of

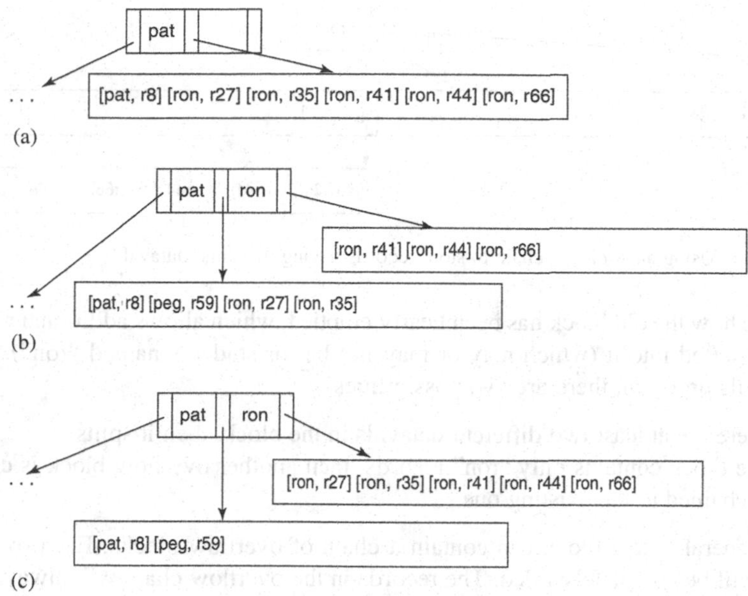

Fig. 12.19 Splitting a leaf block that has duplicate values. (**a**) The original leaf block and its parent, (**b**) an incorrect way to split the block, (**c**) the correct way to split the block

the B-tree, namely, the block that contains "pat." Figure 12.19a shows the contents of that block. Suppose that you insert a record for "peg," and this record causes the block to split. Figure 12.19b shows the result of splitting the block evenly: The records for "ron" wind up in different blocks.

The B-tree of Fig. 12.19b is clearly unacceptable, because the records for Ron that remained in Pat's block are not accessible. We have the following rule: *When you split a block, you must place all records having the same dataval in the same block.* This rule is just common sense. When you use the B-tree directory to look for index records having a particular search key, the directory will always point you to a single leaf block. If index records with that search key exist in other blocks, they will never be found.

The consequence of this rule is that it may not be possible to split an index block evenly. Figure 12.1c depicts the only reasonable way to perform the split, by placing the five "ron" records in the new block.

An index block can always be split if its records contain at least two different datavals. The only real problem occurs when all of the records in the index block have the same dataval. In this case, splitting is of no use. Instead, the best approach is to use an overflow block.

For example, start from Fig. 12.19c and insert records for several more students named "ron." Instead of splitting the block, you should create a new leaf block and move all but one of the "ron" records into it. This new block is the overflow block. The old block links to the overflow block, as shown in Fig. 12.20.

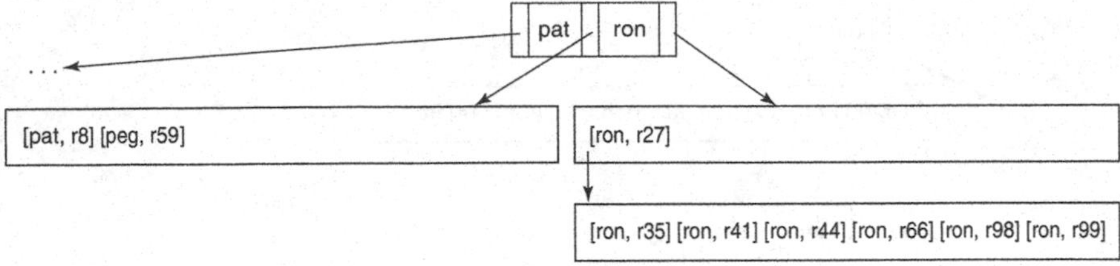

Fig. 12.20 Using an overflow chain to store records having the same dataval

Note how the old block has been nearly emptied, which allows additional records to be inserted into it (which may or may not be for students named "ron"). If the block fills up again, there are two possibilities.

- If there are at least two different datavals in the block, then it splits.
- If the block contains only "ron" records, then another overflow block is created and chained to the existing one.

In general, a leaf block can contain a chain of overflow blocks. Each overflow block will be completely filled. The records in the overflow chain will always have the same dataval, which will always be the same as the dataval of the first record in the non-overflow block.

Suppose that you are searching for index records having a particular search key. You follow the B-tree directory to a particular leaf block. If the search key is not the first key of the block, then you examine the records in the block as before. If the search key is the first one, then you also need to use the records in the overflow chain, if one exists.

Although the index records in the B-tree may contain duplicate datavals, the directory entries will not. The reason is that the only way to get a dataval into a directory entry is to split a leaf block; the first dataval of the new block is added to the directory. But the dataval that is first in its block will never get split again—if the block fills with records having that dataval, an overflow block will be created instead.

12.5.6 Implementing B-Tree Pages

The SimpleDB code to implement B-trees lives in the package `simpledb.index.btree`. This package contains four principal classes: `BTreeIndex`, `BTreeDir`, `BTreeLeaf`, and `BTPage`. Classes `BTreeDir` and `BTreeLeaf` implement the directory and index blocks of a B-tree, respectively.[5] Although the

[5]We use the term *leaf* to denote index blocks, because they form the leaves of the B-tree. The SimpleDB implementation uses "leaf" to avoid confusion with the *BTreeIndex* class, which implements the *Index* interface.

directory and leaf blocks contain different kinds of records and are used in different ways, they have common requirements, such as the need to insert entries in sorted order and to split themselves. The class `BTPage` contains this common code. The class `BTreeIndex` implements the actual B-tree operations, as specified by the `Index` interface.

Consider first the class `BTPage`. Records in a B-tree page have the following requirements:

- The records need to be maintained in sorted order.
- The records do not need to have a permanent id, which means that they can be moved around within the page as needed.
- A page needs to be able to split its records with another page.
- Each page needs an integer to serve as a flag. (A directory page uses the flag to hold its level, and a leaf page uses the flag to point to its overflow block.)

That is, you can think of a B-tree page as holding a sorted list of records (as opposed to a record page, which holds an unsorted array of records). When a new record is inserted into the page, its position in the sort order is determined, and the records following it are shifted one place to the right to make room. Similarly when a record is deleted, the records following it are shifted to the left to fill in the hole. In order to implement this list-like behavior, the page must also store an integer that holds the current number of records in the page.

The code for class `BTPage` appears in Fig. 12.21. The most interesting method in this class is `findSlotBefore`. This method takes a search key `k` as argument finds the smallest slot `x` such that `k` ≤ `dataval(x)`; it then returns the slot before that. The reason for this behavior is that it accommodates all of the ways that pages can be searched. For example, it acts like a `beforeFirst` operation on leaf pages, so that a call to *next* will retrieve the first record having that search key.

Now consider the leaf blocks of the B-tree. The code for the class `BTreeLeaf` appears in Fig. 12.22.

The constructor first creates a B-tree page for the specified block and then calls `findSlotBefore` to position itself immediately before the first record containing the search key. A call to `next` moves to the next record and returns `true` or `false` depending on whether that record has the desired search key. The call to `tryOverflow` handles the possibility that the leaf block contains an overflow chain.

The methods `delete` and `insert` assume that the current slot of the page has already been set by a call to `findSlotBefore`. Method `delete` repeatedly calls `next` until it encounters the index record having the specified rid, and then deletes that record. Method `insert` moves to the next record, which means that it is now positioned at the first record greater than or equal to that search key. The new record is inserted in that spot. Note that if the page already contains records having that search key, then the new record will be inserted at the front of the list. Method `insert` returns an object of type `DirEntry` (i.e., a directory record). If the insertion does not cause the block to split, then this return value is null. If a split occurs, then the return value is the (dataval, blocknumber) entry corresponding to the new index block.

```
public class BTPage {
   private Transaction tx;
   private BlockId currentblk;
   private Layout layout;
   public BTPage(Transaction tx, BlockId currentblk, Layout layout) {
      this.tx = tx;
      this.currentblk = currentblk;
      this.layout = layout;
      tx.pin(currentblk);
   }
   public int findSlotBefore(Constant searchkey) {
      int slot = 0;
      while (slot < getNumRecs() &&
               getDataVal(slot).compareTo(searchkey) < 0)
         slot++;
      return slot-1;
   }
   public void close() {
      if (currentblk != null)
         tx.unpin(currentblk);
      currentblk = null;
   }
   public boolean isFull() {
      return slotpos(getNumRecs()+1) >= tx.blockSize();
   }
   public BlockId split(int splitpos, int flag) {
      BlockId newblk = appendNew(flag);
      BTPage newpage = new BTPage(tx, newblk, layout);
      transferRecs(splitpos, newpage);
      newpage.setFlag(flag);
      newpage.close();
      return newblk;
   }
   public Constant getDataVal(int slot) {
      return getVal(slot, "dataval");
   }
   public int getFlag() {
      return tx.getInt(currentblk, 0);
   }
   public void setFlag(int val) {
      tx.setInt(currentblk, 0, val, true);
   }
   public BlockId appendNew(int flag) {
      BlockId blk = tx.append(currentblk.fileName());
      tx.pin(blk);
      format(blk, flag);
      return blk;
   }
```

Fig. 12.21 The code for the SimpleDB class `BTPage`

```
public void format(BlockId blk, int flag) {
   tx.setInt(blk, 0, flag, false);
   tx.setInt(blk, Integer.BYTES, 0, false);  // #records = 0
   int recsize = layout.slotSize();
   for (int pos=2*Integer.BYTES; pos+recsize<=tx.blockSize();
                                 pos += recsize)
      makeDefaultRecord(blk, pos);
}
private void makeDefaultRecord(BlockId blk, int pos) {
   for (String fldname : layout.schema().fields()) {
      int offset = layout.offset(fldname);
      if (layout.schema().type(fldname) == INTEGER)
         tx.setInt(blk, pos + offset, 0, false);
      else
         tx.setString(blk, pos + offset, "", false);
   }
}
// Methods called only by BTreeDir
public int getChildNum(int slot) {
   return getInt(slot, "block");
}
public void insertDir(int slot, Constant val, int blknum) {
   insert(slot);
   setVal(slot, "dataval", val);
   setInt(slot, "block", blknum);
}
// Methods called only by BTreeLeaf
public RID getDataRid(int slot) {
   return new RID(getInt(slot, "block"), getInt(slot, "id"));
}
public void insertLeaf(int slot, Constant val, RID rid) {
   insert(slot);
   setVal(slot, "dataval", val);
   setInt(slot, "block", rid.blockNumber());
   setInt(slot, "id", rid.slot());
}
public void delete(int slot) {
   for (int i=slot+1; i<getNumRecs(); i++)
      copyRecord(i, i-1);
   setNumRecs(getNumRecs()-1);
   return;
}
public int getNumRecs() {
   return tx.getInt(currentblk, Integer.BYTES);
}
```

Fig. 12.21 (continued)

```
// Private methods
private int getInt(int slot, String fldname) {
   int pos = fldpos(slot, fldname);
   return tx.getInt(currentblk, pos);
}

private String getString(int slot, String fldname) {
   int pos = fldpos(slot, fldname);
   return tx.getString(currentblk, pos);
}

private Constant getVal(int slot, String fldname) {
   int type = layout.schema().type(fldname);
   if (type == INTEGER)
      return new Constant(getInt(slot, fldname));
   else
      return new Constant(getString(slot, fldname));
}

private void setInt(int slot, String fldname, int val) {
   int pos = fldpos(slot, fldname);
   tx.setInt(currentblk, pos, val, true);
}

private void setString(int slot, String fldname, String val) {
   int pos = fldpos(slot, fldname);
   tx.setString(currentblk, pos, val, true);
}

private void setVal(int slot, String fldname, Constant val) {
   int type = layout.schema().type(fldname);
   if (type == INTEGER)
      setInt(slot, fldname, val.asInt());
   else
      setString(slot, fldname, val.asString());
}

private void setNumRecs(int n) {
   tx.setInt(currentblk, Integer.BYTES, n, true);
}
private void insert(int slot) {
   for (int i=getNumRecs(); i>slot; i--)
      copyRecord(i-1, i);
   setNumRecs(getNumRecs()+1);
}
private void copyRecord(int from, int to) {
   Schema sch = layout.schema();
   for (String fldname : sch.fields())
      setVal(to, fldname, getVal(from, fldname));
}
```

Fig. 12.21 (continued)

```
   private void transferRecs(int slot, BTPage dest) {
      int destslot = 0;
      while (slot < getNumRecs()) {
         dest.insert(destslot);
         Schema sch = layout.schema();
         for (String fldname : sch.fields())
            dest.setVal(destslot, fldname, getVal(slot, fldname));
         delete(slot);
         destslot++;
      }
   }

   private int fldpos(int slot, String fldname) {
      int offset = layout.offset(fldname);
      return slotpos(slot) + offset;
   }

   private int slotpos(int slot) {
      int slotsize = layout.slotSize();
      return Integer.BYTES + Integer.BYTES + (slot * slotsize);
   }
}
```

Fig. 12.21 (continued)

The class `BTreeDir` implements directory blocks; its code appears in Fig. 12.23.

Methods `search` and `insert` both start at the root, moving down the tree until the level-0 directory block associated with the search key is located. Method `search` uses a simple while-loop to move down the tree; when the level-0 block is found, it searches that page and returns the block number of the leaf containing the search key. Method `insert` uses recursion to move down the tree. The return value of the recursive call indicates whether the insertion caused its child page to split; if so, then the method `insertEntry` is called to insert a new directory record into the page. If this insertion causes the page to split, the directory record for the new page is passed back to the page's parent. A null value indicates that no split occurred.

The method `makeNewRoot` is invoked when a call to `insert` on the root page returns a non-null value. Since the root must always be at block 0 of the directory file, this method allocates a new block, copies the contents of block 0 to the new block, and initializes block 0 as the new root. The new root will always have two entries: The first entry will refer to the old root; the second entry will refer to the newly split block (that was passed in as an argument to `makeNewRoot`).

12.5.7 Implementing the B-Tree Index

Now that you have seen how B-tree pages are implemented, it is time to see how they are used. The class `BTreeIndex` implements the methods of the `Index` interface, coordinating the use of directory and leaf pages; see Fig. 12.24. Its constructor does

```
public class BTreeLeaf {
   private Transaction tx;
   private Layout layout;
   private Constant searchkey;
   private BTPage contents;
   private int currentslot;
   private String filename;

   public BTreeLeaf(Transaction tx, BlockId blk, Layout layout,
                    Constant searchkey) {
      this.tx = tx;
      this.layout = layout;
      this.searchkey = searchkey;
      contents = new BTPage(tx, blk, layout);
      currentslot = contents.findSlotBefore(searchkey);
      filename = blk.fileName();
   }

   public void close() {
      contents.close();
   }

   public boolean next() {
      currentslot++;
      if (currentslot >= contents.getNumRecs())
         return tryOverflow();
      else if (contents.getDataVal(currentslot).equals(searchkey))
         return true;
      else
         return tryOverflow();
   }
   public RID getDataRid() {
      return contents.getDataRid(currentslot);
   }

   public void delete(RID datarid) {
      while(next())
         if(getDataRid().equals(datarid)) {
            contents.delete(currentslot);
            return;
         }
   }
   public DirEntry insert(RID datarid) {
      if (contents.getFlag() >= 0 &&
          contents.getDataVal(0).compareTo(searchkey) > 0) {
         Constant firstval = contents.getDataVal(0);
         BlockId newblk = contents.split(0, contents.getFlag());
         currentslot = 0;
         contents.setFlag(-1);
         contents.insertLeaf(currentslot, searchkey, datarid);
```

Fig. 12.22 The code for the SimpleDB class BTreeLeaf

```
         return new DirEntry(firstval, newblk.number());
      }
      currentslot++;
      contents.insertLeaf(currentslot, searchkey, datarid);
      if (!contents.isFull())
         return null;
      // else page is full, so split it
      Constant firstkey = contents.getDataVal(0);
      Constant lastkey  = contents.getDataVal(contents.getNumRecs()-1);
      if (lastkey.equals(firstkey)) {
         // create an overflow block to hold all but the first record
         BlockId newblk = contents.split(1, contents.getFlag());
         contents.setFlag(newblk.number());
         return null;
      }
      else {
         int splitpos = contents.getNumRecs() / 2;
         Constant splitkey = contents.getDataVal(splitpos);
         if (splitkey.equals(firstkey)) {
            // move right, looking for the next key
            while (contents.getDataVal(splitpos).equals(splitkey))
               splitpos++;
            splitkey = contents.getDataVal(splitpos);
         }
         else {
            // move left, looking for first entry having that key
            while (contents.getDataVal(splitpos-1).equals(splitkey))
               splitpos--;
         }
         BlockId newblk = contents.split(splitpos, -1);
         return new DirEntry(splitkey, newblk.number());
      }
   }

   private boolean tryOverflow() {
      Constant firstkey = contents.getDataVal(0);
      int flag = contents.getFlag();
      if (!searchkey.equals(firstkey) || flag < 0)
         return false;
      contents.close();
      BlockId nextblk = new BlockId(filename, flag);
      contents = new BTPage(tx, nextblk, layout);
      currentslot = 0;
      return true;
   }
}
```

Fig. 12.22 (continued)

```
public class BTreeDir {
   private Transaction tx;
   private Layout layout;
   private BTPage contents;
   private String filename;

   BTreeDir(Transaction tx, BlockId blk, Layout layout) {
      this.tx = tx;
      this.layout = layout;
      contents = new BTPage(tx, blk, layout);
      filename = blk.fileName();
   }

   public void close() {
      contents.close();
   }

   public int search(Constant searchkey) {
      BlockId childblk = findChildBlock(searchkey);
      while (contents.getFlag() > 0) {
         contents.close();
         contents = new BTPage(tx, childblk, layout);
         childblk = findChildBlock(searchkey);
      }
      return childblk.number();
   }

   public void makeNewRoot(DirEntry e) {
      Constant firstval = contents.getDataVal(0);
      int level = contents.getFlag();
      BlockId newblk = contents.split(0, level); //ie, transfer all the recs
      DirEntry oldroot = new DirEntry(firstval, newblk.number());
      insertEntry(oldroot);
      insertEntry(e);
      contents.setFlag(level+1);
   }

   public DirEntry insert(DirEntry e) {
      if (contents.getFlag() == 0)
         return insertEntry(e);
      BlockId childblk = findChildBlock(e.dataVal());
      BTreeDir child = new BTreeDir(tx, childblk, layout);
      DirEntry myentry = child.insert(e);
      child.close();
      return (myentry != null) ? insertEntry(myentry) : null;
   }

   private DirEntry insertEntry(DirEntry e) {
      int newslot = 1 + contents.findSlotBefore(e.dataVal());
      contents.insertDir(newslot, e.dataVal(), e.blockNumber());
      if (!contents.isFull())
         return null;
      // else page is full, so split it
      int level = contents.getFlag();
```

Fig. 12.23 The code for the SimpleDB class `BTreeDir`

```
      int splitpos = contents.getNumRecs() / 2;
      Constant splitval = contents.getDataVal(splitpos);
      BlockId newblk = contents.split(splitpos, level);
      return new DirEntry(splitval, newblk.number());
   }

   private BlockId findChildBlock(Constant searchkey) {
      int slot = contents.findSlotBefore(searchkey);
      if (contents.getDataVal(slot+1).equals(searchkey))
         slot++;
      int blknum = contents.getChildNum(slot);
      return new BlockId(filename, blknum);
   }
}
```

Fig. 12.23 (continued)

most of the heavy lifting. It constructs the layout of the leaf records from the supplied `Schema` object. It then constructs the schema of the directory records by extracting the corresponding information from the leaf schema, and from there constructs their layout. Finally, it formats the root if necessary, inserting an entry that points to block 0 of the leaf file.

Each `BTreeIndex` object holds an open `BTreeLeaf` object. This leaf object keeps track of the current index record: it is initialized by a call to method `beforeFirst`, incremented by a call to `next`, and accessed by calls to `getDataRid`, `insert`, and `delete`. The method `beforeFirst` initializes this leaf object by calling method `search` from the root directory page. Note that once the leaf page has been located, the directory is no longer needed, and its pages can be closed.

Method `insert` has two parts. The first part locates the appropriate leaf page and inserts the index record into it. If the leaf page splits, then the method inserts the index record for the new leaf into the directory, starting the recursion at the root. A non-null return value from the root means that the root has split, and so `makeNewRoot` is called.

Method `delete` deletes the index record from the leaf but does not try to modify the directory. Another strategy would be to perform the deletion through the B-tree, as with insertions. Such a strategy would allow the directory blocks to coalesce if they became sufficiently empty. However, the algorithm for coalescing blocks is complex and error-prone and is rarely implemented. The reason is that databases rarely get smaller—deletions are usually followed by other insertions. Consequently, it makes sense to leave the nearly empty directory blocks in place, assuming that records will soon be inserted into them.

12.6 Index-Aware Operator Implementations

This section considers the question of how the query planner can take advantage of indexes. Given an SQL query, the planner has two tasks to perform: it must determine the appropriate query tree, and it must choose a plan for each operator

```
public class BTreeIndex implements Index {
   private Transaction tx;
   private Layout dirLayout, leafLayout;
   private String leaftbl;
   private BTreeLeaf leaf = null;
   private BlockId rootblk;
   public BTreeIndex(Transaction tx, String idxname,
                                         Layout leafLayout) {
      this.tx = tx;
      // deal with the leaves
      leaftbl = idxname + "leaf";
      this.leafLayout = leafLayout;
      if (tx.size(leaftbl) == 0) {
         BlockId blk = tx.append(leaftbl);
         BTPage node = new BTPage(tx, blk, leafLayout);
         node.format(blk, -1);
      }
      // deal with the directory
      Schema dirsch = new Schema();
      dirsch.add("block",   leafLayout.schema());
      dirsch.add("dataval", leafLayout.schema());
      String dirtbl = idxname + "dir";
      dirLayout = new Layout(dirsch);
      rootblk = new BlockId(dirtbl, 0);
      if (tx.size(dirtbl) == 0) {
         // create new root block
         tx.append(dirtbl);
         BTPage node = new BTPage(tx, rootblk, dirLayout);
         node.format(rootblk, 0);
         // insert initial directory entry
         int fldtype = dirsch.type("dataval");
         Constant minval = (fldtype == INTEGER) ?
               new Constant(Integer.MIN_VALUE) :
               new Constant("");
         node.insertDir(0, minval, 0);
         node.close();
      }
   }
   public void beforeFirst(Constant searchkey) {
      close();
      BTreeDir root = new BTreeDir(tx, rootblk, dirLayout);
      int blknum = root.search(searchkey);
      root.close();
      BlockId leafblk = new BlockId(leaftbl, blknum);
      leaf = new BTreeLeaf(tx, leafblk, leafLayout, searchkey);
   }
   public boolean next() {
      return leaf.next();
   }
```

Fig. 12.24 The code for the SimpleDB class BTreeIndex

```
   public RID getDataRid() {
      return leaf.getDataRid();
   }

   public void insert(Constant dataval, RID datarid) {
      beforeFirst(dataval);
      DirEntry e = leaf.insert(datarid);
      leaf.close();
      if (e == null)
         return;
      BTreeDir root = new BTreeDir(tx, rootblk, dirLayout);
      DirEntry e2 = root.insert(e);
      if (e2 != null)
         root.makeNewRoot(e2);
      root.close();
   }

   public void delete(Constant dataval, RID datarid) {
      beforeFirst(dataval);
      leaf.delete(datarid);
      leaf.close();
   }

   public void close() {
      if (leaf != null)
         leaf.close();
   }

   public static int searchCost(int numblocks, int rpb) {
      return 1 + (int)(Math.log(numblocks) / Math.log(rpb));
   }
}
```

Fig. 12.24 (continued)

in the tree. This second task was trivial for the basic planner of Chap. 10 because it only knows about one implementation for each operator. For example, it always implements a select node using a `SelectPlan` regardless of whether an appropriate index is available.

For the planner to construct a plan that uses an index, it needs to have operator implementations that use indexes. This section develops such implementations for the select and join operators. Given a query, the planner is then free to incorporate these implementations in its plan.

The planning process becomes much more complicated when relational operators can have more than one implementation. The planner must be able to consider multiple plans for a query, some which use indexes, and some that do not; it then must decide which plan is the most efficient. This feature is addressed in Chap. 15.

```
public class IndexSelectPlan implements Plan {
   private Plan p;
   private IndexInfo ii;
   private Constant val;

   public IndexSelectPlan(Plan p, IndexInfo ii, Constant val) {
      this.p = p;
      this.ii = ii;
      this.val = val;
   }

   public Scan open() {
      // throws an exception if p is not a table plan.
      TableScan ts = (TableScan) p.open();
      Index idx = ii.open();
      return new IndexSelectScan(idx, val, ts);
   }

   public int blocksAccessed() {
      return ii.blocksAccessed() + recordsOutput();

   }

   public int recordsOutput() {
      return ii.recordsOutput();
   }

   public int distinctValues(String fldname) {
      return ii.distinctValues(fldname);
   }

   public Schema schema() {
      return p.schema();
   }
}
```

Fig. 12.25 The code for the SimpleDB class `IndexSelectPlan`

12.6.1 An Indexed Implementation of Select

The SimpleDB class `IndexSelectPlan` implements the select operator. Its code appears in Fig. 12.25. The constructor takes three arguments: the plan for the underlying table, which is assumed to be a `TablePlan`; the information about the applicable index; and the selection constant. The method `open` opens the index and passes it (and the constant) to the `IndexSelectScan` constructor. The methods `blocksAccessed`, `recordsOutput`, and `distinctValues` implement cost-estimation formulas, using methods provided by the `IndexInfo` class.

The code for `IndexSelectScan` appears in Fig. 12.26. The `Index` variable `idx` holds the current index record, and the `TableScan` variable `ts` holds the current data record. The call to `next` moves to the next index record having the

```
public class IndexSelectScan implements Scan {
   private TableScan ts;
   private Index idx;
   private Constant val;

   public IndexSelectScan(TableScan ts, Index idx,
                                            Constant val) {
      this.ts  = ts;
      this.idx = idx;
      this.val = val;
      beforeFirst();
   }

   public void beforeFirst() {
      idx.beforeFirst(val);
   }

   public boolean next() {
      boolean ok = idx.next();
      if (ok) {
         RID rid = idx.getDataRid();
         ts.moveToRid(rid);
      }
      return ok;
   }

   public int getInt(String fldname) {
      return ts.getInt(fldname);
   }

   public String getString(String fldname) {
      return ts.getString(fldname);
   }

   public Constant getVal(String fldname) {
      return ts.getVal(fldname);
   }

   public boolean hasField(String fldname) {
      return ts.hasField(fldname);
   }

   public void close() {
      idx.close();
      ts.close();
   }
}
```

Fig. 12.26 The code for the SimpleDB class `IndexSelectScan`

For each record t1 in T1:

1. Let x be the *A*-value of t1.
2. Use the index on B to find the index records whose *B*-value = x.
3. For each index record:
   a. Obtain the value of its datarid.
   b. Move directly to the T2 record t2 having that RID.
   c. Process the output record (t1, t2).

Fig. 12.27 Implementing a join using an index

specified search constant; the table scan is then positioned at the data record having the datarid value of the current index record.

Note that the table scan is never scanned; its current record is always obtained via the datarid of an index record. The remaining scan methods (`getVal`, `getInt`, etc.) pertain to the current data record and thus are obtained directly from the table scan.

12.6.2 An Indexed Implementation of Join

A *join* operation takes three arguments: two tables T1 and T2 and a predicate *p* of the form "$A = B$", where *A* is a field from T1 and *B* is a field from T2. The predicate specifies which combination of records from T1 and T2 should be in the output table. In particular, the join operation is defined as follows:

```
join(T1, T2, p) ≡ select(product(T1, T2), p).
```

An *index join* is an implementation of a join in the special case where T2 is a stored table having an index on B. Figure 12.27 gives the algorithm.

Note that an index join is implemented similarly to a product; the difference is that instead of repeatedly scanning the inner table, the code only has to repeatedly search the index. Consequently, an index join can be considerably more efficient than taking the product of the two tables.

The classes `IndexJoinPlan` and `IndexJoinScan` implement index joins. The code for `IndexJoinPlan` appears in Fig. 12.28.

The constructor arguments `p1` and `p2` denote plans for the tables T1 and T2 in Fig. 12.27. The variable `ii` denotes T2's index on B, and variable `joinfield` corresponds to the field A. The `open` method converts the plans to scans and the `IndexInfo` object into an index; it then passes these to the `IndexJoinScan` constructor.

The code for `IndexJoinScan` appears in Fig. 12.29. The `beforeFirst` method sets T1's scan to the first record, obtains its value of A, and positions the index before that dataval. The `next` method moves to the next index value, if one exists. If not, it moves to the next value of T1 and resets the index to point to the new dataval.

```
public class IndexJoinPlan implements Plan {
   private Plan p1, p2;
   private IndexInfo ii;
   private String joinfield;
   private Schema sch = new Schema();

   public IndexJoinPlan(Plan p1, Plan p2, IndexInfo ii,
                                                String joinfield) {

      this.p1 = p1;
      this.p2 = p2;
      this.ii = ii;
      this.joinfield = joinfield;
      sch.addAll(p1.schema());
      sch.addAll(p2.schema());
   }

   public Scan open() {
      Scan s = p1.open();
      // throws an exception if p2 is not a table plan
      TableScan ts = (TableScan) p2.open();
      Index idx = ii.open();
      return new IndexJoinScan(s, idx, joinfield, ts);
   }

   public int blocksAccessed() {
      return p1.blocksAccessed()
         + (p1.recordsOutput() * ii.blocksAccessed())
         + recordsOutput();
   }

   public int recordsOutput() {
      return p1.recordsOutput() * ii.recordsOutput();
   }

   public int distinctValues(String fldname) {
      if (p1.schema().hasField(fldname))
         return p1.distinctValues(fldname);
      else
         return p2.distinctValues(fldname);
   }

   public Schema schema() {
      return sch;
   }
}
```

Fig. 12.28 The code for the SimpleDB class `IndexJoinPlan`

```
public class IndexJoinScan implements Scan {
   private Scan lhs;
   private Index idx;
   private String joinfield;
   private TableScan rhs;

   public IndexJoinScan(Scan lhs, Index idx, String joinfld,
                                                    TableScan rhs) {

      this.lhs = lhs;
      this.idx  = idx;
      this.joinfield = joinfld;
      this.rhs = rhs;
      beforeFirst();
   }

   public void beforeFirst() {
      lhs.beforeFirst();
      lhs.next();
      resetIndex();
   }

   public boolean next() {
      while (true) {
         if (idx.next()) {
            rhs.moveToRid(idx.getDataRid());
            return true;
         }
         if (!lhs.next())
            return false;
         resetIndex();
      }
   }

   public int getInt(String fldname) {
      if (rhs.hasField(fldname))
         return rhs.getInt(fldname);
      else
         return lhs.getInt(fldname);
   }

   public Constant getVal(String fldname) {
      if (rhs.hasField(fldname))
         return rhs.getVal(fldname);

      else
         return lhs.getVal(fldname);
   }

   public String getString(String fldname) {
      if (rhs.hasField(fldname))
         return rhs.getString(fldname);
      else
         return lhs.getString(fldname);
   }
```

Fig. 12.29 The code for the SimpleDB class `IndexJoinScan`

```
    public boolean hasField(String fldname) {
       return rhs.hasField(fldname) || lhs.hasField(fldname);
    }

    public void close() {
       lhs.close();
       idx.close();
       rhs.close();
    }

    private void resetIndex() {
       Constant searchkey = lhs.getVal(joinfield);
       idx.beforeFirst(searchkey);
    }
}
```

Fig. 12.29 (continued)

12.7 Index Update Planning

If a database engine supports indexing, then its planner must ensure that whenever a data record is updated, a corresponding change is made to each of its index records. The code fragment of Fig. 12.4 showed the kind of code that the planner needs to execute. This section shows how the planner does it.

Package `simpledb.index.planner` contains the planner class `IndexUpdatePlanner`, which modifies the basic update planner; its code appears in Fig. 12.30.

The method `executeInsert` retrieves the index information of the mentioned table. As in the basic planner, the method calls `setVal` to set the initial value of each specified field. After each call to `setVal`, the planner looks to see if there is an index on that field; if there is, then it inserts a new record into that index.

The method `executeDelete` constructs a scan of records to be deleted, as in the basic planner. Before each of these data records is deleted, the method uses the record's field values to determine which index records need to be deleted. It then deletes those index records, and then the data record.

The method `executeModify` constructs the scan of records to be modified, as in the basic planner. Before modifying each record, the method first adjusts the index of the modified field, if it exists. In particular, it deletes the old index record and inserts a new one.

The methods to create tables, views, and indexes are the same as in the basic planner.

In order to get SimpleDB to use the index update planner, you must change the method `planner` in class `SimpleDB` so that it creates an instance of `IndexUpdatePlanner` instead of `BasicUpdatePlanner`.

```
public class IndexUpdatePlanner implements UpdatePlanner {
   private MetadataMgr mdm;

   public IndexUpdatePlanner(MetadataMgr mdm) {
      this.mdm = mdm;
   }

   public int executeInsert(InsertData data, Transaction tx) {
      String tblname = data.tableName();
      Plan p = new TablePlan(tx, tblname, mdm);

      // first, insert the record
      UpdateScan s = (UpdateScan) p.open();
      s.insert();
      RID rid = s.getRid();

      // then modify each field, inserting index records
      Map<String,IndexInfo> indexes = mdm.getIndexInfo(tblname, tx);
      Iterator<Constant> valIter = data.vals().iterator();
      for (String fldname : data.fields()) {
         Constant val = valIter.next();
         System.out.println("Modify field " + fldname +
                            " to val " + val);
         s.setVal(fldname, val);

         IndexInfo ii = indexes.get(fldname);
         if (ii != null) {
            Index idx = ii.open();
            idx.insert(val, rid);
            idx.close();
         }
      }
      s.close();
      return 1;
   }
   public int executeDelete(DeleteData data, Transaction tx) {
      String tblname = data.tableName();
      Plan p = new TablePlan(tx, tblname, mdm);
      p = new SelectPlan(p, data.pred());
      Map<String,IndexInfo> indexes = mdm.getIndexInfo(tblname, tx);

      UpdateScan s = (UpdateScan) p.open();
      int count = 0;
      while(s.next()) {
         // first, delete the record's RID from every index
         RID rid = s.getRid();
         for (String fldname : indexes.keySet()) {
            Index idx = indexes.get(fldname).open();
            Constant val = s.getVal(fldname);
            idx.delete(val, rid);
            idx.close();
         }
         // then delete the record
         s.delete();
```

Fig. 12.30 The code for the SimpleDB class `IndexUpdatePlanner`

```
         count++;
      }
      s.close();
      return count;
   }
   public int executeModify(ModifyData data, Transaction tx) {
      String tblname = data.tableName();
      String fldname = data.targetField();
      Plan p = new TablePlan(tx, tblname, mdm);
      p = new SelectPlan(p, data.pred());
      IndexInfo ii = mdm.getIndexInfo(tblname, tx).get(fldname);
      Index idx = (ii == null) ? null : ii.open();
      UpdateScan s = (UpdateScan) p.open();
      int count = 0;
      while(s.next()) {
         // first, update the record
         Constant newval = data.newValue().evaluate(s);
         Constant oldval = s.getVal(fldname);
         s.setVal(data.targetField(), newval);
         // then update the appropriate index, if it exists
         if (idx != null) {
            RID rid = s.getRid();
            idx.delete(oldval, rid);
            idx.insert(newval, rid);
         }
         count++;
      }
      if (idx != null) idx.close();
      s.close();
      return count;
   }
   public int executeCreateTable(CreateTableData data,
                                 Transaction tx) {
      mdm.createTable(data.tableName(), data.newSchema(), tx);
      return 0;
   }
   public int executeCreateView(CreateViewData data,
                                Transaction tx) {
      mdm.createView(data.viewName(), data.viewDef(), tx);
      return 0;
   }
   public int executeCreateIndex(CreateIndexData data,
                                 Transaction tx) {
      mdm.createIndex(data.indexName(), data.tableName(),
      data.fieldName(), tx);
      return 0;
   }
}
```

Fig. 12.30 (continued)

12.8 Chapter Summary

- Given a field A of table T, an *index* on A is a file of records, one index record for each record of T. Each index record contains two fields: its *dataval*, which is the A-value of the corresponding record of T, and its *datarid*, which is the rid of the corresponding record.
- An index is able to improve the efficiency of select and join operations. Instead of scanning each block of the data table, the system can do the following:

  – Search the index to find all index records having the selected dataval.
  – For each index record found, use its datarid to access the desired data record.

  In this way, the database system is able to access only the data blocks that contain matching records.
- An index is not necessarily useful. As a rule of thumb, the usefulness of an index on field A is proportional the number of different A-values in the table.
- A query may be indexable in different ways. The query processor determines which of these implementations is best.
- The database engine is responsible for updating the indexes when their table changes. It must insert (or delete) a record in each index whenever a record is inserted (or deleted) from the table. This maintenance cost means that only the most useful indexes are worth keeping.
- Indexes are implemented so that searches require very few disk accesses. The chapter discussed three index implementation strategies: *static hashing, extendable hashing*, and *B-trees*.
- Static hashing stores index records in a fixed number of *buckets*, where each bucket corresponds to a file. A *hash function* determines the bucket assigned to each index record. To find an index record using static hashing, the index manager hashes its search key and examines that bucket. If an index contains B blocks and N buckets, then each bucket is about B/N blocks long, and so traversing a bucket requires about B/N block accesses.
- Extendable hashing allows buckets to share blocks. This improves on static hashing, because it allows for very many buckets without an especially large index file. Block sharing is achieved by means of a *bucket directory*. The bucket directory can be thought of as an array Dir of integers; if an index record hashes to bucket b, then that record will be stored in block Dir[b] of the bucket file. When a new index record does not fit in its block, then the block *splits*, the bucket directory is updated, and the block's records are rehashed.
- A B-tree stores its index records in a file sorted on their dataval. A B-tree also has a file of directory records. Each index block has a corresponding *directory record*, which contains the dataval of the first index record in the block and a reference to that block. These directory records level 0 of the B-tree directory. Similarly, each directory block has its own directory record, which is stored in the next level of the directory. The top level consists of a single block, which is called the *root* of the B-tree. Given a dataval, we can search the directory by examining one block at each level of the directory tree; this search leads us to the index block containing the desired index records.

- B-tree indexes are exceptionally efficient. Any desired data record can be retrieved in no more than five disk accesses, unless its table is unusually large. If a commercial database system implements only one indexing strategy, it almost certainly uses a B-tree.

12.9 Suggested Reading

This chapter treated indexes as auxiliary files. The article Sieg and Sciore (1990) shows how an index can be treated as a special type of table and how indexselect and indexjoin can be treated as relational algebra operators. This approach allows the planner to use indexes in a much more flexible way.

B-trees and hash files are general-purpose index structures, which work best when the query has a single selective search key. They do not work so well when queries have multiple search keys, such as in geographic and spatial databases. (For example, a B-tree cannot help with a query such as "find all restaurants within 2 miles of my home.") *Multidimensional indexes* have been developed to deal with such databases. The article Gaede and Gunther (1998) provides a survey of these indexes.

The cost of a B-tree search is determined by the height of the B-tree, which is determined by the size of the index and directory records. The article Bayer and Unteraurer (1977) gives techniques for reducing the size of these records. For example, if the datavals in a leaf node are strings and these strings have a common prefix, then this prefix can be stored once at the beginning of the page, and the suffix of the dataval is stored with each index record. Moreover, there usually is no need to store the entire dataval in a directory record; the B-tree only needs to store the prefix of that dataval sufficient to determine which child to choose.

The article Graefe (2004) describes a novel implementation of B-trees in which nodes are never overridden; instead, updates to nodes cause new nodes to be created. The article demonstrates that this implementation results in faster updates at the cost of slightly slower reads.

This chapter has focused exclusively on how to minimize the number of disk accesses performed by a B-tree search. Although the CPU cost of a B-tree search is less important, it is often significant and needs to be considered by commercial implementations. The article Lomet (2001) discusses how to structure B-tree nodes to minimize search. The article Chen et al. (2002) shows how to structure B-tree nodes to maximize CPU cache performance.

This chapter also did not consider the issue of how to lock the nodes of a B-tree. SimpleDB simply locks a B-tree node the same as any other data block and holds the lock until the transaction completes. However, it turns out that B-trees do not need to satisfy the lock protocol of Chap. 5 in order to guarantee serializability; instead, locks can be released early. The article Bayer and Schkolnick (1977) addresses this issue.

Web search engines keep databases of web pages, which are primarily text. Queries on these databases tend to be based on string and pattern matching, for which traditional indexing structures are basically useless. Text-based indexing methods are treated in Faloutsos (1985).

An unusual indexing strategy stores a bitmap for each field value; the bitmap contains one bit for each data record and indicates whether the record contains that value. One interesting thing about bitmap indexes is that they can be easily intersected to handle multiple search keys. The article O'Neil and Quass (1997) explains how bitmap indexes work.

Chapter 6 assumed that tables are stored sequentially and are basically unorganized. However, it is also possible to organize a table according to a B-tree, hash file, or any other indexing strategy. There are some complications: for example, a B-tree record may move to another block when its block splits, which means that record ids must be handled carefully; furthermore, the indexing strategy must also support sequential scans of the table (and, in fact, the entire *Scan* and `UpdateScan` interfaces). But the basic principles hold. The article Batory (1982) describes how complex file organizations can be constructed out of the basic indexing strategies.

Batory, D., & Gotlieb, C. (1982). A unifying model of physical databases. *ACM Transactions of Database Systems, 7*(4), 509–539.

Bayer, R., & Schkolnick, M. (1977). Concurrency of operations on B-trees. *Acta Informatica, 9*(1), 1–21.

Bayer, R., & Unterauer, K. (1977). Prefix B-trees. *ACM Transactions of Database Systems, 2*(1), 11–26.

Chen, S., Gibbons, P., Mowry, T., & Valentin, G. (2002). Fractal prefetching B$^+$-trees: Optimizing both cache and disk performance. *Proceedings of the ACM SIGMOD Conference*, pp. 157–168.

Faloutsos, C. (1985). Access methods for text. *ACM Computing Surveys, 17*(1), 49–74.

Graede, V., & Gunther, O. (1998). Multidimensional access methods. *ACM Computing Surveys, 30*(2), 170–231.

Graefe, G. (2004) Write-optimized B-trees. *Proceedings of the VLDB Conference*, pp. 672–683.

Lomet, D. (2001). The evolution of effective B-tree: Page organization and techniques: A personal account. *ACM SIGMOD Record, 30*(3), 64–69.

O'Neil, P., & Quass, D. (1997). Improved query performance with variant indexes. *Proceedings of the ACM SIGMOD Conference*, pp. 38–49.

Sieg, J., & Sciore, E. (1990). Extended relations. *Proceedings of the IEEE Data Engineering Conference*, pp. 488–494.

12.10 Exercises

Conceptual Exercises

12.1. Consider the university database of Fig. 1.1. Which fields would be inappropriate to index on? Explain your reasoning.

12.2. Explain which indexes could be useful for evaluating each of the following queries.

(a)
```
select SName
from STUDENT, DEPT
where MajorId=DId and DName='math' and GradYear<>2001
```
(b)
```
select Prof
from ENROLL, SECTION, COURSE
where SectId=SectionId and CourseId=CId
and Grade='F' and Title='calculus'
```

12.3. Suppose that you have decided to create an index on the field *GradYear* in STUDENT.

(a) Consider the following query:

```
select * from STUDENT where GradYear=2020
```

Calculate the cost of using the index to answer this query, using the statistics of Fig. 7.8 and assuming that students are evenly distributed among 50 different graduation years.

(b) Do the same as in part (b), but instead of 50 different graduation years, assume that there are 2, 10, 20, or 100 different graduation years.

12.4. Show that an index on field A is useless if the number of different A-values is less than the number of table records that fit in a block.

12.5. Does it ever make sense to create an index for another index? Explain.

12.6. Assume that blocks are 120 bytes and that the DEPT table has 60 records. For each field of DEPT, calculate how many blocks are required to hold the index records.

12.7. The interface `Index` contains a method `delete`, which deletes the index record having a specified dataval and datarid. Would it be useful to also have a method `deleteAll`, which deletes all index records having a specified dataval? How and when would the planner use such a method?

12.8. Consider a query that joins two tables, such as

```
select SName, DName
from STUDENT, DEPT
where MajorId = DId
```

Suppose STUDENT contains an index on `MajorId`, and DEPT contains an index on `DId`. There are two ways to implement this query using an index join, one way for each index. Using the cost information from Fig. 7.8, compare the cost of these two plans. What general rule can you conclude from your calculation?

12.9. The example of extendable hashing in Sect. 12.4 stopped after the insertion of only seven records. Continue the example, inserting records for employees having id 28, 9, 16, 24, 36, 48, 64, and 56.

12.10. In an extendable hashed index, consider an index block having local depth `L`. Show that the number of every bucket that points to this block has the same rightmost `L` bits.

12.11. In extendable hashing, the bucket file increases when blocks split. Develop an algorithm for deletion that allows two split blocks to be coalesced. How practical is it?

12.12. Consider an extendable hash index such that 100 index records fit in a block. Suppose that the index is currently empty.

(a) How many records can be inserted before the global depth of the index becomes 1?
(b) How many records can be inserted before the global depth becomes 2?

12.13. Suppose that an insertion into an extendable hash index just caused its global depth to increase from 3 to 4.

(a) How many entries will the bucket directory have?
(b) How many blocks in the bucket file have exactly one directory entry pointing to them?

12.14. Explain why any extensible hash index can be accessed in exactly two block accesses, regardless of its size.

12.15. Suppose you create a B-tree index for `SId`. Assuming that 3 index records and 3 directory records fit into a block, draw a picture of the B-tree that results from inserting records for students 8, 12, 1, 20, 5, 7, 2, 28, 9, 16, 24, 36, 48, 64, and 56.

12.16. Consider the statistics of Fig. 7.8, and suppose that you have a B-tree index on field `StudentId` of ENROLL. Assume that 100 index or directory records fit in a block.

(a) How many blocks are in the index file?
(b) How many blocks are in the directory file?

12.17. Consider again a B-tree index on field `StudentId` of ENROLL, and assume that 100 index or directory records fit in a block. Suppose that the index is currently empty.

(a) How many insertions will cause the root to split (into a level-1 node)?
(b) What is the smallest number of insertions that will cause the root to split again (into a level-2 node)?

12.18. Consider the SimpleDB implementation of B-trees.

(a) What is the maximum number of buffers that will be pinned simultaneously during an index scan?
(b) What is the maximum number of buffers that will be pinned simultaneously during an insertion?

12.19. The SimpleDB `IndexSelectPlan` and `IndexSelectScan` classes assume that the selection predicate is an equality comparison, as in

"*GradYear = 2019.*" In general, however, an index could be used with a range predicate, such as "*GradYear > 2019.*"

(a) Explain conceptually how a B-tree index on `GradYear` could be used to implement the following query:

```
select SName from STUDENT where GradYear > 2019
```

(b) What revisions need to be made to the SimpleDB B-tree code in order to support your answer to part (a)?
(c) Suppose that the database contains a B-tree index on `GradYear`. Explain why this index might not be useful for implementing the query. When would it be useful?
(d) Explain why static and extendable hash indexes are never useful for this query.

Programming Exercises

12.20. The methods `executeDelete` and `executeUpdate` of the SimpleDB update planner use a select scan to find the affected records. Another possibility is to use an index select scan, if an appropriate index exists.

(a) Explain how the planner algorithms would have to change.
(b) Implement these changes in SimpleDB.

12.21. Implement extendable hashing. Choose a maximum depth that creates a directory of at most two disk blocks.

12.22. Consider the following modification to index records: Instead of containing the rid of the corresponding data record, the index record only contains the block number where the data record lives. Thus, there may be fewer index records than data records—if a data block contains multiple records for the same search key, a single index record would correspond to all of them.

(a) Explain why this modification could result in fewer disk accesses during index-based queries.
(b) How do the index delete and insert methods have to change in order to accommodate this modification? Do they require more disk accesses than the existing methods? Write the necessary code, for both B-trees and static hashing.
(c) Do you think that this modification is a good idea?

12.23. Many commercial database systems allow indexes to be specified from within the SQL `create table` statement. For example, the syntax of MySQL looks like this:

```
create table T (A int, B varchar(9), index(A), C int, index(B))
```

That is, items of the form `index(<field>)` can appear anywhere inside the list of field names.

(a) Revise the SimpleDB parser to handle this additional syntax.
(b) Revise the SimpleDB planner to create the appropriate plan.

12.24. One of the problems with the update planner method `executeCreateIndex` is that the newly created index is empty, even if the indexed table contains records. Revise the method so that it automatically inserts an index record for every existing record in the indexed table.

12.25. Revise SimpleDB so that it has a `drop index` statement. Create your own syntax, and modify the parser and planner appropriately.

12.26. Revise SimpleDB so that a user can specify the type of a newly created index.

(a) Develop a new syntax for the create index statement, and give its grammar.
(b) Modify the parser (and possibly the lexer) to implement your new syntax.

12.27. Implement static hashing using a single index file. The first *N* blocks of this file will contain the first block of each bucket. The remaining blocks in each bucket will be chained together, using an integer stored in the block. (For example, if the value stored in block 1 is 173, then the next block in the chain is block 173. A value of −1 indicates the end of the chain.) For simplicity, you can devote the first record slot of each block to hold this chain pointer.

12.28. SimpleDB splits a B-tree block as soon as it becomes full. Another algorithm is to allow blocks to be full and to split them during the `insert` method. In particular, as the code moves down the tree looking for the leaf block, it splits any full block it encounters.

(a) Modify the code to implement this algorithm.
(b) Explain how this code reduces the buffer needs of the `insert` method.

Chapter 13
Materialization and Sorting

This chapter considers the relational algebra operators *materialize*, *sort*, *groupby*, and *mergejoin*. These operators materialize their input records by saving them in temporary tables. This materialization allows the operators to access their records multiple times without recomputation, which can result in query implementations that are much more efficient than could be achieved using only pipelined operators.

13.1 The Value of Materialization

Every operator that you have seen so far has had a *pipelined* implementation. Such implementations have the following characteristics:

- Records are computed one at a time, as needed, and are not saved.
- The only way to access previously seen records is to recompute the entire operation from the beginning.

This chapter considers operators that *materialize* their input. Scans for these operators read their input records when they are opened and save their output records in one or more temporary tables. These implementations are said to *preprocess* their input because they perform all computation before any output records have been requested. The purpose of this materialization is to improve the efficiency of the ensuing scan.

For example, consider the *groupby* operator, to be introduced in Sect. 13.5. This operator groups its input records according to specified grouping fields, calculating aggregation functions for each group. The easiest way to determine the groups is to sort the input records on the grouping fields, which causes the records in each group to be next to each other. A good implementation strategy is therefore to first materialize the input, saving the records in a temporary table sorted on the grouping fields. The calculation of the aggregation functions can then be performed by making a single pass through the temporary table.

E. Sciore, *Database Design and Implementation*, Data-Centric Systems and Applications, https://doi.org/10.1007/978-3-030-33836-7_13

Materialization is a two-edged sword. On one hand, using a temporary table can significantly improve the efficiency of a scan. On the other hand, creating the temporary table incurs significant overhead costs as it writes to and reads from the temporary table. Moreover, creating a temporary table means preprocessing the entire input, even if the client is interested in only a few output records.

A materialized implementation is useful only when these costs are offset by the increased efficiency of the scan. The four operators in this chapter all have highly efficient materialized implementations.

13.2 Temporary Tables

Materialized implementations store their input records in *temporary tables*. A temporary table differs from a regular table in three ways:

- A temporary table is not created using the table manager's `createTable` method, and its metadata does not appear in the system catalog. In SimpleDB, each temporary table manages its own metadata and has its own `getLayout` method.
- Temporary tables are automatically deleted by the database system when they are no longer needed. In SimpleDB, the file manager deletes the tables during system initialization.
- The recovery manager does not log changes to temporary tables. There is no need to recover the previous state of a temporary table, because the table will never be used after its query has completed.

SimpleDB implements temporary tables via the class `TempTable`, whose code appears in Fig. 13.1. The constructor creates an empty table and assigns it a unique name (of the form "`tempN`" for some integer N). The class contains three public methods. The method `open` opens a table scan for the table, and the methods `tableName` and `getLayout` return the temporary table's metadata.

13.3 Materialization

This section introduces a new relational algebra operator, called *materialize*. The materialize operator has no visible functionality. It takes a table as its only argument, and its output records are exactly the same as its input records. That is:

```
materialize(T) ≡ T
```

The purpose of the materialize operator is to save the output of a subquery in a temporary table, to keep those records from being computed multiple times. This section examines its use and implementation of this operator.

```
public class TempTable {
   private static int nextTableNum = 0;
   private Transaction tx;
   private String tblname;
   private Layout layout;

   public TempTable(Transaction tx, Schema sch) {
      this.tx = tx;
      tblname = nextTableName();
      layout = new Layout(sch);
   }

   public UpdateScan open() {
      return new TableScan(tx, tblname, layout);
   }

   public String tableName() {
      return tblname;
   }

   public Layout getLayout() {
      return layout;
   }

   private static synchronized String nextTableName() {
      nextTableNum++;
      return "temp" + nextTableNum;
   }
}
```

Fig. 13.1 The code for the SimpleDB class `TempTable`

13.3.1 An Example of Materialization

Consider the query tree of Fig. 13.2a. Recall that the product operation examines every record of its right subtree for each record in the left subtree. Consequently, the records of the left subtree are accessed once, and the records of the right subtree are accessed many times.

The problem with accessing the right-side records repeatedly is that they will need to be recalculated repeatedly. In Fig. 13.2a, the implementation will need to read the entire ENROLL table multiple times, and each time it will search for records having a grade of "A." Using the statistics of Fig. 7.8, you can calculate the cost of the product as follows: There are 900 students in the class of 2005. The pipelined implementation will read the entire 50,000-block ENROLL table for each of these 900 students, which is 45,000,000 block accesses of ENROLL. Adding this to the 4500 STUDENT blocks results in a total of 45,004,500 block accesses.

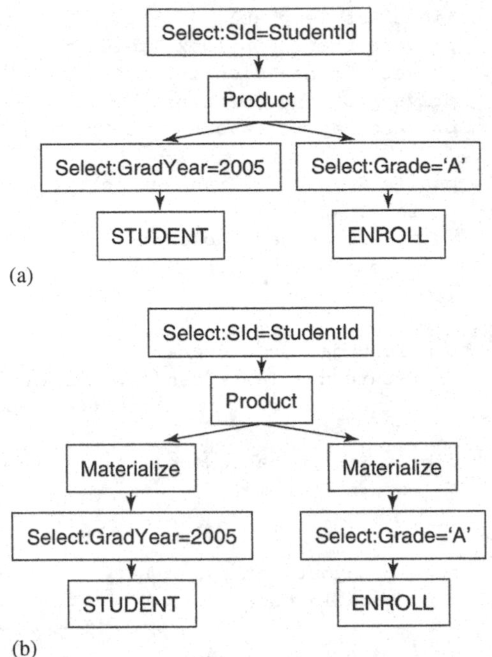

Fig. 13.2 Where to use the materialize operator? (**a**) The original query, (**b**) materializing the left and right sides of the product

The query tree of Fig. 13.2b has two materialize nodes. Consider first the materialize node above the right-side select node. This node creates a temporary table containing the ENROLL records having a grade of "A." Each time that the product node requests a record from its right side, the materialize node will take the record directly from this temporary table instead of searching ENROLL.

This materialization significantly reduces the cost of the product. Consider the following analysis. The temporary table will be 14 times smaller than ENROLL, or 3572 blocks. The right-side materialize node needs 53,572 block accesses to create the table (50,000 accesses to read ENROLL and 3572 accesses to write the table). After the temporary table has been created, it will be read 900 times, for a total of 3,214,800 accesses. Adding the 4500 STUDENT block accesses to these costs results in a combined total of 3,272,872 block accesses. In other words, materialization reduces the cost of the original query tree by 82% (which, at 1 ms per block access, results in a time savings of over 11 hours). The cost of creating the temporary table is miniscule compared to the savings it generates.

Now consider the left-side materialize node in Fig. 13.2b. That node will scan the STUDENT table and create a temporary table containing all students in the class of 2005. The product node will then examine this temporary table once. However, the product node in the original query tree also examines the STUDENT table once. Since the STUDENT records are examined once in each case, the left-side materialize node actually increases the cost of the query. In general, a materialize node is only useful when the node's output will be calculated repeatedly.

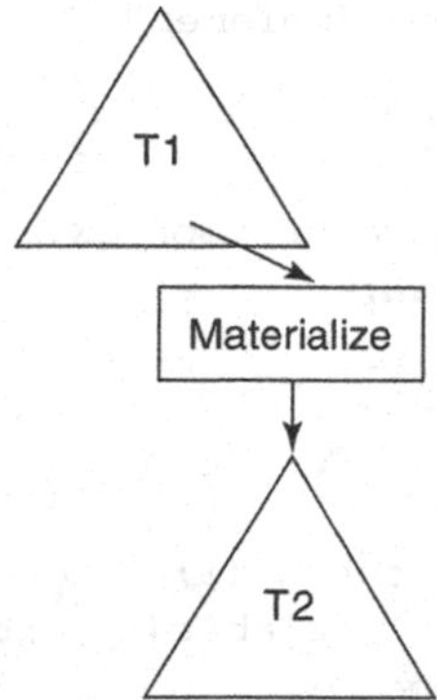

Fig. 13.3 A query tree containing a materialize node

13.3.2 The Cost of Materialization

Figure 13.3 depicts the structure of a query tree that contains a materialize node. The input to the node is the subquery denoted by T2. When a user opens the plan for query T1, its root plan will open its child plans, and so on down the tree. When the materialize plan is opened, it will preprocess its input. In particular, the plan will open a scan for T2, evaluate it, save the output in a temporary table, and close the scan for T2. During the scan of query T1, the materialize scan will respond to a request by accessing the corresponding record from its temporary table. Note that the subquery T2 is accessed once, to populate the temporary table; after that, it is no longer needed.

The cost associated with the materialize node can be divided into two parts: the cost of preprocessing the input and the cost of executing the scan. The preprocessing cost is the cost of T2 plus the cost of writing the records to the temporary table. The scanning cost is the cost of reading the records from the temporary table. Assuming that the temporary table is `B` blocks long, then these costs can be expressed as follows:

- Preprocessing cost = `B` + the cost of its input
- Scanning cost = `B`

13.3.3 Implementing the Materialize Operator

The SimpleDB class `MaterializePlan` implements the materialize operator; its code appears in Fig. 13.4. The `open` method preprocesses the input—it creates a new temporary table, opens scans for the table and for the input, copies the input records into the table scan, closes the input scan, and returns the table scan. The method `blocksAccessed` returns the estimated size of the materialized table. This size is computed by calculating the records per block (RPB) of the new records

```
public class MaterializePlan implements Plan {
   private Plan srcplan;
   private Transaction tx;

   public MaterializePlan(Transaction tx, Plan srcplan) {
      this.srcplan = srcplan;
      this.tx = tx;
   }

   public Scan open() {
      Schema sch = srcplan.schema();
      TempTable temp = new TempTable(tx, sch);
      Scan src = srcplan.open();
      UpdateScan dest = temp.open();
      while (src.next()) {
         dest.insert();
         for (String fldname : sch.fields())
            dest.setVal(fldname, src.getVal(fldname));
      }
      src.close();
      dest.beforeFirst();
      return dest;
   }

   public int blocksAccessed() {
      // create a dummy Layout object to calculate slot size
      Layout y = new Layout(srcplan.schema());
      double rpb = (double) (tx.blockSize() / y.slotSize());
      return (int) Math.ceil(srcplan.recordsOutput() / rpb);
   }

   public int recordsOutput() {
      return srcplan.recordsOutput();
   }

   public int distinctValues(String fldname) {
      return srcplan.distinctValues(fldname);
   }

   public Schema schema() {
      return srcplan.schema();
   }
}
```

Fig. 13.4 The code for the SimpleDB class `MaterializePlan`

and dividing the number of output records by this RPB. The values for methods `recordsOutput` and `distinctValues` are the same as in the underlying plan.

Note that `blocksAccessed` does not include the preprocessing cost. The reason is that the temporary table is built once but may be scanned multiple times.

If you want to include the cost of building the table in your cost formulas, you need to add a new method (say, `preprocessingCost`) to the `Plan` interface and to rework all of the various plan estimation formulas to include it. This task is left to Exercise 13.9. Alternatively, you can assume that the preprocessing cost is sufficiently insignificant and ignore it in your estimates.

Also note that there is no `MaterializeScan` class. Instead, the method `open` returns a table scan for the temporary table.

13.4 Sorting

Another useful relational algebra operator is *sort*. The sort operator takes two arguments: an input table and a list of field names. The output table has the same records as the input table but sorted according to the fields. For example, the following query sorts the STUDENT table by `GradYear`, with students having the same graduation year further sorted by name. If two students have the same name and graduation year, then their records may appear in any order.

```
sort(STUDENT, [GradYear, SName])
```

A planner uses sort to implement the `order by` clause of an SQL query. Sorting will also be used to implement the operators *groupby* and *mergejoin* later in this chapter. A database engine needs to be able to sort records efficiently. This section considers this problem and its SimpleDB solution.

13.4.1 Why Sort Needs to Materialize Its Input

It is possible to implement sorting without using materialization. For example, consider the sort node in the query tree of Fig. 13.5. The input to this node is the set of students and their majors, and the output is sorted by student name. Assume for simplicity that no two students have the same name, so that the input records have distinct sort values.

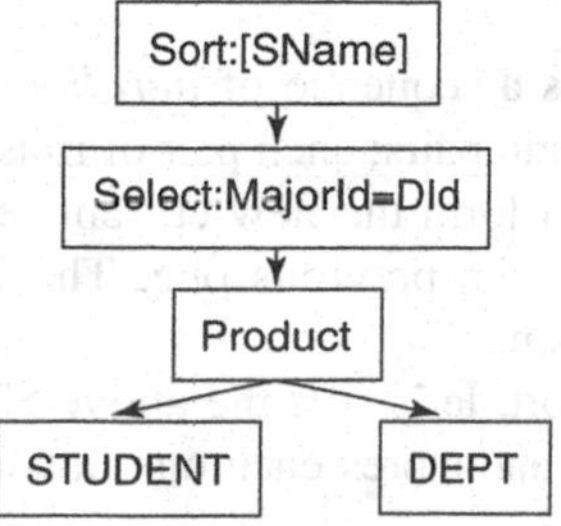

Fig. 13.5 A query tree containing a sort node

In a non-materialized implementation of the sort operator, the `next` method will need to position the scan at the input record having the next largest `SName`-value. To do so, the method will have to iterate through the input records twice: first to find the next largest value and then to move to the record having that value. Although such an implementation is possible, it would be exceptionally inefficient and totally impractical for large tables.

In a materialized implementation of sort, the `open` method will preprocess the input records, saving them in sorted order in a temporary table. Each call to `next` will simply retrieve the next record from the temporary table. This implementation produces a very efficient scan at the cost of some initial preprocessing. Assuming that creating and sorting a temporary table can be performed relatively efficiently (which it can), then this materialized implementation will be considerably less expensive than the non-materialized one.

13.4.2 The Basic Mergesort Algorithm

The standard sorting algorithms taught in beginning programming courses (such as insertion sort and quicksort) are called *internal* sorting algorithms, because they require all of the records to be in memory at the same time. A database engine, however, cannot assume that a table will fit completely into memory; thus it must use *external* sorting algorithms. The simplest and most common external sorting algorithm is called *mergesort*.

The mergesort algorithm is based on the concept of a *run*. A run is a sorted portion of a table. An unsorted table has several runs; a sorted table has exactly one run. For example, suppose you want to sort students by their id, and the `SId`-values of the STUDENT records are currently in the following order:

```
2 6 20 4 1 16 19 3 18
```

This table contains four runs. The first run contains [2, 6, 20], the second contains [4], the third contains [1, 16, 19], and the fourth [3, 18].

Mergesort works in two phases. The first phase, called *split*, scans the input records and places each run into its own temporary table. The second phase, called *merge*, repeatedly merges these runs until a single run remains; this final run is the sorted table.

The merge phase works as a sequence of *iterations*. During each iteration, the current set of runs is divided into pairs; each pair of runs is then merged into a single run. These resulting runs then form the new current set of runs. This new set will contain half as many runs as the previous one. The iterations continue until the current set contains a single run.

As an example of mergesort, let's sort the above STUDENT records. The split phase identifies the four runs and stores each one in a temporary table:

```
Run 1: 2  6  20
Run 2: 4
Run 3: 1  16  19
Run 4: 3  18
```

The first iteration of the merge phase merges runs 1 and 2 to produce run 5 and merges runs 3 and 4 to produce run 6:

```
Run 5: 2  4  6  20
Run 6: 1  3  16  18  19
```

The second iteration merges runs 5 and 6 to produce run 7:

```
Run 7: 1  2  3  4  6  16  18  19  20
```

There is now just one run, so the algorithm stops. It sorted the table using just two merge iterations.

Suppose that a table has 2^N initial runs. Each merge iteration transforms pairs of runs into single runs, that is, it reduces the number of runs by a factor of 2. Thus it will take N iterations to sort the file: the first iteration will reduce it to 2^{N-1} runs, the second to 2^{N-2} runs, and the Nth to $2^0=1$ run. In general, a table with R initial runs will be sorted in $\log_2 R$ merge iterations.

13.4.3 Improving the Mergesort Algorithm

There are three ways to improve the efficiency of this basic mergesort algorithm:

- Increase the number of runs merged at a time
- Reduce the number of initial runs
- Avoid writing the final, sorted table

This section examines these improvements.

Increasing the Number of Runs in a Merge

Instead of merging pairs of runs, the algorithm could merge three runs at a time, or even more. Suppose that the algorithm merges k runs at a time. Then it would open a scan on each of *k* temporary tables. At each step, it looks at the current record of each scan, copies the lowest-valued one to the output table, and moves to the next record of that scan. This step is repeated until the records of all k runs have been copied to the output table.

Merging multiple runs at a time reduces the number of iterations needed to sort the table. If the table starts with R initial runs and k runs are merged at a time, then only $\log_k R$ iterations will be needed to sort the file. How do you know what value of k to use? Why not just merge all of the runs in a single iteration? The answer depends on how many buffers are available. In order to merge k runs, you need k+1 buffers: one buffer for each of the k input scans and one buffer for the output scan.

For now, you can assume that the algorithm picks an arbitrary value for `k`. Chapter 14 will examine how to pick the best value for `k`.

Reducing the Number of Initial Runs

If you want to reduce the number of initial runs, then you need to increase the number of records per run. There are two algorithms you can use.

The first algorithm is shown in Fig. 13.6. That algorithm ignores the runs generated by the input records and instead creates runs that are always one block long. It works by repeatedly storing a block's worth of input records in a temporary table. Since this block of records will be located in a buffer page in memory, the algorithm can use an in-memory sorting algorithm (such as quicksort) to sort these records without incurring any disk accesses. After sorting the block of records into a single run, it saves that block to disk.

The second algorithm is similar, but it uses an additional block of memory as a "staging area" for input records. It begins by filling the staging area with records. For as long as possible, it repeatedly deletes a record from the staging area, writes it to the current run, and adds another input record to the staging area. This procedure will stop when all the records in the staging area are smaller than the last record in the run. In this case, the run is closed, and a new run is begun. The code for this algorithm appears in Fig. 13.7.

The advantage to using a staging area is that you keep adding records to it, which means that you always get to choose the next record in the run from a block-sized applicant pool. Thus each run will most likely contain more than a block's worth of records.

The following example compares these two ways of creating initial runs. Consider again the previous example that sorted STUDENT records by their `SId` values. Assume that a block can hold three records and that the records are initially in the following order:

Repeat until there are no more input records:
1. Read a block's worth of input records into a new temporary table.
2. Sort those records using an in-memory sorting algorithm.
3. Save the one-block temporary table to disk.

Fig. 13.6 An algorithm to create initial runs that are exactly one block long

1. Fill the one-block staging area with input records.
2. Start a new run.
3. Repeat until the staging area is empty:
   a. If none of the records in the staging area fit into the current run, then:
      Close the current run, and start a new one.
   b. Choose the record from the staging area having the lowest value higher than the last record in the current run.
   c. Copy that record to the current run.
   d. Delete that record from the staging area.
   e. Add the next input record (if there is one) to the staging area.
4. Close the current run.

Fig. 13.7 An algorithm to create large initial runs

```
2 6 20 4 1 16 19 3 18
```

These records happen to form four runs, as illustrated earlier. Suppose that you use the algorithm in Fig. 13.6 to reduce the number of initial runs. Then you would read the records in groups of three, sorting each group individually. You therefore wind up with three initial runs, as follows:

```
Run 1: 2  6  20
Run 2: 1  4  16
Run 3: 3  18  19
```

Suppose instead that you use the algorithm in Fig. 13.7 to reduce the number of runs. You begin by reading the first three records into the staging area.

```
Staging area: 2  6  20
Run 1:
```

You next choose the smallest value, 2, add it to the run, remove it from the staging area, and read the next record into the staging area.

```
Staging area: 6  20  4
Run 1: 2
```

The next smallest value is 4, so you add that value to the run, remove it from the staging area, and read in the next input value.

```
Staging area: 6  20  1
Run 1: 2  4
```

Here, the smallest value is 1, but that value is too small to be part of the current run. Instead, the next viable value is 6, so you add it to the run and read the next input value into the staging area.

```
Staging area: 20 1 16
Run 1: 2 4 6
```

Continuing, you will add 16, 19, and 20 to the run. At this point, the staging area consists entirely of records that cannot be added to the run.

```
Staging area: 1 3 18
Run 1: 2 4 6 16 19 20
```

You therefore begin a new run. Since there are no more input records, this run will contain the three records in the staging area.

```
Staging area:
Run 1: 2  4  6 16 19 20
Run 2: 1  3 18
```

This algorithm produced only two initial runs. The first run is two blocks long.

Don't Write the Final Sorted Table
Recall that every materialized implementation has two stages: a preprocessing stage, in which the input records are materialized into one or more temporary tables, and a scanning stage, which uses the temporary tables to determine the next output record.

In the basic mergesort algorithm, the preprocessing stage creates a sorted temporary table, and the scan reads from that table. This is a simple strategy but is not optimal.

Instead of creating a sorted temporary table, suppose that the preprocessing stage stops before the final merge iteration, that is, it stops when the number of temporary tables is ≤k. The scanning stage would take these k tables as input and perform the final merge itself. In particular, the stage would open a scan for each of these k tables. Each call to the method `next` would examine the current record of these scans and choose the record having the smallest sort value.

At each point in time, the scanning stage needs to keep track of which of the k scans contains the current record. This scan is called the *current scan*. When the client requests the next record, the implementation moves to the next record in the current scan, determines the scan containing the lowest record, and assigns that scan to be the new current scan.

To summarize, the job of the scanning stage is to return records in sorted order, as if they were stored in a single, sorted table. However, it does not need to actually create that table. Instead, it uses the k tables it receives from the preprocessing stage. Thus the block accesses needed to write (and read) the final, sorted table can be avoided.

13.4.4 The Cost of Mergesort

Let's calculate the cost of sorting, using analysis similar to that for the materialize operator. Figure 13.8 depicts the structure of a query tree that contains a sort node.

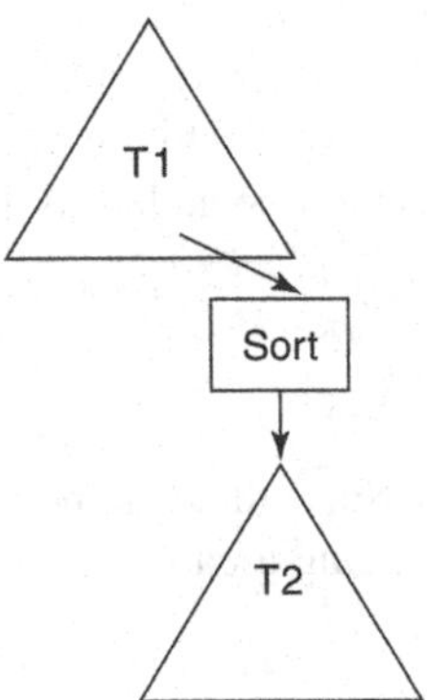

Fig. 13.8 A query tree containing a sort node

The cost associated with the sort node can be divided into two parts: the preprocessing cost and the scanning cost.

- The preprocessing cost is the cost of T2, plus the cost of splitting the records into runs, plus the cost of all but the last merge iteration.
- The scanning cost is the cost of performing the final merge from the records of the temporary tables.

In order to be more specific, assume the following:

- The algorithm merges k runs at a time.
- There are R initial runs.
- The materialized input records require B blocks.

The split phase writes to each of the blocks once, so splitting requires B block accesses plus the cost of the input. The records can be sorted in $\log_k R$ iterations. One of those iterations will be performed by the scanning stage and the rest by the preprocessing stage. During each preprocessing iteration, the records of each run will be read once and written once; thus the iteration requires 2B block accesses. During the scanning stage, the records in each run will be read once, for a cost of B block accesses. Putting these values together and simplifying give the following cost formulas:

Preprocessing cost = $2B\log_k R$ - B + the cost of its input
Scanning cost = B

For a concrete example, suppose that you want to sort a 1000-block stored table having 1-block long initial runs (that is, B = R = 1000). The table is stored, so the cost of the input is 1000 blocks. If you merge 2 runs at a time, then you need 10 merge iterations to completely sort the records (because $\log_2 1000 \leq 10$). The above formula states that it takes 20,000 block accesses to preprocess the records, plus another 1000 for the final scan. If you merge 10 runs at a time (that is, k = 10), then you would need only 3 iterations, and preprocessing would require only 6000 block accesses.

Continuing this example, suppose that you merge 1000 runs at a time (that is, k = 1000). Then $\log_k R = 1$, so the preprocessing cost is B plus the cost of the input, or 2000 block accesses. Note that the cost of sorting in this case is identical to the cost of materialization. In particular, the preprocessing stage does not need to perform any merging, because the split phase already results in k runs. The cost of preprocessing is therefore the cost of reading the table and splitting the records, which is 2B block accesses.

13.4.5 Implementing Mergesort

The SimpleDB classes SortPlan and SortScan implement the sort operator.

The Class SortPlan

The code for SortPlan appears in Fig. 13.9.

The open method performs the mergesort algorithm. In particular, it merges two runs at a time (i.e., k = 2) and does not try to reduce the number of initial runs. (Instead, Exercises 13.10 to 13.13 ask you to make these improvements.)

The private method splitIntoRuns performs the split phase of the mergesort algorithm, and method doAMergeIteration performs one iteration of the merge phase; this method is called repeatedly until it returns no more than two runs. At that point, open passes the list of runs to the SortScan constructor, which will handle the final merge iteration.

Method splitIntoRuns starts by creating a temporary table and opening a scan on it (the "destination scan"). The method then iterates through the input scan. Each input record is inserted into the destination scan. Each time a new run begins, the destination scan is closed, and another temporary table is created and opened. At the end of this method, several temporary tables will have been created, each containing a single run.

The method doAMergeIteration is given a list of the current temporary tables. It repeatedly calls the method mergeTwoRuns for each pair of temporary tables in the list and returns a list containing the resulting (merged) temporary tables.

Method mergeTwoRuns opens a scan for each of its two tables and creates a temporary table to hold the result. The method repeatedly chooses the smallest-valued record from the input scans, copying that record to the result. When one of the scans completes, then the remaining records of the other scan are added to the result.

The cost estimation methods are straightforward. The methods recordsOutput and distinctValues return the same values as the input table, because the sorted table contains the same records and value distribution. The method blocksAccessed estimates the number of block accesses required to iterate through the sorted scan, which is equal to the number of blocks in the sorted table. Since sorted and materialized tables are exactly the same size, this computation will be exactly the same as in MaterializePlan. Thus the method creates a "dummy" materialized plan for the sole purpose of calling its blocksAccessed method. The preprocessing cost is not included in the blocksAccessed method, for the same reasons as with MaterializePlan.

The job of comparing records is performed by the class RecordComparator, whose code appears in Fig. 13.10. The class compares the current records of two scans. Its compare method iterates through the sort fields, using compareTo to compare the values in each scan's current record. If all values are equal, then compareTo returns 0.

The Class SortScan

The class SortScan implements the scan; its code appears in Fig. 13.11. The constructor expects a list containing one or two runs. It initializes the runs by opening their tables and moving to their first record. (If there is only one run, then the variable hasmore2 is set to false, and the second run will never get considered.)

```
public class SortPlan implements Plan {
   private Plan p;
   private Transaction tx;
   private Schema sch;
   private RecordComparator comp;

   public SortPlan(Plan p, List<String> sortfields, Transaction tx) {
      this.p = p;
      this.tx = tx;
      sch = p.schema();
      comp = new RecordComparator(sortfields);
   }

   public Scan open() {
      Scan src = p.open();
      List<TempTable> runs = splitIntoRuns(src);
      src.close();
      while (runs.size() > 2)
         runs = doAMergeIteration(runs);
      return new SortScan(runs, comp);
   }

   public int blocksAccessed() {
      // does not include the one-time cost of sorting
      Plan mp = new MaterializePlan(tx, p);
      return mp.blocksAccessed();
   }

   public int recordsOutput() {
      return p.recordsOutput();
   }

   public int distinctValues(String fldname) {
      return p.distinctValues(fldname);
   }

   public Schema schema() {
      return sch;
   }

   private List<TempTable> splitIntoRuns(Scan src) {
      List<TempTable> temps = new ArrayList<>();
      src.beforeFirst();
      if (!src.next())
         return temps;
      TempTable currenttemp = new TempTable(tx, sch);
      temps.add(currenttemp);
      UpdateScan currentscan = currenttemp.open();
      while (copy(src, currentscan))
         if (comp.compare(src, currentscan) < 0) {
         // start a new run
         currentscan.close();
         currenttemp = new TempTable(tx, sch);
         temps.add(currenttemp);
         currentscan = (UpdateScan) currenttemp.open();
      }
```

Fig. 13.9 The code for the SimpleDB class `SortPlan`

```
      currentscan.close();
      return temps;
   }

   private List<TempTable> doAMergeIteration(List<TempTable> runs) {
      List<TempTable> result = new ArrayList<>();
      while (runs.size() > 1) {
         TempTable p1 = runs.remove(0);
         TempTable p2 = runs.remove(0);
         result.add(mergeTwoRuns(p1, p2));
      }
      if (runs.size() == 1)
         result.add(runs.get(0));
      return result;
   }

   private TempTable mergeTwoRuns(TempTable p1, TempTable p2) {
      Scan src1 = p1.open();
      Scan src2 = p2.open();
      TempTable result = new TempTable(tx, sch);
      UpdateScan dest = result.open();

      boolean hasmore1 = src1.next();
      boolean hasmore2 = src2.next();
      while (hasmore1 && hasmore2)
         if (comp.compare(src1, src2) < 0)
         hasmore1 = copy(src1, dest);
      else
         hasmore2 = copy(src2, dest);

      if (hasmore1)
         while (hasmore1)
         hasmore1 = copy(src1, dest);
      else
         while (hasmore2)
         hasmore2 = copy(src2, dest);
      src1.close();
      src2.close();
      dest.close();
      return result;
   }

   private boolean copy(Scan src, UpdateScan dest) {
      dest.insert();
      for (String fldname : sch.fields())
         dest.setVal(fldname, src.getVal(fldname));
      return src.next();
   }
}
```

Fig. 13.9 (continued)

```
public class RecordComparator implements Comparator<Scan> {
   private Collection<String> fields;

   public RecordComparator(Collection<String> fields) {
      this.fields = fields;
   }

   public int compare(Scan s1, Scan s2) {
      for (String fldname : fields) {
         Constant val1 = s1.getVal(fldname);
         Constant val2 = s2.getVal(fldname);
         int result = val1.compareTo(val2);
         if (result != 0)
            return result;
      }
      return 0;
   }
}
```

Fig. 13.10 The code for the SimpleDB class `RecordComparator`

The variable `currentscan` points to the scan containing the most recent record in the merge. The `get` methods obtain their values from that scan. The `next` method moves to the next record of the current scan and then chooses the lowest-value record from the two scans. The variable `currentscan` then points to that scan.

The class also has the two public methods `savePosition` and `restorePosition`. These methods allow a client (in particular, the mergejoin scan of Sect. 13.6) to move back to a previously seen record and continue the scan from there.

13.5 Grouping and Aggregation

The *groupby* relational algebra operator takes three arguments: an input table, a set of grouping fields, and a set of aggregation expressions. It organizes its input records into groups, where records having the same values for the grouping fields are in the same group. Its output table contains one row for each group; the row has a column for each grouping field and aggregation expression.

For example, the following query returns, for each student major, the minimum and maximum graduation year of students having that major. Figure 13.12 displays the output of this query, given the STUDENT table of Fig. 1.1.

```
groupby (STUDENT, {MajorID}, {Min(GradYear), Max(GradYear)})
```

In general, an aggregation expression specifies an *aggregation function* and a field. In the above query, the aggregation expression `Min(GradYear)` returns the

```
public class SortScan implements Scan {
   private UpdateScan s1, s2=null, currentscan=null;
   private RecordComparator comp;
   private boolean hasmore1, hasmore2=false;
   private List<RID> savedposition;

   public SortScan(List<TempTable> runs, RecordComparator comp) {
      this.comp = comp;
      s1 = (UpdateScan) runs.get(0).open();
      hasmore1 = s1.next();
      if (runs.size() > 1) {
         s2 = (UpdateScan) runs.get(1).open();
         hasmore2 = s2.next();
      }
   }

   public void beforeFirst() {
      s1.beforeFirst();
      hasmore1 = s1.next();
      if (s2 != null) {
         s2.beforeFirst();
         hasmore2 = s2.next();
      }
   }

   public boolean next() {
      if (currentscan == s1)
         hasmore1 = s1.next();
      else if (currentscan == s2)
         hasmore2 = s2.next();

      if (!hasmore1 && !hasmore2)
         return false;
      else if (hasmore1 && hasmore2) {
         if (comp.compare(s1, s2) < 0)
            currentscan = s1;
         else
            currentscan = s2;
      }
      else if (hasmore1)
         currentscan = s1;
      else if (hasmore2)
         currentscan = s2;
      return true;
   }

   public void close() {
      s1.close();
      if (s2 != null)
         s2.close();
   }
```

Fig. 13.11 The code for the SimpleDB class `SortScan`

```
   public Constant getVal(String fldname) {
      return currentscan.getVal(fldname);
   }

   public int getInt(String fldname) {
      return currentscan.getInt(fldname);
   }

   public String getString(String fldname) {
      return currentscan.getString(fldname);
   }

   public boolean hasField(String fldname) {
      return currentscan.hasField(fldname);
   }

   public void savePosition() {
      RID rid1 = s1.getRid();
      RID rid2 = s2.getRid();
      savedposition = Arrays.asList(rid1,rid2);
   }

   public void restorePosition() {
      RID rid1 = savedposition.get(0);
      RID rid2 = savedposition.get(1);
      s1.moveToRid(rid1);
      s2.moveToRid(rid2);
   }
}
```

Fig. 13.11 (continued)

MajorId	MinOfGradYear	MaxOfGradYear
10	2021	2022
20	2019	2022
30	2020	2021

Fig. 13.12 The output of the example groupby query

minimum value of `GradYear` for the records in the group. The available aggregation functions in SQL include `Min`, `Max`, `Count`, `Sum`, and `Avg`.

The main issue in implementing the groupby operator is how to create the groups of records. The best solution is to create a temporary table in which the records are sorted on the grouping fields. The records in each group will then be next to each other, and so the implementation can calculate the information on every group by making a single pass through the sorted table. Figure 13.13 gives the algorithm.

1. Create a temporary table containing the input records, sorted by the grouping fields.
2. Move to the first record in the table.
3. Repeat until the temporary table is exhausted:
   a. Let the "group value" be the values of the grouping fields for the current record.
   b. For each record whose grouping field values equals the group value:
      Read the record into the group list.
   c. Calculate the specified aggregation functions for the records in the group list.

Fig. 13.13 An algorithm to perform aggregation

The cost of the aggregation algorithm can be split into its preprocessing cost and its scanning cost. These costs are straightforward. The preprocessing cost is the cost of the sort, and the scanning cost is a single iteration through the sorted records. In other words, the groupby operator has the same cost as sort.

SimpleDB uses the classes `GroupByPlan` and `GroupByScan` to implement the groupby algorithm; see Figs. 13.14 and 13.15.

The `open` method in `GroupByPlan` creates and opens a sort plan for the input records. The resulting sort scan is passed into the constructor of `GroupByScan`. The groupby scan reads the records of the sort scan as needed. In particular, the method `next` reads the records in the next group each time it is called. This method recognizes the end of a group when it reads a record from another group (or when it detects that there are no more records in the sorted scan); consequently, each time `next` is called, the current record in the underlying scan will always be the first record in the next group.

The class `GroupValue` holds information about the current group; its code appears in Fig. 13.16. A scan is passed into its constructor, together with the grouping fields. The field values of the current record define the group. The method `getVal` returns the value of a specified field. The `equals` method returns `true` when the two `GroupValue` objects have the same values for the grouping fields, and the `hashCode` method assigns a hash value to each `GroupValue` object.

SimpleDB implements each aggregation function (such as `MIN`, `COUNT`, etc.) as a class. An object of the class is responsible for keeping track of the relevant information about the records in a group, for calculating the aggregate value for this group, and for determining the name of the calculated field. These methods belong to the interface `AggregationFn`, whose code is in Fig. 13.17. Method `processFirst` starts a new group using the current record as the first record of that group. Method `processNext` adds another record to the existing group.

An example of an aggregation function class is `MaxFn`, which implements `MAX`; see Fig. 13.18. The client passes the name of the aggregated field into the constructor. The object uses this field name to examine the field value from each record in the group, and it saves the maximum one in its variable `val`.

```
public class GroupByPlan implements Plan {
   private Plan p;
   private List<String> groupfields;
   private List<AggregationFn> aggfns;
   private Schema sch = new Schema();

   public GroupByPlan(Transaction tx, Plan p,
                      List<String> groupfields,
                      List<AggregationFn> aggfns) {
      this.p = new SortPlan(tx, p, groupfields);
      this.groupfields = groupfields;
      this.aggfns = aggfns;
      for (String fldname : groupfields)
         sch.add(fldname, p.schema());
      for (AggregationFn fn : aggfns)
         sch.addIntField(fn.fieldName());
   }

   public Scan open() {
      Scan s = p.open();
      return new GroupByScan(s, groupfields, aggfns);
   }

   public int blocksAccessed() {
      return p.blocksAccessed();
   }

   public int recordsOutput() {
      int numgroups = 1;
      for (String fldname : groupfields)
         numgroups *= p.distinctValues(fldname);
      return numgroups;
   }

   public int distinctValues(String fldname) {
      if (p.schema().hasField(fldname))
         return p.distinctValues(fldname);
      else
         return recordsOutput();
   }

   public Schema schema() {
      return sch;
   }
}
```

Fig. 13.14 The code for the SimpleDB class `GroupByPlan`

```
public class GroupByScan implements Scan {
   private Scan s;
   private List<String> groupfields;
   private List<AggregationFn> aggfns;
   private GroupValue groupval;
   private boolean moregroups;

   public GroupByScan(Scan s, List<String> groupfields,
                      List<AggregationFn> aggfns) {
      this.s = s;
      this.groupfields = groupfields;
      this.aggfns = aggfns;
      beforeFirst();
   }

   public void beforeFirst() {
      s.beforeFirst();
      moregroups = s.next();
   }

   public boolean next() {
      if (!moregroups)
         return false;
      for (AggregationFn fn : aggfns)
         fn.processFirst(s);
      groupval = new GroupValue(s, groupfields);
      while(moregroups = s.next()) {
         GroupValue gv = new GroupValue(s, groupfields);
         if (!groupval.equals(gv))
            break;
         for (AggregationFn fn : aggfns)
            fn.processNext(s);
      }
      return true;
   }

   public void close() {
      s.close();
   }

   public Constant getVal(String fldname) {
      if (groupfields.contains(fldname))
         return groupval.getVal(fldname);
      for (AggregationFn fn : aggfns)
         if (fn.fieldName().equals(fldname))
         return fn.value();
      throw new RuntimeException("no field " + fldname)
   }

   public int getInt(String fldname) {
      return getVal(fldname).asInt();
   }
```

Fig. 13.15 The code for the SimpleDB class `GroupByScan`

```
   public String getString(String fldname) {
      return getVal(fldname).asString();
   }

   public boolean hasField(String fldname) {
      if (groupfields.contains(fldname))
         return true;
      for (AggregationFn fn : aggfns)
         if (fn.fieldName().equals(fldname))
         return true;
      return false;
   }
}
```

Fig. 13.15 (continued)

```
public class GroupValue {
   private Map<String,Constant> vals = new HashMap<>();

   public GroupValue(Scan s, List<String> fields) {
      for (String fldname : fields)
         vals.put(fldname, s.getVal(fldname));
   }

   public Constant getVal(String fldname) {
      return vals.get(fldname);
   }

   public boolean equals(Object obj) {
      GroupValue gv = (GroupValue) obj;
      for (String fldname : vals.keySet()) {
         Constant v1 = vals.get(fldname);
         Constant v2 = gv.getVal(fldname);
         if (!v1.equals(v2))
            return false;
      }
      return true;
   }
   public int hashCode() {
      int hashval = 0;
      for (Constant c : vals.values())
         hashval += c.hashCode();
      return hashval;
   }
}
```

Fig. 13.16 The code for the SimpleDB class `GroupValue`

```
public interface AggregationFn {
   void processFirst(Scan s);
   void processNext(Scan s);
   String fieldName();
   Constant value();
}
```

Fig. 13.17 The code for the SimpleDB `AggregationFn` interface

```
public class MaxFn implements AggregationFn {
   private String fldname;
   private Constant val;

   public MaxFn(String fldname) {
      this.fldname = fldname;
   }

   public void processFirst(Scan s) {
      val = s.getVal(fldname);
   }

   public void processNext(Scan s) {
      Constant newval = s.getVal(fldname);
      if (newval.compareTo(val) > 0)
         val = newval;
   }

   public String fieldName() {
      return "maxof" + fldname;
   }

   public Constant value() {
      return val;
   }
}
```

Fig. 13.18 The code for the SimpleDB class `MaxFn`

1. For each input table:
   Sort the table, using its join field as the sort field.
2. Scan the sorted tables in parallel, looking for matches between the join fields.

Fig. 13.19 The *mergejoin* algorithm

13.6 Merge Joins

Chapter 12 developed an efficient indexjoin operator for joining two tables when the join predicate is of the form "A = B" where A is in the left-side table and B is in the right-side table. These fields are called the *join fields*. The indexjoin operator is applicable when the right-side table is stored and has an index on its join field. This section examines an efficient join operator, called *mergejoin*, which is always applicable. Its algorithm appears in Fig. 13.19.

Consider step 2 of the algorithm. If you assume for the moment that the table on the left side of the join has no duplicate values in its join field, then the algorithm is similar to a product scan. That is, it scans the left-side table once. For each left-side record, it searches the right-side table looking for matching records. However, the fact that the records are sorted simplifies the search considerably. In particular, note that:

- The matching right-side records must begin after the records for the previous left-side record.
- The matching records are next to each other in the table.

Consequently, each time a new left-side record is considered, it suffices to continue scanning the right-side table from where it left off and to stop when it reaches a join value greater than the left-side join value. That is, the right-side table need only be scanned once.

13.6.1 An Example of Mergejoin

The following query uses mergejoin to join the DEPT and STUDENT tables.

```
mergejoin(DEPT, STUDENT, DId=MajorId)
```

The first step of the merge join algorithm creates temporary tables to hold the contents of DEPT and STUDENT, sorted on fields `DId` and `MajorId`, respectively. Figure 13.20 shows these sorted tables, using the sample records from Fig. 1.1 but extended with a new department (the Basketry department, `DId` = 18).

The second step of the algorithm scans through the sorted tables. The current DEPT record is department 10. It scans STUDENT, finding a match at the first three records. When it moves to the fourth record (for Amy), it discovers a different `MajorId`-value, and so it knows it is done with department 10. It moves to the next DEPT record (for the Basketry department) and compares the record's `DId`-value with the `MajorId`-value of the current STUDENT record (i.e., Amy). Since Amy's `MajorId`-value is larger, the algorithm knows that there are no matches for that department and therefore moves to the next DEPT record (for the Math department). This record matches Amy's record, as well as the next three STUDENT records. As the algorithm moves through STUDENT, it eventually gets to Bob's record, which does not match with the current department. So it moves to the next DEPT record

DEPT	DId	DName
	10	compsci
	18	basketry
	20	math
	30	drama

STUDENT	SId	SName	MajorId	GradYear
	1	joe	**10**	2021
	3	max	**10**	2022
	9	lee	**10**	2021
	2	amy	**20**	2020
	4	sue	**20**	2022
	6	kim	**20**	2020
	8	pat	**20**	2019
	5	bob	**30**	2020
	7	art	**30**	2021

Fig. 13.20 The sorted DEPT and STUDENT tables

(for the Drama department) and continues its search through STUDENT, where the records for Bob and Art match. The join can finish as soon as one of the tables has run out of records.

What happens if the left side of a merge join has duplicate join values? Recall that the algorithm moves to the next left-side record when it reads a right-side record that no longer matches. If the next left-side record has the same join value, then the algorithm needs to move back to the first matching right-side record. That is, all of the right-side blocks containing matching records will have to be re-read, potentially increasing the cost of the join.

Fortunately, duplicate left-side values rarely occur. Most joins in a query tend to be based on a key-foreign key relationship. For example, in the above join, `DId` is a key of DEPT, and `MajorId` is its foreign key. Since keys and foreign keys are declared when the table is created, the query planner can use this information to ensure that the table having the key is on the left side of the merge join.

To calculate the cost of the mergejoin algorithm, note that the preprocessing phase sorts each input table and the scanning phase iterates through the sorted tables. If there are no duplicate left-side values, then each sorted table gets scanned once, and the cost of the join is the sum of the cost of the two sort operations. If there are duplicate left-side values, then the corresponding records in the right-side scan will be read multiple times.

For example, you can use the statistics of Fig. 7.8 to calculate the cost of a merge join of STUDENT and DEPT. Assume that the algorithm merges pairs of runs and that each initial run is 1-block long. The preprocessing cost includes sorting the 4500-block STUDENT table (for $9000 \times \log_2(4500) - 4500 = 112{,}500$ block accesses, plus 4500 for the cost of the input), and sorting the 2-block DEPT table (for $4 \times \log_2(2) - 2 = 2$ block accesses, plus 2 for the cost of the input). The total preprocessing cost is thus 117,004 block accesses. The scanning cost is the sum of the sizes of the sorted tables, which is 4502 block accesses. The total cost of the join is thus 121,506 block accesses.

Compare this cost with the cost of performing the join as a product followed by a selection, as in Chap. 8. That cost formula is B1 + R1*B2, which comes to 184,500 block accesses.

13.6.2 *Implementing Mergejoin*

The SimpleDB classes `MergeJoinPlan` and `MergeJoinScan` implement the merge join algorithm.

The Class `MergeJoinPlan`

The code for `MergeJoinPlan` appears in Fig. 13.21. The method `open` opens a sort scan for each of the two input tables, using the specified join fields. It then passes these scans to the `MergeJoinScan` constructor.

The method `blocksAccessed` assumes that each scan will be traversed once. The idea is that even if there are duplicate left-side values, the matching right-side records will either be in the same block or a recently accessed one. Thus it is likely that very few (or possibly zero) additional block accesses will be needed.

The method `recordsOutput` calculates the number of records of the join. This value will be the number of records in the product, divided by the number of records filtered out by the join predicate. The code for the method `distinctValues` is straightforward. Since the join does not increase or decrease field values, the estimate is the same as in the appropriate underlying query.

The Class MergeJoinScan

The code for `MergeJoinScan` appears in Fig. 13.22. Method `next` performs the difficult work of looking for matches. The scan uses variable `joinval` to keep track of the most recent join value. When `next` is called, it reads the next right-side record. If this record has a join value equal to `joinval`, a match is found, and the method returns. If not, then the method moves to the next left-side record. If this record's join value equals `joinval`, then we have a duplicate left-side value. The method repositions the right-side scan to the first record having that join value and returns. Otherwise, the method repeatedly reads from the scan having the lowest join value, until either a match is found or a scan runs out. If a match is found, the variable `joinval` is set, and the current right-side position is saved. If a scan runs out, the method returns `false`.

13.7 Chapter Summary

- A *materialized implementation* of an operator preprocesses its underlying records, storing them in one or more temporary tables. Its scan methods are thus more efficient, because they only need to examine the temporary tables.

```
public class MergeJoinPlan implements Plan {
   private Plan p1, p2;
   private String fldname1, fldname2;
   private Schema sch = new Schema();

   public MergeJoinPlan(Transaction tx, Plan p1, Plan p2,
                        String fldname1, String fldname2) {
      this.fldname1 = fldname1;
      List<String> sortlist1 = Arrays.asList(fldname1);
      this.p1 = new SortPlan(tx, p1, sortlist1);

      this.fldname2 = fldname2;
      List<String> sortlist2 = Arrays.asList(fldname2);
      this.p2 = new SortPlan(tx, p2, sortlist2);

      sch.addAll(p1.schema());
      sch.addAll(p2.schema());
   }

   public Scan open() {
      Scan s1 = p1.open();
      SortScan s2 = (SortScan) p2.open();
      return new MergeJoinScan(s1, s2, fldname1, fldname2);
   }

   public int blocksAccessed() {
      return p1.blocksAccessed() + p2.blocksAccessed();
   }

   public int recordsOutput() {
      int maxvals = Math.max(p1.distinctValues(fldname1),
                             p2.distinctValues(fldname2));
      return (p1.recordsOutput()*p2.recordsOutput())/maxvals;
   }

   public int distinctValues(String fldname) {
      if (p1.schema().hasField(fldname))
         return p1.distinctValues(fldname);
      else
         return p2.distinctValues(fldname);
   }

   public Schema schema() {
      return sch;
   }
}
```

Fig. 13.21 The code for the SimpleDB class `MergeJoinPlan`

```
public class MergeJoinScan implements Scan {
   private Scan s1;
   private SortScan s2;
   private String fldname1, fldname2;
   private Constant joinval = null;

   public MergeJoinScan(Scan s1, SortScan s2,
                        String fldname1, String fldname2) {
      this.s1 = s1;
      this.s2 = s2;
      this.fldname1 = fldname1;
      this.fldname2 = fldname2;
      beforeFirst();
   }

   public void close() {
      s1.close();
      s2.close();
   }

   public void beforeFirst() {
      s1.beforeFirst();
      s2.beforeFirst();
   }

   public boolean next() {
      boolean hasmore2 = s2.next();
      if (hasmore2 && s2.getVal(fldname2).equals(joinval))
         return true;

      boolean hasmore1 = s1.next();
      if (hasmore1 && s1.getVal(fldname1).equals(joinval)) {
         s2.restorePosition();
         return true;
      }

      while (hasmore1 && hasmore2) {
         Constant v1 = s1.getVal(fldname1);
         Constant v2 = s2.getVal(fldname2);
         if (v1.compareTo(v2) < 0)
            hasmore1 = s1.next();
         else if (v1.compareTo(v2) > 0)
            hasmore2 = s2.next();
         else {
            s2.savePosition();
            joinval  = s2.getVal(fldname2);
            return true;
         }
      }
      return false;
   }
```

Fig. 13.22 The code for the SimpleDB class `MergeJoinScan`

```
    public int getInt(String fldname) {
       if (s1.hasField(fldname))
          return s1.getInt(fldname);
       else
          return s2.getInt(fldname);
    }

    public String getString(String fldname) {
       if (s1.hasField(fldname))
          return s1.getString(fldname);
       else
          return s2.getString(fldname);
    }

    public Constant getVal(String fldname) {
       if (s1.hasField(fldname))
          return s1.getVal(fldname);
       else
          return s2.getVal(fldname);
    }

    public boolean hasField(String fldname) {
       return s1.hasField(fldname) || s2.hasField(fldname);
    }
}
```

Fig. 13.22 (continued)

- Materialized implementations compute their input once and can take advantage of sorting. However, they must compute their entire input table even if the user is interested in only a few of those records. Although it is possible to write materialized implementations for any relational operator, a materialized implementation will be useful only if its preprocessing cost is offset by the savings of the resulting scan.
- The *materialize* operator creates a temporary table containing all of its input records. It is useful whenever its input is executed repeatedly, such as when it is on the right side of a product node.
- A database system uses an *external* sorting algorithm to sort its records into a temporary table. The simplest and most common external sorting algorithm is called *mergesort*. The mergesort algorithm splits the input records into runs and then repeatedly merges the runs until the records are sorted.
- Mergesort is more efficient when the number of initial runs is smaller. A straightforward approach is to create initial runs that are one block long, by reading the input records into a block and then using an internal sorting algorithm to sort them. Another approach is to read input records into a one-block-long *staging area* and to construct runs by repeatedly selecting the lowest-valued record in the area.

- Mergesort is also more efficient when it merges more runs at a time. The more runs that are merged, the fewer iterations that are needed. A buffer is needed to manage each merged run, so the maximum number of runs is limited by the number of available buffers.
- Mergesort requires $2B\log_k(R)-B$ block accesses (plus the cost of the input) to preprocess its input, where B is the number of blocks required to hold the sorted table, R is the number of initial runs, and k is the number of runs that are merged at one time.
- The implementation of the *groupby* operator sorts the records on the grouping fields, so that the records in each group are next to each other. It then calculates the information on each group by making a single pass through the sorted records.
- The *mergejoin* algorithm implements the join to two tables. It begins by sorting each table on its join field. It then scans the two sorted tables in parallel. Each call to the *next* method increments the scan having the lowest value.

13.8 Suggested Reading

File sorting has been an important (even crucial) operation throughout the history of computing, predating database systems by many years. There is an enormous literature on the subject and numerous variations on mergesort that were not considered here. A comprehensive overview of the various algorithms appears in Knuth (1998).

The SimpleDB `SortPlan` code is a straightforward implementation of the mergesort algorithm. The article Graefe (2006) describes several interesting and useful techniques for improving upon this implementation.

The article Graefe (2003) explores the duality between sort algorithms and B-tree algorithms. It shows how to use a B-tree to usefully store the intermediate runs of a mergesort and how merge iterations can be used to create a B-tree index for an existing table.

Materialized algorithms are discussed in Graefe (1993) and are compared with non-materialized algorithms.

Graefe, G. (1993) Query evaluation techniques for large databases. *ACM Computing Surveys, 25*(2), 73–170.

Graefe, G. (2003) Sorting and indexing with partitioned B-trees. *Proceedings of the CIDR Conference.*

Graefe, G. (2006) Implementing sorting in database systems. *ACM Computing Surveys, 38*(3), 1–37.

Knuth, D. (1998) *The art of computer programming, Vol 3: Sorting and searching.* Addison-Wesley.

13.9 Exercises

Conceptual Exercises

13.1. Consider the query tree of Fig. 13.2b.

(a) Suppose that there was only one student in the class of 2005. Is the right-hand materialize node worthwhile?
(b) Suppose that there were only two students in the class of 2005. Is the right-hand materialize node worthwhile?
(c) Suppose that the right and left subtrees of the product node were swapped. Calculate the savings of materializing the new right-hand select node.

13.2. The basic mergesort algorithm of Sect. 13.4 merges the runs iteratively. Using the example of that section, it merged runs 1 and 2 to produce run 5 and runs 3 and 4 to produce run 6; then it merged runs 5 and 6 to produce the final run. Suppose instead that the algorithm merged the runs sequentially. That is, it merges runs 1 and 2 to produce run 5, then merges runs 3 and 5 to produce run 6, and then merges runs 4 and 6 to produce the final run.

(a) Explain why the final run produced by this "sequential merging" will always require the same number of merges as with iterative merging.
(b) Explain why sequential merging requires more (and usually many more) block accesses than iterative merging.

13.3. Consider the run-generation algorithms of Figs. 13.6 and 13.7.

(a) Suppose that the input records are already sorted. Which algorithm will produce the fewest initial runs? Explain.
(b) Suppose that the input records are sorted in reverse order. Explain why the algorithms will produce the same number of initial runs.

13.4. Consider the university database and the statistics of Fig. 7.8.

(a) For each table, estimate the cost of sorting it using 2, 10, or 100 auxiliary tables. Assume that each initial run is one block long.
(b) For each pair of tables that can be meaningfully joined, estimate the cost of performing a mergejoin (again, using 2, 10, or 100 auxiliary tables).

13.5. The method `splitIntoRuns` in the class `SortPlan` returns a list of `TempTable` objects. If the database is very large, then this list might be very long.

(a) Explain how this list might be a source of unexpected inefficiency.
(b) Propose a solution that would be better.

Programming Exercises

13.6. Section 13.4 described a non-materialized implementation of sorting.

(a) Design and implement the classes `NMSortPlan` and `NMSortScan`, which provide sorted access to records without the creation of temporary tables.
(b) How many block accesses are required to fully traverse such a scan?
(c) Suppose that a JDBC client wants to find the record having the minimum value for a field; the client does so by executing a query that sorts the table on that field and then choosing the first record. Compare the number of block accesses required to do this, using the materialized and non-materialized implementations.

13.7. When the server restarts, temporary table names begin again from 0. The SimpleDB file manager constructor deletes all temporary files.

(a) Explain what problem will occur in SimpleDB if temporary table files were allowed to remain after the system restarts.
(b) Instead of deleting all temporary files when the system restarts, the system could delete the file for a temporary table as soon as the transaction that created it has completed. Revise the SimpleDB code do this.

13.8. What problem occurs when `SortPlan` and `SortScan` are asked to sort an empty table? Revise the code to fix the problem.
13.9. Revise the SimpleDB `Plan` interface (and all of its implementing classes) to have a method `preprocessingCost`, which estimates the one-time cost of materializing a table. Modify the other estimation formulas appropriately.
13.10. Revise the code for `SortPlan` so that it constructs initial runs of one block long, using the algorithm of Fig. 13.5.
13.11. Revise the code for `SortPlan` so that it constructs initial runs using a staging area, using the algorithm of Fig. 13.6.
13.12. Revise the code for `SortPlan` so that it merges three runs at a time.
13.13. Revise the code for `SortPlan` so that it merges `k` runs at a time, where the integer `k` is supplied in the constructor.
13.14. Revise the SimpleDB `Plan` classes so that they keep track of whether their records are sorted, and if so on what fields. Then revise the code for `SortPlan` so that it sorts the records only if necessary.
13.15. An `order by` clause in an SQL query is optional. If it exists, it consists of the two keywords "order" and "by," followed by a comma-separated list of field names.

(a) Revise the SQL grammar of Fig. 9.7 to include `order by` clauses.
(b) Revise the SimpleDB lexical analyzer and query parser to implement your syntax changes.
(c) Revise the SimpleDB query planner to generate an appropriate sort operation for queries containing an `order by` clause. The `SortPlan` object should be the topmost node in the query tree.

13.16. SimpleDB only implements the aggregation functions `COUNT` and `MAX`. Add classes that implement `MIN`, `AVG`, and `SUM`.

13.17. Look up the syntax of SQL aggregation statements.

(a) Revise the SQL grammar of Fig. 9.7 to include this syntax.
(b) Revise the SimpleDB lexical analyzer and query parser to implement your syntax changes.
(c) Revise the SimpleDB query planner to generate an appropriate groupby operation for queries containing a `group by` clause. The `GroupBy` object should be above the select and semijoin nodes but below the extend and project nodes in the query plan.

13.18. Define a relational operator *nodups*, whose output table consists of those records from its input table but with duplicates removed.

(a) Write code for `NoDupsPlan` and `NoDupsScan`, similar to how `GroupByPlan` and `GroupByScan` are written.
(b) Duplicate removal can also be performed by a groupby operator with no aggregation functions. Write code for `GBNoDupsPlan`, which implements nodups operator by creating the appropriate `GroupByPlan` object.

13.19. The keyword "distinct" can optionally appear in the select clause of an SQL query. If it exists, the query processor should remove duplicates from the output table.

(a) Revise the SQL grammar of Fig. 9.7 to include the `distinct` keyword.
(b) Revise the SimpleDB lexical analyzer and query parser to implement your syntax changes.
(c) Revise the basic query planner to generate an appropriate nodups operation for `select distinct` queries.

13.20. Another way to sort a table on a single field is to use a B-tree index. The `SortPlan` constructor would first create an index for the materialized table on the sort field. It then would add an index record into the B-tree for each data record. The records can then be read in sorted order by traversing the leaf nodes of the B-tree from the beginning.

(a) Implement this version of `SortPlan`. (You will need to modify the B-tree code so that all index blocks are chained.)
(b) How many block accesses does it require? Is it more or less efficient than using mergesort?

Chapter 14
Effective Buffer Utilization

Different operator implementations have different buffer needs. For example, the pipelined implementation of the select operator uses a single buffer very efficiently and has no need for additional buffers. On the other hand, the materialized implementation of the sort operator merges several runs at a time and needs a buffer for each.

This chapter considers the various ways in which operator implementations can use additional buffers, and gives efficient multibuffer algorithms for the sort, product, and join operators.

14.1 Buffer Usage in Query Plans

The relational algebra implementations discussed so far have been very frugal when it comes to buffer usage. For example, each table scan pins one block at a time; when it finishes with the records in a block, it unpins that block before pinning the next one. The scans for the operators select, project, and product do not pin any additional blocks. Consequently, given an N-table query, the scan produced by the SimpleDB basic query planner uses N simultaneous pinned buffers.

Consider the index implementations of Chap. 12. A static hash index implements each bucket as a file and scans it sequentially, pinning one block at a time. And a B-tree index works by pinning one directory block at a time, starting at the root. It scans the block to determine the appropriate child, unpins the block, and pins the child block, continuing until the leaf block is found.[1]

Now consider the materialized implementations of Chap. 13. The implementation of the materialize operator requires one buffer for the temporary table, in addition to

[1]This analysis is certainly true for queries. Inserting a record into a B-tree may require several buffers to be pinned simultaneously, to handle block splitting and the recursive insertion of entries up the tree. Exercise 12.16 asked you to analyze the buffer requirements for insertions.

E. Sciore, *Database Design and Implementation*, Data-Centric Systems and Applications, https://doi.org/10.1007/978-3-030-33836-7_14

the buffers needed by the input query. The split phase of the sort implementation requires one or two buffers (depending on whether it uses a staging area), and the merge phase requires k + 1 buffers: one buffer for each of the k runs being merged and one buffer for the result table. And the implementations of groupby and mergejoin require no additional buffers beyond those used for sorting.

This analysis shows that, with the exception of sorting, the number of simultaneous buffers used by a query plan is roughly equal to the number of tables mentioned in the query; this number is usually less than 10 and almost certainly less than 100. The total number of available buffers is typically much larger. Server machines these days typically have at least 16 GB of physical memory. If only a paltry 400 MB of that is used for buffers, then the server would have 100,000 4K-byte buffers. So even if the database system supports hundreds (or thousands) of simultaneous connections, there are still plenty of buffers available for executing any given query, if only the query plan were able to use them effectively. This chapter considers how the sort, join, and product operators can take advantage of this abundance of buffers.

14.2 Multibuffer Sorting

Recall that the mergesort algorithm has two phases: The first phase splits the records into runs, and the second phase merges the runs until the table is sorted. Chapter 13 discussed the benefits of using multiple buffers during the merge phase. It turns out that the split phase can also take advantage of additional buffers.

Suppose that k buffers are available. The split phase can read k blocks of the table at a time into the k buffers, use an internal sorting algorithm to sort them into a single k-block run, and then write those blocks to a temporary table. That is, instead of splitting the records into one-block-long runs, it splits the records into k-block-long runs. If k is large enough (in particular, if $k \geq \sqrt{B}$), then the split phase will produce no more than k initial runs, which means that the preprocessing stage will not need to do anything. The *multibuffer mergesort* algorithm incorporates these ideas; see Fig. 14.1.

Step 1 of this algorithm produces B/k initial runs. Using the cost analysis of Sect. 13.4.4, it follows that multibuffer mergesort requires $\log_k(B/k)$ merge iterations. This is one fewer merge iteration than basic mergesort (where the initial runs are of size 1). Put another way, multibuffer mergesort saves 2B block accesses during the preprocessing stage, which means that multibuffer sorting a B-block table, using k buffers, has the following costs:

- Preprocessing cost = $2B\log_k B - 3B$ + the cost of its input
- Scanning cost = B

How to choose the best value of k? The value of k determines the number of merge iterations. In particular, the number of iterations performed during preprocessing is equal to $(\log_k B)-2$. It follows that:

```
// The split phase, which uses k buffers
1. Repeat until there are no more input records:
      a. Pin k buffers, and read k blocks of input records into them.
      b. Use an internal sorting algorithm to sort these records.
      c. Write the contents of the buffers to a temporary table.
      d. Unpin the buffers.
      e. Add the temporary table to the run-list.
// The merge phase, which uses k+1 buffers
2. Repeat until the run-list contains one temporary table:
      // Do an iteration
      a. Repeat until the run-list is empty:
            i.   Open scans for k of the temporary tables.
            ii.  Open a scan for a new temporary table.
            iii. Merge the k scans into the new one.
            iv.  Add the new temporary table to list L.
      b. Add the contents of L to the run-list.
```

Fig. 14.1 The Multibuffer Mergesort Algorithm

# buffers	1000	100	32	16	10	8	6	5	4	3	2
# iterations	0	1	2	3	4	5	6	7	8	11	18

Fig. 14.2 The number of preprocessing iterations required to sort a 4 GB table

- There will be 0 iterations when $k=\sqrt{B}$.
- There will be 1 iteration when $k=\sqrt[3]{B}$.
- There will be 2 iterations when $k=\sqrt[4]{B}$.

And so on.

This calculation should make intuitive sense to you. If $k=\sqrt{B}$, then the split phase will produce k runs of size k. These runs can be merged during the scanning phase, which means that no merge iterations are needed during preprocessing. And if $k=\sqrt[3]{B}$, then the split phase will produce k^2 runs of size k. One merge iteration will produce k runs (of size k^2), which can then be merged during the scanning phase.

For a concrete example, suppose that you need to sort a 4 GB table. If blocks are 4 KB, then the table contains about one million blocks. Figure 14.2 lists the number of buffers required to obtain a specific number of merge iterations during preprocessing.

At the lower end of this figure, note how adding just a few more buffers results in dramatic improvements: 2 buffers require 18 iterations, but 10 buffers bring it down to only 4 iterations. This tremendous difference in cost implies that it would be a very bad idea for the database system to sort this table using less than ten buffers.

The upper end of this figure illustrates how efficient sorting can be. It is quite possible that 1000 buffers are available, or at least 100. The figure shows that with 1000 buffers (or equivalently, 4 MB of memory), it is possible to sort a 4 GB table by performing 1000 internal sorts during the preprocessing stage, followed by a single 1000-way merge during the scanning phase. The total cost is three million block accesses: one million to read the unsorted blocks, one million to write to the temporary tables, and one million to read the temporary tables. This efficiency is both unexpected and remarkable.

This example also shows that for a given table size B, multibuffer mergesort can effectively use only certain numbers of buffers, namely, $\sqrt{B}$, $\sqrt[3]{B}$, $\sqrt[4]{B}$, and so on. Figure 14.2 listed those values for B = 1,000,000. What about other buffer values? What happens if you have, say, 500 buffers available? We know that 100 buffers result in 1 preprocessing merge iteration. Let's see if those extra 400 buffers can be put to good use. With 500 buffers, the split phase will result in 2000 runs of 500 blocks each. The first merge iteration will merge 500 runs at a time, resulting in 4 runs (of 250,000 blocks each). These runs can then be merged during the scanning phase. So in fact the extra 400 buffers don't help, because you still need the same number of iterations as 100 buffers.

This analysis can be expressed as the following rule: *If you use k buffers to sort a table that is B blocks long, then k should be a root of B.*

14.3 Multibuffer Product

The basic implementation of the product operator involves numerous block accesses. For example, consider the SimpleDB implementation of the query:

```
product(T1, T2)
```

That implementation will examine all of T2 for each record of T1, using a single buffer to hold the records from T2. That is, after the code examines the last record of a T2 block, it unpins the block and pins the next block of T2. This unpinning allows the buffer manager to replace each T2 block, which means that they all may need to be re-read from disk when the next record of T1 is examined. In the worst case, each block of T2 will be read as many times as there are records in T1. If we assume that T1 and T2 are both 1000-block tables containing 20 records per block, then the query will require 20,001,000 block accesses.

Suppose instead that the implementation did not unpin any blocks from T2. The buffer manager would then be compelled to place each block of T2 in its own buffer. The blocks of T2 will thus get read once from disk and remain in memory during the entire query. This scan would be exceptionally efficient, because it would read each block of T1 once and each block of T2 once.

Of course, this strategy will work only if there are enough buffers to hold all of T2. What should you do if T2 is too large? For example, suppose that T2 has 1000 blocks, but only 500 buffers are available. The best thing to do is to process T2 in two stages. First, read the first 500 blocks into the available buffers and compute the product of T1 with those blocks; then read the remaining 500 blocks of T2 into those buffers and compute their product with T1.

This strategy is very efficient. The first stage requires reading T1 once and the first half of T2 once, and the second stage requires reading T1 again and the second half of T2 once. In total, T1 gets read twice and T2 gets read once, for a total of only 3000 block accesses.

The *multibuffer product* algorithm generalizes these ideas; see Fig. 14.3. In this algorithm, the blocks of T1 will be read once for each chunk. Since there are `B2/k` chunks, the product operation will require `B2 + (B1*B2/k)` block accesses.

Note how the multibuffer product implementation treats T1 and T2 opposite from how they are treated by the basic product implementation of Chap. 8. In that chapter, T2 is scanned multiple times, whereas here, T1 is scanned multiple times.

Assume again that T1 and T2 are both 1000-block tables. Figure 14.4 lists the block accesses required by the multibuffer product algorithm for various numbers of buffers. If 1000 buffers are available, then T2 can be processed in a single chunk, resulting in only 2000 block accesses. On the other hand, if 250 buffers are available, then the multibuffer product algorithm would use 4 chunks of 250 blocks each; thus table T1 would be scanned 4 times and T2 would be scanned once, for a total of 5000 block accesses. If only 100 buffers are available, then the algorithm would use 10 chunks and thus 11,000 total block accesses. All of these values are much less than what the basic product implementation requires.

As with sorting, Fig. 14.4 also demonstrates that not all values of `k` are useful. In this example, if 300 buffers are available, then the multibuffer product algorithm can only make use of 250 of them.

Let T1 and T2 be the two input tables. Assume that T2 is stored (as either a user-defined table or a materialized temporary table) and contains `B2` blocks.

1. Let `k` = `B2/i` for some integer `i`. That is, `k` is a fraction of `B2`.
2. Treat T2 as consisting of `i` *chunks* of `k` blocks each. For each chunk C:
   a) Read all of C's blocks into `k` buffers.
   b) Take the product of T1 and C.
   c) Unpin C's blocks.

Fig. 14.3 The multibuffer product algorithm

# buffers	1,000	500	334	250	200	167	143	125	112	100
# chunks	1	2	3	4	5	6	7	8	9	10
# block accesses	2,000	3,000	4,000	5,000	6,000	7,000	8,000	9,000	10,000	11,000

Fig. 14.4 The block accesses required to take the product of two 1000-block tables

14.4 Determining Buffer Allocation

Each of the multibuffer algorithms chooses k buffers but does not specify the exact value of k. The proper value of k is determined by the number of available buffers, the size of the input tables, and the operator involved. For sorting, k is a root of the input table size; for the product, k is a factor of the table size.

The goal is to choose k to be the largest root (or factor) that is less than the number of available buffers. The SimpleDB class `BufferNeeds` contains methods to calculate these values; its code appears in Fig. 14.5.

The class contains the public static methods `bestRoot` and `bestFactor`. These two methods are almost identical. The inputs to each method are the number of available buffers the size of the table. The methods calculate the optimum number of buffers, either as the largest root or the largest factor that is less than `avail`. The method `bestRoot` initializes the variable k to `MAX_VALUE` in order to force the loop to be executed at least once (so that k cannot be more than √B).

Note that the methods in `BufferNeeds` do not actually reserve the buffers from the buffer manager. Instead, they simply ask the buffer manager how many buffers

```
public class BufferNeeds {
  public static int bestRoot(int available, int size) {
     int avail = available - 2; //reserve a couple of buffers
     if (avail <= 1)
        return 1;
     int k = Integer.MAX_VALUE;
     double i = 1.0;
     while (k > avail) {
        i++;
        k = (int)Math.ceil(Math.pow(size, 1/i));
     }
     return k;
  }

  public static int bestFactor(int available, int size) {
     int avail = available - 2;  //reserve a couple of buffers
     if (avail <= 1)
        return 1;
     int k = size;
     double i = 1.0;
     while (k > avail) {
        i++;
        k = (int)Math.ceil(size / i);
     }
     return k;
  }
}
```

Fig. 14.5 The code for the SimpleDB class `BufferNeeds`

are currently available and choose a value for k less than that. When the multibuffer algorithms attempt to pin those k blocks, some of the buffers may no longer be available. In that case, the algorithms will wait until the buffers become available again.

14.5 Implementing Multibuffer Sorting

In the SimpleDB class SortPlan, the methods splitIntoRuns and doAMergeIteration determine how many buffers to use. Currently, splitIntoRuns creates its runs incrementally, using one buffer attached to a temporary table, and doAMergeIteration uses three buffers (two buffers for the input runs and one buffer for the output run). This section considers how these methods need to change to implement multibuffer sorting.

Consider splitIntoRuns. This method does not actually know how large the sorted table will be, because the table has not yet been created. However, the method can use the method blocksAccessed to make this estimate. In particular, splitIntoRuns can execute the following code fragment:

```
int size = blocksAccessed();
int available = tx.availableBuffs();
int numbuffs = BufferNeeds.bestRoot(available, size);
```

It can then pin numbuffs buffers, fill them with input records, sort them internally, and write them to a temporary table, as shown in Fig. 14.1.

Now consider the method doAMergeIteration. The best strategy is for the method to remove k temporary tables from the run list, where k is a root of the number of initial runs:

```
int available = tx.availableBuffs();
int numbuffs = BufferNeeds.bestRoot(available, runs.size());
List<TempTable> runsToMerge = new ArrayList<>();
for (int i=0; i<numbuffs; i++)
   runsToMerge.add(runs.remove(0));
```

The method can then pass the runsToMerge list to the method mergeTwoRuns (which could be renamed mergeSeveralRuns) to be merged into a single run.

The SimpleDB distribution code does not contain a version of SortPlan that performs multibuffer sorting. That task is left to Exercises 14.15–14.17.

Finally, note that code that uses SortPlan, such as GroupByPlan and MergeJoinPlan, cannot tell whether it is using the regular sorting algorithm or the multibuffer algorithm. Thus those classes do not need to be changed. (However, there are some minor issues related to the number of buffers used by `MergeJoinPlan`; see Exercise 14.5.)

14.6 Implementing Multibuffer Product

To implement the multibuffer product algorithm, you need to implement the notion of a chunk. Recall that a chunk is a `k`-block portion of a materialized table having the property that all blocks of the chunk fit into the available buffers. The class `ChunkScan` implements a chunk as a scan of records; see Fig. 14.6.

The `ChunkScan` constructor is given the stored table's metadata together with the block number of the first and last blocks of the chunk. The constructor opens record pages for each block in the chunk and stores them in a list. The scan also keeps track of a current record page; initially, the current page is the first page in the list. The `next` method moves to the next record in the current page. If the current page has no more records, then the next page in the list becomes current. Unlike table scans, moving between blocks in a chunk scan does not close the previous record page (which would unpin its buffer). Instead, the record pages in a chunk are unpinned only when the chunk itself is closed.

The class `MultibufferProductPlan` implements the multibuffer product algorithm; its code appears in Fig. 14.7. The method `open` materializes both the left-side and right-side records—the left side as a `MaterializeScan` and the right side as a temporary table. The method `blocksAccessed` needs to know the size of the materialized right-side table, so that it can calculate the number of chunks. Since this table does not exist until the plan is opened, the method estimates the size by using the estimate provided by `MaterializePlan`. The code for the methods `recordsOutput` and `distinctValues` is the same as in `ProductPlan` and is straightforward.

The code for `MultibufferProductScan` appears in Fig. 14.8. Its constructor determines the chunk size by calling `BufferNeeds.bestFactor` on the size of the right-side file. It then positions its left-side scan at the first record, opens a `ChunkScan` for the first chunk of the right side, and creates a `ProductScan` from these two scans. That is, the variable `prodscan` contains a basic product scan between the left-side scan and the current chunk. Most of the scan methods use this product scan. The exception is the method `next`.

The `next` method moves to the next record in the current product scan. If that scan has no more records, then the method closes that scan, creates a new product scan for the next chunk, and moves to its first record. The method returns `false` when there are no more chunks to process.

```
public class ChunkScan implements Scan {
   private List<RecordPage> buffs = new ArrayList<>();
   private Transaction tx;
   private String filename;
   private Layout layout;
   private int startbnum, endbnum, currentbnum;
   private RecordPage rp;
   private int currentslot;

   public ChunkScan(Transaction tx, String filename,
            Layout layout, int startbnum, int endbnum) {

      this.tx = tx;
      this.filename = filename;
      this.layout = layout;
      this.startbnum = startbnum;
      this.endbnum   = endbnum;
      for (int i=startbnum; i<=endbnum; i++) {
         BlockId blk = new BlockId(filename, i);
         buffs.add(new RecordPage(tx, blk, layout));
      }
      moveToBlock(startbnum);
   }

   public void close() {
      for (int i=0; i<buffs.size(); i++) {
         BlockId blk = new BlockId(filename, startbnum+i);
         tx.unpin(blk);
      }
   }

   public void beforeFirst() {
      moveToBlock(startbnum);
   }

   public boolean next() {
      currentslot = rp.nextAfter(currentslot);
      while (currentslot < 0) {
         if (currentbnum == endbnum)
            return false;
         moveToBlock(rp.block().number()+1);
         currentslot = rp.nextAfter(currentslot);
      }
      return true;
   }

   public int getInt(String fldname) {
      return rp.getInt(currentslot, fldname);
   }

   public String getString(String fldname) {
      return rp.getString(currentslot, fldname);
   }
```

Fig. 14.6 The code for the SimpleDB class `ChunkScan`

```
    public Constant getVal(String fldname) {
       if (layout.schema().type(fldname) == INTEGER)
          return new Constant(getInt(fldname));
       else
          return new Constant(getString(fldname));
    }

    public boolean hasField(String fldname) {
       return layout.schema().hasField(fldname);
    }

    private void moveToBlock(int blknum) {
       currentbnum = blknum;
       rp = buffs.get(currentbnum - startbnum);
       currentslot = -1;
    }
}
```

Fig. 14.6 (continued)

14.7 Hash Joins

Section 13.6 examined the mergejoin algorithm. Because that algorithm sorts both its input tables, its cost is determined by the size of the larger input table. This section considers a different join algorithm, called *hashjoin*. This algorithm has the property that its cost is determined by the size of the smaller input table. Thus this algorithm will be preferable to mergejoin when the input tables are of very different sizes.

14.7.1 The Hashjoin Algorithm

The idea behind the multibuffer product algorithm can be extended to computing the join two tables. This algorithm is called *hashjoin*, and appears in Fig. 14.9.

The hashjoin algorithm is recursive, based on the size of T2. If T2 is small enough to fit in the available buffers, then the algorithm joins T1 and T2 using a multibuffer product. If T2 is too large to fit into memory, then the algorithm uses hashing to reduce T2's size. It creates two sets of temporary tables: a set $\{V_0,...,V_{k-1}\}$ for T1 and a set $\{W_0,...,W_{k-1}\}$ for T2. These temporary tables act as buckets for the hash function. Each T1 record is hashed on its join field and placed in the bucket associated with the hash value. Each T2 record is hashed similarly. The corresponding tables (V_i, W_i) are then joined recursively.

It should be clear that all records having the same join value will hash to the same bucket. Thus you can perform the join of T1 and T2 by independently joining Vi with Wi, for each `i`. Since each Wi will be smaller than T2, the recursion will eventually stop.

```
public class MultibufferProductPlan implements Plan {
   private Transaction tx;
   private Plan lhs, rhs;
   private Schema schema = new Schema();

   public MultibufferProductPlan(Transaction tx, Plan lhs, Plan rhs) {
      this.tx = tx;
      this.lhs = new MaterializePlan(tx, lhs);
      this.rhs = rhs;
      schema.addAll(lhs.schema());
      schema.addAll(rhs.schema());
   }

   public Scan open() {
      Scan leftscan = lhs.open();
      TempTable t = copyRecordsFrom(rhs);
      return new MultibufferProductScan(tx, leftscan, t.tableName(),
                                        t.getLayout());
   }

   public int blocksAccessed() {
      // this guesses at the # of chunks
      int avail = tx.availableBuffs();
      int size = new MaterializePlan(tx, rhs).blocksAccessed();
      int numchunks = size / avail;
      return rhs.blocksAccessed() +
             (lhs.blocksAccessed() * numchunks);
   }

   public int recordsOutput() {
      return lhs.recordsOutput() * rhs.recordsOutput();
   }

   public int distinctValues(String fldname) {
      if (lhs.schema().hasField(fldname))
         return lhs.distinctValues(fldname);
      else
         return rhs.distinctValues(fldname);
   }

   public Schema schema() {
      return schema;
   }

   private TempTable copyRecordsFrom(Plan p) {
      Scan   src = p.open();
      Schema sch = p.schema();
      TempTable tt = new TempTable(tx, sch);
      UpdateScan dest = (UpdateScan) tt.open();
      while (src.next()) {
         dest.insert();
         for (String fldname : sch.fields())
```

Fig. 14.7 The code for the SimpleDB class `MultibufferProductPlan`

```
                dest.setVal(fldname, src.getVal(fldname));
            }
            src.close();
            dest.close();
            return tt;
        }
    }
```

Fig. 14.7 (continued)

Note that each recursive call to the hashjoin algorithm must use a different hash function. The reason is that all of the records in a temporary table are there because they all hashed to the same value. A different hash function ensures that those records will be evenly distributed among the new temporary tables.

The code of Fig. 14.9 also says to re-choose the value for `k` for each recursive call. You could instead choose `k` once and use it throughout all of the calls. Exercise 14.11 asks you to consider the trade-offs involved in these two options.

You can improve the efficiency of the multibuffer product somewhat, by being careful how you search the blocks for matching records. Given a record of T1, the algorithm needs to find the matching records from T2. The strategy taken by multibuffer product is to simply search all of T2. Although this search does not incur any additional disk accesses, it could certainly be made more efficient by means of appropriate internal data structures. For example, you could store references to the T2 records in a hash table or binary search tree. (In fact, any implementation of the Java *Map* interface would work.) Given a T1 record, the algorithm would look up its join value in the data structure and find the references to the records of T2 having this join value, thereby avoiding the need to search T2.

14.7.2 An Example of Hashjoin

As a concrete example, let's use hashjoin to implement the join of the ENROLL and STUDENT tables, using the records from Fig. 1.1. Make the following assumptions:

- The STUDENT table is on the right side of the join.
- Two STUDENT records fit in a block, and two ENROLL records fit in a block.
- Three buckets are used; that is, `k` = 3.
- The hash function is `h(n)` = `n%3`.

The nine STUDENT records fit into five blocks. Since `k` = 3, the STUDENT records cannot all fit into memory at once, and so you hash. The resulting buckets appear in Fig. 14.10.

The student ID values 3, 6, and 9 have a hash value of 0. Thus the ENROLL records for those students are placed in V0, and the STUDENT records for those students are placed in W0. Similarly, the records for students 1, 4, and 7 are placed in

```
public class MultibufferProductScan implements Scan {
   private Transaction tx;
   private Scan lhsscan, rhsscan=null, prodscan;
   private String filename;
   private Layout layout;
   private int chunksize, nextblknum, filesize;

   public MultibufferProductScan(Transaction tx, Scan lhsscan,
                                 String filename, Layout layout) {
      this.tx = tx;
      this.lhsscan = lhsscan;
      this.filename = filename;
      this.layout = layout;
      filesize = tx.size(filename);
      int available = tx.availableBuffs();
      chunksize = BufferNeeds.bestFactor(available, filesize);
      beforeFirst();
   }

   public void beforeFirst() {
      nextblknum = 0;
      useNextChunk();
   }

   public boolean next() {
      while (!prodscan.next())
         if (!useNextChunk())
         return false;
      return true;
   }

   public void close() {
      prodscan.close();
   }

   public Constant getVal(String fldname) {
      return prodscan.getVal(fldname);
   }

   public int getInt(String fldname) {
      return prodscan.getInt(fldname);
   }

   public String getString(String fldname) {
      return prodscan.getString(fldname);
   }

   public boolean hasField(String fldname) {
      return prodscan.hasField(fldname);
   }
```

Fig. 14.8 The code for the SimpleDB class `MultibufferProductScan`

```
    private boolean useNextChunk() {
        if (rhsscan != null)
            rhsscan.close();
        if (nextblknum >= filesize)
            return false;
        int end = nextblknum + chunksize - 1;
        if (end >= filesize)
            end = filesize - 1;
        rhsscan = new ChunkScan(tx, filename, layout, nextblknum, end);
        lhsscan.beforeFirst();
        prodscan = new ProductScan(lhsscan, rhsscan);
        nextblknum = end + 1;
        return true;
    }
}
```

Fig. 14.8 (continued)

Let T1 and T2 be the tables to be joined.

1. Choose a value `k` that is less than the number of available buffers.
2. If the size of T2 is no more than `k` blocks, then:
   a) Join T1 and T2, using a multibuffer product followed by a selection on the join predicate.
   b) Return.

// Otherwise:

3. Choose a hash function that returns a value between 0 and `k-1`.
4. For the table T1:
   a) Open a scan for `k` temporary tables.
   b) For each record of T1:
      i. Hash the record's join field, to get the hash value `h`.
      ii. Copy the record to the `h`th temporary table.
   b) Close the temporary table scans.
5. Repeat Step 4 for the table T2.
6. For each `i` between 0 and `k-1`:
   a) Let `Vi` be the `i`th temporary table of T1.
   b) Let `Wi` be the `i`th temporary table of T2.
   c) Recursively perform the hashjoin of `Vi` and `Wi`.

Fig. 14.9 The *hashjoin* algorithm

V1 and W1, and the records for students 2, 5, and 8 are placed in V2 and W2. You now are able to recursively join each Vi table with its corresponding Wi table.

Since each Wi table has two blocks, they will each fit into memory; thus each of the three recursive joins can be performed as a multibuffer product. In particular, join Vi with Wi by reading all of Wi into memory. Then scan Vi; for each record, search Wi for any matching records.

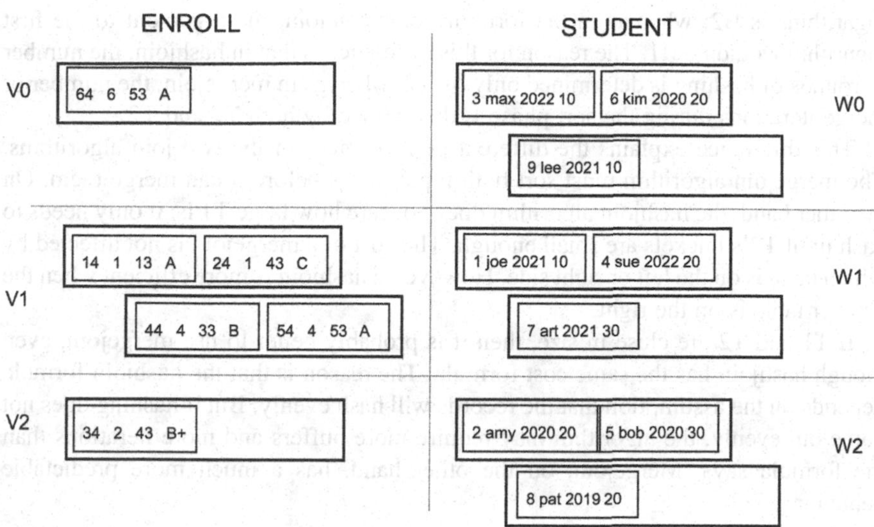

Fig. 14.10 Using hashjoin to join ENROLL with STUDENT

14.7.3 Cost Analysis

To analyze the cost of using hashjoin to join T1 with T2, suppose that the materialized records in T1 require B1 blocks and that the records in T2 require B2 blocks. Choose k to be an nth root of B2; that is, B2 = k^n. Then assuming that the records hash evenly, you can calculate the costs as follows:

The first round of hashing will produce *k* temporary tables; each of T2's tables will have k^{n-1} blocks. When you recursively hash these temporary tables, you will be left with k^2 temporary tables, each of which will have k^{n-2} blocks. Continuing, T2 will eventually wind up with k^{n-1} temporary tables, having k block each. These tables can then be joined (together with their corresponding tables from T1) using multibuffer product.

Consequently, there will be n-1 rounds of hashing. The first round has cost B1 + B2, plus the cost of reading the input. During subsequent rounds, each block of each temporary table will be read once and written once; thus the cost for those rounds is 2(B1 + B2). The multibuffer products occur during the scanning phase. Each block of the temporary tables will be read once, for a cost of B1 + B2.

Combining these values implies that using hashjoin to join tables of size B_1 and B_2 using k buffers has the following costs:

- Preprocessing cost = $(2B_1\log_k B_2 - 3B_1) + (2B_2\log_k B_2 - 3B_2)$ + the cost of the input
- Scanning cost = $B_1 + B_2$

Amazingly enough, this cost is almost identical to the cost of a multibuffer mergejoin! There is one difference: in this formula, the argument to both of the logarithms is B2; whereas in the formula for mergejoin, the argument to the first logarithm would be B1. The reason for this difference is that in hashjoin, the number of rounds of hashing is determined only by T2, whereas in mergejoin, the number of merge iterations during the sort phase is determined by both T1 and T2.

This difference explains the different performances of the two join algorithms. The mergejoin algorithm must sort both input tables before it can merge them. On the other hand, the hashjoin algorithm does not care how large T1 is; it only needs to hash until T2's buckets are small enough. The cost of a mergejoin is not affected by which table is on the left or right side. However, a hashjoin is more efficient when the smaller table is on the right.

If T1 and T2 are close in size, then it is probably better to use mergejoin, even though hashjoin has the same cost formula. The reason is that the hashjoin formula depends on the assumption that the records will hash evenly. But if hashing does not come out evenly, the algorithm may require more buffers and more iterations than the formula says. Mergejoin, on the other hand, has a much more predictable behavior.

14.8 Comparing the Join Algorithms

This chapter has examined two ways to implement a join of two tables, mergejoin and hashjoin, and Chap. 12 examined indexjoin. This section uses the following join query to investigate the relative benefits of these three implementations:

```
select SName, Grade from STUDENT, ENROLL where SId=StudentId
```

Assume that the tables have the sizes given in Fig. 7.8, 200 buffers are available and that ENROLL has an index on `StudentId`.

Consider the mergejoin algorithm. This algorithm needs to sort both ENROLL and STUDENT before merging them. The ENROLL table has 50,000 blocks. The square root of 50,000 is 244, which is more than the number of available buffers. Thus you must allocate the cube root, which is 37 buffers. The split phase will create 1352 runs, each of which is 37 blocks. A single merge iteration will result in 37 runs of size 1352 blocks. Thus preprocessing the ENROLL table requires two reads and two writes of the records, or 200,000 total block accesses. The STUDENT table has 4500 blocks. The square root of 4500 is 68, and 68 buffers are available. So you can use 68 buffers to split the 4500 STUDENT blocks into 68 runs of size 68. This splitting takes 9000 block accesses and is all the preprocessing that is needed. Merging the two sorted tables requires another 54,500 block accesses, for a total cost of 263,500 block accesses.

Consider now the hashjoin algorithm. This algorithm is most efficient when the smallest table is on the right; thus ENROLL will be the left-side table and STUDENT will be the right-side table. You can use 68 buffers to hash STUDENT into 68 buckets, each of which will contain about 68 blocks. Similarly, you can use the same 68 buffers to hash ENROLL into 68 buckets, each of which will contain about 736 blocks. Then recursively join the corresponding buckets. Each of these sub-joins can be performed using multibuffer product. That is, allocate 68 buffers to hold the entire STUDENT bucket, and allocate another buffer for a sequential scan through the ENROLL bucket. Each bucket gets scanned once. Summing the costs, the ENROLL and STUDENT records have been read once, and the buckets have been written once and read once, for a total of 163,500 block accesses.

The indexjoin implementation scans through the STUDENT table; for each STUDENT record, it uses the record's `SId` value to search the index and look up the matching ENROLL records. Thus the STUDENT table will be accessed once (for 4500 block accesses), and the ENROLL table will be accessed once for each matching record. However, since every ENROLL record matches some STUDENT record, the ENROLL table will potentially require 1,500,000 block accesses. The query therefore requires 1,504,500 block accesses.

This analysis shows that under these assumptions, hashjoin is the fastest, followed by mergejoin and then indexjoin. The reason why hashjoin is so efficient is that one of the tables (i.e., STUDENT) is reasonably small compared to the number of available buffers, and the other (i.e., ENROLL) is much larger. Suppose instead that 1000 buffers were available. Then mergejoin would be able to sort ENROLL without any merge iterations, and the total cost would be 163,500 block accesses, the same as hashjoin. The indexjoin algorithm is by far the least efficient implementation for this query. The reason is that indexes are not useful when there are many matching data records, and in this query, every ENROLL record matches.

Now consider a variation of this query that has an additional selection on *GradYear*:

```
select SName, Grade from STUDENT, ENROLL
where SId=StudentId and GradYear=2020
```

Consider first the mergejoin implementation. There are only 900 relevant STUDENT records, which fit into 90 blocks. Thus it is possible to sort the STUDENT records by reading them into 90 buffers and using an internal sort algorithm to sort them. Thus only 4500 block accesses are needed. But the cost of processing ENROLL is unchanged, so the query would require a total of 204,500 block accesses, only a slight improvement over mergejoin on the original query.

The hashjoin implementation would recognize that the 90 blocks of STUDENT records will fit directly into 90 buffers, with no hashing required. Thus the join can be performed by a single scan of both tables, which is 54,500 block accesses.

The indexjoin implementation would read all 4500 STUDENT records to find the 900 students from 2020. These records will match with 1/50th (or 50,000) of the ENROLL records, resulting in about 50,000 block accesses of ENROLL, or 54,500 total block accesses.

Thus, hashjoin and indexjoin are comparable, but mergejoin is significantly worse. The reason is that mergejoin is forced to preprocess both tables, even though one is considerably smaller.

For a final example, modify the above query so that there is an even more restrictive selection on STUDENT:

```
select SName, Grade from STUDENT, ENROLL
where SId=StudentId and SId=3
```

Now the output table consists of the 34 records corresponding to the enrollments for this single student. In this case, indexjoin will be the most efficient. It scans the entire 4500 blocks of STUDENT, traverses the index, and looks up the 34 ENROLL records, for a total of about 4534 block accesses (not counting index traversal costs). The hashjoin implementation has the same cost as before. It will need to scan STUDENT once (to materialize the single record) and ENROLL once (to find all of the matching records), for a total of 54,500 block accesses. And mergejoin will have to preprocess ENROLL and STUDENT the same as before, for a total of 204,500 block accesses.

This analysis demonstrates that mergejoin is most efficient when both of its input tables are relatively the same size. Hashjoin is often better when at the input tables are of disparate sizes. And indexjoin is better when the number of output records is small.

14.9 Chapter Summary

- Non-materialized scans are very frugal when it comes to buffer usage. In particular:
  - A table scan uses exactly one buffer.
  - Scans for select, project, and product use no additional buffers.
  - A static hash or B-tree index requires one additional buffer (for queries).
- The *mergesort* algorithm can take advantage of multiple buffers when it creates the initial runs and when it merges them. It chooses $k = \sqrt[n]{B}$, where B is the size of the input table and n is the smallest integer such that k is less than the number of available buffers. The resulting algorithm is called *multibuffer mergesort*, and is as follows:
  - Allocate k buffers from the buffer manager.
  - Read k blocks of the table at a time into the k buffers, and use an internal sorting algorithm to sort them into a k-block run.
  - Perform merge iterations on the resulting runs using k temporary tables, until there are no more than k runs remaining. Since the splitting phase results in B/k runs, there will be n-2 merge iterations.
  - Merge the final k runs during the scanning phase.
- The *multibuffer product* algorithm is an efficient implementation of the product operator and works as follows:

1. Materialize the RHS table as temporary table T2. Let `B2` be the number of blocks in T2.
2. Let `i` be the smallest number such that `B2/i` is less than the number of available buffers.
3. Treat T2 as `i` *chunks* of `k` blocks each. For each chunk *C*:
   (a) Read all of *C*'s blocks into `k` buffers.
   (b) Take the product of T1 and *C*.
   (c) Unpin *C*'s blocks.

That is, T1's blocks will be read once for each chunk. Consequently, the number of blocks in the product is

```
B2 + B1*B2/k
```

- Not all buffer allocations are useful. Multibuffer mergesort can only use a buffer allocation that is a root of the size of its table. Multibuffer product can only use an allocation that is a factor of the size of its right-side table.
- The *hashjoin* algorithm is an extension of multibuffer product that works as follows:
  1. Choose a value `k` that is less than the number of available buffers.
  2. If T2 fits into `k` buffers, use a multibuffer product to join T1 and T2.
  3. Otherwise, hash T1 and T2, using `k` temporary tables each.
  4. Recursively perform hashjoin on the corresponding hashed buckets.

14.10 Suggested Reading

The article Shapiro (1986) describes and analyzes several join algorithms and their buffer requirements. The article Yu and Cornell (1993) considers the cost-effectiveness of buffer usage. It argues that buffers are a valuable global resource and that instead of allocating as many buffers as it can (which is what SimpleDB does), a query should allocate the number of buffers that will be most cost-effective for the entire system. The article gives an algorithm that can be used to determine the optimal buffer allocation.

Shapiro, L. (1986) Join processing in database systems with large main memories. *ACM Transactions on Database Systems, 11*(3), 239–264.

Yu, P., & Cornell, D. (1993) *Buffer management based on return on consumption in a multi-query environment. VLDB Journal,* 2(1), 1–37.

14.11 Exercises

Conceptual Exercises

14.1. Suppose that a database system contains so many buffers that they never all are pinned at the same time. Is this just a waste of physical memory, or is there an advantage to having an excess number of buffers?

14.2. Large amounts of RAM are becoming increasingly cheap. Suppose that a database system has more buffers than there are blocks in the database. Can all the buffers be used effectively?

14.3. Suppose that the database system contains enough buffers to hold every block of the database. Such a system is called a *main-memory* database system, because it can read the entire database into buffers once and then execute queries without any additional block accesses.

(a) Does any component of the database system become unnecessary in this case?
(b) Should the functioning of any component be significantly different?
(c) The query plan estimation functions certainly need changing, because it no longer makes sense to evaluate queries based on the number of block accesses. Suggest a better function, which would more accurately model the cost of evaluating a query.

14.4. Consider the description of multibuffer sorting in Sect. 14.5, which suggests that the methods `splitIntoRuns` and `doAMergeIteration` should each determine how many buffers to allocate.

(a) Another option would be for the `open` method to determine a value for `numbuffs` and pass it into both methods. Explain why this is a less desirable option.
(b) Yet another option would be to allocate the buffers in the `SortPlan` constructor. Explain why this is an even worse option.

14.5. Suppose that the class `SortPlan` has been revised to implement the multibuffer sorting algorithm of Fig. 14.2, and consider the first mergejoin example in Sect. 14.6.

(a) How many buffers are used in the scanning phase of that mergejoin scan?
(b) Suppose that only 100 buffers were available (instead of 200). Suppose that buffers were allocated for ENROLL before STUDENT. How would they be allocated?
(c) Suppose that only 100 buffers were available (instead of 200). Suppose that buffers were allocated for STUDENT before ENROLL. How would they be allocated?
(d) Another option would be to fully materialize either of the sorted tables, before joining them. Calculate the cost of this option.

14.6. Consider the following algorithm for implementing the groupby operator:

1. Create and open k temporary tables.
2. For each input record:
   (a) Hash the record on its grouping fields.
   (b) Copy the record to the corresponding temporary table.
3. Close the temporary tables.
4. For each temporary table:
   Perform the sort-based groupby algorithm on that table.

(a) Explain why this algorithm works.
(b) Calculate the preprocessing and scanning costs of this algorithm.
(c) Explain why this algorithm is in general not as good as the sort-based groupby algorithm of Fig. 13.14.
(d) Explain why this algorithm might be useful in a parallel-processing environment.

14.7. Consider the example of multibuffer product in Sect. 14.3 that took the product of two 1000-block tables. Suppose that only one buffer were available for table T2, that is, suppose that $k = 1$.

(a) Calculate the number of block accesses required to take the product.
(b) This number is significantly less than the block accesses required by the basic product algorithm of Chap. 8, even though it uses the same number of buffers. Explain why.

14.8. The multibuffer product algorithm requires that the RHS table be materialized (so that it can be chunked). However, the `MultibufferProductPlan` code also materializes the LHS scan. Not materializing the left side can cause problems with buffer use and with efficiency. Explain why, and give an example of each.

14.9. Rewrite the hashjoin algorithm of Fig. 14.9 so that it is nonrecursive. Make sure that all of the hashing is performed during the preprocessing stage and that the merging is performed during the scanning stage.

14.10. The hashjoin algorithm of Fig. 14.9 uses the same value of k to hash the records of both T1 and T2. Explain why using different values of k will not work.

14.11. The hashjoin algorithm of Fig. 14.9 re-chooses the value of k each time it is called.

(a) Explain why it would also be correct to choose the value of *k* once, and pass it into each recursive call.
(b) Analyze the trade-offs of these two possibilities. Which do you prefer?

14.12. Suppose that you revise the hashjoin algorithm of Fig. 14.9 so that step 6 uses mergejoin to join the individual buckets, instead of calling hashjoin recursively. Give a cost analysis of this algorithm, and compare the block accesses to the original hashjoin algorithm.

14.13. Suppose that the STUDENT table has indexes on `SId` and `MajorId`. For each of the following SQL queries, use the statistics of Fig. 7.8 to calculate the cost of implementations that use mergejoin, hashjoin, or indexjoin.

```
(a) select SName, DName from STUDENT, DEPT
    where MajorId=DId
(b) select SName, DName from STUDENT, DEPT
    where MajorId=DId and GradYear=2020
(c) select DName from STUDENT, DEPT
    where MajorId=DId and SId=1
(d) select SName from STUDENT, ENROLL
    where SId=StudentId and Grade='F'
```

Programming Exercises

14.14. The SimpleDB class `BufferNeeds` does not reserve buffers from the buffer manager.

(a) List some possible problems that could occur in SimpleDB that would be alleviated if the buffers were actually reserved. Are there any advantages to not reserving buffers?
(b) Redesign the SimpleDB buffer manager so that it allows transactions to reserve buffers. (Be sure to consider the case where transaction T1 pins block b to a reserved buffer and then transaction T2 wants to pin b. What should you do?)
(c) Implement your design, and modify `BufferNeeds` appropriately.

14.15. In Exercise 13.10, you modified the class `SortPlan` so that it constructs initial runs that are one block long. Modify the code so that it constructs initial runs that are `k` blocks long, as discussed in Sect. 14.5.

14.16. In Exercise 13.11, you modified the class `SortPlan` to use a one-block long staging area for computing the initial runs. Modify the code so that it uses a `k`-block long staging area.

14.17. In Exercise 13.13, you modified the class `SortPlan` to merge `k` runs at a time, where the value of *k* was passed into the constructor. Modify the code so that the value of `k` is determined by the number of initial runs, as discussed in Sect. 14.5.

14.18. The multibuffer product algorithm is usually most efficient when its smallest input table is on the right side.

(a) Explain why.
(b) Revise the code for `MultiBufferProductPlan` so that it always chooses the smaller input table to be on the right side of the scan.

14.19. Revise the code for `MultiBufferProductPlan` so that it materializes its left-side and right-side tables only when necessary.

14.20. Write SimpleDB code to implement the hashjoin algorithm.

Chapter 15
Query Optimization

The basic planner of Chap. 10 uses a simple algorithm to create its query plans. Unfortunately, those plans often entail significantly more block accesses than they need, for two basic reasons: the operations are performed in a suboptimal order, and they do not take advantage of the indexed, materialized, or multibuffer implementations of Chaps. 12–14.

This chapter examines how the planner can address these problems and generate efficient plans. This task is called *query optimization*. The most efficient plan for a query can be several orders of magnitude faster than a naïve plan, which is the difference between a database engine that can respond to queries in a reasonable amount of time and a database engine that is completely unusable. A good query optimization strategy is therefore a vital part of every commercial database system.

15.1 Equivalent Query Trees

Two tables are *equivalent* if an SQL query cannot tell them apart. That is, two equivalent tables contain exactly the same records, although not necessarily in the same order. Two queries are *equivalent* if their output tables are always equivalent, regardless of the contents of the database. This section considers equivalences between relational algebra queries. Since these queries can be expressed as trees, an equivalence between two queries can often be thought of as a transformation between their trees. The following subsections consider these transformations.

15.1.1 Rearranging Products

Let T1 and T2 be two tables. Recall that the product of T1 and T2 is the table containing all combinations of records from T1 and T2. That is, whenever there are

E. Sciore, *Database Design and Implementation*, Data-Centric Systems and Applications, https://doi.org/10.1007/978-3-030-33836-7_15

records r1 in T1 and r2 in T2, then the combined record (r1, r2) is in the output table. Note that this combined record is essentially the same as (r2, r1), since the order in which fields appear in a record is irrelevant. But since (r2, r1) is the record produced by the product of T2 and T1, the product operator must be commutative. That is:

```
product(T1, T2) ≡ product(T2, T1)
```

A similar argument (see Exercise 15.1) can show that the product operator is associative. That is:

```
product(product(T1, T2), T3) ≡ product(T1, product(T2, T3))
```

In terms of query trees, the first equivalence swaps the left and right children of a product node. The second equivalence applies when two product nodes are next to each other. In that case, the inner product node moves from being the left child of the outer product node to being its right child; the ordering of the other child nodes stays the same. Figure 15.1 illustrates these equivalences.

These two equivalences can be used repeatedly to transform trees of product nodes. For example, consider Fig. 15.2, which consists of two trees corresponding to the query:

```
select SName
from STUDENT, ENROLL, SECTION, COURSE, DEPT
```

The tree in Fig. 15.2a is created by the basic planner. Two steps are required to transform this tree into the tree of Fig. 15.2b. The first step applies the commutative

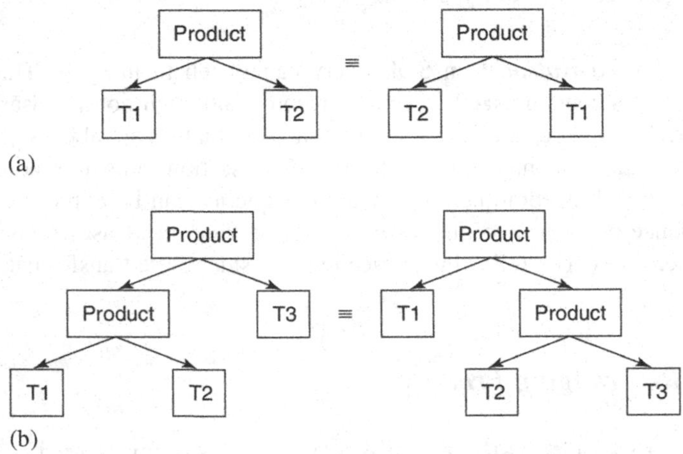

Fig. 15.1 Equivalences involving the product operator. (**a**) The *product* operator is commutative, (**b**) the *product* operator is associative

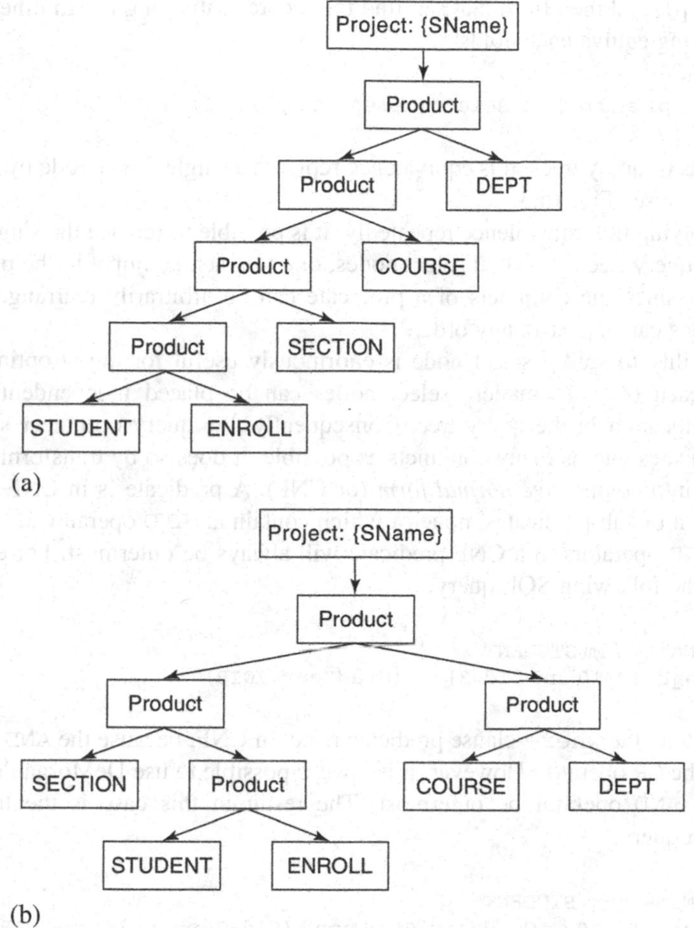

Fig. 15.2 Rearranging product nodes to produce an equivalent query tree. (**a**) A tree produced by the basic planner, (**b**) the result of applying associative and commutative transformations

rule to the product node above SECTION; the second step applies the associative rule to the product node above DEPT.

In fact, it can be shown (see Exercise 15.2) that you can use these two rules to transform any tree of product nodes into any other tree having the same nodes. That is, product operations can be performed in any order.

15.1.2 Splitting Selections

Suppose that a selection predicate p is the conjunction of two predicates p1 and p2. It is possible to find the records satisfying p in two steps: First, find the records satisfying p1, and then from that set, find the records satisfying p2. In other words, the following equivalence holds:

```
select(T, p1 and p2) ≡ select(select(T, p1), p2)
```

In terms of query trees, this equivalence replaces a single select node by a pair of select nodes; see Fig. 15.3.

By applying this equivalence repeatedly, it is possible to replace the single select node in a query tree by several select nodes, one for each conjunct in the predicate. Moreover, since the conjuncts of a predicate can be arbitrarily rearranged, these select nodes can appear in any order.

The ability to split a select node is enormously useful for query optimization, because each of the "smaller" select nodes can be placed independently at its optimum location in the query tree. Consequently, the query optimizer strives to split predicates into as many conjuncts as possible. It does so by transforming each predicate into *conjunctive normal form* (or CNF). A predicate is in CNF if it is a conjunction of sub-predicates, none of which contain an AND operator.

The AND operators in a CNF predicate will always be outermost. For example, consider the following SQL query:

```
select SName from STUDENT
where (MajorId=10 and SId=3) or (GradYear=2018)
```

As written, the `where`-clause predicate is not in CNF, because the AND operator is inside the OR operator. However, it is always possible to use DeMorgan's laws to make the AND operator be outermost. The result in this case is the following equivalent query:

```
select SName from STUDENT
where (MajorId=10 or GradYear=2018) and (SId=3 or GradYear=2018)
```

The predicate of this query has two conjuncts, which can now be split.

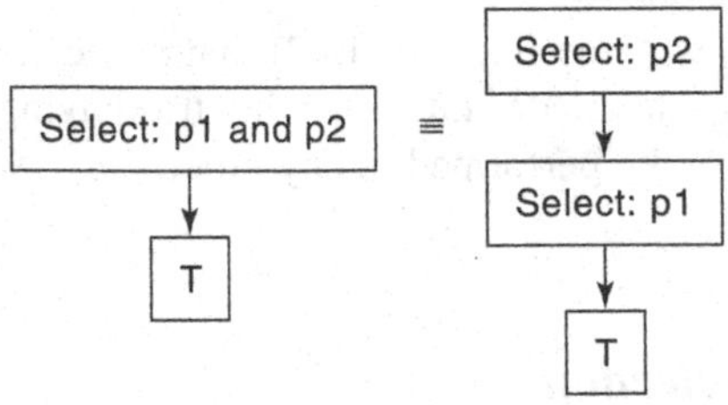

Fig. 15.3 Splitting a select node

15.1.3 Moving Selections Within a Tree

The following query retrieves the name of every student majoring in math:

```
select SName from STUDENT, DEPT
where DName = 'math' and MajorId = DId
```

Its where-clause predicate is in CNF and contains two conjuncts. Figure 15.4a depicts the query tree created by the basic planner, modified so that there are two select nodes. Consider first the selection on DName. The product node below it outputs all combinations of STUDENT and DEPT records; the select node then retains only those combinations in which DName has the value "math." This is exactly the same set of records you would get if you first selected the math-department record from DEPT and then returned all combinations of STUDENT records with that record. In other words, since the selection applies only to the DEPT table, it is possible to "push" the selection inside the product, giving the equivalent tree depicted in Fig. 15.4b.

Now consider the join predicate MajorId=DId. It is not possible push this selection inside the product, because the predicate mentions fields from both STUDENT and DEPT. For example, pushing the selection above STUDENT would produce a meaningless query because the selection would reference a field that is not in STUDENT.

The following equivalence generalizes this discussion. It holds when predicate p refers only to fields of T1:

```
select(product(T1, T2), p) ≡ product(select(T1, p), T2)
```

This equivalence is depicted in Fig. 15.5.

This equivalence can be applied repeatedly to a select node, pushing it down the query tree as far as possible. For example, consider Fig. 15.6. The query of part

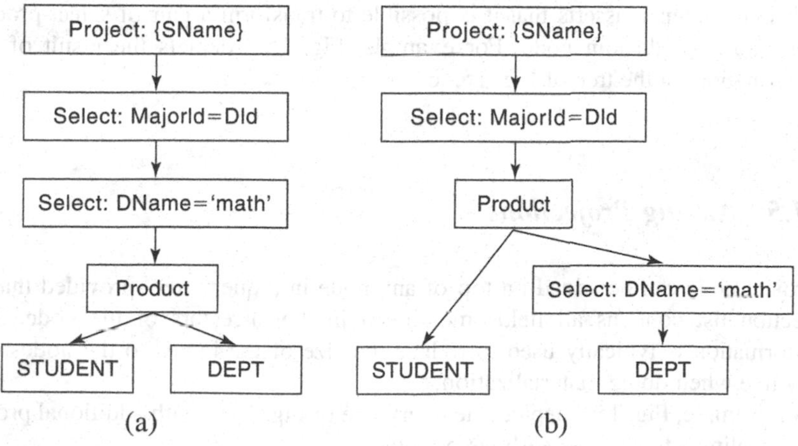

Fig. 15.4 Pushing a select node down the query tree

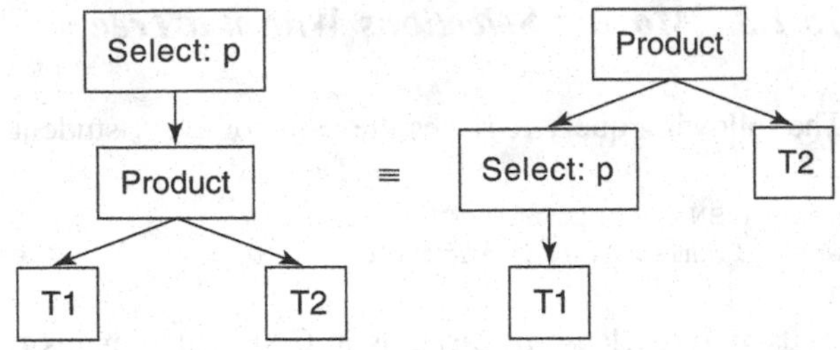

Fig. 15.5 Pushing a select node inside a product

(a) returns the name of those students who failed a math course in 2018. Parts (b) and (c) depict two equivalent trees for this query. Figure 15.6b depicts the query tree created by the basic planner. Figure 15.6c depicts the query tree resulting from splitting the select node and pushing the smaller select nodes down the tree.

The equivalence of Fig. 15.5 can also be applied in reverse, moving a select node up the tree past one or more product nodes. Moreover, it is easily shown that a select node can always be moved past another select node in either direction and that a select node can be moved past a project or groupby node whenever it is meaningful to do so (see Exercise 15.4). It therefore follows that a select node can be placed anywhere in the query tree, provided that its predicate only mentions fields of the underlying subtree.

15.1.4 Identifying Join Operators

Recall that the join operator is defined in terms of the select and product operators:

```
join(T1, T2, p) ≡ select(product(T1, T2), p)
```

This equivalence asserts that it is possible to transform a pair of select-product nodes into a single join node. For example, Fig. 15.7 depicts the result of this transformation on the tree of Fig. 15.6c.

15.1.5 Adding Projections

A project node can be added on top of any node in a query tree, provided that its projection list contains all fields mentioned in the ancestors of the node. This transformation is typically used to reduce the size of the inputs to the nodes of a query tree when doing materialization.

For example, Fig. 15.8 depicts the query tree of Fig. 15.7, with additional project nodes to eliminate fields as early as possible.

```
select SName
from STUDENT, ENROLL, SECTION, COURSE, DEPT
where SId=StudentId and SectionId=SectId and CourseId=CId
and DeptId=DId and DName='math' and Grade='F'
and YearOffered=2018
```

(a)

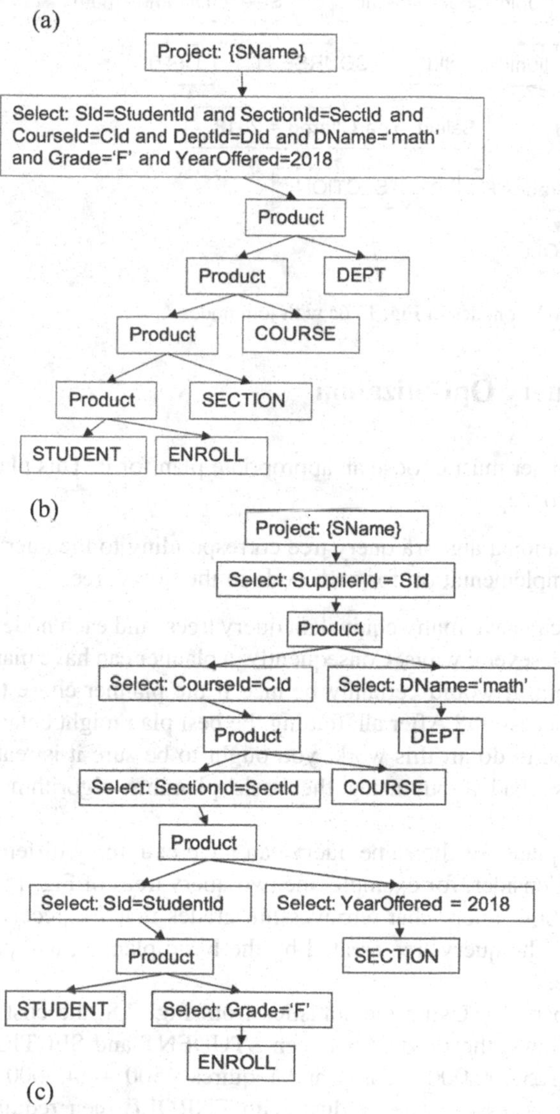

Fig. 15.6 Pushing several selections down a query tree. (**a**) The SQL query, (**b**) the query tree created by the basic planner, (**c**) the query tree resulting from pushing select nodes

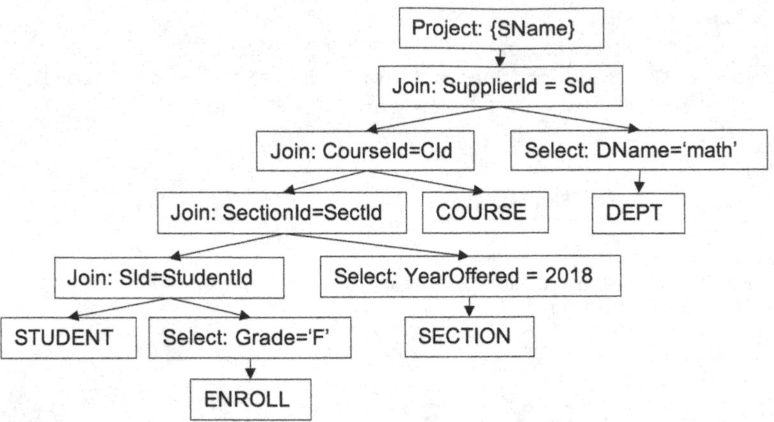

Fig. 15.7 Replacing the select-product nodes in Fig. 15.6c with join nodes

15.2 The Need for Query Optimization

Given an SQL query, the planner must choose an appropriate plan for it. This plan-generation activity entails two steps:

- The planner chooses a relational algebra query tree corresponding to the query.
- The planner chooses an implementation for each node in the query tree.

In general, an SQL query can have many equivalent query trees, and each node in the tree can be implemented in several ways. Consequently, a planner can have many potential plans to choose from. It would certainly be nice if the planner chose the most efficient plan, but is it necessary? After all, finding the best plan might entail a lot of work. Before you agree to do all this work, you ought to be sure it is really worth the effort. What is so bad about using the basic planning algorithm of Chap. 10?

It turns out that different plans for the same query can have extremely different numbers of block accesses. Consider, for example, the two query trees of Fig. 15.9. Part (a) of this figure is an SQL query that retrieves the grades that Joe received during 2020. Part (b) depicts the query tree created by the basic planner, and part (c) depicts an equivalent tree.

Consider the plan from part (b). Using the statistics from Fig. 7.8, the cost of this plan is calculated as follows: the product between STUDENT and SECTION has 45,000 × 25,000 = 1,125,000,000 records and requires 4500 + (45,000 × 2500) = 112,504,500 block accesses. The product with ENROLL then requires 112,504,500 + (1,125,000,000 × 50,000) = 56,250,112,504,500 block accesses. The select and project nodes require no additional block accesses. Thus, this plan requires over 56 trillion block accesses! If you assume just 1 ms per block access, a database engine would take about 1780 years to answer this query.

Now consider the query tree from part (c). Assume that there is one student named "joe." In this case, the selection on STUDENT requires 4500 block accesses

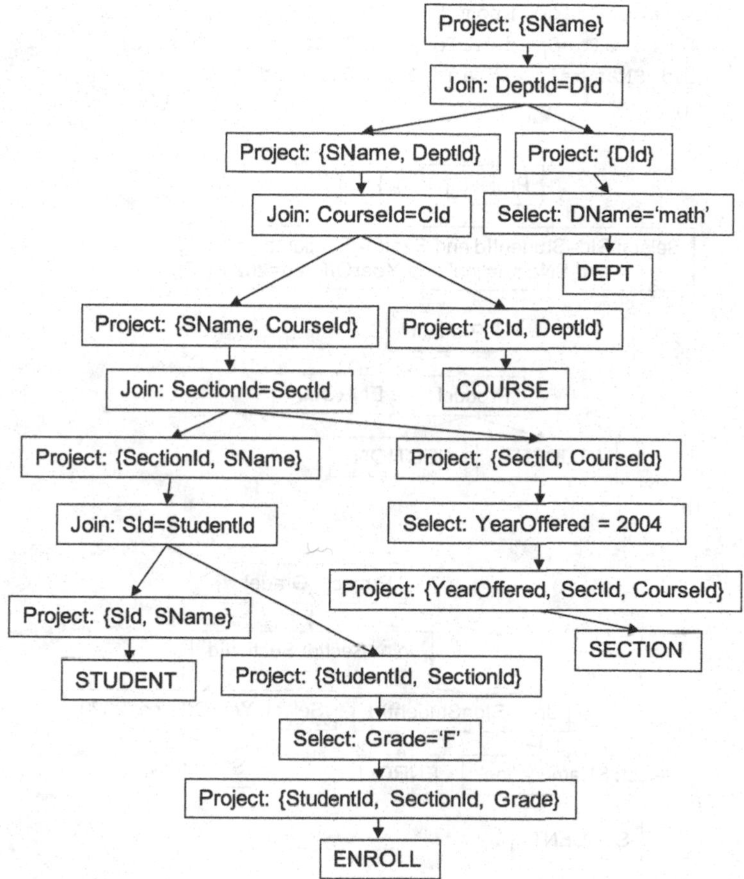

Fig. 15.8 Adding projections to the query tree of Fig. 15.7

and outputs 1 record. The join with ENROLL requires 4500 + (1 × 50,000) = 54,500 block accesses and outputs 34 records. And the join with SECTION requires 54,500 + (34 × 2500) = 139,500 block accesses. At 1 ms per block access, executing this plan would take about 2.3 minutes.

The cost reduction from 1780 years to 2.3 minutes is nothing short of amazing and demonstrates how utterly worthless the basic planning algorithm is. No client can afford to wait a thousand years to get the answer to a query. If a database engine is to be useful, its planner must be sophisticated enough to construct reasonable query trees.

Although 2.3 minutes is not an intolerable execution time, the planner can do even better by using other implementations for the nodes in the query tree. Consider again the query tree from part (c), and assume that ENROLL has an index on `StudentId`. The plan of Fig. 15.10 is then possible.

Most of the plans in this figure use the basic plan classes of Chap. 10. The two exceptions are `p4` and `p7`. Plan `p4` performs an index join. For each selected

```
select Grade from STUDENT, SECTION, ENROLL
where SId=StudentId and SectId=SectionId
and SName='joe' and YearOffered=2020
```

(a)

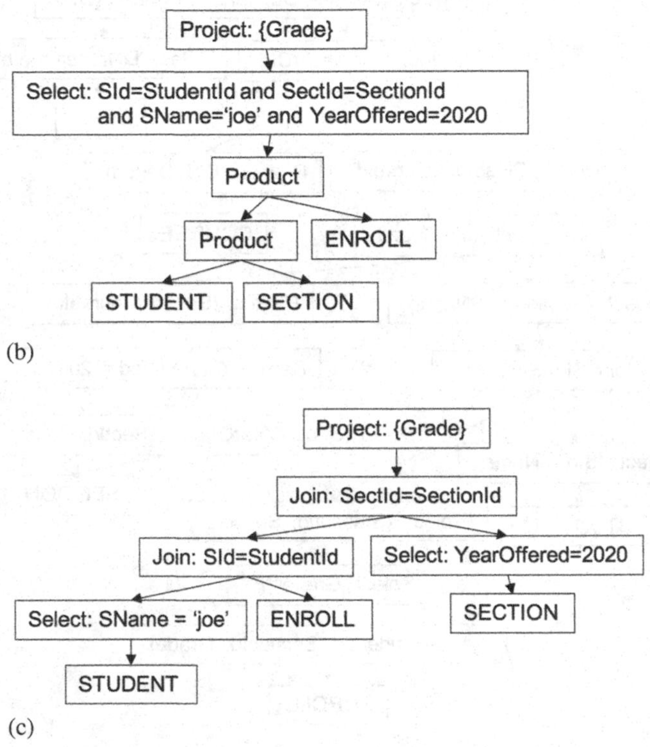

Fig. 15.9 Which query tree results in the better plan? (**a**) The SQL query, (**b**) the query tree produced by the basic planner, (**c**) an equivalent query tree

STUDENT record, the index on `StudentId` is searched to find the matching ENROLL records. Plan `p7` performs the join using a multibuffer product. It materializes its right side table (i.e., the sections from 2020), divides them into chunks, and performs the product of `p4` with these chunks.

Let's calculate the block accesses required by this plan. Plan `p2` requires 4500 block accesses and outputs 1 record. The index join accesses ENROLL once for each of the 34 records matching Joe's STUDENT record; that is, the join requires 34 additional block accesses and outputs 34 records. Plan `p6` (which finds the sections from 2020) requires 2500 block accesses and outputs 500 records. The multibuffer product materializes these records, which requires 50 additional blocks to create a 50-block temporary table. Assuming that there are at least 50 buffers available, this temporary table fits into a single chunk, and so the product requires 50 more block accesses to scan the temporary table, in addition to the cost of computing the left-side records. The remaining plans require no additional block

```
SimpleDB db = new SimpleDB("studentdb");
MetadataMgr mdm = db.mdMgr();
Transaction tx = db.newTx();

// the plan for the STUDENT node
Plan p1 = new TablePlan(tx, "student", mdm);

// the plan for the select node above STUDENT
Predicate joepred = new Predicate(...); //sname='joe'
Plan p2 = new SelectPlan(p1, joepred);

// the plan for the ENROLL node
Plan p3 = new TablePlan(tx, "enroll", mdm);

// an indexjoin plan between STUDENT and ENROLL
Map<String,IndexInfo> indexes = mdm.getIndexInfo("enroll", tx);
IndexInfo ii = indexes.get("studentid");
Plan p4 = new IndexJoinPlan(p2, p3, ii, "sid");

// the plan for the SECTION node
Plan p5 = new TablePlan(tx, "section", mdm);

// the plan for the select node above SECTION
Predicate sectpred = new Predicate(...); //yearoffered=2020
Plan p6 = new SelectPlan(p5, sectpred);

// a multibuffer product plan between the indexjoin and SECTION
Plan p7 = new MultiBufferProductPlan(tx, p4, p6);

// the plan for the select node above the multibuffer product
Predicate sectpred = new Predicate(...); //sectid=sectionid
Plan p8 = new SelectPlan(p7, sectpred);

// the plan for the project node
List<String> fields = Arrays.asList("grade");
Plan p9 = new ProjectPlan(p8, fields);
```

Fig. 15.10 An efficient plan for the tree of Fig. 15.9c

accesses. Thus the plan requires 7134 total block accesses, which takes a little more than 7 seconds.

In other words, a careful choice of node implementations reduced the execution time of the query by a factor of almost 20, using the same query tree. This reduction may not be as dramatic as the difference from using different query trees, but it is nevertheless substantial and important. A commercial database system that is 20 times slower than its competition will not last long in the marketplace.

15.3 The Structure of a Query Optimizer

Given an SQL query, the planner must try to find the plan for that query that requires the fewest block accesses. This process is called *query optimization.*

But how can the planner determine that plan? An exhaustive enumeration of all possible plans is daunting: If a query has n product operations, then there are (2n)!/n! ways to arrange them, which means that the number of equivalent plans grows super-exponentially with the size of the query. And that's not even considering the different ways to place the nodes for the other operators and the different ways to assign implementations to each node.

One way that a query planner can deal with this complexity is to perform the optimization in two independent stages:

- Stage 1: Find the *most promising tree* for the query, that is, the query tree that seems most likely to produce the most efficient plan.
- Stage 2: Choose the best implementation for each node in that tree.

By performing these stages independently, the planner reduces the choices it needs to make at each stage, which allows each stage to be simpler and more focused.

During each of these two optimization stages, the planner can reduce complexity even further by using *heuristics* to restrict the set of trees and plans that it considers. For example, query planners typically use the heuristic "perform selections as early as possible." Experience has shown that in the optimal plan for a query, the select nodes are always (or nearly always) placed as early as possible. Thus by following this heuristic, a query planner does not need to consider any other placement of select nodes in the query trees it considers.

The following two sections examine the two stages of query optimization and their relevant heuristics.

15.4 Finding the Most Promising Query Tree

15.4.1 The Cost of a Tree

The first stage of query optimization is to find the "most promising" query tree, that is, the tree that the planner thinks will have the lowest-cost plan. The reason that the planner cannot actually determine the best tree is that cost information is not available during the first stage. Block accesses are associated with plans, and plans are not considered until the second stage. Consequently, the planner needs a way to compare query trees without actually computing block accesses. The insight is to note that:

Query Tree	Size of the inputs to the bottom product node	Size of the inputs to the top product node	Total cost of the tree
Figure 15.9(b)	45,000 + 25,000	1,125,000,000 + 1,500,000	1,126,570,000
Figure 15.9(c)	1 + 1,500,000	34 + 25,000	1,525,035

Fig. 15.11 Calculating the cost of two query trees

- Nearly all of the block accesses in a query are due to product and join operations.
- The number of block accesses required by these operations is related to the size of their inputs.[1]

The planner therefore defines the *cost* of a query tree to be the sum of the sizes of the inputs to each product/join node in the tree.

For example, let's calculate the cost of the two query trees in Fig. 15.9. These trees have two *product* nodes, so you should sum the sizes of the inputs to each one. The results appear in Fig. 15.11 and indicate that the second query tree is much better than the first one.

You can think of the cost of a query tree as a "quick and dirty" approximation of its execution time. The cost does not help you estimate block accesses, but it does help determine the relative value of two trees. In particular, given two query trees, you can expect that the most efficient plan will come from the lower-cost tree. This expectation is not always correct (see Exercise 15.8). However, experience shows that it is correct most of the time, and even when it is not, the cheapest plan for the lower-cost tree tends to be good enough.

15.4.2 Pushing Select Nodes Down the Tree

The planner uses heuristics to search for the most promising query tree. The first heuristic concerns the placement of select nodes in the tree. The selection predicate comes from the `where` clause of an SQL query. Recall that the equivalences of Sect. 15.1.2 allow the planner to place a select node anywhere in the tree that it wants, provided that the predicate is meaningful at that point.

Which placement of select nodes leads to the lowest-cost tree? The output of a select node cannot have more records than its input. So if you place a select node inside of a product or join, the inputs to those nodes will likely be smaller, and the cost of the tree will be reduced. This leads to the following heuristic.

- Heuristic 1: The planner only needs to consider query trees whose selections are pushed down as far as possible.

Suppose that after pushing selections completely, two selections are next to each other in the query tree. Heuristic 1 does not specify the order these selections should

[1] An exception is the index join, whose cost is basically unrelated to the size of the indexed table. The planner ignores that exception at this point.

appear in. However, the order makes no difference in the cost of the tree, and so the planner is free to choose any order or to combine them into a single select node.

Heuristic 1 reduces the planner's task so that it doesn't have to worry about where to place select nodes. Given a query plan for the other operators, the placement of these nodes is well specified.

15.4.3 Replacing Select-Product Nodes by Join

Consider a join predicate involving fields from tables T1 and T2. When a select node containing this predicate is pushed down the tree, it will come to rest at a particular spot in the tree, namely ,the product node for which T1 appears in one subtree and T2 appears in the other subtree. This pair of select-product nodes can be replaced by a single join node.

- Heuristic 2: The planner should replace each select-product node pair in the query tree with a single join node.

Although this heuristic does not change the cost of the query tree, it is an important step towards finding the best plan. This book has examined several efficient implementations of the join operator. By identifying the joins in the query tree, the planner allows these implementations to be considered during the second stage of optimization.

15.4.4 Using Left-Deep Query Trees

The planner must choose the order in which the product/join operations should be performed. For an example, consider Fig. 15.12. The SQL query of part (a) retrieves the name of the students graduating in 2018 and the titles of the math courses they took. Parts (b)–(f) depict five equivalent trees for this query.

These trees have different *skeletons*. The trees of parts (b)–(d) are called *left-deep*, because the right-side of each product/join node contains no other product/join nodes. Similarly, the tree of part (e) is called *right-deep*. The tree of part (f) is called *bushy*, because it is neither left-deep nor right-deep. Many query planners adopt the following heuristic:

- Heuristic 3: The planner only needs to consider left-deep query trees.

The reasoning behind this heuristic is not obvious. For example, consider Fig. 15.13, which computes the cost of each tree using the statistics of Fig. 7.8. The lowest-cost tree of Fig. 15.12 is the bushy one. Moreover, that tree turns out to be the most promising one (see Exercise 15.9). So why would the planner deliberately choose to ignore a large set of trees that might contain the most promising one? There are two reasons.

```
select SName, Title
from STUDENT, ENROLL, SECTION, COURSE
where SId=StudentId and SectId=SectionId
and CId=CourseId and GradYear=2018 and DeptId=10
```

(a)

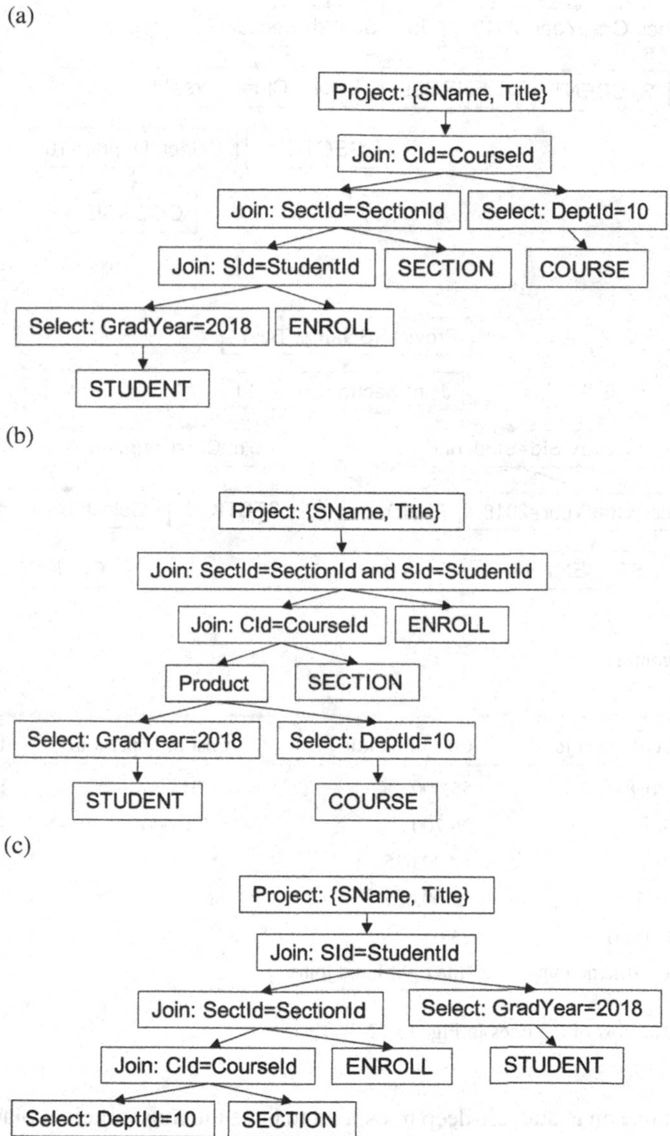

Fig. 15.12 Equivalent query trees having different skeletons. (**a**) The SQL query, (**b**) a left-deep query tree, (**c**) another left-deep query tree, (**d**) yet another left-deep query tree, (**e**) a right-deep query tree, (**f**) a bushy query tree

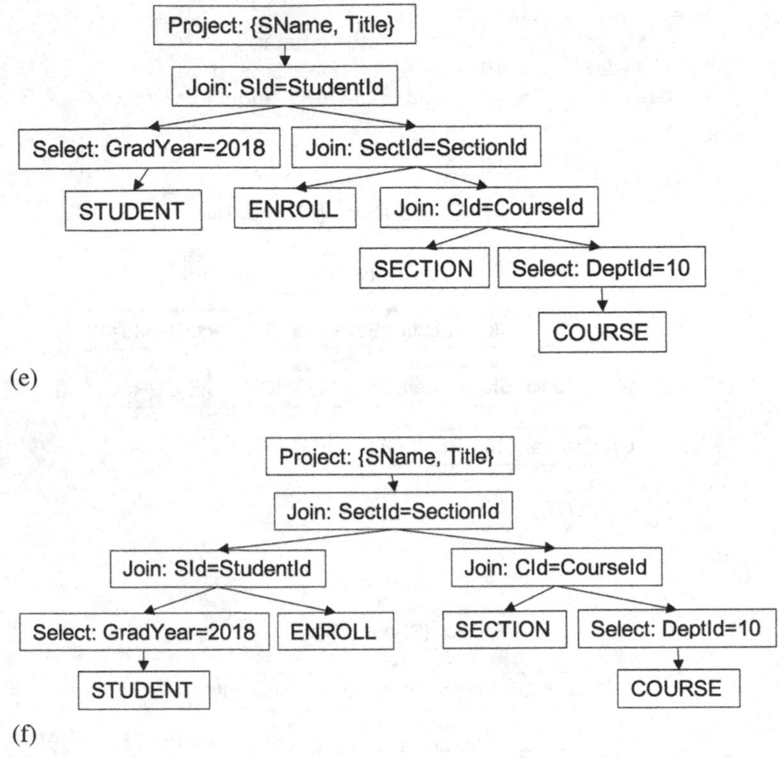

Fig. 15.12 (continued)

Tree	Cost of lower join	Cost of middle join	Cost of upper join	Total cost
(b)	1,500,900	55,000	30,013	1,585,913
(c)	913	36,700	3,750,000	3,787,613
(d)	25,013	1,500,625	38,400	1,564,038
(e)	25,013	1,500,625	38,400	1,564,038
(f)	1,500,900 (the left-hand join)	25,013 (the right-hand join)	30,625	1,556,538

Fig. 15.13 The cost of the trees in Fig. 15.12

The first reason is that left-deep trees tend to have the most efficient plans, even if they don't have the lowest cost. Think back to the join algorithms you have seen; they all work best when the right-side of the join is a stored table. For example, multibuffer product needs its right-side table to be materialized, so additional materialization will not be necessary when the table is already stored. And an index join is possible only when its right side is a stored table. Therefore by using a left-deep tree, the planner increases the likelihood that it will be able to use more efficient implementations when it generates the final plan. Experience has shown that the best left-deep plan for a query tends to be either optimal or close enough to it.

The second reason is convenience. If a query has n product/join nodes, then there are only n! left-deep trees, which is far fewer than the (2n)!/n! possible trees. Heuristic 3 thus allows the planner to work much more quickly (which is important), with little risk of getting stuck with a bad plan.

A left-deep tree can be specified by listing its tables in order. The first table is the table that appears on the left-side of the bottommost product/join node, and the subsequent tables come from the right sides of each product/join node moving up the tree. This order is called the *join order* of the left-deep tree.

For example, the left-deep tree of Fig. 15.12b has the join order (STUDENT, ENROLL, SECTION, COURSE), and the tree of Fig. 15.12c has the join order (STUDENT, COURSE, SECTION, ENROLL). Heuristic 3 therefore simplifies the job of the query planner—all the planner has to do is determine the best join order. Heuristics 1 to 3 then completely determine the corresponding query tree.

15.4.5 Choosing a Join Order Heuristically

The task of finding the best join order for a given query is the most critical part of the query optimization process. By "critical", I mean two things:

- The choice of join order dramatically effects the cost of the resulting query tree. An example is in Fig. 15.12, where tree (b) is so much better than tree (c).
- There are so many possible join orders that it is usually not feasible to examine them all. In particular, a query that mentions n tables can have n! join orders.

Thus the planner must be very clever about which join orders it considers, so as not to get stuck with a bad one. Two general approaches have been developed for determining good join orders: an approach that uses heuristics and an approach that considers all possible orders. This section examines the heuristic approach; the next section considers exhaustive search.

The heuristic approach constructs the join order incrementally. That is, the planner begins by choosing one of the tables to be first in the join order. It then chooses another table to be next in the join order and repeats until the join order is complete.

The following heuristic helps the planner to weed out the "obviously bad" join orders:

- Heuristic 4: Each table in the join order should join with previously chosen tables, whenever possible.

In other words, this heuristic states that the only product nodes in a query tree should correspond to joins. The query tree of Fig. 15.12c violates this heuristic because it begins by taking the product of the STUDENT and COURSE tables.

Why are join orders that violate Heuristic 4 so bad? Recall that the role of a join predicate is to filter out the meaningless output records generated by a product operation. So when a query tree contains a non-join product node, its intermediate tables will continue to propagate these meaningless records until the join predicate is encountered. For example, consider again the query tree of Fig. 15.12c. The product between STUDENT and COURSE results in 11,700 output records, because each of the 13 COURSE records from the math department is repeated 900 times (once for each student graduating in 2018). When this output table is joined with SECTION, each COURSE record is matched with its SECTION record; however, these matchings are repeated 900 times. Consequently, the output of that join is 900 times larger than it should be. It is only when ENROLL is added to the join order that the join predicate with STUDENT finally kicks in and the repetition is eliminated.

This example demonstrates that the output of a query tree involving a product node can start out small, but eventually the repetition caused by the product leads to a very high-cost tree. Thus Heuristic 4 asserts that product operations should be avoided if at all possible. Of course, if the user specifies a query that does not completely join all of the tables, then a product node will be inevitable. In this case, the heuristic ensures that this node will be as high in the tree as possible, so the repetition will have the smallest possible effect.

Heuristic 4 is a commonly used heuristic. It is possible to find queries whose most promising query tree violates this heuristic (see Exercise 15.11), but such queries rarely occur in practice.

It is now time to address the questions of which table to choose first and which of the joinable tables to choose next. These are tough questions. The database community has proposed many heuristics, with very little consensus on which is most appropriate. I shall consider two logical possibilities, which I will call Heuristics 5a and 5b:

- Heuristic 5a: Choose the table that produces the smallest output.

This heuristic is the most direct, straightforward approach. Its intention is this: since the cost of a query tree is related to the sum of the sizes of its intermediate output tables, a good way to minimize this sum is to minimize each of those tables.

Let's use this heuristic on the query of Fig. 15.12a. The first table in the join order would be COURSE, because its selection predicate reduces it to 13 records. The remaining tables are determined by Heuristic 4. That is, SECTION is the only table that joins with COURSE, and then ENROLL is the only table that joins with SECTION, which leaves STUDENT to be last in the join order. The resulting query tree appeared in Fig. 15.12d.

An alternative heuristic is the following:

- Heuristic 5b: Choose the table having the most restrictive selection predicate.

Heuristic 5b arises from the insight that a selection predicate will have the greatest impact when it appears lowest in the query tree. For example, consider the query tree of Fig. 15.12b and its selection predicate on STUDENT. That selection predicate has the obvious benefit of reducing the number of STUDENT records, which lowers the cost of the join node immediately above it. But it has an even more important benefit—the predicate also reduces the output of that join from 1,500,000 records to just 30,000 records, which lowers the cost of each subsequent join node in the tree. In other words, the cost savings produced by a select node is compounded all the way up the tree. In contrast, the selection predicate on COURSE at the top of the tree has much less of an impact.

Since the selection predicates that are lower in a query tree have the greatest effect on its cost, it makes sense for the optimizer to choose the table whose predicate has the largest reduction factor. This is exactly what Heuristic 5b does. For example, the query tree of Fig. 15.12b satisfies this heuristic. The first table in its join order is STUDENT, because its selection predicate reduces the table by a factor of 50 whereas the selection predicate for COURSE reduces it by only a factor of 40. The remaining tables in the join order, as before, are determined by Heuristic 4.

In this example, it turns out that using Heuristic 5b results in a lower-cost query tree than Heuristic 5a. This is typical. Studies (such as Swami [1989]) have shown that although Heuristic 5a makes intuitive sense and produces reasonable query trees, these trees tend to have higher cost than those from Heuristic 5b.

15.4.6 Choosing a Join Order by Exhaustive Enumeration

Heuristics 4 and 5 tend to produce good join orders but are not guaranteed to produce the best one. If a vendor wants to be sure that its planner finds the optimum join order, its only alternative is to enumerate all of them. This section considers such a strategy.

A query that mentions `n` tables can have as many as `n!` join orders. A well-known algorithmic technique, known as *dynamic programming*, can reduce the time needed to find the most promising join order to $O(2^n)$. If `n` is reasonably small (say, not more than 15 or 20 tables), then this algorithm is efficient enough to be practical.

For an illustration of how this technique can save time, consider a query that joins all five tables in the university database. Four of its 120 possible join orders are:

```
(STUDENT, ENROLL, SECTION, COURSE, DEPT)
(STUDENT, SECTION, ENROLL, COURSE, DEPT)
(STUDENT, ENROLL, SECTION, DEPT, COURSE)
(STUDENT, SECTION, ENROLL, DEPT, COURSE)
```

The first two join orders differ only on their second and third tables. Suppose we determine that the partial join order (STUDENT, ENROLL, SECTION) has a lower cost than (STUDENT, SECTION, ENROLL). Then it follows, without any further calculation, that the first join order must have lower cost than the second one. Moreover, we also know that the third join order requires fewer block accesses than the fourth one. And in general, we know that any join order that begins (STUDENT, SECTION, ENROLL) is not worth considering.

The dynamic programming algorithm uses an array variable named `lowest`, which has an entry for each possible set of tables. If `S` is a set of tables, then `lowest [S]` contains three values:

- The lowest-cost join order involving the tables in `S`
- The cost of the query tree corresponding to that join order
- The number of records output by that query tree

The algorithm begins by computing `lowest [S]` for each set of two tables, then each set of three tables, and continues until it reaches the set of all tables in the query. The optimum join order is the value of `lowest [S]` when `S` is the set of all tables.

Computing Sets of Two Tables
Consider a set of two tables, say {T1, T2}. The value of `lowest [{T1, T2}]` is determined by computing the cost of the query tree that takes the join (or product, if there is no join predicate) of the two tables and their selection predicates. The cost of the query tree is the sum of the sizes of the two inputs to the product/join node. Note that the cost is the same regardless of which table is first. Thus, the planner must use some other criterion to determine the first table. A reasonable choice is to use Heuristic 5a or 5b.

Computing Sets of Three Tables
Consider a set of three tables, say {T1, T2, T3}. Their lowest-cost join order can be computed by considering the following join orders:

```
lowest [{T2, T3}] joined with T1
lowest [{T1, T3}] joined with T2
lowest [{T1, T2}] joined with T3
```

The join order having the lowest cost will be saved as the value of *lowest[{T1, T2, T3}]*.

Computing Sets of `n` Tables
Now suppose that the variable `lowest` has been calculated for each set of `n-1` tables. Given the set {T1, T2, . . ., Tn}, the algorithm considers the following join orders:

```
lowest [{T2, T3 ,..., Tn}] joined with T1
lowest [{T1, T3 ,..., Tn}] joined with T2
. . .
lowest [{T1, T2 ,..., Tn-1}] joined with Tn
```

The join order having the lowest cost is the best join order for the query.

As an example, let's use the dynamic programming algorithm on the query of Fig. 15.12. The algorithm begins by considering all six sets of two tables, as shown in Fig. 15.14a.

Each set of two tables has two partial join orders, which are listed in the row corresponding to that set. The join orders for each set are listed in terms of

S	Partial Join Order	Cost	#Records
{ENROLL,STUDENT}	(STUDENT,ENROLL)	1,500,900	30,000
	(ENROLL,STUDENT)	1,500,900	
{ENROLL,SECTION}	(SECTION,ENROLL)	1,525,000	1,500,000
	(ENROLL,SECTION)	1,525,000	
{COURSE,SECTION}	(COURSE,SECTION)	25,500	25,000
	(SECTION,COURSE)	25,500	
{SECTION,STUDENT}	(STUDENT,SECTION)	25,900	22,500,000
	(SECTION,STUDENT)	25,900	
{COURSE,STUDENT}	(COURSE,STUDENT)	1,400	450,000
	(STUDENT,COURSE)	1,400	
{COURSE,ENROLL}	(COURSE,ENROLL)	1,500,500	450,000,000
	(ENROLL,COURSE)	1,500,500	

(a)

S	Partial Join Order	Cost	#Records
{ENROLL,SECTION,STUDENT}	(STUDENT,ENROLL,SECTION)	1,555,900	30,000
	(SECTION,ENROLL,STUDENT)	3,025,900	
	(STUDENT,SECTION,ENROLL)	24,025,900	
{COURSE,ENROLL,STUDENT}	(STUDENT,ENROLL,COURSE)	1,531,400	15,000,000
	(COURSE,STUDENT,ENROLL)	1,951,400	
	(COURSE,ENROLL,STUDENT)	451,501,400	
{COURSE,ENROLL,SECTION}	(SECTION,ENROLL,COURSE)	1,500,500	1,500,000
	(COURSE,SECTION,ENROLL)	1,550,500	
	(COURSE,ENROLL,SECTION)	450,025,000	
{COURSE,SECTION,STUDENT}	(COURSE,SECTION,STUDENT)	25,900	22,500,000
	(COURSE,STUDENT,SECTION)	475,000	
	(STUDENT,SECTION,COURSE)	22,500,500	

(b)

Join Order	Cost
(STUDENT,ENROLL,SECTION,COURSE)	1,586,400
(COURSE,SECTION,ENROLL,STUDENT)	3,051,400
(STUDENT,ENROLL,COURSE,SECTION)	16,556,400
(COURSE,SECTION,STUDENT,ENROLL)	24,051,400

(c)

Fig. 15.14 Calculating the best join order for Fig. 15.12. (**a**) All sets of two tables, (**b**) all sets of three tables, (**c**) all sets of four tables

desirability. In this case, they have the same cost, so they are listed according to Heuristic 5a. The first partial join order for each set is chosen as the representative of that set in subsequent calculations.

The algorithm then considers all four sets of three tables. Figure 15.14b lists the partial join orders for these sets and their costs. Each set has three possible join orders. The first two tables in the join order are the lowest-cost representative of their set from Fig. 15.14a. The costs are listed from lowest to highest cost, so the first partial join order for each set is chosen as the representative of that set.

Figure 15.14c considers sets of four tables. There are four join orders to consider. The first three tables in each join order represent the lowest-cost join order from Fig. 15.14b; the fourth table in the join order is the missing table. This table shows that the join order (STUDENT, ENROLL, SECTION, COURSE) is optimum.

Note that at each stage, the algorithm must compute the value of `lowest` for every possible set of prefix tables, because there is no way of knowing how the costs will change during subsequent stages. It may be that the prefix that has highest cost at one stage will produce the lowest-cost join order overall, because of how the remaining tables join with it.

15.5 Finding the Most Efficient Plan

The first stage of query optimization was to find the most promising query tree. The second stage is to turn that query tree into an efficient plan. The planner constructs the plan by choosing an implementation for each node in the query tree. It chooses these implementations bottom-up, starting from the leaves. The advantage of proceeding bottom-up is that when a given node is considered, the planner will have already chosen the lowest-cost plan for each of its subtrees. The planner can thus consider each possible implementation of the node, use the implementation's `blocksAccessed` method to calculate the cost of that implementation, and choose the implementation having the lowest cost.

Note that the planner chooses the implementation of each node independently of the implementations of the other nodes. In particular, it does not care how the subtrees of a node are implemented; it only needs to know the cost of that implementation. This lack of interaction between nodes significantly reduces the computational complexity of plan generation. If the query tree has `n` nodes, and each node has at most `k` implementations, then the planner needs to examine at most `k*n` plans, which is certainly reasonable.

Nevertheless, the planner can also take advantage of heuristics to speed up plan generation. These heuristics tend to be operation specific. For example:

- Heuristic 6: If possible, use indexselect to implement a select node.
- Heuristic 7: Implement a join node according to the following priority:
  - Use indexjoin if possible.
  - Use hashjoin if one of the input tables is small.
  - Use mergejoin otherwise.

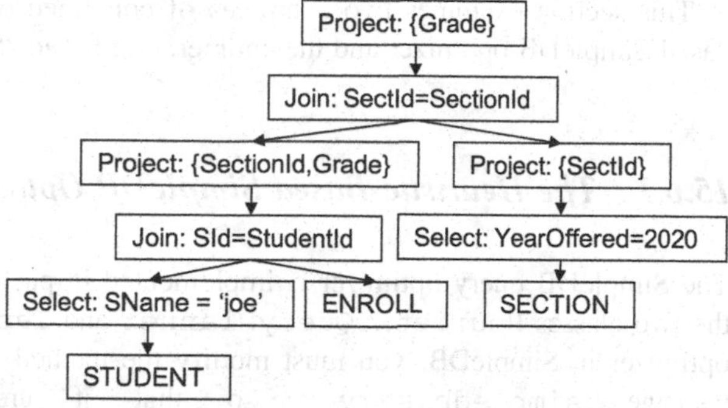

Fig. 15.15 A query tree for the query of Fig. 15.9, with added project nodes

There is one more issue to consider. Whenever the planner chooses to implement a node using a materialized plan, then it should also insert project nodes into the query tree, as follows:

- Heuristic 8: The planner should add a project node as the child of each materialized node, to remove fields that are no longer needed.

Heuristic 8 ensures that the temporary tables created by a materialized implementation are as small as possible. There are two reasons why this is important: a larger table takes more block accesses to create, and a larger table also takes more block accesses to scan. The planner therefore should determine which fields will be needed by the materialized node and its ancestors and insert a project node to remove the other fields from its input.

For example, consider the query tree of Fig. 15.15. This tree returns the grades that Joe received in 2020 and is equivalent to the trees of Fig. 15.9.

The plan of Fig. 15.10 chose to implement the upper join node with multibuffer product, which is materialized. Heuristic 8 asserts that project nodes need to be added to the query tree as children of that join node; these nodes are shown in Fig. 15.15. The right-hand project node is especially important, because it reduces the size of the temporary table by about 75%, thereby allowing the algorithm to run using fewer chunks.

15.6 Combining the Two Stages of Optimization

The easiest way to understand query optimization is as two separate stages: a first stage that constructs the query tree from the SQL query and a second stage that constructs the plan from the query tree. In practice, however, these stages are often combined. There are two good reasons in favor of combining optimization stages:

- *Convenience*: The plan can be created directly, without having to create an explicit query tree.
- *Accuracy*: Since the plans are created concurrently with the query tree, it may be possible to calculate the cost of the tree in terms of actual block accesses.

This section examines two examples of combined optimization: the heuristic-based SimpleDB optimizer and the enumeration-based "Selinger-style" optimizer.

15.6.1 *The Heuristic-Based SimpleDB Optimizer*

The SimpleDB query optimizer is implemented in package `simpledb.opt` via the two classes `HeuristicQueryPlanner` and `TablePlanner`. To use this optimizer in SimpleDB, you must modify the method `SimpleDB.planner` in package `simpledb.server` so that it creates an instance of `HeuristicQueryPlanner` instead of `BasicQueryPlanner`.

The Class `HeuristicQueryPlanner`
The class `HeuristicQueryPlanner` uses Heuristic 5a to determine the join order. Every table has a `TablePlanner` object. When a table is added to the join order, its `TablePlanner` object creates the corresponding plan, adding appropriate selection and join predicates, and using indexes when possible. In this way, the plan is built simultaneously with the join order.

The code for `HeuristicQueryPlanner` appears in Fig. 15.16. The collection `tableinfo` contains a `TablePlanner` object for each table in the query. The planner begins by choosing (and removing) the object from this collection corresponding to the smallest table and uses its select plan as the *current plan*. It then repeatedly chooses (and removes) from the collection the table having the lowest-cost join. The planner sends the current plan to that table's `TablePlanner` object, which creates and returns the join plan. This join plan then becomes the current plan. This process is continued until the collection is empty, at which point the current plan is the final one.

The Class `TablePlanner`
An object of class `TablePlanner` is responsible for creating plans for a single table; its code appears in Fig. 15.17. The `TablePlanner` constructor creates a table for the specified table, obtains the information about the indexes for the table, and saves the query predicate. The class has public methods `makeSelectPlan`, `makeProductPlan`, and `makeJoinPlan`.

The method `makeSelectPlan` creates a select plan for its table. The method first calls `makeIndexSelect` to determine if an index can be used; if so, an `IndexSelect` plan is created. The method then calls `addSelectPred` to determine the portion of the predicate that applies to the table and create a select plan for it.

Method `makeProductPlan` adds a select plan to the table plan and then creates a `MultiBufferProductPlan` to implement the product of the specified plan with this plan.[2]

---

[2]Ideally, the method should create a hashjoin plan, but SimpleDB does not support hash joins. See Exercise 15.17.

```
public class HeuristicQueryPlanner implements QueryPlanner {
   private Collection<TablePlanner> tableplanners = new ArrayList<>();
   private MetadataMgr mdm;

   public HeuristicQueryPlanner(MetadataMgr mdm) {
      this.mdm = mdm;
   }

   public Plan createPlan(QueryData data, Transaction tx) {

      // Step 1, Create a TablePlanner object for each mentioned table
      for (String tblname : data.tables()) {
         TablePlanner tp = new TablePlanner(tblname, data.pred(),
         tx, mdm);
         tableplanners.add(tp);
      }

      // Step 2, Choose the lowest-size plan to begin the join order
      Plan currentplan = getLowestSelectPlan();

      // Step 3, Repeatedly add a plan to the join order
      while (!tableplanners.isEmpty()) {

         Plan p = getLowestJoinPlan(currentplan);
         if (p != null)
            currentplan = p;
         else  // no applicable join
            currentplan = getLowestProductPlan(currentplan);
      }

      // Step 4.  Project on the field names and return
      return new ProjectPlan(currentplan, data.fields());
   }

   private Plan getLowestSelectPlan() {
      TablePlanner besttp = null;
      Plan bestplan = null;
      for (TablePlanner tp : tableplanners) {
         Plan plan = tp.makeSelectPlan();
         if (bestplan == null ||
             plan.recordsOutput() < bestplan.recordsOutput()) {
            besttp = tp;
            bestplan = plan;
         }
      }
      tableplanners.remove(besttp);
      return bestplan;
   }
```

Fig. 15.16 The code for the SimpleDB class `HeuristicQueryPlanner`

```
   private Plan getLowestJoinPlan(Plan current) {
      TablePlanner besttp = null;
      Plan bestplan = null;
      for (TablePlanner tp : tableplanners) {
         Plan plan = tp.makeJoinPlan(current);
         if (plan != null && (bestplan == null ||
             plan.recordsOutput() < bestplan.recordsOutput())) {
            besttp = tp;
            bestplan = plan;
         }
      }
      if (bestplan != null)
         tableplanners.remove(besttp);
      return bestplan;
   }

   private Plan getLowestProductPlan(Plan current) {
      TablePlanner besttp = null;
      Plan bestplan = null;
      for (TablePlanner tp : tableplanners) {
         Plan plan = tp.makeProductPlan(current);
         if (bestplan == null ||
             plan.recordsOutput() < bestplan.recordsOutput()) {
               besttp = tp;
               bestplan = plan;
         }
      }
      tableplanners.remove(besttp);
      return bestplan;
   }

   public void setPlanner(Planner p) {
      // for use in planning views, which
      // for simplicity this code doesn't do.
   }
}
```

Fig. 15.16 (continued)

Method `makeJoinPlan` first calls the predicate's `joinPred` method to determine if a join exists between the specified plan and this plan. If no join predicate exists, the method returns `null`. If a join predicate does exist, the method looks to see if an `IndexJoinScan` can be created. If not, then the join is implemented by creating a multibuffer product followed by a select.

Records Output Versus Blocks Accessed

The `HeuristicQueryPlanner` code calculates the lowest-cost plan using the method `recordsOutput`. That is, it attempts to find the plan needing the smallest number of block accesses without ever examining the block requirements of its subplans. This situation deserves explanation.

```
class TablePlanner {
   private TablePlan myplan;
   private Predicate mypred;
   private Schema myschema;
   private Map<String,IndexInfo> indexes;
   private Transaction tx;

   public TablePlanner(String tblname, Predicate mypred,
                       Transaction tx, MetadataMgr mdm) {
      this.mypred  = mypred;
      this.tx  = tx;
      myplan   = new TablePlan(tx, tblname, mdm);
      myschema = myplan.schema();
      indexes  = mdm.getIndexInfo(tblname, tx);
   }

   public Plan makeSelectPlan() {
      Plan p = makeIndexSelect();
      if (p == null)
         p = myplan;
      return addSelectPred(p);
   }


   public Plan makeJoinPlan(Plan current) {
      Schema currsch = current.schema();
      Predicate joinpred = mypred.joinSubPred(myschema, currsch);

      if (joinpred == null)
         return null;
      Plan p = makeIndexJoin(current, currsch);
      if (p == null)
         p = makeProductJoin(current, currsch);
      return p;
   }

   public Plan makeProductPlan(Plan current) {
      Plan p = addSelectPred(myplan);
      return new MultiBufferProductPlan(current, p, tx);
   }

   private Plan makeIndexSelect() {
      for (String fldname : indexes.keySet()) {
         Constant val = mypred.equatesWithConstant(fldname);
         if (val != null) {
            IndexInfo ii = indexes.get(fldname);
            return new IndexSelectPlan(myplan, ii, val, tx);
         }
      }
      return null;
   }
```

Fig. 15.17 The code for the SimpleDB class `TablePlanner`

```
   private Plan makeIndexJoin(Plan current, Schema currsch) {
      for (String fldname : indexes.keySet()) {
         String outerfield = mypred.equatesWithField(fldname);
         if (outerfield != null && currsch.hasField(outerfield)) {
            IndexInfo ii = indexes.get(fldname);
            Plan p = new IndexJoinPlan(current, myplan, ii,
                                       outerfield, tx);
            p = addSelectPred(p);
            return addJoinPred(p, currsch);
         }
      }
      return null;
   }

   private Plan makeProductJoin(Plan current, Schema currsch) {
      Plan p = makeProductPlan(current);
      return addJoinPred(p, currsch);
   }

   private Plan addSelectPred(Plan p) {
      Predicate selectpred = mypred.selectSubPred(myschema);
      if (selectpred != null)
         return new SelectPlan(p, selectpred);
      else
         return p;
   }

   private Plan addJoinPred(Plan p, Schema currsch) {
      Predicate joinpred = mypred.joinSubPred(currsch, myschema);
      if (joinpred != null)
         return new SelectPlan(p, joinpred);
      else
         return p;
   }
}
```

Fig. 15.17 (continued)

As you have seen, the problem with using heuristic optimization is that partial join orders that start out cheap can wind up very expensive, and the best join order may have a very expensive beginning. It is therefore important for the optimizer to not get sidetracked by a join that seems better than it is. Figure 15.18 illustrates this problem.

The query of Fig. 15.18a returns the grades given and the title for each course taught by Professor Einstein. Assume the statistics of Fig. 7.8, and suppose that ENROLL has an index on `SectionId`. The SimpleDB optimizer will choose SECTION to be first in the join order because it is smallest (as well as most selective). The question is which table it should choose next. If your criterion is to minimize records output, then you should choose COURSE. But if your criterion is to minimize blocks accessed, then you should choose ENROLL because the index join will be more efficient. However, ENROLL turns out to be the wrong choice

```
select Title, Grade
from ENROLL, SECTION, COURSE
where SectId=SectionId and CId=CourseId and Prof='einstein'
```

(a)

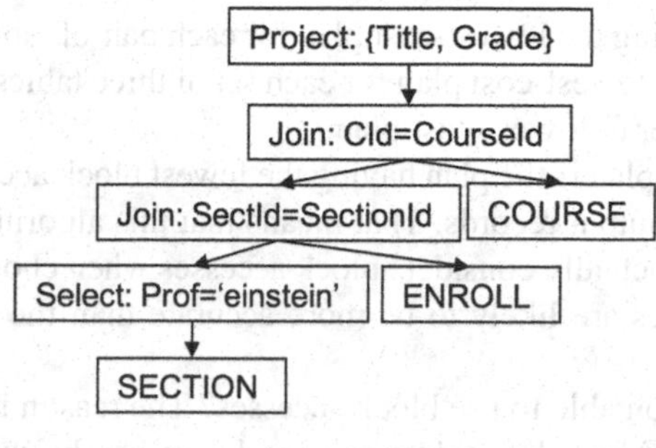

(b)

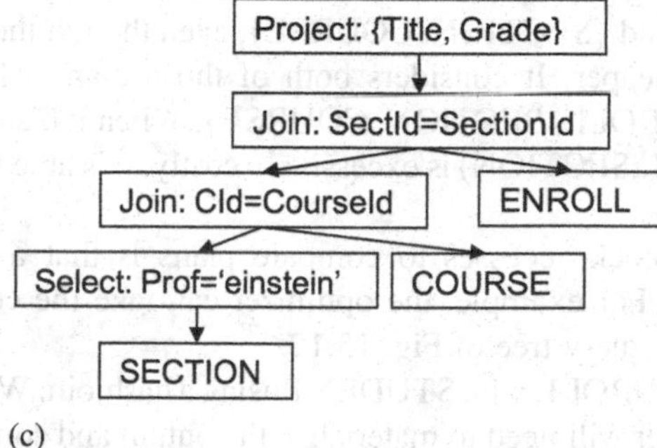

(c)

Fig. 15.18 Which table should be second in the join order? (**a**) The SQL query, (**b**) choosing ENROLL second in the join order, (**c**) choosing COURSE second in the join order

because the high number of output records causes the subsequent join with COURSE to be much more expensive.

This example demonstrates that the large number of matching ENROLL records has a significant effect on the cost of subsequent joins; thus ENROLL should appear as late as possible in the join order. By minimizing records output, the optimizer ensures that ENROLL winds up at the end. The fact that the join with ENROLL has a fast implementation is misleading and irrelevant.

15.6.2 Selinger-Style Optimization

The SimpleDB optimizer uses heuristics for choosing the join order. In the early 1970s, researchers at IBM wrote an influential optimizer for the System-R prototype database system; this optimizer chose its join orders using dynamic programming.

That optimization strategy is often called "Selinger style," in reference to Pat Selinger, who headed the optimizer team.

Selinger-style optimization combines dynamic programming with plan generation. In particular, the algorithm calculates `lowest[S]` for each set of tables `S`. But instead of saving a join order in `lowest[S]`, the algorithm saves the lowest-cost plan.

The algorithm begins by calculating the lowest-cost plan for each pair of tables. It then uses these plans to calculate the lowest-cost plan for each set of three tables, and so on, until it has calculated the overall lowest-cost plan.

In this algorithm, the lowest-cost plan is the plan having the fewest block accesses and not the plan having the fewest output records. That means that this algorithm is the only algorithm in this book that actually considers block accesses when choosing its join order; therefore, its estimates are likely to be more accurate than the other algorithms.

Why is Selinger-style optimization able to use block accesses? The reason is that unlike heuristic optimization, it considers all left-deep trees and does not throw out a partial join order until it is sure that the order is not useful. Look back at the example of Fig. 15.18. The Selinger-style algorithm will calculate and store the lowest plans for both {SECTION, ENROLL} and {SECTION, COURSE}, even though the plan for {SECTION, ENROLL} is cheaper. It considers both of those plans when it calculates the lowest plan for {ENROLL, SECTION, COURSE}. When it discovers that joining COURSE to (ENROLL,SECTION) is excessively costly, it is able to use an alternative plan.

Another advantage to using block accesses to compare plans is that a more detailed cost analysis is possible. For example, the optimizer can take the cost of sorting into account. Consider the query tree of Fig. 15.19.

Suppose that the planner joins ENROLL with STUDENT using a hashjoin. When it goes to do the grouping, the planner will need to materialize the output and sort it on `StudentId`. Alternatively, suppose instead that the planner uses a mergejoin to join the tables. In this case, it would not need to preprocess the output because it would already be sorted on `StudentId`. In other words, it is possible that using a mergejoin could result in the best final plan, even if it was less efficient than the hashjoin!

The point of this example is that the planner also needs to keep track of sort order if it wants to generate the best plan. A Selinger-style optimizer can do so by saving

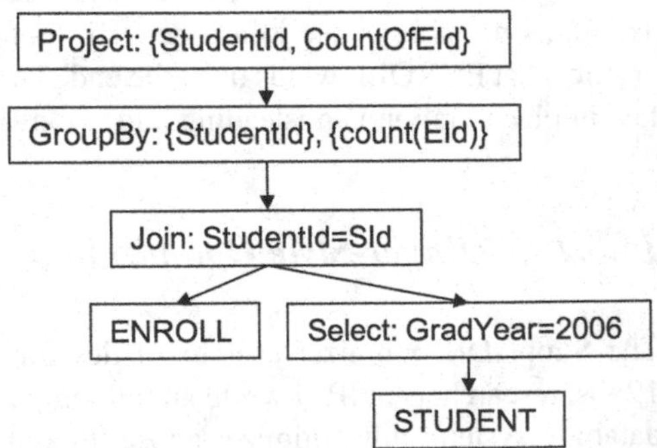

Fig. 15.19 What is the best way to join ENROLL with STUDENT?

the lowest-cost plan for each sort order in `lowest[S]`. In the above example, the value of `lowest[{ENROLL,STUDENT}]` will contain both the mergejoin and the hashjoin plans, because each has a different sort order.

15.7 Merging Query Blocks

This section examines the optimization of queries that mention views. Consider, for example, the query of Fig. 15.20a, which uses a view to retrieve the names of the students who received an "A" in a course taught by Professor Einstein. The basic query planner of Chap. 10 creates the plan for such a query by planning the view definition and the query separately and then hooking the plan for the view into the plan for the query. That plan appears in Fig. 15.20b.

The plan associated with each query and view definition is called a *query block*. The plan for Fig. 15.20b illustrates the simplest way that an optimizer can deal with view queries—it can optimize each query block separately before combining them

```
create view EINSTEIN as
select SectId from SECTION
where Prof = 'einstein'

select SName from STUDENT, ENROLL, EINSTEIN
where SId = StudentId and SectionId = SectId
and Grade = 'A'
```

(a)

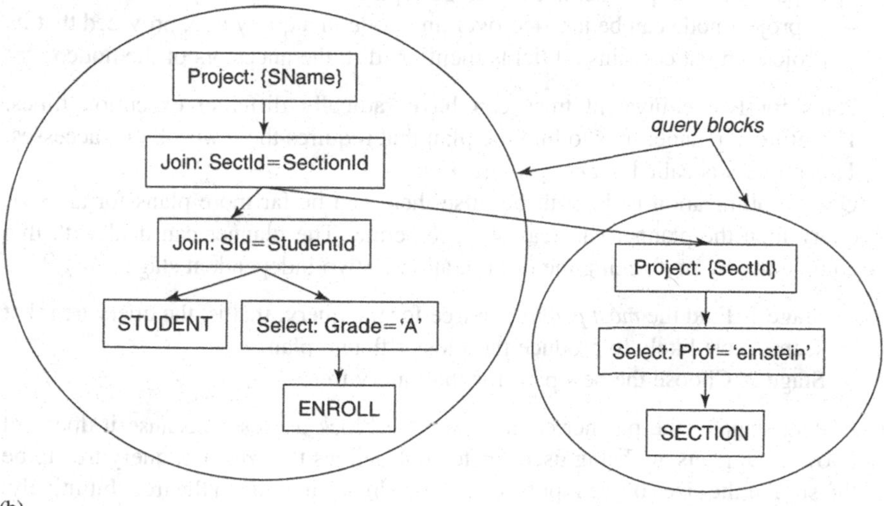

(b)

Fig. 15.20 Planning a view query. (**a**) A view definition and a query that uses it, (**b**) planning each query block separately

into the final plan. Although separate optimization is simple to implement, the plans that get created are not necessarily very good. The plan of Fig. 15.20 is a case in point. The best join order is (SECTION, ENROLL, STUDENT), but this join order is not possible given these query blocks.

A solution to this problem is to *merge* the query blocks and plan their contents as a single query. For example, in Fig. 15.20, the planner can ignore the project node of the view definition block and add its select and table nodes to the main query. Such a strategy is possible if the view definition is sufficiently simple. The situation becomes much more complex when the view definition contains grouping or duplicate removal, and merging may not be possible.

15.8 Chapter Summary

- Two queries are *equivalent* if their output tables contain exactly the same records (although not necessarily in the same order), regardless of the contents of the database.
- An SQL query may have many equivalent query trees. These equivalences are inferred from properties of the relational algebra operators.
  - The product operator is commutative and associative. These properties imply that the product nodes in a query tree can be computed in any order.
  - A select node for predicate p can be split into several select nodes, one for each conjunct of p. Writing p in conjunctive normal form (CNF) allows it to be split into the smallest pieces. The nodes for each conjunct can be placed anywhere within the query tree, as long as their selection predicate is meaningful.
  - A pair of select-product nodes can be replaced by a single join node.
  - A project node can be inserted over any node in a query tree, provided that its projection list contains all fields mentioned in the ancestors of the node.
- Plans for two equivalent trees can have radically different execution times. Therefore, a planner tries to find the plan that requires the fewest block accesses. This process is called *query optimization*.
- Query optimization is difficult because there can be far more plans for an SQL query than the planner can feasibly enumerate. The planner can deal with this complexity by performing the optimization in two independent stages:
  - Stage 1: Find the *most promising* tree for the query, that is, the query tree that seems most likely to produce the most efficient plan.
  - Stage 2: Choose the best plan for that query tree.
- During stage 1, the planner cannot estimate block accesses because it does not know what plans are being used. Instead, it defines the *cost* of a query tree to be the sum of the sizes of the inputs to each product/join node in the tree. Intuitively, a low-cost query tree minimizes the size of intermediate joins. The idea is that the output of each join will be the input to the subsequent join, and so the larger the intermediate outputs, the more expensive it will be to execute the query.

- The planner also adopts *heuristics* to limit the set of trees and plans that it considers. Common heuristics are:

  - Place select nodes as deep as possible in the query tree.
  - Replace each select-product node pair by a join node.
  - Place a project node above the inputs to each materialized plan.
  - Consider only left-deep trees.
  - Whenever possible, avoid product operations that are not joins.

- Each left-deep tree has an associated *join order*. Finding a good join order is the most difficult part of query optimization.
- One way to choose a join order is to use heuristics. Two reasonable (but conflicting) heuristics are:

  - Choose the table that produces the smallest output.
  - Choose the table that has the most restrictive predicate.

This second heuristic strives to create a query tree in which the most restrictive *select* nodes are maximally deep, the intuition being that such trees tend to have the lowest cost.

- Another way to choose a join order is to exhaustively examine all possible join orders, using dynamic programming. The dynamic programming algorithm calculates the lowest join order for each set of tables, starting with sets of two tables, then sets of three tables, and continues until it reaches the set of all tables.
- During the second optimization stage, the planner constructs the plan by choosing an implementation for each node in the query tree. It chooses each implementation independently of the implementations of the other nodes and calculates its cost in terms of blocks accessed. The planner can determine the lowest-cost plan either by examining all possible implementations of each node or by following heuristics such as:

  - Use indexing whenever possible.
  - If indexing is not possible for a join, then use a hashjoin if one of the input tables is small; otherwise use a mergejoin.

- An implementation of a query optimizer can combine its two stages, constructing the plan in conjunction with the query tree. The SimpleDB optimizer uses heuristics to determine the join order and incrementally constructs the plan as each table is chosen. A *Selinger-style* optimizer uses dynamic programming—instead of saving the lowest cost join order for each set of tables, it saves the lowest-cost plan. The advantage of a Selinger-style optimizer is that, unlike any of the other techniques, it can use estimated block accesses to calculate thc best join order.
- A query that uses a view will have a plan consisting of multiple *query blocks*. The most straightforward way to handle multiple query blocks is to optimize each one separately and then combine them. However, more efficient plans are possible if the query blocks can be optimized together. Such as strategy is possible if the view definition is sufficiently simple.

15.9 Suggested Reading

This chapter gives a basic introduction to query optimization; the articles Graefe (1993) and Chaudhuri (1998) go into considerably more detail. The paper Swami (1989) contains an experimental comparison of various join-order heuristics. The System-R optimizer is described in Selinger et al. (1979).

One difficulty with traditional query planners is that their heuristics and optimization strategy are hard-coded into their methods. Consequently, the only way to change the heuristics or to add new relational operators is to rewrite the code. An alternative approach is to express operators and their transformations as *rewrite rules* and to have the planner repeatedly use the rules to transform the initial query into an optimum one. To change the planner, one then only needs to change the rule set. A description of this strategy appears in Pirahesh (1992).

The optimization strategies in this chapter have a sharp distinction between query planning and query execution—once a plan is opened and executed, there is no turning back. If the planner has mistakenly chosen an inefficient plan, there is nothing to be done. The article Kabra and DeWitt (1998) describes how a database system can monitor the execution of a plan, collecting statistics about its behavior. If it thinks that the execution is less efficient than it should be, it can use the statistics to create a better plan and "hot-swap" the old plan with the new one.

Chaudhuri, S. (1998). An overview of query optimization in relational systems. *Proceedings of the ACM Principles of Database Systems Conference*, pp. 34–43.

Graefe, G. (1993). Query evaluation techniques for large databases. *ACM Computing Surveys, 25*(2), pp. 73–170.

Kabra, N., & DeWitt, D. (1998). Efficient mid-query re-optimization of sub-optimal query execution plans. *Proceedings of the ACM SIGMOD Conference*, pp. 106–117.

Pirahesh, H., Hellerstein, J., & Hasan, W. (1992). Extendable/rule based query rewrite in starburst. *Proceedings of the ACM SIGMOD Conference*, pp. 39–48.

Selinger, P., Astrahan, M., Chamberlin, D., Lorie, R., & Price, T. (1979). Access-path selection in a relational database management system. *Proceedings of the ACM SIGMOD Conference*, pp. 23–34.

Swami, A. (1989) Optimization of large join queries: Combining heuristics and combinatorial techniques. *ACM SIGMOD Record, 18*(2), 367–376.

15.10 Exercises

Conceptual Exercises

15.1. Show that the product operator is associative.

15.2. Consider a query that takes the product of several tables and any two query trees equivalent to this query. Show that it is possible to use the equivalences of Sect. 15.1.1 to transform one tree into the other.

15.3. Consider the query tree of Fig. 15.2a.

(a) Give a sequence of transformations that will create the following tree:

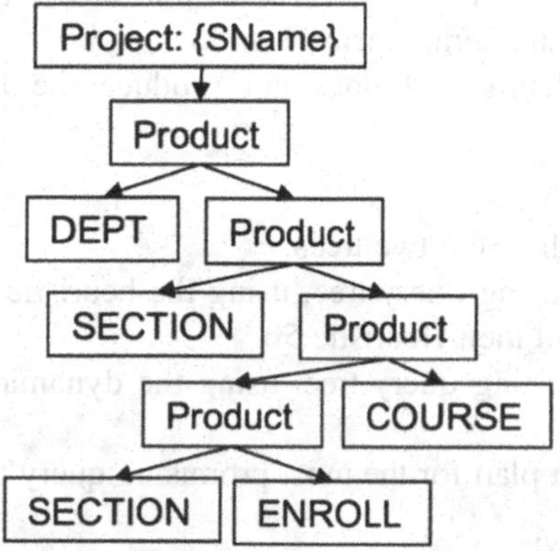

(b) Give a sequence of transformations that will create a left-deep tree having the join order (COURSE, SECTION, ENROLL, STUDENT, DEPT).

15.4. Consider a query tree containing a select node.

(a) Show that moving the select node past another select node results in an equivalent query tree.
(b) When can the select node be moved above a project node?
(c) Show that a select node can be moved above or below a groupby node if meaningful to do so.

15.5. Consider the *union* relational algebra operator from Exercise 8.16.

(a) Show that the operator is associative and commutative, and give transformations for these equivalences.
(b) Give a transformation that allows a selection to be pushed inside of a union.

15.6. Consider the *antijoin* and *semijoin* relational algebra operators of Exercise 8.17.

(a) Are these operators associative? Are they commutative? Give any appropriate transformations.
(b) Give transformations that allow selections to be pushed inside of an antijoin or semijoin.

15.7. Consider adding the selection predicate of Fig. 15.6b to the query tree of Fig. 15.2b. Give the query tree that results from pushing the selections as far as possible.

15.8. Give two equivalent query trees such that the lowest-cost plan comes from the higher-cost tree.

15.9. Show that the bushy tree of Fig. 15.12e is the most promising tree for its SQL query.

15.10. The query tree of Fig. 15.6c has the join order (STUDENT, ENROLL, SECTION, COURSE, DEPT). There are 15 other join orders that do not require product operations. Enumerate them.

15.11. Give a query such that Heuristic 4 does not produce the lowest-cost query tree.

15.12. Consider Fig. 15.6.

(a) Calculate the cost of each of the two trees.
(b) Calculate the most promising query tree, using the heuristic algorithm, first with Heuristic 5a and then Heuristic 5b.
(c) Calculate the most promising query tree, using the dynamic programming algorithm.
(d) Calculate the lowest-cost plan for the most promising query tree.

15.13. Consider the following query:

```
select Grade
from ENROLL, STUDENT, SECTION
where SId=StudentId and SectId=SectionId and SId=1 and SectId=53
```

(a) Show that the join order (ENROLL, STUDENT, SECTION) has a lower cost tree than (ENROLL, SECTION, STUDENT).
(b) Calculate the most promising query tree, using the heuristic algorithm, first with Heuristic 5a and then Heuristic 5b.
(c) Calculate the most promising query tree, using the dynamic programming algorithm.
(d) Calculate the lowest-cost plan for the most promising query tree.

15.14. The dynamic programming algorithm given in Sect. 15.4 only considers left-deep trees. Extend it to consider all possible join trees.

Programming Exercises

15.15. Revise the SimpleDB heuristic planner so that it uses Heuristic 5b to choose the tables in the join order.

15.16. Implement a Selinger-style query planner for SimpleDB.

15.17. Exercise 14.15 asked you to implement the hashjoin algorithm in SimpleDB. Now modify the class `TablePlanner` so that it creates a hashjoin plan instead of a multibuffer product, when possible.

Index

E. Sciore, *Database Design and Implementation*, Data-Centric Systems and Applications, https://doi.org/10.1007/978-3-030-33836-7

M

N

O

P

Q

R

S

Printed in the United States
By Bookmasters